OPERA!

The Guide to

Western Europe's

Great Houses

Karyl Lynn Zietz

JOHN MUIR PUBLICATIONS
SANTA FE, NEW MEXICO

John Muir Publications, P.O. Box 613, Santa Fe, NM 87504

First edition. First printing April 1991

Library of Congress Cataloging-in-Publication Data
Zietz, Karyl Lynn.
  Opera! : the guide to Western Europe's great houses / Karyl Lynn Zietz — 1st ed.
    p. cm.
  Includes bibliographical references and index.
  ISBN 0-945465-81-5
  1. Opera—Europe. 2. Theaters—Europe—Guide-books. 3. Europe—Description and travel—1971- —Guide-
books. I. title.
ML1720.Z53 1991
792.5'09—dc20
                                                                                        91-4427
                                                                                        CIP
                                                                                        MN

Designer: Sally Blakemore/Ellen Olmsted
Cover Illustration: Nancy Sutor
Typeface: Galliard, Venetian Script
Typesetter: Copygraphics, Inc.
Printer: McNaughton & Gunn

Distributed to the book trade by
W. W. Norton & Co., Inc.
New York, New York

CONTENTS

FOREWORD

A present day traveler would undoubtedly expect to have a great deal more information in advance about his ports of call than any of the fabled great adventurers of yore—Ulysses, Columbus, and Marco Polo or, more appropriately, those staunch operatic voyagers such as the Flying Dutchman, Tristan, Bacchus, Otello, B. F. Pinkerton, and Captain Vere. Although in several notable cases they had significant rendezvous to keep, few, aside from B. F. Pinkerton, had critical deadlines to meet or an 8:30 p.m. curtain.

The fact is that until now there has been woefully inadequate information in one source book for the sophisticated traveler wanting to sample the riches of La Scala, Staatsoper Wien, and so forth. This volume that I have been privileged to help nurture for well over a year provides not only a vast amount of practical information and procedures but also a storehouse of fascinating history of opera houses, their cities, and the richness of musical life over the centuries that has made them centers of operatic culture. In fact, this is an absorbing overview of European opera, even if you are only fantasizing the best of all possible operatic adventures.

As an avid opera fan and peripatetic operagoer, Karyl Lynn Zietz is filled with enthusiasm and a natural curiosity about opera performances and opera theaters. It is not at all strange that this combination of traits should give birth to a richly documented companion for the world opera traveler.

This book is not only a splendid idea but the answer to a specific need. As an opera administrator, I have been bombarded for years with frantic requests for information about performance schedules and how to go about securing tickets for La Scala, Bayreuth, Salzburg, and so on (the list is very long), and from a most practical point of view I welcomed the idea that such detailed information might be available under one cover.

The end result is a rich compilation of useful factual information and historical background, organized meticulously and peppered with the wisdom of the experienced (and, I suspect, oft-wounded) opera traveler. Brava to Karyl Lynn Zietz for filling an important need with flair, with thoroughness, and with her personal love for her subject.

—EDWARD C. PURRINGTON
Administrative Director,
The Washington Opera
Washington, D. C.

ACKNOWLEDGMENTS

*T*his book would not have been possible without the collaboration of the opera houses and the assistance of numerous people, institutions, and organizations.

I want to thank British Airways for providing transportation to England and the Continent, making it possible for me to revisit almost every opera house in the book. I would highly recommend flying British Airways on your next opera journey.

I am deeply indebted to Edward C. Purrington, administrative director of the Washington Opera, whose comments and suggestions helped me shape and mold the guide; to Carlos A. Ott and Shirley N. Roberts of NORR Partnership Limited, whose books and photographs made possible the Opéra Bastille chapter; to Stevan Bradley, who also contributed to the Opéra Bastille chapter and provided indispensable information on the Bayreuther Festspiele; to the staff of the performing arts section of the Library of Congress and especially Charles Sens; to Hella Roth at Inter Nationes, whose archives provided most of the photographs for Germany's opera houses; to the Austrian Press and Information Service, whose archives provided most of the photographs for the Salzburger Festspiele and Staatsoper Wien; to Traudl Lisey of the Wiener Fremdenverkehrsverband and to the Austrian National Tourist Office, New York, for providing the remaining photographs of the Staatsoper; to Shawn Wright of SBM, who provided all the photographs for Salle Garnier; to Marleen Bervoets of the Belgian Tourist Office for some of the photographs of La Monnaie; and to Andrea Murphy of the Embassy of Belgium, Nardone Silverio of the Italian Government Travel Office, New York, and the Istituto Italiano di Cultura, New York, for their booklets and pamphlets.

At the opera houses, I particularly want to thank M. Philippe Girard, Grand Théâtre de Genève; Egidio Saracino, Teatro Comunale; Elisabetta Navarbi, La Fenice; Patrizia Biffi, La Scala; Pino Cuccia, Teatro Bellini; the press offices of Teatro Regio Torino, Teatro Regio di Parma, and Teatro dell'Opera; Adelita Rocha, Gran Teatre del Liceu; Barbara Hering, Deutsche Oper Berlin; Barbara Wagner Galdea, Bayerische Staatsoper; Pablo Fernandez, Théâtre Royal de la Monnaie; Helen O'Neill, Glyndebourne; Katharine Wilkinson, The Royal Opera; Per Forsström, Drottningholms Slottsteater; Staffan Carlweitz and Lars Carlsson, Operan; Ole Knudsen and Marianne Hallar, Det Kongelige Teater; Joyce Snoek, De Nederlandse Opera; Martina von Brüning, Alte Oper Frankfurt; Norbert Abels, Oper Frankfurt; Erika Borgwardt, Hamburgische Staatsoper; and Ester Widmer, Opernhaus Zürich, for their extra efforts in helping provide material.

Last but certainly not least, I want to dedicate this book to Joachim, whose support and advice during the stressful months of its creation and whose solutions to my endless number of computer problems helped make *Opera! The Guide to Western Europe's Great Houses* a reality.

INTRODUCTION

A guide for a journey through Europe's great opera houses can take many shapes. The one I have chosen is based on what I wish had been available when I took my opera journeys: a spicy blend of facts on history, architecture, and performances, with practical travel information, and, sprinkled throughout, the meanings of essential foreign words.

Although opera originated as entertainment for the aristocracy and the royal court, the label "elitist" no longer applies, nor should it. Granted, the enjoyment of an opera performance requires more preparation and effort than does enjoyment of a symphony or theater performance. Nevertheless, for opera lovers, the emotional reward is much more intense and the enjoyment reaches significantly greater heights.

The main purpose of attending opera in Europe is to experience its great opera houses, which are impregnated with history and overflowing with architectural delights. Yet almost no books are available in English which unlock this rich treasure chest. I am not cognizant of any other book that has tried to unravel the mysteries of Europe's great opera houses in the manner that this book does. The purpose of the Historical Overview sections in each chapter is to offer the reader information that otherwise would be inaccessible. Much of the material was culled from books in Italian, German, and French. Furthermore, the American attending opera in Europe might not feel at ease with the languages and customs. The Practical Informa-

tion sections in this work lighten the ordeal of the foreign journey, enabling the opera lover to concentrate on enjoying the opera.

In the **Historical Overview** for each chapter, first, the **Background** recounts the building of all the opera houses that have stood in the city, from the first wooden structure to the most recently built or renovated edifice, concentrating on the happenings that were the most captivating and integral to the development of the present opera house. The **Theater** section describes, in some detail, the architectural features and decorative elements that characterize the various opera houses. **Performance History** traces the presentation of operas in the city from the first work ever heard to the 1990 performances, with emphasis on native composers, singers, and world premières, both known and forgotten. Since entire books have been written tracking performances, I have limited my coverage. I feel this emphasis imparts the best understanding of the opera houses. However, some great composers and conductors, along with a few superstars and exciting performances, are mentioned.

Practical Information treats, first, **Tickets**, which offers essential information on getting tickets, from box office locations and hours to hints on obtaining tickets for "sold out" performances to the most famous opera houses and festivals. The addresses and telephone numbers for ordering tickets, a complete ticket table with all the seating locations (in the language of that country and in English), and current ticket prices

1

for every opera house are included. Seating plans and translations of sample tickets (so you can be sure you received what you paid for) are included with every opera house. Second, **Finding Your Way** leads you, step by step, to and through each opera house, from the streets that border the theater and public transportation to how to find your seat, the rest room, the bar, the cloakroom, and the programs. The foreign words for each are included. Facilities for the disabled, where available, are noted. In **Planning Your Trip**, the Opera Schedule gives you the current list of operas being performed at each opera house, noting the new productions, so you have an idea of the range of works produced, when the season opens and closes, and whether the house is a repertory or *stagione* house; and Travel Information anticipates any problems you could encounter in the city, recommends one or two luxury hotels in each city where you are guaranteed a trouble-free stay, notes restaurants located near the opera house, and lists whom to write for further travel information. Finally, **Box Office Survival** lists the essential "box office" words you should understand in Italian, German, French, Flemish, Catalan, Danish, Swedish, and Dutch, as well as sentences and phrases in Italian, German, and French to use when dealing with the box offices.

I am also responsible for the photographs and illustrative materials in the book. My intent was to re-create the atmosphere of operagoing, not only with photographs of the opera houses and their performances but also with pictures of their posters, season programs, and tickets. There are also occasional glimpses into the past. Collecting all these photographs was a major undertaking, and I hope the final selection, which was partially determined by what the opera houses and other organizations provided, is enjoyable. I have supplemented those photographs with many of my own, taken on my opera journeys.

When gathering information for the historical overview, I sometimes encountered conflicting accounts of the same events and differing dates or versions of performances or singers. This led to the dilemma of deciding who was correct. I judged the books offered by the opera houses as the most accurate. However, if the opera house was unable or unwilling to provide such material, I relied on my own judgment and experience in deciding which account was the most accurate.

The practical information is as up to date as possible. I revisited almost every opera house in the book within the past couple of months and incorporated the latest schedules and ticket prices. However, these situations inevitably change, so please reconfirm schedules and prices. I would be delighted to hear from anyone who encounters a situation different from what I have described.

I hope this guide satisfies the needs of seasoned opera lovers on their trips and entices the uninitiated to undertake such a journey.

Italy

Luciano Pavarotti and Dolora Zajich in *Il trovatore* at Comunale (Courtesy of Teatro Comunale di Firenze)

FLORENCE
Teatro Comunale
Teatro della Pergola

*T*he city that gave birth to opera proudly carries forth the tradition in the Teatro Comunale. Originally called Politeama Fiorentino Vittorio Emanuele, the theater was inaugurated on May 17, 1862, with a gala production of Gaetano Donizetti's *Lucia di Lammermoor.* Designed by Telemaco Bonaiuti, the open-air amphitheater survived barely a year before fire consumed it. Undaunted, Bonaiuti rebuilt the 6,000-seat arena. A century later, the architect, Bartolini, with the engineer, Giuntoli, forged the theater into a modern opera house, inaugurated on May 8, 1961, with a splendid production of Giuseppe Verdi's *Don Carlo.*

HISTORICAL OVERVIEW
Background

In 1656, Florence's first opera house, Teatro della Pergola, was opened by the Accademia degli Immobili, which was founded by Giovanni Carlo de' Medici. Designed by Ferdinando Tacca and located on via della Pergola, the wooden structure was built as a private theater for Florence's aristocrats and noblemen. When the Grand Duke Cosimo III de' Medici married Marguerite Louise d'Orleans in 1661, the occasion was celebrated in the Pergola with Jacopo Melani's *Ercole in Tebe.* Two years later, Giovanni Carlo died and the Pergola was closed, a victim of estate squabbling. Eventually, the problems were resolved, but the new Accademia head, Cosimo de' Medici, was not interested in mu-

sic, so the Pergola was left like an orphan. In 1688, Ferdinando de' Medici took control of the Accademia. He decided to remodel the Pergola for his marriage to Violante Beatrice di Baviera in 1689, putting Ferdinando Sengher in charge of the effort. The occasion was celebrated with Giovanni Maria Pagliardi's *Il greco in Troia.* However, Pergola's glory was short-lived. After the festivities, the theater was deserted and its debt left unpaid. The Grand Duke Cosimo III came to the rescue and prevented foreclosure, enabling the Pergola to resume operation. However, on September 19, 1721, the theater was closed to observe a year of mourning after the death of the Grand Duchess Marguerite Louise d'Orleans, the estranged wife of Cosimo III.

After the death in July 1737 of Gian Gastone, the last Medici, Duke Francesco di Lorena became the protector of the Immobili. The Pergola's situation improved, and the opera house was renovated by Antonio Galli-Bibiena the following year. By 1740, there were fourteen theaters in Florence, but only La Pergola was devoted exclusively to *opera seria.* Around the same time, rules were established governing the theaters. Some of the more interesting ones follow:

1. One doctor, policemen, and enough servants to attend to the *Palco dei Principi* (Royal Box) were to receive free passes for each performance.

2. "Extraordinary applause" could be found to be "indecent to the dignity of the theater,"

in which case the deputy of the Accademia had to intervene. (What constituted "extraordinary applause" was not defined.)

3. If the audience formed claques, showing preference to one particular artist, soldiers could be called on to eject the disorderly spectators. In addition, the performer who caused the noise could be ejected and even arrested.

4. The curtain could not be raised later than one-quarter hour after the posted curtain time, except if the sovereign or his representatives were to attend the performance.

Opera seria at the Pergola vied with gambling for the noblemen's attention. Gambling played a big role in the financial health of theaters in those days, so when steps were taken to abolish gambling in 1748, profits plummeted while opera concentration soared.

Although La Pergola was remodeled again in 1857, resulting in the theater's current appearance, it had passed its prime. Like an aging prima donna, the theater soon relinquished its role as Florence's number one opera house. Today it hosts theatrical productions, although for the Maggio Musicale, it also hosts opera.

Florence's new prima donna, Politeama Fiorentino Vittorio Emanuele, was located a block from the Arno River near the Parco delle Cascine. The architect, Bonaiuti, according to one local paper, "tried to join ancient magnificence with the demands of modern art." The result was a horseshoe-shaped, open-air arena with stone gallery seats. Tragically, fire erupted during a gala ball the following year, killing several ball goers and gutting the stage and part of the auditorium. The theater was rebuilt and reopened on April 7, 1864. It became apparent that not having a roof was impractical, so in 1883 one was added, along with thirty-four support columns. The columns, unfortunately, blocked the view from many gallery seats.

In 1932, the city of Florence took over the theater, renaming it Teatro Comunale. Near the end of the 1950s, the Comunale suffered from "stability problems," forcing its closure on January 9, 1958. The reconstruction, which included the addition of a second gallery, lasted three years and gave the theater the appearance it has today. On November 4, 1966, the *Fiume Arno* overflowed its banks, and the orchestra level of the Comunale was filled with water instead of people. Through cooperative efforts, the Comunale rebounded and by November 27, was back in all its glory.

The Theaters

Teatro della Pergola's orange-coral stucco façade, displaying a plaque commemorating the world première of Verdi's *Macbeth*, is lined with shuttered windows, wooden doors, and wrought-iron electrified "gas" lights. Posters advertising the theater's fare and a glass and wrought-iron awning complete the front, which does not even hint at the grand theater behind. The palatial entrance hall, illuminated by a large crystal and gold chandelier, features a black and white marble floor and beige walls adorned with reliefs and two enormous paintings. An intricately decorated archway, flanked by pairs of salmon marble Corinthian columns, leads into the grand lobby. Additional salmon marble Corinthian columns, majestically rising from the black and white marble floor, line the lobby. Three tiers of boxes, topped by a gallery, soar above plush red velvet orchestra seats. In the center, ivory and white pilasters flank the royal box, while golden scrolls and angels embellish the parapets. A glorious chandelier hangs from a ceiling populated by angels and other celestial beings. La Pergola seats 1,000.

The Teatro Comunale is a spacious building with an unpretentious façade. Arched windows mingle with Ionic pilasters, and glass doors sport "TEATRO COMUNALE, PALCHI/ PLATEA" and gold fleurs-de-lis on their transoms. A modern, plant-filled foyer with a charcoal marble floor leads into a striking, stark white and red horseshoe-shaped auditorium. Starlike lights in a perfectly formed sky dome illuminate

the warm wood and white paneling. A dark and light gray proscenium complements the plush red velvet seats. The Comunale accommodates 2,600.

Performance History

Opera was born at the Palazzo Corsi in 1597 with Jacopo Peri's *Dafne*. Unfortunately, the music from the opera, except for six arias, is lost. The earliest surviving opera is Peri's *Euridice*, introduced at the Palazzo Pitti on October 6, 1600. Giulio Caccini's *Euridice* followed on December 5, 1602. Marco da Gagliano's *La Flora* appeared in 1628 at the Uffizi and Francesco Cavalli's *Egisto* in 1646 at the Palazzo Pitti.

This new art form was created by a group of men known as the *Camerata*, which included

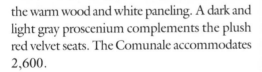

Upper left: Façade of La Pergola (Photo by author)
Lower left: Auditorium, La Pergola (Photo by author)
Upper right: Façade entrance, Comunale during 53° Maggio Musicale (Photo by author)
Lower right: Auditorium, Comunale (Courtesy of Teatro Comunale, Photo by Marchiori)

composers Peri, Caccini, Emilio de Cavalieri, and Vincenzo Galilei, noblemen Jacopo Corsi and Giovanni Bardi, and poet Ottavio Rinuccini. The Camerata's first efforts were pastorals by Cavalieri, *Il Satiro* and *La disperazione di Fileno*, introduced at Carnival in 1590. Five years later, Cavalieri's *Il giuoco della cieca* appeared at the Palazzo Pitti.

Melani's *Il potestà di Colognole* inaugurated the Teatro della Pergola during Carnival 1656. Two years later, his *Il passo per forza* and Cavalli's *L'Hipermestra* entertained the noble opera crowd. Actually, *L'Hipermestra* was scheduled to inaugurate the Pergola, but stage machinery problems caused delays and the task fell to Melani. His opera *Amor vuol inganno* closed the theater after Giovanni Carlo de' Medici's death.

The première of Antonio Vivaldi's *Scanderbegh* reopened the theater in 1718. A second première, Luc Antonio Pedieri's *La fède ne' tradimenti*, followed a couple of months later. For Carnival 1719, La Pergola offered the première of Pedieri's *La finta pazzia di Diana*, followed by his *Il trionfo di Solimano*, *Il trionfo della virtù*, and *Astarto*. In 1728, Vivaldi's *L'Atenaide* was introduced, with Giovanni Porta's *Il gran Tamerlano* coming two years later. Carnival 1736 saw Vivaldi's *Ginevra, Principessa di Scozia* staged. Each season, three to four different operas were offered, sharing the stage with the occasional ballet and masked ball. Unlike the other theaters in Florence, La Pergola was never rented to troupes, even troupes that only performed opera.

On March 17, 1833, Donizetti's *Parisina* had its world première, with his *Rosmonda d'Inghilterra* following the next year on February 27. Verdi's *Macbeth*, composed especially for La Pergola, was introduced on March 14, 1847. Verdi received a tumultuous reception, accepting thirty-eight curtain calls. In 1892, Pietro Mascagni's *I Rantzau* graced the stage for the first time.

Four years later, Mascagni moved to Florence's "new opera house," Politeama Vittorio Emanuele, where he conducted for fourteen years. However, no regular opera season was scheduled, and opera shared the stage with circuses, baby contests, and gymnastic demonstrations. Only in 1928, with the formation of the *Stabile Orchestrale Fiorentina* directed by Vittorio Gui, was the future of opera in Firenze assured.

Maggio Musicale, the oldest and most important music festival in Italy, was born on April 22, 1933, with Verdi's *Nabucco*. During the first few decades, under the leadership of Guido Gatti, Mario Labroca, and Francesco Siciliani, Maggio Musicale gained a reputation for presenting important *prime assolute* (world premières). A list of them follows in chronological order: Gian Francesco Malipiero's *Deserto tentato* on May 8, 1937, *Antonio e Cleopatra* on May 4, 1938, *Figliol prodigo* on May 14, 1957, and *Venere prigioniera* on May 14, 1957; Anonimo's *Vergini savie e vergini folli* on May 21, 1938; Vito Frazzi's *Re Lear* on April 29, 1939, and *Don Chisciotte* on April 27, 1952; Orazio Vecchi's *Amfiparnaso* on May 21, 1938; Luigi Dallapiccola's *Volo di notte* on May 18, 1940 (Pergola), and *Il prigioniero* on May 20, 1950 (first staging); Franco Alfano's *Don Juan de Manara* on May 28, 1941; Ildebrando Pizzetti's *Vanna Lupa* on May 4, 1949; Valentino Bucchi's *Il contrabbasso* on May 20, 1954, and *Notte in Paradiso* on May 11, 1960; Mario Castelnuovo-Tedesco's *Aucassin ed Nicolette* on June 2, 1952, and *Mercante di Venezia* on May 25, 1961; Luciano Chailly's *Il mantello* on May 11, 1960; Testi's *Celestina* on May 28, 1963; Salvatore Sciarrino's *Aspern* on June 8, 1978; and Fabio Vacchi's *Girotondo* on June 16, 1982.

In addition, many festival productions of familiar operas are so imaginative and creative, as well as controversial, that the opera is seen in a totally new light. For example, on June 21, 1986, Giacomo Puccini's *Tosca* was stripped of tradition and impregnated with symbolism: it was *Tosca* 1943, set in Rome during the Nazi occupation. Seven years earlier on May 23,

Upper left: Samuel Ramey in *Mefistofele* (Courtesy of Teatro Comunale di Firenze archives)
Lower left: Bruno Bartoletti, artistic director Maggio Musicale (Courtesy of Teatro Comunale di Firenze archives)
Upper right: *Der Rosenkavalier* (Courtesy of Teatro Comunale di Firenze archives)
Lower right: Zubin Mehta, principal conductor Maggio Musicale (Courtesy of Teatro Comunale di Firenze archives)

Richard Wagner's *Das Rheingold* opened with the *Rhein* maidens stark naked, a symbol of their innocence.

The festival is also known for its delightful revivals of long-forgotten scores. Among these are Cavalli's *Didone,* awakened from the seventeenth century on June 21, 1952, and Da Gagliano's *Dafne,* also resuscitated from the seventeenth century on June 17, 1965. Tommaso Traetta's *Antigone,* from the eighteenth century, was revitalized on May 12, 1962.

The greatest names in opera have graced the Maggio Musicale stage. In 1951, Maria Callas delighted the audience with her first Violetta in Verdi's *La traviata.* She returned on April 26 the following year for Gioacchino Rossini's *Armida* and again for Maria Luigi Cherubini's *Médée* on May 7, 1953. The 53° Maggio Musicale featured Luciano Pavarotti as Manrico in Verdi's *Il trovatore.*

At the 53° festival, I witnessed a marvelous revival of Donizetti's long-forgotten *Parisina*. It was a historic occasion, the first time *Parisina* had been performed at La Pergola since its world première in 1833. Mariella Devia displayed the perfect *bel canto* voice for the role of Parisina, for which she was enthusiastically cheered. Dalmacio Gonzales as Ugo, Giorgio Zancanaro as Azzo, and Dimitri Kavrakos as Ernesto all sang admirably in a superb production under the expert guidance of Bruno Bartoletti. There are surtitles for all operas not sung in Italian.

PRACTICAL INFORMATION
Tickets

The Teatro Comunale box office (*biglietteria*), located at Corso Italia 16, is to the right of the main theater entrance. It is open Tuesday

TICKET TABLES
Prezzi (Prices in Lit.)

STAGIONE AUTUNNALE - COMUNALE

Location	Prima rappresentazione	Repliche
Platea (orchestra)	100.000	80.000
Prima galleria (1st balcony)	65.000	50.000
Seconda galleria (2nd balcony)	25.000	20.000

MAGGIO MUSICALE - COMUNALE

	Ante prima	Prima rappresentazione	Repliche
Platea	250.000	150.000	100.000
Prima galleria	100.000	80.000	70.000
Seconda galleria	40.000	30.000	30.000

MAGGIO MUSICALE - PERGOLA

	Prima rappresentazione	Repliche
Platea (orchestra)	150.000	100.000
Palchi (boxes—seat)	80.000	50.000
Galleria (gallery)	30.000	20.000

Anteprima ("Status" performance), Prima rappresentazione (First performance), Repliche (Repeat performances)
$1 = Lit. 1.200, but can vary due to the fluctuating value of the dollar.
Lit. is an abbreviation for Italian Lire.

through Sunday from 9:00 a.m. to 1:00 p.m. and one hour before the beginning of the performances (*dal martedì al domenica dalle ore 9 alle ore 13 e un'ora prima dell'inizio delle manifestazioni*). Maggio Musicale tickets go on sale two weeks before the festival opens for the entire festival. Fall season tickets go on sale one week before the season opens for the first six weeks and one month later for the remainder of the season. Monitors by the box office window show the seating plan with available seats indicated in blue. Stacks of programs are piled on the shelf ahead as you enter. Unfortunately, the personnel are unfriendly, so read the program before going to the window to avoid their wrath.

Although plays are the usual fare at the Pergola, opera takes the stage during the Maggio Musicale. The box office, located at via della Pergola 32, inside the entrance lobby on the right side, is open Tuesday through Saturday from 9:30 a.m. to 1:00 p.m. and from 3:45 p.m. to 6:45 p.m., Sunday 10:00 a.m. to 1:00 p.m., and one hour before curtain time (*dal martedì al sabato dalle ore 9,30 alle 13 e dalle ore 15,45 alle 18,45, la*

domenica dalle ore 10 alle 13 e un'ora prima dell'inzio delle manifestazioni). You can buy tickets seven days before the performance. A price chart and seating plan are located by the box office window. Although the box office personnel cannot speak English, they try to be helpful.

Tickets can be reserved through the mail for both theaters. The box ofice begins accepting reservations for the entire Maggio Musicale one month before the festival opens and for the fall schedule two weeks before the season opens. Send your name, address, telephone number, opera, date, location, number of seats (maximum four), and a check in Italian Lire to:

Biglietteria Teatro Comunale
Via Solferino 15
50123-Florence
Italy

It is not possible to reserve tickets by telephone.

Ticket prices are higher for Maggio Musicale than for the fall season, reflecting the star quality of the festival casts.

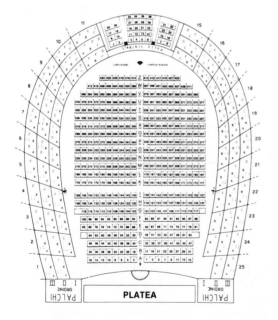

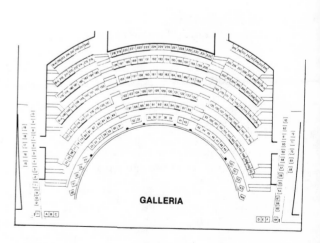

Pergola Seating Plan (Courtesy of Teatro Comunale di Firenze)

Tickets are extremely difficult to find for Maggio Musicale. Most operas are *tutto esaurito* (sold out) before the festival starts. Your best chance for tickets is as follows: mail your request as soon as reservations are accepted, choose a *fuori abbonamento* (nonsubscription) performance, avoid opening nights, and accept poor visibility side seats if necessary. Tickets are easier to obtain during the fall season.

Comunale and Pergola are well marked, so understanding your ticket (shown below) will help you find your seat.

Evening performances begin at 8:00 p.m. (*ore* 20), Sunday matinees at 4 p.m. (*ore* 16). However, there are exceptions. The starting times are listed on the posters outside the theater and in the bimonthly *English/Italian Florence Concierge Information*.

Finding Your Way

TEATRO COMUNALE

Teatro Comunale faces Corso Italia, bordered on the north by via Solferino and on the west by via Magenta. It is a fifteen-minute walk from the *Stazione Centrale* (central railroad station). Bus 16 stops in front of the theater.

The main entrance to Teatro Comunale is located at 16 Corso Italia. *Platea* and *Palchi* are written in gold letters above the main entrance. Those seated in the orchestra and boxes use those doors. Those in the *prima galleria* (first gallery) use the entrance to the right marked *1° galleria*, next to the box office. Those seated in the *seconda galleria* (second gallery) use the via Magenta entrance.

From the entrance foyer, follow the sign *Ingresso Platea* down a flight of stairs if you hold tickets in the front of the orchestra. For even-

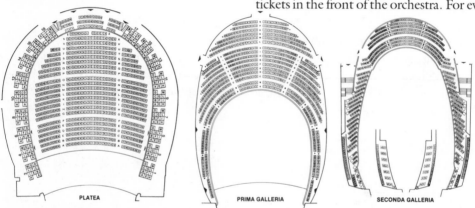

Comunale Seating Plan (Courtesy of Teatro Comunale di Firenze)

TICKET TRANSLATION			
Teatro Comunale		Communal Theater	
1° Galleria	68	First Balcony	(Performance Number)
Fila B	**No. 19**	**Row B**	**Seat 19**
Il Trovatore		(Opera)	
19.6.90	Ore 20,00	June 19, 1990	8:00 P.M.
ETI Teatro della Pergola Firenze		Pergola Theater Florence	
	Balconata		Balcony (Section)
N. 11	**II°**	**Box 11**	**2nd Tier** **Seat B**
	Posto B		
24 Mag. 1990		May 24, 1990	

Note: on *Poltrone* (orchestra) tickets at Pergola, *Fila* (row) is a letter and *N.* (seat) is a number.

Top: Luciano Pavarotti in *Il trovatore* (Courtesy of Teatro Comunale di Firenze)
Lower left: Dimitri Kavrakos and Dano Raffanti in *Parisina* (Courtesy of Teatro Comunale di Firenze)
Lower right: Mariella Devia and Tiziana Tramonti in *Parisina* (Courtesy of Teatro Comunale di Firenze)

numbered seats, go right and follow the *platea N° pari* sign; for odd-numbered seats, go left and follow the *platea N° dispari*. If you are seated in the rear orchestra, continue straight after entering. Use the right side entrance down a few steps for even numbers and the left side for odd numbers. Seats 1 and 2 are in the middle of each row. Gold and black seat numbers are on the backs of chairs and row letters are on the floor.

The *palchi* are on the same level as the entrance foyer. Turn left for odd numbers and right for even numbers. Boxes 1 and 2 are closest to the stage on the left and right sides, respectively. The center section of the box tier is called *balconata centrale*. Walk straight ahead for those seats. Ushers are recognizable by their red jackets, black skirts, and white blouses.

Programs are for sale in the entrance foyer and cost Lit. 12.000. The program (in Italian) contains the complete libretto, a synopsis in English, articles, and pictures relating to the opera. A marvelous program book (in Italian) on all the operas presented at the festival is also available for Lit. 25.000. The book is filled with photographs and illustrations as well as articles pertaining to all the festival operas. The ladies' room (*signore*) and men's room (*signori*) are located down one flight of stairs from the entrance foyer on both the right and left sides (follow the sign *Guardaroba—Ingresso Platea*). The cloakroom (*guardaroba*) is next to the rest rooms and costs Lit. 1.000. (Umbrellas cost Lit. 500 to check.) The bar is located at the right end of the hall in a huge room. During intermissions, the bars and foyers are so filled with smoke, it is impossible to breathe. There is a special entrance for the disabled, between the *biglietteria* and the *1° galleria* entrance.

TEATRO DELLA PERGOLA
Teatro della Pergola faces via della Pergola. The nearest cross streets are via San Egidio and via degli Alfani. It is a twenty-minute walk from the *Stazione Centrale*.

The main entrance to Teatro della Pergola is located at 32 via della Pergola. The *galleria* entrance is two doors to the right of the main entrance. Those holding tickets in the *poltrone* and *palchi* should enter through the main entrance, continue up the stairs, and turn right into the magnificent grand lobby. Those seated in the *poltrone* should continue straight ahead through the center doors. Seat numbers are on the backs of the chairs in red. Row letters are on the floor. If you are seated in the *palchi*, take the stairs on the right for boxes 1-11, and on the left for boxes 15-25. Each tier is identified with gold letters as *ordine primo, ordine secondo,* or *ordine terzo* (first tier, second tier, or third tier). Ushers wear black suits or dresses with an ETI pin on the left side.

Programs are sold by the entrance stairs and cost Lit. 12.000. The program (in Italian) contains a synopsis in English, the complete libretto, articles, and pictures relating to the opera. A marvelous program book (in Italian) on all the operas presented at the festival is also available at a cost of Lit. 25.000. The book is filled with color and black and white photographs and illustrations as well as articles pertaining to all the festival operas. The cloakroom (*guardaroba*) is located on the left side of the grand foyer and costs Lit. 1.000. (Umbrellas cost Lit. 500 to check.) The bar is on the right side of the foyer, down some steps, in a huge room. The room is so smoke laden, as is the foyer during intermission, that it is difficult to breathe. The ladies' room (*signore*) is upstairs on the right. The men's room (*signori*) is on the left off the foyer.

Planning Your Trip
OPERA SCHEDULE
There are two performance seasons: the spring festival, Maggio Musicale Fiorentino, from the end of April to the beginning of July and the fall season from the end of September to the end of December. The 53° Maggio Musicale opened on April 28, 1990, with a new production of Nikolai Rimsky-Korsakov's *Skazaniye o nevidimom grade Kitezhe* (The Legend of the Invisible City of Kitezh) and closed on July 4 with the world

première of three dances, *Alternativa*, *Jeux* and *Sport*. The last opera was a new production of Mozart's *Don Giovanni* on June 29. The operas completing the schedule were all new productions: Donizetti's *Parisina*, Verdi's *Il trovatore*, and Kurt Weill's *Aufstieg und Fall der Stadt Mahagonny*. The first opera of the fall season was Verdi's *Rigoletto*, opening on October 29. Arrigo Boïto's *Mefistofele* closed the season on December 23. Leoš Janáček's *Kát'a Kabanová* completed the opera program. The 1990/91 season is abbreviated because of repairs to the roof and heating and air-conditioning systems at the Teatro Comunale and is not representative of the opera season in Florence.

Teatro Comunale is a *stagione* house, which means only one opera is performed at a time. During the Maggio Musicale, different operas are scheduled at different theaters on consecutive nights. During both seasons, opera shares the stage with concerts and ballets. To be sure your visit corresponds with an opera, contact the Italian Government Travel Offices (ENIT), 630 Fifth Avenue, New York, NY 10011, 212-245-4822, for an opera schedule. They respond promptly. It takes a long time to get the schedule from the opera house, but if you are not in a hurry, here is the address:

Informazioni Ufficio Biglietteria
Teatro Comunale
Corso Italia 16
50123 Firenze, Italy

You can call (39)(55)277-9236 for information between 3:30 p.m. and 5:30 p.m., Tuesday through Saturday. (39) = country code; (55) = city code. In Italy, dial (055)277-9236. You should speak Italian. Florence is six hours ahead of Eastern Standard Time.

TRAVEL INFORMATION

The best hotel in Florence is the Savoy Hotel, Piazza della Repubblica 7, 50123 Florence, Italy; telephone (39)(55)283-313, fax (39)(55)284-840. From the United States, call toll-free, 1-800-223-6800 (member of the Leading

Daniela Dessí in *Mefistofele* (Courtesy of Teatro Comunale di Firenze archives)

Hotels of the World). Singles start at $180, doubles at $370. A delicious buffet breakfast is included. The Savoy is a luxurious five-star hotel with 101 rooms and overlooks the Piazza della Repubblica. Claiming the best location in Florence, the hotel offers impeccable service and delightfully furnished rooms. If you enjoy fresh flowers and fin-de-siècle atmosphere, the Savoy has both. For a special treat, order a bottle of Italian champagne and watch the happenings on the Piazza della Repubblica. The Savoy is the only hotel convenient to both *teatri*, Comunale and Pergola. It is an enjoyable twenty-minute walk along the Arno River to Comunale and ten minutes to La Pergola. Contact the concierge for all your last-minute ticket needs.

You will find eating places on Il Prato, a few blocks from Comunale. For La Pergola, there is a wide range of restaurants on the via de Calzaiuoli (pedestrian street) behind the hotel. For a gourmet meal, try the Savoy's restaurant (expensive).

You can also contact the Italian Government Travel Offices (address above) for travel information. They respond promptly.

MILAN
Teatro alla Scala

Teatro alla Scala was inaugurated on August 3, 1778, with Antonio Salieri's *Europe riconosciuta* and two ballets, *Pafio e Mirra* and *Apollo placato*. The resplendent program dazzled the opening night crowd, which included Il Serenissimo Arciduca Ferdinando and his wife, La Serenissima Archiduchessa Maria Ricciarda Beatrice d'Este. On the program, their names were larger than the title of the opera, and the composers' names were not even mentioned. Bravos for Maria Balducci, Francesca Lebrun Danzi, and the celebrated *castrato* Gasparo Pachiarotti echoed throughout the house. Thirty-six horses appeared on the stage. La Scala, designed by Giuseppe Piermarini, stood majestically until August 16, 1943, when bombs reduced it to rubble. Under the careful eye of Luigi L. Secchi, La Scala was rebuilt following the original plans of Piermarini. On May 11, 1946, Arturo Toscanini conducted music by Giuseppe Verdi, Gioacchino Rossini, Arrigo Boïto, and Giacomo Puccini for the reopening of the "shrine of opera." Verdi's *Nabucco* inaugurated the regular opera season on December 26, 1946.

HISTORICAL OVERVIEW
Background

Milan's first theater, Salone Margherita, built in honor of Princess Margherita of Austria, opened in the Ducal Palace in 1598. Flames engulfed the theater in 1708, but nine years later, Teatro Regio Ducale replaced the Salone Margherita in the *palazzo dell'Archiduca*. This magnificent theater featured long seasons and was managed in an aristocratic style. However, on the night of February 25, 1776, the theater was destroyed by fire. Within five months, Maria Theresa, Empress of Austria and Duchess of Milan, granted the building site and permission to reconstruct to the *palchettisti* (box owners of the destroyed theater who belonged to Milan's rich nobility). However, the Church of Santa Maria della Scala had claimed the spot first. Not a problem: the church was simply demolished. Construction began on August 15, 1776. During the excavation, the ancient bas-relief of Pilade was uncovered, which was interpreted as a good omen. During the construction, Maria Theresa bragged, "*S'alza già il nuovo teatro, destinato ad offuscare la celebrità dei più famosi d'Italia*" (Already the new theater is destined to obscure the prominence of the most famous in Italy). After excellent results from two acoustics tests, the opera house, named Il nuovo Regio Ducale Teatro di Santa Maria della Scala was opened. Since this was cumbersome, it was simply called Teatro alla Scala.

The *palchettisti* paid for the new opera house and reserved their boxes, which were adorned as they wished. Some decorated the walls with tapestry or silk, others painted them with scenes from their favorite operas. Ceilings were embellished with mirrors, carved wood, or frescoes. Their family coats of arms were affixed to the front. The *palchettisti* used their boxes as private salons, enjoying *la dolce vita*. They passed the evening eating, drinking, socializing, gossiping, and even gambling, emerging only for the climactic events of the opera to applaud and whistle at the singers of the moment.

During the first ten years, the theater was illuminated by candlelight. Then 84 oil lamps were placed on the stage, and 996 lights of every type were suspended from the ceiling. In 1821, a grand chandelier of Argand lamps was hung in the center of the room. Thirty-one years later, the first arc lamps appeared on the stage, and in 1883, all lighting became electric.

In the early days, the orchestra seats were uncomfortable wooden benches reserved for the military and the servants of the rich. Most spectators were drunk and boisterous, their shouts drowning out the performers on stage. They showed their approval by whacking sticks against the benches. The ordinary folks, seated upstairs in the galleries, demonstrated their approval by showering the stage with paper. The behavior of La Scala's early audiences was more befitting a sports arena than an opera house. Then bylaws were passed governing audience behavior:

1. Displaying disapproval of a performance either during or after was forbidden.

2. Applauding "in a manner which did not represent the true worth of the performance" was forbidden.

3. Encores were forbidden.

4. Calling singers back onto the stage more than once was forbidden.

When the French arrived on May 14, 1796, bringing with them the Cisalpine Republic, the frivolity of Milan's nobility was temporarily ended. The French lost no time in removing the family coats of arms from the boxes, claiming they were "relics from an age of barbarity and slavery," and defacing the boxes. Fortunately, the French did not remain too long, and when the Austrians returned, so did the family coats of arms and the magnificently decorated boxes.

In 1807, the first general renovation took place. New decorations were added to the dome and boxes, and the stage was enlarged. Alessandro Sanquirico redecorated in 1830, but the original decor of Piermarini was restored in 1879. Meanwhile, in 1867, the *Comune* of Milan had taken over the opera house. Thirty years later, they withdrew its subsidy, and La Scala did not open. A sign was nailed to the door: "La Scala, closed on the occasion of the death of all feeling for art, of civic pride, and of good sense." You can imagine the outrage. Soon Guido Visconti di Modrone and a group of *palchettisti* founded the *Società Anonima* to get the season under way.

Meanwhile, a year after La Scala was inaugurated, the Teatro della Cannobiana opened its doors. Built by Piermarini, the theater accommodated 2,000. In 1894, the Cannobiana was bought by Edoardo Sonzogno and renamed Teatro Lirico. Reconstructed by Achille Sfondrini, the Lirico is still in use today. Two other theaters hosted opera as well: the Teatro Carcano, which opened in 1803, and Teatro dal Verme, which opened in 1872. Both are movie houses today.

The Museo Teatrale, joined to La Scala by the grand foyer, was inaugurated on March 8, 1913, and eight years later the descendants of the *palchettisti* surrendered their boxes (for a price) to the municipality. Teatro alla Scala became an *Ente Autonomo* (autonomous corporation).

War came to La Scala in 1943, when hundreds of bombs rained from the nighttime sky. Only the outer shell and stage area survived. The sets and costumes for more than one hundred operas were also lost. After the war, a 2 percent amusement tax imposed in the Lombardy region (of which Milan was the capital), combined with part of the gate money from football matches, helped pay for the reconstruction of the opera house. La Scala gave birth to a daughter known as Piccola Scala in 1955. The 500-seat theater, adjoining La Scala, was built primarily as a home for sixteenth- and seventeenth-century chamber works as well as certain twentieth-century pieces that were better suited to a small space. In 1978, La Scala celebrated its 200th birthday.

The Theater

The Teatro alla Scala is a severe but elegant neoclassical building, blending harmoniously with its surroundings. Its façade of "soft" copper-colored stucco is embellished with white and salmon stone Corinthian columns and pilasters, which flank seven Empire windows topped by tympanums. Above, an entablature encircles the façade, which is crowned by a chariot relief pediment. The arched former carriage entrance leads into a narrow vestibule, which flows into the marble-floored entrance foyer. Divided by eight white- and black-veined marble columns sporting gold Corinthian capitals, the foyer is home to large white marble statues of Verdi and Gaetano Donizetti on the left and Vincenzo Bellini and Rossini on the right. Upstairs, the grand foyer accommodates busts of Umberto Giordano, Puccini, and Pietro Mascagni.

Façade of La Scala (Courtesy of Teatro alla Scala archives)

Four tiers of boxes topped by two galleries soar in gold, ivory, and red splendor around the beautifully proportioned horseshoe-shaped auditorium. Cherubs frolic and pairs of gilded griffins flank lyres on the ivory parapets. Golden caryatids guard the royal box. A glorious Bohemian crystal chandelier with 365 bulbs illuminates the vast room, complemented by clusters of white glass globes around the parapets. Separate lights glow from the galleries and boxes. The boxes were uniformly redecorated with red damask in 1921 when the *palchettisti* relinquished

their ownership. A clock with no hands resides high over the proscenium. Flanked by gilded, winged maidens and encircled by a wreath of laurels, the clock displays the hours in Roman numerals and the minutes in Arabic numerals, changing only at five-minute intervals.

The magic of La Scala starts right before the performance: the center chandelier and light clusters on the tiers dim, giving the darkened theater a bewitching atmosphere from the still-glowing box and gallery lights. As those lights fade, a magic ripples through the auditorium and the curtain rises. Then you know why La Scala is the world's greatest opera house.

Performance History

In 1644, Francesco Manelli's *Andromeda* was the first opera performed in Milan. Three years short of a century later, Christoph Willibald Gluck's *Artaserse* was premiered at the Teatro Regio Ducale, the scene of the world premières of Wolfgang Amadeus Mozart's *Mitridate, Re di Ponto* on December 26, 1770, his *Ascanio in Alba* on October 17, 1771, and his *Lucio Silla* on December 26, 1772.

Gluck was offered the commission to compose the inaugural work for Teatro alla Scala but declined, so the task fell to Salieri. Another Salieri opera, *Fiera di Venezia*, inaugurated the Teatro della Cannobiana in 1779, where the world première of Donizetti's *L'elisir d'amore* took place on May 12, 1832. Meanwhile, the world première of Giuseppe Sarti's *I due litiganti* was given at La Scala on September 14, 1782. Six years later, two independent impresarios, Gaetano Maldonati and Francesco Benedetti Ricci, took over managing the opera house and published the theater's first regular season program, with works by Sarti, Giovanni Paisiello, Domenico Cimarosa, and Niccolò Antonio Zingarelli in the repertory.

On September 26, 1812, Rossini's *La pietra del paragone* had its world première, followed by his *Aureliano in Palmira* the next year and *Il turco*

Top: *Aida* (Courtesy of Teatro alla Scala, Photo by Lelli & Masotti)
Lower left: *Madama Butterfly* (Courtesy of Teatro alla Scala, Photo by Lelli & Masotti)
Lower right: Auditorium with view of royal box (Courtesy of Teatro alla Scala, Photo by Lelli & Masotti)

in Italia on August 14, 1814. Although the world première of his *La gazza ladra* on May 31, 1817, was a success, his *Bianca e Falliero*, composed for the inauguration of La Scala's 1819 season, was soon forgotten. Two years later, Saverio Mercadante's *Elisa e Claudio* was premiered, followed by his *Il giuramento* on March 10, 1837.

Domenico Barbaia took over as impresario in 1826, commissioning Bellini to write three operas. The world première of *Il pirata* took place on October 27, 1827, *La straniera* on February 14, 1829, and *Norma* on December 26, 1831. The première of *Norma* was a disaster. As the story goes, Marchesa Bianchi was in love with Bellini, but Bellini did not reciprocate her affections. Bent on revenge, Bianchi paid spectators to yell, whistle, hiss, and boo during the first performance. Fortunately for Bellini, she did not have enough money to pay for the disturbances to continue. Donizetti's operas took center stage next, with the world premières of *Chiara e Serafina* on October 26, 1822, *Ugo, conte di Parigi* on March 13, 1832, *Lucrezia Borgia* on December 26, 1833, *Gemma di Vergy* on December 26, 1834, and *Maria Padilla* seven years later.

In September 1803, Vincenzo Federici's *Zaira* inaugurated the Teatro Carcano. The world première of Donizetti's *Anna Bolena* took place there on December 26, 1830, and Bellini's *La sonnambula* followed on March 6, 1831. Bartolomeo Merelli took over La Scala in 1836, presenting Verdi's first opera, *Oberto, Conte di San Bonifacio*, on November 17, 1839. Merelli then commissioned Verdi to write three more operas, the first one a comic opera. Tragically, while Verdi was trying to compose the opera, both his children died. Then his wife, Margherita, died. How could he possibly write a comic opera? Verdi asked to be released from his contract, but Merelli refused. *Un giorno di regno* was premiered on September 5, 1840. It was a dismal failure, and Verdi sank into a deep depression, refusing to compose anymore. Merelli returned the contract, but he did not give up. One chilly winter night he met Verdi and forced

a libretto by Temistocle Solera into the composer's hands. When Verdi arrived home, he threw the libretto on the table. It opened to *"Va, pensiero sull'ali dorate"* (Fly, thought, on wings of gold). Inspired, Verdi composed *Nabucco*, which was premiered triumphantly on March 9, 1842, with Giuseppina Strepponi (his future wife) as Abigaille. The next year, Verdi's *I Lombardi alla prima crociata* was introduced on February 11, followed by *Giovanna d'Arco* on February 15, 1845. After *Giovanna d'Arco*, Verdi's association with La Scala ended. His relations had been fraught with tension and conflict, so Verdi decided to première his operas elsewhere, although they remained a staple of La Scala's repertory.

On March 5, 1868, the scandalous world première of Boïto's *Mefistofele* took place during violent protests between Boïto's admirers and his enemies. When the demonstrations disrupted the second performance as well, Milan's chief of police ordered the opera withdrawn from the repertory. By contrast, the world première of Amilcare Ponchielli's *La Gioconda* on April 8, 1876, was a quiet affair.

Near the end of his career, Verdi returned to La Scala for the world premières that were his crowning glory. *Otello* graced the stage for the first time on February 5, 1887, and *Falstaff* followed on February 9, 1893. With the resounding triumph of *Falstaff*, Verdi's second era at La Scala drew to a close. On January 27, 1901, La Scala shut its doors as thousands gathered outside the Grand Hotel nearby, where the world's greatest Italian opera composer had died of a stroke at the age of eighty-eight. A few days later, Toscanini conducted a concert of Verdi's music, with Enrico Caruso singing. As Verdi was buried, those at the grave site spontaneously sang *"Va, pensiero sull'ali dorate"* in hushed tones.

Next, Puccini arrived in Milan, where his first opera, *Le Villi*, was introduced on May 31, 1884, at Teatro dal Verme, a theater that had been inaugurated in 1872 with Giacomo Meyerbeer's *Les Huguenots*. Dal Verme also staged the

Top: *Falstaff* (Courtesy of Teatro alla Scala, Photo by Lelli & Masotti)
Bottom: *Fetonte* (Courtesy of Teatro alla Scala, Photo by Lelli & Masotti)

world première of Ruggero Leoncavallo's *Pagliacci* on May 21, 1892, and Riccardo Zandonai's *Conchita* nineteen years later.

La Scala hosted the world première of Puccini's second opera, *Edgar*, on April 21, 1889. It was a disaster, but it was nothing compared with the hostile reaction to *Madama Butterfly*, which was practically hooted off the stage at its première on February 17, 1904. *Madama Butterfly* was not repeated until 1925. Unfortunately, Puccini did not live to see his only La Scala triumph, *Turandot*, which was completed by Franco Alfano and introduced on April 25, 1926. Toscanini conducted the première, and when he came to the point where Puccini stopped composing, he put down his baton, turned to the audience, and said, *"Qui finisce l'opera, perché a questo punto il maestro è morto"* (Here the opera ends, because at this point the maestro died) and left the podium.

Alfredo Catalani's *La Wally* graced the stage for the first time on January 20, 1892, followed the next year by Leoncavallo's *I Medici*. The world premières of Giordano's *Andrea Chénier* took place on March 28, 1896, Alberto Franchetti's *Germania* on March 11, 1902, and Mascagni's *Parisina* on December 15, 1913. Italo Montemezzi's *L'amore dei tre Re* was introduced on April 10, 1913. His *La nave* followed on November 3, 1918, three years after the world première of Ildebrando Pizzetti's *Fedra* on March 20, 1915.

In 1894, Samara's *La martire* opened the Teatro Lirico. The world première of Francesco Cilèa's *L'Arlesiana* took place there on November 27, 1897, with Caruso creating the role of Federico. The next year, Giordano's *Fedora* was introduced on November 17, followed by Leoncavallo's *Zazà* on November 10, 1900, and Cilèa's *Adriana Lecouvreur* on November 26, 1902.

When Toscanini was appointed permanent conductor at La Scala in 1898, the opera house was transformed into a battleground between the audience and the conductor. He would not allow in the theater any ladies who wore large hats, and he strictly enforced the no-encore rule. The coup de grace came on the closing night of the 1903 season, when Toscanini was conducting Verdi's *Un ballo in maschera*. Enraged by the continual demands of the audience for encores, he threw down his baton and stormed out of the theater. The performance was never completed, and three years passed before he set foot again in La Scala.

La Scala was closed during World War I, reopening on December 26, 1921, with Toscanini conducting Verdi's *Falstaff*. It was the same season he took "absolute" control, turning La Scala into the "shrine of opera," until his legendary clashes with Italian dictator Benito Mussolini forced him to resign in 1929. Six years later, Mascagni's *Nerone*, which glorified Mussolini and Fascism, was premiered.

Most of opera's greatest voices have been heard from La Scala's stage, but probably the most memorable was that of Maria Callas. In 1950, she made her debut in Verdi's *Aida*, sub-

Foyer with statue of Giuseppe Verdi (Courtesy of Teatro alla Scala, Photo by Lelli & Masotti)

stituting for Renata Tebaldi. For an unforgettable decade she captivated La Scala's audiences. All of opera's greatest artists continue to sing at La Scala.

Since 1947, world premières have become almost an annual event, with some years seeing two or three. What follows is a random sampling. Ildebrando Pizzetti's *L'oro* was introduced on January 2, 1947; Giorgio Federico Ghedini's *Baccanti* on February 21, 1948, and Renzo Bianchi's *Gli incatenati* on May 7 of the same year; Giulio Cesare Sonzogno's *Regina Uliva* on March 17, 1949, and Goffredo Petrassi's *Il Cordovano* on May 12, 1949. On March 17, 1952, Juan José Castro's *Proserpina e lo straniero* graced the stage. A double bill of Virgilio Mortari's *La figlia del Diavolo* and Mario Peragallo's *La gita in campagna* was performed on March 24, 1954. *La gita* aroused some hostile feelings; a shoe was even thrown from the balcony. Francis Poulenc's *Dialogues des Carmélites* as *Dialoghi delle Carmelitane* was premiered on January 26, 1957, and Pizzetti's *Assassinio nella cattedrale* took the stage on March 1, 1958. His *Il calzare d'argento* ushered in the 1960s on March 23, 1960, followed by Guido Turchi's *Il buon soldato Svejk* on April 5, 1962, and Renzo Rossellini's *La leggenda del ritorno* on March 10, 1966.

La Piccola Scala was inaugurated on December 26, 1955, with Cimarosa's *Il matrimonio segreto*. The theater's first world première took place on March 10, 1956, with Ghedini's *L'ipocrita felice*. Riccardo Malipiero's *La donna è mobile* followed on February 22, 1957, and Mortari's *La scuola delle mogli* was introduced on March 17, 1959. During the 1960s, world premières continued to be an almost annual event, with Nino Rota's *La notte di un nevrastenico* on February 8, 1960, starting the decade. The 1970s were ushered in with Bruno Bettinelli's *Count Down* and Gino Negri's *Pubblicità ninfa gentile* on March 26, 1970, and, later that year, Angelo Paccagnini's *La misura, il mistero* on November 12. Five additional world premières were presented during the decade. Sylvano Bussotti's *Le Racine*, first performed on December 9, 1980, greeted the 1980s.

Karlheinz Stockhausen's *Donnerstag aus Licht* on March 15, 1981, ushered in the world premières of the 1980s at La Scala. Stockhausen's *Samstag aus Licht* followed on May 25, 1984, and his *Montag aus Licht* on May 7, 1988. Giacomo Manzoni's *Doktor Faustus* closed the decade on May 16, 1989.

A couple of years ago, I saw a superb production of Verdi's *Nabucco*, which had opened the 1986/87 season. With flawless precision, the people of Jerusalem climbed up and down the most incredible number of steps, while never missing a beat. Splendid singing by Ghena Dimitrova as Abigaille, Giorgio Zancanaro as Nabucodonosor, Ezio di Cesare as Ismaele, Paata Burchuladze as Zaccaria, and Luciana D'Intino as Fenena was combined with stunning sets and costumes by Mauro Carosi and Odette Nicoletti, respectively. Riccardo Muti's conducting gave new meaning to the word perfection.

Nabucco (Courtesy of Teatro alla Scala, Photo by Lelli & Masotti)

PRACTICAL INFORMATION
Tickets

The box office (*biglietteria*) is located on via Giuseppe Verdi, along the right side of the opera house through an unmarked door and down a flight of stairs. The box office is open Tuesday through Sunday 10:00 a.m. to 1:00 p.m. and from 3:30 p.m. to 5:30 p.m. (*dal martedì al domenica, dalle ore 10 alle ore 13 e dalle 15,30 alle 17,30*). A metal detector and a guard stand between the entrance and the box office windows. There is usually a line. Bimonthly schedules (*Calendario*) are found on the shelf. On performance days, the evening box office, at via Filodrammatici 2 along the left side of the opera house, is open from 5:30 p.m. to 9:30 p.m. (*dalle ore 17,30 alle ore 21,30*). If the clerk likes you, he or she will ''understand'' English. Otherwise they pretend to understand nothing. The box office opens on Mondays when there is a Monday performance. You can purchase tickets starting seven days before the performance.

Tickets can be reserved by mail or telegram. Reservations are accepted for all performances of one opera for five days only, Tuesday through Saturday, beginning six weeks before the opera's first performance. Include your name, address, telephone number, opera, three different choices of performance dates (in order of preference), seat location, and number of tickets (maximum is two) on your reservation request. If your reservation is accepted, you will receive confirmation in the mail. Tickets can be paid for and picked up at the box office beginning two days before the performance until noon on performance day. Tickets not picked up by that time will be released. Mail your ticket requests to:

E.A. Teatro alla Scala
Ufficio Biglietteria
Via Filodrammatici 2
20121 Milan
Italy

Tickets cannot be reserved by telephone. However, you can call (39)(2)809-160 or 809-

TICKET TABLE

Location	Prezzi (Prices in Lit.)	
	Subscription turni A,B,C,D	Nonsubscription fuori abbonamento
Poltrona di platea (front orchestra)	180.000	115.000
Poltroncina di platea (rear orchestra)	145.000	93.000
Posto in palco (seat in box)	145.000	93.000
Ingresso suppl.re palco (standing in box)	72.500	46.500
Prima Galleria (first gallery)		
Poltroncina (front seats)	42.000	33.000
Numerato (rear seats)	30.000	26.000
Ingresso (standing room)	4.000	4.000
Seconda Galleria (second gallery)		
Poltroncina (front seats)	33.000	25.000
Numerato (rear seats)	15.000	15.000
Ingresso (standing room)	4.000	4.000

$1 = Lit. 1.200, but can vary due to the fluctuating value of the dollar.
Lit. is an abbreviation for Italian Lire.

169 for schedule information, ticket availability, and prices between 10:00 a.m. and 1:00 p.m. and 3:00 p.m. and 6:00 p.m. daily. (39) = country code; (2) = city code. In Italy, dial (02)809-160 or 809-169. You should speak Italian. Milan is six hours ahead of Eastern Standard Time.

Reservations can be made in the United States for nonsubscription performances only, within ten days of the performance, through the following CIT (Compagnia Italiana Turismo) offices: CIT , 666 Fifth Avenue, New York, N.Y., 212-397-2666; CIT, 333 North Michigan Avenue, Chicago, Ill., 312-332-5334; CIT, 5670 Wilshire Blvd, Los Angeles, Calif., 213-938-2921.

Your best chance for tickets is *fuori abbonamento* (nonsubscription) performances and contemporary operas. *Prima rappresentazione* (opening night), *nuovo allestimento* (new production), *turni* A and B (subscription series A and B), and, of course, star-studded casts are always *tutto esaurito* (sold out). If you see *serata riservata* (closed performance), think of another date.

If you want to see an opera in one of the *tutto esaurito* categories, here are some suggestions: cable your request the first day that tickets go on sale for that opera; arrive in Milan seven days ahead and stand in line, or get in line the night before. Go to the box office during the day of the performance to see if someone has turned in tickets; pressure the concierge at the hotel (only possible at the better hotels). But avoid the scalpers, who hang around the front of the theater on the Filodrammatici Street side.

Remember when buying tickets that La Scala was built in the era when opera houses were more a social gathering place than a place to hear fine opera. Except for the first row in the side boxes, your view of the stage might be limited. However, La Scala's mystique will capture you, no matter where you are seated.

La Scala's new computer-generated tickets look like stock certificates and cost almost as much! They are delightful multicolored affairs but a bit confusing to understand, so a translation appears below.

Seating Plan (Courtesy of Teatro alla Scala)

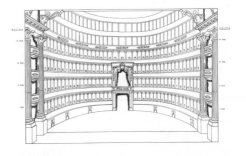

Seating Plan (Courtesy of Teatro alla Scala)

TICKET TRANSLATION		
Teatro alla Scala	Theater at the Scala	
Poltroncina	Rear Orchestra	
Fila V **n. 4/S**	**Row V** Seat 4	Left
Madama Butterfly	(Opera)	
19/05/90 20,00 £93.000	May 19, 1990 8:00 p.m. (Price)	

Most operas begin at 8:00 p.m. (*ore* 20,00). Check the posters outside the theater or the *Calendario* for any change in starting times. No one is admitted once the performance has begun.

Finding Your Way

La Scala faces the Piazza della Scala, bordered on the east by via Giuseppe Verdi and on the west by via Filodrammatici. *Tranvie* 1, 4, and 12 stop in front of the opera house, exit Piazza della Scala. Line 1 also stops at the *Stazione Centrale F.F.S.A.* (Central Railroad Station).

The main entrance is on the Piazza della Scala. Those holding tickets in the *poltrona* (front orchestra), *poltroncina* (rear orchestra), or *palchi* (boxes) should use the main entrance. If you hold tickets in the *prima galleria* or *seconda galleria*, enter on the via Giuseppe Verdi side for *destra* and via Filodrammatici for *sinistra*. After passing through the narrow entrance vestibule, those seated in the *palchi* should take the stairs going up on either side of *la porta grande*. If you hold tickets in the *poltrona* and *poltroncina*, take the outer stairs leading down on the right side for *destra* and on the left side for *sinistra*. You will be in the hallway surrounding the orchestra. Use the first entrance for *poltroncina* (entrance between rows S, T) and the second entrance for *poltrona* (entrance between rows L, M). Since the seats are numbered identically on both sides of the orchestra (beginning with 1 on the sides and increasing sequentially to the center aisle), it is crucial that you enter on the correct side. Boxes also have the same numbers on both sides. Box 1 is closest to the stage, and boxes 18, 19, and 20 are in the center. Seat numbers in the galleries begin with 1 on the left and continue sequentially. The ushers can be recognized by their black slacks, black turtleneck shirts, and black jackets (tails). They wear La Scala medallions on heavy chains draped around their necks. The young ushers speak some English and are friendlier than the older ones.

Programs are sold by the ushers in the entrance foyer and in the auditorium. Price varies according to the opera, ranging between Lit. 15.000 and 25.000. The program (in Italian) contains a synopsis in English and the complete libretto. It is also filled with articles, illustrations, and photographs relating to the opera and the composer. You will find the cloakroom (*guardaroba*) in the hallway surrounding the auditorium on all tiers. The cost is Lit. 2.000. Ladies' rooms (*signore*) and men's rooms (*signori*) are past the cloakrooms on each *ordine* (tier). The doors are unmarked, but a *signora* in black and white attire stands outside the ladies' room. A bar is on the via Verdi side of the entrance foyer. (You must buy a drink chit first.) A cappuccino/coffee

Die Frau ohne Schatten (Courtesy of Teatro alla Scala, Photo by Lelli & Masotti)

bar is on the via Filodrammatici side of the grand foyer. To visit the Museo Teatrale from the grand foyer, continue walking toward the via Filodrammatici side, and soon you will see MDCCCCXIII in bronze imbedded in marble. That is the entrance to the museum, where white marble busts of Jules Massenet, Jean-Baptiste Lully, and Cilèa greet you. The room farthest in the back is devoted to Verdi. Listen for the warning bells so you are not locked out of the next act.

La Scala reserves several seats in the *poltroncina* for the disabled and their escorts at the price of gallery seats. Contact the box office for more information.

Planning Your Trip

OPERA SCHEDULE

The opera season runs from early December to the beginning of July. The 1989/90 season opened on December 7 with Verdi's *I vespri siciliani* and closed on July 2 with Verdi's *La traviata*. Giovanni Battista Pergolesi's *Lo frate'-nnamorato*, Ludwig van Beethoven's *Fidelio*, Richard Wagner's *Die Meistersinger von Nürnberg*, Wolfgang Amadeus Mozart's *La clemenza di Tito*, Puccini's *Madama Butterfly*, and Pyotr Il'yich Tchaikovsky's *Pikovaya dama* (The Queen of Spades) completed the schedule.

La Scala is a *stagione* house, which means only one opera is presented at a time. Opera shares the stage with ballet. To be sure your visit coincides with an opera, write ahead for a schedule. However, it will only cover a two-month period.

If you are interested in receiving the opera schedule on a regular basis for the year, send an international postal money order payable to Teatro alla Scala for Lit. 20.000 along with your name and address to the theater address given at the beginning of the ticket section.

TRAVEL INFORMATION

Milan is a marvelous but extremely expensive city. Taxis are exorbitant: a five-block ride costs almost $8. Fortunately, public transportation is clean and safe, even late at night. However,

be sure to buy a ticket at the kiosk before you board the tram and validate it with the machine inside.

The best hotel in Milan for those attending the opera is Hotel Palace, Piazza della Repubblica 20, 20124 Milan, Italy; telephone (39)(2)6336, fax (39)(2)654-485. For reservations in the United States, call toll-free, 1-800-223-6800 (member of the Leading Hotels of the World). Singles begin at $225, doubles at $280. The hotel is a palatial five-star luxury establishment, with 230 rooms and 10 suites. Conveniently near the *Stazione Centrale F.F.S.A.* but in a quiet, tree-lined location, the Palace offers royally decorated rooms and superb service. It is the ideal place to complement your trip to La Scala. *Tranvie* 1 and 4 stop at the piazza, putting the opera house only eight minutes away. The concierge can take care of all your last-minute ticket needs.

Finding a place to dine before the performance is difficult, because most restaurants do not start serving until curtain time. However, you can get a good spaghetti platter at the Downtown Restaurant/Spaghetti Bar in the Galleria or a snack at Bar Ezio Filodrammatici 1 before the performance.

Contact the Italian Government Travel Offices (ENIT), 630 Fifth Avenue, New York, NY 10011, 212-245-4822, for travel information as well as opera schedules. They respond promptly.

Riccardo Muti, music director La Scala (Photo by Romano)

NAPLES
Teatro di San Carlo

The glorious Teatro di San Carlo, originally called Reale Teatro di San Carlo, was inaugurated on November 4, 1737, with Domenico Sarri's *Achille in Sciro*. The gala production regaled an illustrious opening night audience that included King Charles III of Bourbon. Designed by Giovanni Antonio Medrano and built by Angelo Carasale, the opera house survived seventy-nine years before succumbing to a fire in 1816. Within six days, King Ferdinand ordered the theater rebuilt, under the direction of Antonio Niccolini. The opera house was inaugurated on the king's birthday, January 12, 1817, with a work written for the occasion: Johannes Simon Mayr's *Il sogno di Partenope*. Teatro di San Carlo is the oldest European opera house with a regular season.

HISTORICAL OVERVIEW
Background

Opera in Naples was first performed privately in the Palazzo Reale. The first public performances took place at the Teatro di San Bartolomeo in 1654. The early 1700s saw three more theaters opened: Teatro dei Fiorentini in 1709 (until 1820), Teatro Pace in 1724 (until 1749), and Teatro Nuovo in 1724 (until 1828). On March 4, 1737, Charles III commissioned a new royal theater to replace the Teatro di San Bartolomeo. Completed in less than nine months at a cost of 100,000 ducats, Teatro di San Carlo, named after the king's patron saint,

was inaugurated on the saint's day. On opening night, San Carlo looked splendid, its auditorium bathed in light from oil lamps and more than a thousand candles; the ladies were decked in their finest. However, its builder, Carasale, was not so fortunate. The royal auditors were not satisfied with his accounting of the construction money and imprisoned him in the San Elmo fortress, where he died a year later. In 1799, another theater was built in Naples, Teatro del Fondo. Primarily for opera buffa, the opera house was renamed Teatro Mercadante a century later and is still in use today.

Disaster struck San Carlo on February 12, 1816. Rehearsals had just finished when a spark escaped from an oil lamp, igniting a fire that raced through the opera house, burning it to the ground. The theater was rebuilt in six months, following Medrano's original plans, with Camillo Guerra and Gennaro Maldarelli responsible for the inside decorations. The stage was enlarged and the acoustics improved. When Teatro di San Carlo reopened in 1817, it was back in all its blue and gold glory. After the unification of Italy, plush red velvet replaced the royal blue.

An orchestra pit appeared in 1872 at the suggestion of Giuseppe Verdi. When electricity was installed in 1890, the central chandelier was removed. A new foyer was added in 1937. The only damage World War II inflicted on San Carlo was to the foyer area, which the British army quickly repaired. The Allied forces played a big role in keeping the theater open during the

Italian campaign and subsequent occupation of Italy, when almost two million troops visited the opera house. San Carlo was closed in 1989 because of structural problems and reopened in 1990 for an abbreviated season. The restoration work will continue over the next few seasons.

The Theater

The Reale Teatro di San Carlo blazoned its regality: the royal palace was connected by a private corridor to the opera house, and two gilded

Top: Façade of San Carlo (Photo by author)
Bottom: Auditorium with view of royal box
(Courtesy of Teatro di San Carlo, Photo by Romano)

palms supported the royal box. Displayed above the stage were the House of Bourbon's three lilies on a blue background and the Kingdom of the Two Sicilies' coat of arms. The royal blue and gold auditorium boasted five tiers crowned by a gallery rising majestically around the horseshoe-shaped room. Oil lamps and a thousand candles illuminated the room. But the candles played another role as well: they revealed the social rank of the occupants of each box. The greater the number of candles in front of the box, the higher the social rank.

The grandeur of San Carlo today is diminished by the surrounding noise, dirt, and pollution, as well as the traffic passing constantly in front of its stucco and stone façade. The classic façade, inscribed with the names of famous Italian composers and writers, Pergolesi, Iommelli, and Piccinni on the left and Alfieri, Metastasio, and Goldini on the right, boasts a peristyle of fourteen Ionic columns. On top, "Reale Teatro di San Carlo" is inscribed, flanked by winged maidens and lyres. Friezes adorn the arched former carriage entrance.

Four tiers of boxes topped by a *galleria* and *loggione* soar in gold, ivory, and red splendor around the auditorium. Intricately carved allegorical beings and scrolls decorate the parapets, while a gold-crowned royal box, flanked by two gilded winged maidens holding red velvet drapes, resides over the entrance to the orchestra. This magnificence is illuminated by pairs of electric candles and glass globes that ring the parapets. Guerra and Maldarelli created the bas-relief resting in the pier arch of the proscenium: seven gold Muses gliding around a Roman numeral clock, above which two gold Genii hold the Bourbons' royal emblem. The ceiling, painted by Giuseppe Cammarano, presents Apollo introducing the world's greatest poets to Minerva. The curtain that Cammarano incorporated in his design was replaced in 1854 with one designed by Giuseppe Mancinelli depicting Parnassus, the sacred mountain of Apollo and the Muses. San Carlo accommodates around 3,500.

Performance History

Opera first came to Naples in 1650, with a performance of Francesco Cavalli's *Didone*. The first public performance of an opera was Francesco Cirillo's *L'Orontea, Regina d'Egitto*, presented on April 3, 1654, in the Teatro di San Bartolomeo. However, it was Alessandro Scarlatti's relocation to Naples in 1682 that transformed *Napoli* into an important operatic center. He founded the Neapolitan school, where his operas thrived. Then operatic history of sorts was made on August 28, 1733, with the world première of Giovanni Battista Pergolesi's *La serva padrona*. Pergolesi had just created what would become an important tradition in Italian opera: opera buffa. *La serva padrona* helped shape the style and form of subsequent comic operas.

After the Teatro di San Carlo opened in 1737, operas by Niccolò Piccinni and Giovanni Paisiello were staged. Domenico Cimarosa's first opera, *Le stravaganze del conte*, was produced in 1772, and the première of Niccolò Antonio Zingarelli's *Montezuma* took place in 1781. Teatro di San Carlo's golden age started when impresario Domenico Barbaia, who was also running Teatro alla Scala in Milan, took the helm. In 1813, he commissioned Mayr to write an opera. *Medea in Corinto*, the most acclaimed of Mayr's sixty-one operas, was premiered in 1813. Vincenzo Bellini was also commissioned to compose an opera. The *prima assoluta* of *Bianca e Fernando* took place on May 30, 1826. But Barbaia's biggest coup was commissioning Gioacchino Rossini as house composer. His first opera, *Elisabetta Regina d'Inghilterra*, was introduced on October 4, 1815. He had written it for the Spanish soprano Isabella Colbran, whom he married seven years later. *La gazzetta* followed at the Teatro dei Fiorentini. Teatro del Fondo hosted the première of *Otello* on December 4, 1816, and *Armida* was premiered on November 11, 1817, in the rebuilt San Carlo. *Mosè in Egitto* was introduced on March 5, 1818, followed by *Riccardo e Zoraide* on December 3, 1818, and *Ermione* on March 27,

1819. The world première of *La donna del lago* took place on October 24, 1819, and *Maometto II*, better known under its French title *Le Siège de Corinthe*, was staged for the first time on December 3, 1820. The last première was *Zelmira*, two years later, after which Rossini fled Naples.

Gaetano Donizetti followed in Rossini's footsteps, composing more than a dozen operas for San Carlo, with many more works introduced in other theaters around Naples. He arrived in 1822, remaining until 1838. Between 1827 and 1838, he also served as director of the royal opera house. Many of Donizetti's lesser-known operas that were written for San Carlo or received their *prime assolute* in Naples are listed here: *La zingara*, May 12, 1822 (Nuovo); *La lettera anonima*, June 29, 1822 (Fondo); *Alfredo il Grande*, July 2, 1823; *Il fortunato inganno*, September 3, 1823 (Nuovo); *Elvida*, July 6, 1826; *Il borgomastro di Saardaam*, August 19, 1827 (Fondo); *L'esule di Roma*, January 1, 1828; *Il castello di Kenilworth*, July 6, 1829; *Francesca di Foix*, May 30, 1831; *Fausta*, January 12, 1832; *Sancia di Castiglia*, November 4, 1832; *Il campanello*, June 1, 1836; *L'assedio di Calais*, November 19, 1836; and *Caterina Cornaro* on January 12, 1844. The censored *Poliuto*, which was introduced in Paris on April 10, 1840, surfaced at San Carlo on November 30, 1848, seven months after Donizetti's death.

The first "familiar" Donizetti opera was premiered on October 18, 1834—the censored version of *Maria Stuarda*, known as *Buondelmonte*. The following year, while Naples was suffering from a cholera epidemic, *Lucia di Lammermoor* was introduced on September 26. For Donizetti, 1837 was a devastatingly tragic year: both his last surviving child and his twenty-eight-year-old wife died. Nevertheless, he completed the score for *Roberto Devereux*, which was premiered on October 29, 1837.

Saverio Mercadante succeeded Donizetti as director of the royal opera house, and many of his operas saw the stage for the first time in Naples. Among them were *L'apoteosi d'Ercole* on

Lorin Maazel, frequent conductor at San Carlo
(Courtesy of Teatro di San Carlo, Photo by
Romano)

Gianluigi Gelmetti, frequent conductor at San
Carlo (Photo by Romano)

August 19, 1819, and *Virginia* in 1866. Mercadante, however, was overshadowed by the musical giants of his time—Bellini, Donizetti, and later Verdi. Bitter, he was determined to make Verdi's life miserable when he came to Naples. Calling Verdi "the newly rich farmer of Sant'Agata," he connived and schemed against him, thereby playing a key role in the disastrous reception of Verdi's *Oberto* and the *novità assoluta* of his *Alzira* on August 12, 1845. The world première of Verdi's *Luisa Miller* on December 8, 1849, nearly ended in disaster as well, but for a different reason: San Carlo could not pay him his fee. Verdi, feeling his contract was broken, almost canceled the opening. In return, he was virtually put under house arrest just for threatening the cancellation. But these problems paled in comparison to what transpired after Teatro di San Carlo commissioned him to write what is known today as *Un ballo in maschera*. Born as *Gustavo III*, then rechristened *Una vendetta in domino*, the opera was rejected by the censors,

partly because Mercadante had begun an opera on the same subject called *Il reggente*. Verdi reworked the piece, conforming to most of their demands, but as fate would have it, the Italian anarchist Felice Orsini attempted to assassinate Napoleon III the day before Verdi arrived in Naples. The result was the ban of regicidal plots from the stage. Verdi was provided with a new libretto and title, *Adelia degli Ademari*, for his opera. After months of problems, Verdi refused to present the opera as the censors dictated. San Carlo sued him, and Verdi countersued. The case was finally settled out of court, and Rome's Teatro Apollo was the beneficiary of this feud.

The glory of San Carlo waned after the unification of Italy in 1860. Even the world's most famous Neapolitan tenor, Enrico Caruso, had little to do with San Carlo: he sang there only once in 1901. Another Neapolitan, Ruggero Leoncavallo, experienced his greatest success, *Pagliacci*, in Milan. The English composer Frederick d'Erlanger did not fare much better in Naples. After the first act in the world première of his *Tess* on April 10, 1906, Mount Vesuvius erupted, sending the audience fleeing in all directions. The world première of Riccardo Zandonai's *Francesca da Rimini* on January 15, 1921, at least was completed. Ildebrando Pizzetti's *Fedra* was introduced on April 16, 1924, and Franco Alfano's *L'ultimo Lord* was premiered six years later. *Aida*, the inaugural opera of the 1937/38 season, was one opening night San Carlo would rather forget: Adolf Hitler was a guest of the royal couple.

After the war, some glorious soprano voices rang out in the theater. Renata Tebaldi made her debut as Violetta in Verdi's *La traviata* on February 21, 1948, and Maria Callas opened the 1949/50 season as Abigaille in Verdi's *Nabucco*. Recently, contemporary works have appeared on stage, and revivals of little-known operas from Neapolitan tradition have emerged.

I was in Naples to see Jules Massenet's *Manon*. However, the date of the performance was moved, and no one bothered to inform me, although they had my address and my telephone and fax numbers. (Keep this in mind when planning to attend the opera at San Carlo.) Therefore, I am unable to give an account of a performance or to report whether the behavior of the reputedly ill-mannered Neapolitan audiences has improved.

PRACTICAL INFORMATION
Tickets

The box office (*biglietteria*) is located at via San Carlo 101, to the left of the main entrance. Decorated with gold masks of comedy and tragedy, it is open Tuesday through Sunday from 10:00 a.m. to 1:00 p.m. and from 4:30 p.m. to 7:30 p.m. (*dal martedì al domenica dalle ore 10 alle ore 13 e dalle ore 16,30 alle ore 19,30*). On performance days, it remains open until a half hour after curtain time. A booklet of the season's schedule, *Programma-Calendario*, is found on the ledge by the box office. Tickets can be purchased beginning thirty days before the performance.

You can also order tickets by mail at the beginning of the season for the entire season, but keep in mind that there are frequent schedule changes, about which you will not be informed. On your ticket order, include your name, address, telephone number, opera, date of performance, seating section, and number of tickets. Enclose a bank draft or money order in Italian Lire and send it by **registered mail** to:

Biglietteria del Teatro San Carlo
101 via San Carlo
80133 Naples, Italy

Tickets can be ordered by telephone at 797-2412 or 797-2370 only if you reside in the Naples area. However, you can telephone either

TICKET TABLE Prezzi (Prices in Lit.)				
Location	Turno A	Turno B	Turni C-F	Turno D
Poltrona (orchestra)	130.000	100.000	80.000	70.000
Posto palco I fila (box seat 1st tier)	90.000	70.000	60.000	50.000
Posto palco II fila (box seat 2nd tier)	100.000	80.000	70.000	60.000
Posto palco III fila (box seat 3rd tier)	80.000	60.000	50.000	40.000
Posto palco IV fila (box seat 4th tier)	60.000	50.000	40.000	30.000
Balconata V fila (balcony - 5th tier)	35.000	25.000	20.000	15.000
Balconata VI fila (balcony - 6th tier)	25.000	20.000	15.000	12.000

Balconata V is also called Galleria. Balconata VI is also called Loggione.
$1 = Lit. 1.200, but can change due to the fluctuating value of the dollar.
Lit. is an abbreviation for Italian Lire.

number for ticket availability. You must speak fluent Italian. Naples is six hours ahead of Eastern Standard Time. From outside Italy, use (39) country code and (81) city code.

Your best chance for tickets is the *fuori abbonamento* (nonsubscription) performances. *Turno A* (series A) is usually *tutto esaurito* (sold out). If you do get tickets, keep in mind that evening dress is requested for the A series.

When Teatro di San Carlo was built, it was more important to see who was seated in the other boxes than what was being performed on stage. As a result, the side box seats have great views of the other boxes. Keep that in mind when buying tickets.

Understanding your ticket will help you find your seat easily, so a translation appears below.

Turni A and C begin at 8:30 p.m. (*ore* 20,30), *Turni* B and D begin at 6:00 p.m. (*ore* 18), and

Turno F begins at 5:30 p.m. (*ore* 17,30). Curtain time for *fuori abbonamento* performances varies, so pick up a schedule at the box office or check the poster in front of the opera house for starting times. Performances at San Carlo used to begin a half hour to an hour late. However, a sign now is posted in the box office stating that performances start on time and latecomers must wait in the foyer, where there are television monitors.

Finding Your Way

Teatro San Carlo faces via San Carlo, bordered on the east by the Biblioteca Nazionale and on the west by Piazza Trieste e Trento. I would not recommend taking any public transportation unless your money is well hidden and you are not carrying a purse or suitcase or wearing any jewelry. Naples is a dangerous and crime-ridden

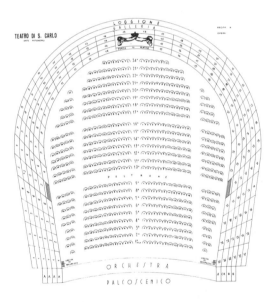

Seating Plan San Carlo (Courtesy of Teatro di San Carlo)

Gustav Kuhn, frequent conductor at San Carlo (Courtesy of Teatro di San Carlo, Photo by Romano)

TICKET TRANSLATION

	Teatro di San Carlo		Theater of Saint Charles
	Stagione Lirica 1990		1990 Opera Season
Maggio 30		May 30	
Ore 18,00	Poltrona	6:00 p.m.	Orchestra Seat
1ª Fila	**N. 8**	**1st Row**	**Seat 8**
	Lire 100.000		(Price)

city. Bus 24 stops in front of the opera house. Buses 106, 131, 150, 406D, and 523 stop on via Verdi, one block from the opera house. Buses 150 and 406D stop at the *Stazione Centrale FS Napoli* (Naples Central Railway Station) as well.

The main entrance is at via San Carlo 101, 102, and 103. Immediately after you enter, a twin grand staircase will lead you into a marble hallway. If you hold tickets in the *poltrone*, go through the doors and up more steps into the auditorium. Even seats are on the right, and odd seats on the left. Seat numbers 1, 2 flank the center aisle, increasing sequentially to the sides. *Palchi* 14-17 are in the center, with boxes 1 and 28 closest to the stage. *Palchi* 1-14 are on the right side, and boxes 15-28 are on the left side. The elevators to the upper tiers are located to the right at the top of the grand staircase.

Programs are for sale at the cloakroom for Lit. 10.000. The program (in Italian) contains the complete libretto, illustrations, and articles relating to the opera. To find the cloakroom (*guardaroba*), turn left in the marble hallway at the top of the grand staircase and then left again. The cost is Lit. 1.000. The bar is past the *guardaroba* at the end of the hallway in the beautiful grand foyer. A white marble bust of Verdi guards the entrance. Three ladies' rooms (*signore*} and one men's room (*signori*) are located through the doors off the left side of the marble hallway and down a flight of stairs. They are unmarked. The entrance for the disabled is on the Piazza Trieste e Trento side and leads directly to the elevators.

Planning Your Trip
OPERA PROGRAM

The season usually runs from mid-December to the beginning of July. However, the Teatro di San Carlo is undergoing renovations due to structural problems, resulting in abbreviated seasons. The first half of the 1990 season took place at the Teatro Mercadante. The only operas performed at San Carlo were Massenet's *Manon* and Giacomo Puccini's *Madama Butterfly*. San Carlo is a *stagione* house, which means that only one opera is performed at a time. Opera shares the stage with ballet. You can write for a schedule, but keep in mind that it changes without notice. The address is:

Teatro San Carlo
Via San Carlo
80133 Naples, Italy

TRAVEL INFORMATION

It is unfortunate that one of the world's most beautiful opera houses is in a city plagued by crime, pollution, and overwhelming numbers of cars and people. The streets are dirty and dangerous. Do not carry a purse or wear jewelry that you want to see again. It is even unsafe to cross the street. Traffic signals are merely colorful decorations; cars do not stop for red lights. When you need to cross the street, wait until a Neapolitan starts to cross and follow him, or her, placing that person between you and the car. And as one might expect in such a city, the taxi drivers are rip-off artists.

The best hotel for operagoers in Naples is the Hotel Mediterraneo, via Nuova Ponte di Tappia 25, 80133, Napoli, Italy; telephone (39)(81)551-2240, fax (39)(81) 552-5868. It is located only three blocks from the opera house, with only one dangerous street to cross. It is close enough that you can walk quickly to the hotel after the performance. Do not carry a purse, and hide any jewelry you might be wearing. Singles are $150 and doubles $225. A filling buffet breakfast is included in the price. It is a comfortable four-star establishment. The hotel can assist with opera tickets.

For a light supper before the opera, there are the Gran Caffe Verdi on via Giuseppe Verdi and a couple of cafes inside a partially cleaned Galleria.

You can contact the Italian Government Travel Offices at 630 Fifth Avenue, New York, NY 10011, 212-245-4822, for travel and opera information. They respond quickly.

PARMA
Teatro Regio

*T*he stately Teatro Regio di Parma, originally called Il Nuovo Teatro Ducale, was inaugurated on May 16, 1829, with Vincenzo Bellini's *Zaira* and the ballet, *Oreste*. The gala opening night, unlike those of most opera houses, was not as lively an occasion as one might expect. The audience gave *Zaira* a cool reception. The Regio, designed by Nicola Bettòli and modeled after Teatro alla Scala, was one of the most modern theaters of its time.

HISTORICAL OVERVIEW
Background

Theater tradition in Parma dates back to Roman times, when both a theater and an amphitheater existed. In 1617, Ranuccio Farnese commissioned the building of the first "modern" theater, Teatro Farnese. Ranuccio wanted to impress the visiting Grand Duke Cosimo II, because he hoped to arrange a marriage between his son, Odoardo, and Cosimo II's daughter, Margherita de' Medici. The theater, designed by Gian Battista Aleotti, was opened in 1628 in honor of that marriage. Used mainly for wedding celebrations until 1732, the Farnese was almost lost in 1857, when civil servant and architect Pier Luigi Montecchini requested its demolition because of its neglected state. Fortunately, no one paid much attention to Montecchini. World War II nearly fulfilled Montecchini's request when a bomb crashed through the roof on May 13, 1944. Although the Farnese suffered extensive damage to its decorations, it survived. Painstakingly restored in 1965, the Farnese stands today in all its classic beauty as a superb example of a seventeenth-century aristocratic theater.

Ranuccio Farnese's heir, Ranuccio II, built three theaters in Parma: Teatro della Rocchetta, opened in 1674 and demolished in 1822, Teatrino di Corte, opened in 1689 and demolished in 1832, and the Teatro Ducale, opened in 1688 and demolished in 1829. The Teatro Ducale, designed by the Court architect, Stefano Lolli, occupied the spot where the central post office now stands. Constructed of wood with a beautiful entrance hall, the Ducale boasted four tiers topped by a gallery. In the center stood a splendid *palco Ducale* (ducal box). The auditorium accommodated 1,200. The Ducale was renowned in all Europe for its grand performances and superb singers.

The Teatro Regio, called Il Nuovo Teatro Ducale until 1849, was the idea of La principessa Imperiale and Arciduchessa d'Austria Marie Louise, also the duchessa di Parma, who happened to be the divorced second wife of Napoleon. The idea of accompanying her husband into exile did not appeal to Marie Louise, daughter of Francis I of Austria, so instead she divorced and settled in Parma. Since she paid for the Regio, she picked out the architect, Nicola Bettòli, and the interior designers, Gian Battista Borghesi and Paolo Toschi. Marie Louise also managed to incorporate some of her Austrian and French Empire background into the undertaking. Taking eight years to build, the Regio opened in 1829. After the first unsuccessful fight for independence, the opera house underwent restoration in 1849. Four years later, the auditorium was modified by Gerolamo Magnani and gas lighting was installed. In 1890 electric lights replaced the gas ones in the auditorium. Seventeen years later, the stage lights were electrified. For the centennial of Giuseppe Verdi's birth, the rest of the theater was converted to electricity.

The Regio managed to survive both world wars relatively unscathed but succumbed to an earthquake on November 9, 1983. It has since been resurrected and is back in all its glory.

Façade of Regio (Photo by author)

The Theaters

The Teatro Farnese was a wooden structure of enormous proportions constructed near the Palazza Pilotta. It resembled the Teatro Olimpico in Vicenza. As many as 4,500 spectators were crammed in the horseshoe-shaped auditorium containing two balcony levels and fourteen rows of stadium "bleachers" that wrapped around the stage. Decorated by Lionello Spada and embellished with statues of stucco and straw by Luca Reti, the Farnese was painted to look like marble and gold, giving the illusion of great wealth and power to its owner, Ranuccio Farnese.

In contrast, the Teatro Regio is an imposing classic building of "soft" mustard-colored stucco, which harmonizes with the surrounding area. Its severe façade, with a peristyle supported by ten unadorned Ionic columns, boasts five elegant Empire windows. Above rests a large semicircular window, flanked by two winged maidens, that gives light to the foyer. On the tympanum, masks of Comedy and Tragedy stare in opposite directions. Parmesan sculptor Tommaso Bandini executed the façade's decorations.

The entrance foyer, with its eight towering Ionic columns, black and white checkered marble floor, and copper-colored walls, leads into a striking red, ivory, and gold elliptical auditorium of perfect proportions and linear harmony.

Four tiers of boxes capped by a gallery rise above plush red velvet orchestra seats. In the center looms a gold- and maroon-draped ducal box topped by the crown of the Holy Roman Empire. Medallions of composers and gold horn-blowing cherubs lavishly embellish the parapets. The boxes, each with a private anteroom, are decorated according to the tastes of the original owners.

The ceiling, originally decorated by Paolo Toschi, was repainted by Borghesi in 1853. Lino, Aristophanes, Euripides, Plautus, Seneca, Metastasio, Alfieri, and Goldini swirled around the spectacular two-and-a-half-ton, twelve-foot-high golden bronze astral lamp. The chandelier, the work of Lacarrière of Paris, was adorned with three statuettes representing Tragedy, Comedy, and Dance. (They have since been removed to allow better stage visibility from the gallery.) The original curtain, painted by Borghesi, represented the *Trionfo della Sapienza* (Triumph of Knowledge). Marie Louise was portrayed as Minerva, sitting on her throne and holding a spear. Around her were Justice, Hercules, and Deianira. Fame and Immortality descended from the sky to crown the goddess, while nymphs danced. Parnassus sat to the left by Orpheus, playing the lyre to honor the goddess's triumph. The three Graces stood behind Parnassus to the left while the great poets Virgil, Dante, Ovid, Homer, and Pindar were grouped to the right. In the background a procession of immortal spirits disappeared into the clouds. Today the curtain is red velvet. On top of the proscenium rests a clock, the top numerals telling the hour, the bottom minutes. They change in five-minute intervals. The auditorium seats 1,244.

Performance History

The Teatro Farnese opened on December 21, 1628, for the wedding celebration of Odoardo Farnese and Margherita de' Medici. The program consisted of a *torneo* entitled *Mercurio e Marte*, with music by Claudio Monteverdi and text by Claudio Archillini. A short time later, Monteverdi's *Gli amori di Diana e di Endimione* graced the stage. The last performance took place on October 6, 1732, to honor Carlo I di Borbone.

Teatro Ducale opened in 1688 with Antonio Zannettini's *Teseo in Atene*. Giovanni Battista Pergolesi's *La serva padrona* surfaced in 1738, and, fifty years later, Giovanni Paisiello's *Il barbiere di Siviglia* was presented. The following year, the first opera by the Parma-born composer Ferdinando Paër, *La locanda dei vagabondi*, was produced. The Ducale hosted the premières of several of Paër's operas, including *Agnese*. Gioacchino Rossini arrived in Parma in 1814. Some of his operas, such as *Tancredi* and *La Cenerentola*, were hits with the critical Parma audience, and others, such as *L'italiana in Algeri* and *Il turco in Italia*, were misses. His *Il barbiere di Siviglia* was both: it started successfully but ended a failure. One could never predict the reception a performance would receive at Teatro Ducale. But despite the mercurial behavior of the audience, almost every important artist of the era appeared on its stage. The Teatro Ducale closed in 1828 with a performance of Rossini's *Zelmira*.

For the inauguration of Teatro Regio, Rossini was invited to compose an opera. However, he was too busy, so the task fell to Bellini. A libretto written by a member of the board of directors of the Regio was sent to Bellini as the basis of the inaugural opera, but Bellini refused to use it. This incident, compounded by the fact that Bellini

Auditorium with view of royal box (Courtesy of Teatro Regio di Parma)

was only the board's second choice, led to the hostile reception *Zaira* received from the opening night crowd. However, contrary to what has been written, *Zaira* received seven more performances before sinking into oblivion. Four additional operas graced the stage during the inaugural season: Luigi Ricci's *Colombo* and Rossini's *Mosè e Faraone*, *Semiramide*, and *Il barbiere di Siviglia*. Two ballets were also performed. During the first few years, Rossini operas dominated the stage, but soon thereafter, works by Bellini and Gaetano Donizetti works joined the repertory. Then Verdi operas were staged.

Verdi was born less than thirty miles from Parma at Le Roncole, so Parma adopted him as its native son, with his operas playing a dominant role in the Regio's repertory. Every one of Verdi's twenty-seven operas has been staged there, including his adaptation of *I Lombardi* for the Paris Opéra, called *Jérusalem*. The first Regio performance of *Jérusalem* took place on January 7, 1986. The first Verdi opera at the Regio

Peristyle of Regio (Courtesy of Teatro Regio di Parma)

was *Nabucodonosor* (*Nabucco*) on April 17, 1843. Verdi journeyed to Parma to direct the opera, which received twenty-three performances. He traveled to the Regio again in April 1872 to direct his *Aida*, which opened on April 20 and received seventeen performances. By the end of the first fifty years of the Regio's existence, almost a quarter of all the performances had been of Verdi operas. Parma operagoers had taken it on themselves to know each note and word of every Verdi opera, and woe to the director, singer, or conductor who did not.

In 1885, Amilcare Ponchielli came to Parma to direct the opening on December 26 of his *La Gioconda*. The Parma première of his *Marion Delorme* followed on February 13, 1886. Ten years later, Umberto Giordano traveled to Parma to lead the opening of his *Andrea Chénier* on December 26, 1896. But Giacomo Puccini's presence did not ensure the success of *La bohème* when it played on January 29, 1898, and Pietro Mascagni's *Amica* fared even worse. It was laughed off the stage when it opened on January 6, 1908.

For the centennial of Verdi's birth, the 1913 winter season offered only works by Verdi. *Oberto, Conte di San Bonifacio* opened the celebration on September 6, 1913. *Nabucco, Un ballo in maschera*, *Aida*, *Falstaff*, and *Don Carlo* followed. The celebration ended on October 11, 1913, with his *Messa da Requiem*. In 1951, a second Verdi celebration took place, commemorating the fiftieth anniversary of his death. The festival opened on his birthday, October 10, with *Ernani*. *Don Carlo*, *La battaglia di Legnano*, and *Falstaff* completed the schedule. In September 1990, the Regio hosted another Verdi festival with *Alzira*, *Il trovatore*, and *Le trouvère* on the program.

Recently, the Regio hosted some world premières: Renato Falavigna's *Ubu Re* on December 2, 1982, and Franco Battiato's *Genesi* on April 26, 1987.

The opera season at the Regio is short, contrasting with the large number of artists the audience has run out of town. Many opera performances end prematurely, the work of the *intenditori* (experts). The 1989/90 season experienced two sudden deaths (out of only twenty-four performances); one opera was breathing only thirty minutes!

As you can see, the Regio's audience plays a big role in the theater's performance history. The penchant for displaying animosity toward substandard performances and singers dates back to the final decade at the Teatro Ducale. The first reported incident took place in 1816, when a tenor named Alberico Curioni performed in Vincenzo Federici's *Zaira*. His singing went unappreciated and was loudly hissed and booed. Undaunted, the tenor responded by yelling obscenities back at the audience. Pandemonium followed. Order was restored only when the chief of police mounted the stage and announced that the tenor had been arrested and a ballet would replace the opera. At the end of the ballet, Curioni returned to the stage and apologized. Then the opera was continued, starting at the point where it had been interrupted. This was not the last the audience heard from Curioni. At the season's final performance, he decided to take his revenge. In the middle of the opera, he sauntered

to the front of the stage and began to whistle. A riot ensued, and the police were summoned once again. This time he was not only arrested but served eight days in jail. Upon his release, he was escorted to the frontier and banished from Parma forever. The audience caused the same fate to befall a hapless impresario two years later. The opening night of the 1818 season was an abysmal failure. The opera house was summarily closed and the impresario sent to jail for "offending the public sensibilities." He was released a short time later on the condition that he improve his operas and presentations. He failed once again and was fired.

When the Regio opened, hostility continued to greet substandard performances (chairs were thrown on stage to stop the show), and ill-prepared singers were treated mercilessly. The acclaimed Parma-born tenor Italo Campanini once forgot his lines, and someone yelled, "Hey, Campanini, this is how it goes," and sang the aria. The audience finally met its match with soprano Emma Carelli. It was February 14, 1903, the opening night of Ponchielli's *La Gioconda*. Several members of the cast already had been jeered when Carelli began Gioconda's second-act aria with Laura, "*L'amo come il fulgor del creato*." The audience was unimpressed and booed her as well. She simply walked off the stage and went straight to the train station, still dressed in her costume and makeup.

Most of the heckling rains down from the top balcony where the *intenditori* sit. However, the audience knows every singer and how much he or she is being paid. The higher the fee, the more ruthless their reaction to a bad note. No singer survives a bad night at the Regio. Although the days of chair throwing to stop a bad performance are over, program throwing has taken its place. But before programs land on the stage, you might hear these noises leading to that climactic event: extended throat clearing; loud sighs; murmurs; groans; whistles; hisses; boos; shouts.

Top: Leona Mitchell and Renato Bruson in *Ernani* (Courtesy of Teatro Regio di Parma)
Bottom: *La donna del lago* (Courtesy of Teatro Regio di Parma)

PRACTICAL INFORMATION
Tickets

The box office (*biglietteria*) is located at via Garibaldi 16/A inside the opera house on the left side, where you see the sign: *Orario di Biglietteria—Mattino 9,30-12,30 Pomeriggio 16,30-19,00* (Box office hours—Morning 9:30 a.m. to 12:30 p.m. Afternoon 4:30 p.m. to 7:00 p.m.). The box office is closed Mondays. On performance days, the box office remains open until one-half hour after curtain time. A bronze bust of Verdi stands opposite the box office windows. Tickets can be purchased around two weeks before the season begins for the entire season.

Tickets can be reserved by mail. Ticket orders are accepted beginning five weeks before the season starts for the entire season. However, your request must arrive at least five days before the performance. Enclose a bank or postal money order in Italian Lire made out to "Teatro Regio," with your name, address, telephone number, opera(s), date(s), seating location, and number of tickets desired. List alternative dates and locations to increase your chances for tickets. If your order cannot be fulfilled, your money will be returned. Mail your request to:

Biglietteria del Teatro Regio
via Garibaldi 16
43100 Parma, Italy

Tickets cannot be reserved by telephone. However, you can call (39)(521)795-678 for ticket information during box office hours. (39) = country code; (521) = city code. In Italy, dial (0521)795-678. You must speak Italian. Parma

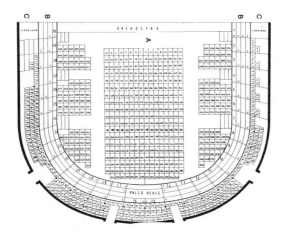

Seating Plan (Courtesy of Teatro Regio di Parma)

TICKET TABLE Prezzi per Serate d'Opera (Prices in Lit. for Opera Evenings)				
Location	prime rappr.	seconde rappr.	alle altre rappr.	popol. rappr.
Poltrona (orchestra)	65.000	45.000	35.000	25.000
Ingresso ai palchi (standing in box)	25.000	20.000	15.000	10.000
Galleria numerata (numbered gallery)	25.000	20.000	15.000	10.000
Posto palco centrale (center box seat)	60.000	40.000	30.000	22.000
Posto palco laterale (side box seat)	50.000	34.000	25.000	20.000

Galleria is also called Loggione.
$1 = Lit. 1.200, but can vary due to the fluctuating value of the dollar.
Lit. is an abbreviation for Italian Lire.

is six hours ahead of Eastern Standard Time.

Your best chance for tickets is the *fuori abbonnement* (nonsubscription) performances, which fall under *alle altre rappresentazioni* price column. *Prime rappresentazioni* (opening nights) and *seconde rappresentazioni* (second performances) of each opera are always *tutto esaurito* (sold out). If you want to attend the opening night or following performance, send your reservation request as early in the season as possible. The higher prices for the first and second performances are mainly status driven. The casts are usually the same, although the risk increases in the later performances that one or more of the première singers will have departed.

Finding your place can be confusing, since every seat in the *poltrone* and *loggione* has a different number and there is no row identification. Below is the information you will find on your ticket.

Evening performances start at either 8:00 p.m. (*ore* 20) or 8:30 p.m. (*ore* 20,30). Matinees begin at 3:30 p.m. (*ore* 15,30). Latecomers must wait in the smoking room, where television monitors are set up.

Finding Your Way

Il Teatro Regio faces via Garibaldi, bordered on the south by Piazzale Antonio Barezzi, on the north by Piazza della Pace, and on the west by via Carducci. The opera house is a pleasant fifteen-minute walk from the *Stazione F.S.* (train station). Buses 1, 2, and 8 stop in front of the Regio.

The main entrance to Teatro Regio is at via Garibaldi 16. After entering, turn left past the box office, then loop back into the entrance foyer. If you are seated in *poltrone numeri pari* (orchestra even numbers), take the stairs down on the right. For the *poltrone numeri dispari*, take the stairs down on your left. Those holding tickets in the *palchi 1a fila* (first tier boxes) continue straight ahead. Those in the remaining box tiers, take the stairs up (right for *pari* and left for *dispari*). You will find the seat numbers on the backs of the seats. If you are seated in the *galleria*, take the stairs next to the box office before entering the grand entrance foyer.

Programs are sold in the entrance foyer and cost Lit. 10.000. The program (in Italian) includes the entire libretto, photographs, prints, and articles relevant to the opera and composer. An abbreviated program is given out at each performance as you enter the auditorium. You will find a ladies' room (*servizi signore*) on the right side of the entrance foyer and a men's room (*servizi signori*) and another ladies' room in the hallway around the orchestra. Follow the sign *servizi* on the right. A cloakroom (*guardaroba*) is on the right side of the entrance foyer, with additional cloakrooms in the hallway around the orchestra on both sides. The cost is Lit. 1.000. The bar and a separate smoking room are off the right side of the entrance foyer.

Planning Your Trip
OPERA SCHEDULE

The season runs from the end of December to the beginning of May. The repertory is predominantly Italian with strong emphasis on Verdi operas. The *serata inaugurale* (opening night) of the 1989/90 season was December 26 with Rossini's *La donna del lago*. The season

---

TICKET TRANSLATION

Città di Parma - Teatro Regio		City of Parma - Royal Theater	
Poltrona N.320	**Pari**	**Orchestra Seat 320**	**Even (Side)**
Werther	Seconde	(Opera)	2nd Presentation
27/4/90	20,30	April 27, 1990	8:30 p.m.
	45.000		(Price)

closed on May 6 with Jules Massenet's *Werther*. Puccini's *La fanciulla del West* and Verdi's *La traviata* and *Ernani* completed the schedule. Every opera was a new production.

Teatro Regio is a *stagione* house, which means only one opera is performed at a time. The opera shares the stage with ballets, concerts, and recitals. To be sure your visit coincides with an opera, write for a schedule to:

Biglietteria e Ufficio Informazioni
del Teatro Regio
via Garibaldi 16
43100 Parma, Italy

Detail of façade (Photo by author)

TRAVEL INFORMATION
The best hotel for operagoers in Parma is the Park Hotel Stendhal, via Bodoni 3, 43100 Parma PR I, Italy; telephone (39)(521)208-057, fax (39)(521)285-655. Singles cost $118, doubles $175. A continental breakfast is included. It is a pleasant, small hotel with 60 rooms, near the Piazza Pilotta and close to the center of town. The hotel is only a ten-minute walk from the train station and a five-minute walk to the opera house. Several opera stars have stayed at the Park Hotel Stendhal.

There are a few places across from the opera house where you can get a light meal: Specialitá Panini e Vini, 17 Strada Garibaldi, Caffé Teatro Regio, 11A via Garibaldi, and Pane e Pasta, 11D via Garibaldi.

The Italian Government Travel Offices (ENIT) at 630 Fifth Avenue, New York, NY 10011, 212-245-4822, can send you travel information as well as some opera information. They reply very promptly.

Poster of 1989/90 season (Courtesy of Teatro Regio di Parma)

ROME
Teatro dell'Opera

The Teatro dell'Opera, originally called Teatro Costanzi, was inaugurated on November 27, 1880, with a gala performance of Gioacchino Rossini's *Semiramide*. The show dazzled an illustrious opening night crowd, which included King Umberto I and Queen Margherita. Their majesties arrived with much fanfare, flanked by cuirassiers, while the orchestra played the *Royal March*. The king stayed only a short time, but the queen, wearing a brilliant diadem around her blonde hair, remained until the end.

Domenico Costanzi, a wealthy builder who wanted his name to live in perpetuity, had commissioned Achille Sfondrini to design the new opera house. The distinguished audience greeted Costanzi and Sfondrini with waves of applause in recognition of their accomplishment.

The city of Rome acquired the building on May 20, 1926, and Italian dictator Benito Mussolini's favorite architect, Marcello Piacentini, supervised its renovation. The opera house reopened on February 27, 1928, with a spectacular performance of Arrigo Boïto's *Nerone*.

HISTORICAL OVERVIEW
Background

Opera was first performed in Rome in the Palazzo Barberini, which opened in 1632 and seated 3,000. In 1669, Pope Clement IX, who wrote librettos for many of the operas given at the Palazzo Barberini, authorized Count Giacomo d'Alibert to erect Rome's first public opera house,

Teatro Torre di Nona (commonly called Teatro Torinona). The theater was inaugurated the following year. The next pope did not have the same enthusiasm for opera and ordered the theater closed six years later. New life was breathed into Teatro Torinona in 1690, but Pope Innocent XII snuffed that out in 1697 when he ordered the theater demolished. Meanwhile, Teatro Caprinaca opened in 1679 as a private theater, admitting the public sixteen years later. Teatro Caprinaca's swan song took place in 1881, with Giuseppe Verdi's *Ernani*.

In 1717, the Teatro delle Dame was constructed by Count d'Alibert's son for *opera seria*. Ten years later, Domenico Valle built the Teatro Valle, which eventually became a playhouse. The largest of the three opera houses constructed during this time was Teatro Argentina, built by Duke Sforza-Cesarini. The theater, which was inaugurated in 1732, functions today as a concert hall. The following year, the demolished Teatro Torinona was resurrected, and its checkered history continued. A fire claimed it in 1781, but the theater was again resurrected six years later. Renovated in 1795 and renamed Teatro Apollo, the opera house was refurbished once again in 1821. Its chronicle finally ended in 1879, when a demolition team arrived and a Tiber River embankment was constructed in its place.

Two years earlier, Costanzi had presented his idea of building a *Grande Politeama* "for the people," a building seating more than 3,000 on a site next to the Hotel Quirinale, which he owned. His proposal met with indifference and scorn and was soon dropped. However, the demolition of the glorious Teatro Apollo created an urgent need for a *Teatro Regio*, so a compromise was reached. A *Teatro Nazionale* was built, accommodating the aristocrats in three splendid box tiers and the working classes in two enormous top galleries. The foundation for Teatro Costanzi was poured in 1879, and the theater opened the following November.

Costanzi died on October 8, 1898, and his son Enrico took over running the opera house. When his son died nine years later on June 24, the doors were opened for its sale to the Società Teatrale Internazionale (STIN), which occurred on July 29, 1908. Eventually the STIN experienced insurmountable financial difficulties and sold the theater to the city of Rome. The city closed the building for two years to convert one gallery into a box tier, to install better stage machinery, and to hang a giant chandelier. The most dramatic change, however, was the moving of its main entrance from via Firenze, a small narrow side street, to the main avenue of via Viminale. The opera house was rechristened Teatro Reale dell'Opera. When Italy became a republic in 1946, the ''Reale'' was quietly dropped from the theater's name. Recently, under the supervision of the architects Italo Ceccarelli and Luigia Zoli, further renovation took place. ''Teatro dell'Opera'' in bronze letters was added to the façade, and four glass showcases were installed to exhibit photographs and relevant materials from operas presented there.

The Theater

Teatro Costanzi was a grand and elegant theater, built in the Renaissance style with a touch of baroque. Its façade, lined with Ionic ''Muse'' pilasters flanking rounded arches, overlooked via Firenze. Costly gilded stucco filled the interior. To the left of the entrance was a splendid room where the ladies could await their carriages. The main vestibule was located to the right. The lavish gold and red horseshoe-shaped auditorium was characterized by harmonious architectural lines. It boasted a majestic royal box, elaborate gilded stucco, fancy imbrication, and arabesque arches buttressing the top gallery's ceiling. Boggio worked the stucco, and Pavone was the gilder. The dome ceiling, painted by Annibale Brugnoli, swirled with allegorical figures of the theater arts and of Olympic games and races. In the center hung a glittering chandelier. Teatro Costanzi accommodated 2,293.

Teatro Costanzi's descendant, Teatro dell' Opera, is a majestic if somewhat pretentious building of travertine stone. Gone are the rounded

Façade of Dell'Opera (Photo by author)

arches and pilasters. In its place are the severe lines of its whitish stone block façade, interrupted by nine elongated rectangular windows. The only embellishment is a bronze bas-relief of the Muses affixed atop the building and the letters Teatro dell'Opera on the portico. Busts of Volpi and Gigli greet you in the entrance foyer, along with a plaque commemorating Domenico Costanzi. A bust of Verdi watches over the grand staircase, which leads up to a grand foyer of rigid lines and gray charcoal marble borders. The gold and rose auditorium, adorned with lavish gilded frescoes of Muses and scrolls, boasts four tiers of boxes topped by a gallery and a prominent royal *loge*. ''Vittorio Emanuele III Rege, Benito Mussolini Duce, Lodovicus Spada Potenziani, Romae Gubernator Restituit MCMXXVIII-VI'' is inscribed on the proscenium, where a maroon-and-gold-fringed curtain hangs. Allegorical figures surround a massive circular chandelier attached to the cupola's center. The opera house seats 2,112.

Performance History

Rome heard its first "opera" in 1600: Cavalieri's *Rappresentazione di anima e di corpo.* Agostino Agazzari's *Eumelio* followed six years later, and Filippo Vitali's *Aretusa* was given in 1620. The Palazzo Barberini opened with Stefano Landi's *Sant' Alessio* in 1632, while Francesco Cavalli's *Scipione Africano* opened Teatro Torre di Nona in 1670.

Domenico Sarri's *Berenice* inaugurated the Teatro Argentina in 1732. This opera house hosted the *novità assoluta* (world première) of Rossini's *Il barbiere di Siviglia* on February 20, 1816. Although *Il barbiere di Siviglia* is one of Rossini's best-loved comic operas, the opening night audience was anything but amused. Giovanni Paisiello also had written an opera called *Il barbiere di Siviglia* that was still popular, and the Roman audience resented this young composer Rossini "stealing" Paisiello's subject. Their boos and catcalls were deafening, and hisses greeted Rossini's curtain call. Gaetano Donizetti's *Zoraide in Granata* was world premiered on January 28, 1822, followed by Verdi's *I due Foscari* on November 3, 1844, and his *La battaglia di Legnano* on January 27, 1849. For *La battaglia di Legnano*, the theater was patriotically decorated, and the opening night audience went wild, forcing Act IV to be repeated. Meanwhile, another Rossini opera, *La Cenerentola*, was introduced at the Teatro Valle on January 25, 1817. Seven years later, Donizetti's *L'ajo nell'imbarazzo* graced the stage for the first time, and his *Torquato Tasso* was premiered on September 9, 1833.

Twelve years earlier, Rossini's *Mathilde di Shabran*, conducted by Nicolò Paganini, had inaugurated the renovated Teatro Apollo. Donizetti's *Adelia* first saw the stage at the Apollo on February 11, 1841. The world première of Verdi's great opera, *Il trovatore*, took place on January 19, 1853, the day the *Fiume Tevere* spilled over its banks, and the elegantly attired opening night crowd sloshed their way to the opera house. Despite an almost incomprehensible story, *Il trovatore* aroused such fervor that the crowd demanded an encore at the end of the Act III and forced the entire Act IV to be repeated. Teatro Apollo was the beneficiary of Verdi's Neapolitan problems (see Teatro di San Carlo), but only after *Un ballo in maschera* was reset in Boston. The première of *Un ballo in maschera* took place on February 17, 1859. (Since almost no Italian operagoer had even heard of Boston, the incongruity of such a lavish ball taking place in a Puritan city did not matter.)

When the Teatro Costanzi opened, Cencio Jacovacci was its first impresario. During his tenure, two world premières took place: Alessandro Orsini's *I Burgravi* on December 10, 1881 (personally supervised by the composer), and Ferdinando Caronna Pellegrino's *Fayel* on June 10, 1882. The following year Edoardo Sonzogno took the helm. He initiated a competition for one-act operas, which Pietro Mascagni's *Cavalleria rusticana* won in 1890. The world première on May 17, 1890, was heralded as Teatro Costanzi's first important *novità assoluta*. That same year, Stanislao Gastaldon's *Mala Pasqua* was premiered on April 9, Nicola Spinelli's *Labilia* on May 9, and Vincenzo Ferroni's *Rudello* on May 28. The following year, Mascagni conducted the première of his *L'amico Fritz* on October 31, but it still failed. In 1893, the tradition of pairing his *Cavalleria rusticana* with Ruggero Leoncavallo's *Pagliacci* was born at Costanzi.

Meanwhile, impresario Guglielmo Canori had taken the helm. He imported La Scala's world première production of Verdi's *Otello* lock, stock, and barrel but *senza* Verdi in April 1887. The production arrived by a special train nicknamed "*il treno Otello*." Six years later, La Scala's *novità assoluta* production of *Falstaff* appeared at Costanzi, but this time Verdi came along. The performance took place on April 15, 1893. When the curtain fell on Act II, Falstaff had just

Top: Auditorium with view of
royal box (Courtesy of Teatro
dell'Opera, Photo by Falsini)
Left: Aprile Millo in *Luisa Miller*
(Courtesy of Teatro dell'Opera,
Photo by Falsini)

been dumped into the Thames with a pile of dirty laundry. Then King Umberto I and Queen Margherita summoned Verdi to their royal box and accompanied him to the front of the box. Slowly they stepped back, leaving Verdi alone to savor the applause.

On November 27, 1894, Teatro Costanzi hosted the world première of Pietro Vallini's *Il voto*. Giacomo Setaccioli's *La sorella di Mark* was premiered on May 6, 1896, Mascagni's *Iris* on November 22, 1898, and Pietro Floridia's *La colonia libera* on May 7, 1899. Meanwhile, Titta Ruffo made his debut in 1898 as the King's Herald in Richard Wagner's *Lohengrin*, and Enrico Caruso made his debut the following year as Osaka in *Iris*.

The next important *prima assoluta*, Giacomo Puccini's *Tosca*, took place on January 14, 1900. And what a tumultuous première it was. The conductor, Leopoldo Mugnone, was shaking like a leaf because of a bomb threat to Queen Margherita, who was in the audience. Mugnone had good reason to be scared: recently a bomb

had been thrown backstage while Arturo Toscanini conducted *Otello*. The bomb did not explode. It has been speculated that Mugnone himself inadvertently instigated the unrest that evening by trying to emulate Toscanini: he insisted on starting the performance on time. Since only half the audience was seated, chaos resulted and someone shouted for the curtain to be lowered. Eventually order was restored, and *Tosca* began again. Since it was the custom for the composer to take a curtain call after the first aria, Puccini appeared after Cavaradossi's ''*Recondita armonia di bellezze diverse*'' to accept the applause, and all was well again.

Mascagni's *Le maschere* was introduced on January 17, 1901. Nine years later, on January 15, he conducted the world première of Leoncavallo's *Majà*. Vincenzo Tommasini's *Uguale fortuna*, Alberto Gasco's *La leggenda delle sette torri*, and Domenico Monleone's *Arabesca* were all premiered in 1913.

On December 26, 1916, Beniamino Gigli, after whom the piazza in front of the opera

View toward stage at Terme di Caracalla (Courtesy of Teatro dell'Opera, Photo by Falsini)

house is named, made his debut as Faust in Boïto's *Mefistofele*. The following year, Camille Saint-Saëns directed his *Samson et Dalila* with a company of French artists. The celebrated bass singer, Ezio Pinza, first appeared at Costanzi in Jules Massenet's *Manon* on January 3, 1920. Meanwhile, Mascagni directed the world première of his *Lodoletta* on April 30, 1917, and his *Il piccolo Marat* on May 2, 1921. Riccardo Zandonai directed the first performance of his *Giulietta e Romeo* on February 14, 1922. The last world première at Teatro Costanzi was Guido Laccetti's *Carnasciali* on February 13, 1925. All told, Teatro Costanzi had hosted fifty *novità assolute* in its forty-five years of existence.

The Teatro Reale dell'Opera had the support of Mussolini, so it thrived during the Fascist era, hosting at least one world première a year, with many years seeing two or three. Some of those premières are: Giuseppe Mulè's *Dafni*, March 14, 1928; Franco Casavola's *Il gobbo del Califfo*, May 4, 1929; Ildebrando Pizzetti's *Lo straniero*, April 29, 1930; Ermanno Wolf-Ferrari's *La vedova scaltra*, March 5, 1931; Franco Alfano's *Cyrano di Bergerac*, January 22, 1936; Alberto Ghislanzoni's *Re Lear*, April 24, 1937; and Gian Francesco Malipiero's *I capricci di Callot*, on October 24, 1942. Several of the composers journeyed to dell'Opera to conduct their world premières: Alfredo Casella for his *La donna serpente* on March 17, 1932; Zandonai for his *La farsa amorosa* on February 22, 1933; Ottorino Respighi for his *La fiamma* on January 23, 1934; and Giuseppe Savagnone for his *Il drago rosso* on March 28, 1935.

Acclaimed Russian bass Feodor Chaliapin made his debut on April 18, 1929, in Modest Mussorgsky's *Boris Godunov*. The winds of World War II also blew home many of Italy's international circuit singers, who brought glory to dell'Opera during Tullio Serafin's tenure. However, the *direttore* overstepped his boundary on November 3, 1942, when Rome was filled with Nazis and he staged the Italian première of Alban Berg's *Wozzeck*. The opera had been banned by the Nazis as "depraved" and its composer as "degenerate." Serafin made a quick retreat to his villa outside of Florence, where he awaited the end of the war.

After World War II, Franco Casavola's *Salammbò*, with Renata Tebaldi in the title role, was introduced on April 27, 1948. Franco Alfano's *Il Dottore Antonio* was premiered on April 30, 1949. Guido Guerrini's *Enea* on March 11, 1953, with Franco Corelli, Pizzetti's *La Pisanella* on February 24, 1955, and Jacopo Napoli's *Il tesoro* on February 26, 1958, are just a few of the many world premières the opera house hosted during the decade or so following the war. At the same time, many stars twinkled from the stage, among them, Maria Callas, Tito Gobbi, Giuseppe di Stefano, and Mario del Monaco.

Since 1960, more than forty additional world premières have been staged. Some of the more recent arrivals were Lorenzo Ferrero's *Salvatore Giuliano* on January 25, 1986, Sylvano Bussotti's *Fedra* on April 19, 1988, and Ferrero's *Charlotte Corday* on February 21, 1989. Dell' Opera does not have as many stars as in earlier times, but occasionally a few come out.

I saw an interesting production of Verdi's *Luisa Miller*, with *sufficente* singing by Adelisa Tabiadon as Luisa and Dino di Domenico as Rodolfo. When Roberto Abbado finally appeared on the podium a half hour late, his conducting was admirable, despite the distraction of loud talking and laughter from the wings. You never know what to expect from opera in Rome.

In 1937, the Teatro dell'Opera experimented with open-air opera at the Terme di Caracalla. The response was so overwhelming that an annual summer event resulted. The operas, given by the singers, conductors, orchestra, and chorus of the Opera di Roma, take place during July and August on a stage reputed to be the world's largest, in a sports arena atmosphere. The *gelati* is great!

PRACTICAL INFORMATION
Tickets

The box office (*biglietteria*) is located at Piazza Beniamino Gigli 1, to the left of the main entrance. It is open Tuesday through Saturday 9:30 a.m. to 2:00 p.m. and 4:00 p.m. to 7:00 p.m. and on performance days from 7:30 p.m. until curtain time; Sunday from 9:30 a.m. to 1 p.m., and on performance days, one hour before curtain time (*dal martedì al sabato dalle 9,30 alle 14 dalle 16 alle 19 e nei giorni di rappresentazione dalle 19,30 sino all'inizio dello spettacolo; domenica dalle 9,30 alle 13 e un'ora prima dello spettacolo*). You will find ticket prices and a seating plan in the bimonthly schedules on the shelf in the box office. The box office gentlemen speak some English and are quite helpful. Tickets can be purchased beginning seven days before the performance.

You can order tickets by mail, but send your request by **registered mail** only. Faxes, telegrams, and telexes are not accepted. These are the requirements: the letter must arrive in Rome between forty and seven days before the performance. Write your name, address, telephone number, opera, date, seat location, and number of desired tickets on your request. You may request tickets for one opera only, giving three alternate dates to increase the likelihood of getting tickets. Enclose a bank or postal money order in Italian Lire made out to "Teatro dell'Opera di Roma" and mail to:

Teatro dell'Opera
Servizio Biglietteria
Piazza B. Gigli 1
00184-Rome, Italy

You can reserve tickets by calling (39)(6) 6759-5721 (English) or (39)(6)6759-5720 (Italian) Tuesday through Saturday from 10:00 a.m. to 12:30 p.m. and from 4:30 p.m. to 7:00 p.m. (39) = country code; (6) = city code. In Italy, dial (06)6759-5721. Rome is six hours ahead of Eastern Standard Time.

The ticket prices accurately reflect how well you can see the stage. The prices of the box seats vary according to their position in relation to the stage (center or side).

Your best chance for tickets is *fuori abbonamento* (nonsubscription) performances. *Prime* (opening nights) are always *tutto esaurito* (sold out), as are many *repliche* performances as well. If you want to see a *prima* or star-studded cast performance, order your tickets as soon as reservations are accepted, or arrive in Rome seven days ahead and get on line very early in the morning.

Understanding your ticket will help you find your seat with no problem, so a translation appears below.

Evening performances usually start at 8:30 p.m. (*ore 20,30*) and afternoon performances at either 5:00 p.m. (*ore 17*) or 4:00 p.m. (*ore 16*). The starting times are listed in the bimonthly calendar, available in the box office. Unfortunately, the tourist brochure, *Ospite di Rome*, only lists the operas. The performance I attended started a half hour late, because the conductor, Roberto Abbado, was caught in a traffic jam.

Finding Your Way

Il Teatro dell'Opera faces Piazza Beniamino Gigli, bordered by via Torino to the east and via Firenze to the west. Via Viminale runs in front of the piazza. The nearest subway stop, Repubblica, is a five-minute walk from the opera house. Take Line A. It is around a ten-minute walk from *Stazioni Termini* (central train station) to the opera house.

TICKET TRANSLATION					
Teatro dell'	Poltrona di Platea		Theater of the	Orchestra	
Opera	**Fila**	**Numero**	**Opera**	**Row**	**Seat**
di Roma	8	18	of Rome	8	18

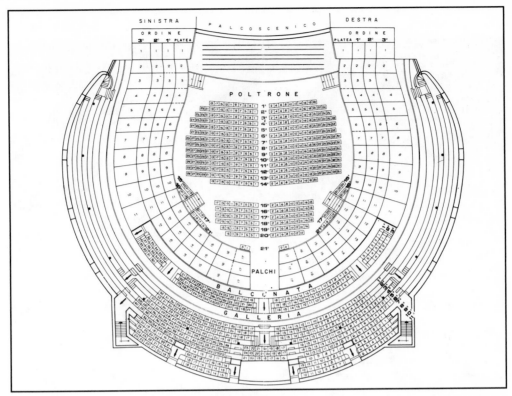

Seating Plan Teatro dell'Opera (Courtesy of Teatro dell'Opera)

TICKET TABLE
Prezzi (Prices in Lit.)

Location	Prime (First)	Repliche (Repeat)
Poltrone di platea (front orchestra)	104.000	71.500
Poltroncine di platea (rear orchestra)	83.000	54.000
Posto in palco di platea e 1°ordine da 6 posti (box seat in orchestra & 1st tier - center)	104.000	71.500
Posto in palco di platea e 1°ordine da 5 posti (box seat in orchestra & 1st tier - partial side)	83.000	54.000
Posto in palco di platea e 1°ordine da 4 posti (box seat in orchestra & 1st tier - side)	75.000	50.500
Posto in palco di 2°ordine da 6 posti (box seat in 2nd tier - center)	65.000	42.500
Posto in palco di 2°ordine da 5 posti (box seat in 2nd tier - partial side)	54.000	34.500
Posto in palco di 2°ordine da 4 posti (box seat in 2nd tier - side)	47.500	32.500
Posto in palco di 3°ordine da 5 posti (box seat in 3rd tier - partial side)	34.500	21.500
Posto in palco di 3°ordine da 4 posti (box seat in 3rd tier - side)	32.500	19.500
Balconata 1ª fila (3rd tier center row 1)	44.000	32.500
Balconata 2ª e 3ª fila (3rd tier center rows 2,3)	32.500	19.500
Galleria dalla 1ª alla 12ª fila (4th tier rows 1-12)	13.000	13.000

$1 = Lit. 1.200, but can vary due to the fluctuating value of the dollar.
Lit. is an abbreviation for Italian Lire.

Aida at Terme di Caracalla (Courtesy of Teatro dell'Opera, Photo by Falsini)

The main entrance to Teatro dell'Opera is at Piazza B. Gigli 2-7. Those seated in the *poltrone*, *poltroncine*, and *palchi* use this entrance, which leads into the right side of the opera house, because the original entrance was on via Firenze. Those seated in the *gallerie* (*balconata* and *galleria*) use the entrance on via Firenze. If you have tickets in the *poltrone pari* (front orchestra, even seats), continue straight ahead to the door on the extreme right, which goes to the first row orchestra. Those with tickets in *poltroncine pari* (rear orchestra, even seats) should use the second door, which leads into the fifteenth row orchestra. If you are seated in the *poltroncine* with a low seat number, continue around to the center rear doors. Seats 1 and 2 flank the center aisle. For *poltrone dispari*, continue farther around before entering. Black seat numbers are affixed to the backs of the seats. If you are seated in the *palcho di platea* (orchestra boxes), go up the grand staircase guarded by men dressed in white. You will be on the *destra* (right) side. Walk left for center and *sinistra* (left) boxes. (Box 1 is the closest to the stage on both sides, and box 17 flanks the center royal loge.) If you are seated in the *palchi I° ordine* (boxes 1st tier), *II° ordine* (2nd tier), or *III° ordine* (3rd tier), continue up the stairs. The ushers wear black skirts and sweaters with white blouses.

Programs are for sale on both the right and left sides of the entrance foyer. They cost Lit. 15.000. The program (in Italian) contains a synopsis in English, the complete libretto, articles, photographs, and illustrations relating to the opera. An excellent book (in Italian) on the opera house, *Il Teatro dell'Opera di Roma*, is available for Lit. 25.000. The cloakroom (*guardaroba*) is on the right side as you enter the lobby and costs Lit. 1.000. (An umbrella costs Lit. 500 to check.) The main bar is in the grand foyer on the *I° ordine*. The grand staircase leads up to the bar, which is around to the left facing B. Gigli Piazza.

Left: Carlo Colombara and Danilo Serraiocco in *Luisa Miller* (Courtesy of Teatro dell'Opera, Photo by Falsini)
Right: *Luisa Miller* (Courtesy of Teatro dell'Opera, Photo by Falsini)

Another bar is on the entrance level all the way around to the left. Ladies' (*signore*) and men's (*signori*) rooms are near each of the bars.

Planning Your Trip

OPERA SCHEDULE

The opera season runs from the middle of November to the end of May. The 1990/91 season opened on November 20 with Wolfgang Amadeus Mozart's *Die Entführung aus dem Serail* and closes on June 11 with Verdi's *Rigoletto*. Puccini's *Tosca*, Mozart's *Le nozze di Figaro* and *Don Giovanni*, Rossini's *Ermione*, Richard Strauss's *Ariadne auf Naxos*, Verdi's *Il trovatore*, Francis Poulenc's *Dialogues des Carmélites*, and Niccolò Piccinni's *Iphigénie en Tauride* complete the season.

Teatro dell'Opera is a *stagione* house, which means only one opera is performed at a time. Opera shares the stage with ballet. To be sure your visit coincides with an opera, contact the Italian Government Travel Offices (ENIT) at 630 Fifth Avenue, New York, NY 10011, 212-245-4822, for a schedule. It takes forever to get the program from the opera house.

TRAVEL INFORMATION

The best hotel for operagoers in Rome is the Hotel Bernini Bristol, Piazza Barberini 23, 00187 Rome, Italy; telephone (39)(6)463-051, fax (39)(6)482-4266. For reservations in the United States, call toll-free, 1-800-223-6800 (member of the Leading Hotels of the World). Singles start at $160, doubles at $220. A continental breakfast is included. It is an elegant five-star hotel, with 113 rooms and 11 suites, ideally located in the city center. The hotel, which overlooks the Piazza Barberini, offers impeccable service. It is a pleasant twenty-minute walk from the opera house, and you can walk back safely after the performance. The concierge provides outstanding opera ticket service. He can even find tickets for those hard-to-get performances.

Several cafes and restaurants offering a wide range of food and prices are located on the streets bordering the opera house. Some of the closest are Caffe dell'Opera and Ristorante del Gigli on via Torino, Ristorante Esperia on via Firenze, and La Matriciana Ristorante on via Viminale.

You can contact the Italian Government Travel Offices for travel information at the address and telephone number given above.

CATANIA, SICILY
Teatro Massimo Bellini

On the evening of May 31, 1890, Catania dedicated a magnificent opera house to native son and renowned composer Vincenzo Bellini, with a lavish production of his *Norma*. The gala occasion attracted dignitaries from all over Italy to this small town on the eastern shore of Sicily. The opera house was designed by Carlo Sada and took ten years to build. Teatro Massimo Bellini celebrated its centennial on May 31, 1990, with another lavish production of *Norma*. Bathed in bright lights for the celebration, with the dates "1890-1990" fashioned in red and pink flowers in the piazza garden, Catania's opera house began its second century in grand style.

HISTORICAL OVERVIEW
Background

The Cantanese had felt the need for an opera house for a long time, and the city's Senate had petitioned for one repeatedly. Finally in 1812, the senators approved the architectural project of Zahra-Buda. Soon thereafter, unwelcome Algerian pirates decided to visit the city and work was suspended on the opera house so that the city could strengthen its defenses instead. Nothing remains of Zahra-Buda's project except a description of his grandiose plan. When the city council decided to continue work on an opera house, Zahra-Buda's project was set aside and a public competition announced. But no one accepted the task. Finally in 1874, Sada came up with a design that was approved by the city

council. Work began in 1880, but the usual legal and political battles ensued. Ten years later, the opera house was completed.

During its hundred-year existence, this small regional opera house has attracted such dignitaries as King Vittorio Emanuele III on April 13, 1907, the king and the queen on May 30, 1911, and Giovanni Gronchi, president of the Republic, on November 3, 1955. The most significant event of its history took place in 1986, when the management was wrestled from an inept bunch of local administrators and given to the *Ente Autonomo* (autonomous corporation) that governs all major Italian opera houses. This change has paved the way for a brighter future in which the opera house is striving to gain international recognition.

The Theater

The Teatro Massimo Bellini is a masterpiece of eclectic styles, a superb blend of neoclassical, Renaissance, and baroque. The façade boasts Ionic columns and pilasters, rounded arches and lyre etched windows, and cornices and friezes with lyres and masks of Tragedy and Comedy. Cherubs and nymphs look down from lofty positions, while busts of composers sit in niches. The opera house extends over the bordering streets with graceful archways. On the top, TEATRO BELLINI is etched in gold on white marble.

The lavish exterior hints at the opulence of the interior. Busts of Sada and Giuseppe Sciuti

Top: Teatro Massimo Bellini from Piazza Bellini
(Photo by author)
Bottom: Detail of façade (Courtesy of Teatro Massimo Bellini, Photo by Angelo)

greet you in the gold-rimmed oval foyer. The horseshoe-shaped auditorium, oozing with the elegance of a bygone era, is perfectly balanced with frescoes and gilded stucco. Four tiers of boxes capped by a large gallery rise from the orchestra level. In the center, a red and gold draped royal box is topped by two cherubs holding a crown. Pairs of glass globes float in front of each box, and elegant chandeliers hover overhead. The light fixtures are the original gas ones, converted for electricity in 1929. The box lighting is pink, lending a rosy glow to the auditorium when the other lights are dimmed. Intricately carved stucco on the parapets, executed by Andrea Stella, complements elaborate decorations on the proscenium, where a clock with Roman numerals resides. The ceiling, painted by Andrea Bellandi, presents the apotheosis of Bellini, surrounded by allegorical illustrations from four Bellini operas, *Norma*, *Il pirata*, *La sonnambula*, and *I Capuleti e i Montecchi*. Around the rim are small medallions of Giovanni Pacini, Gaetano Donizetti, Giuseppe Verdi, Domenico Cimarosa, Gioacchino Rossini, and other Italian composers. The curtain, painted in 1883 by Sciuti, depicts the Cantanese victory over the Libyans, with Mount Etna smoking in the background. The ivory and gold grand salon, dominated by a larger-than-life bronze statue of Bellini by Cantanese sculptor Salvo Giordano, is filled with teak-colored marble columns supporting carved archways and gold pilasters flanking arched windows. The floor is a rich marble. The Teatro Bellini seats 1,266.

Performance History

Teatro Massimo Bellini has repeatedly staged all of Bellini's operas. In November 1951, for the 150th anniversary celebration of Bellini's birth, the theater sponsored a festival where gala productions of *Norma*, *Il pirata*, *I Puritani*, and *La sonnambula* were staged. However, Teatro Bellini has not limited its repertory to Bellini operas. Composers of many nationalities have had their works presented, and artists possessing the most glorious voices have graced the stage: Beniamino Gigli, Gina Cigna, Maria Callas, and, of course, Giuseppe di Stefano, who was born at Motta Santa Anastasia, six miles away.

I was fortunate to attend the centennial celebration performance of *Norma* on May 31, 1990. It was a gala occasion. For an emerging opera house in a small city, it was a splendid production. Most of the credit for this achievement goes to the conductor, Daniel Oren. In fact, the orchestra sounded better than some of the singing. Lucia Aliberti, in the title role of Norma, experienced difficulties with the coloratura. However, the supporting roles were admirably sung by Nicola Martinucci as Polline, Roberto Scandiuzzi as Oroveso, and Anna Caterina Antonacci as Adalgisa. Piero Guccione was responsible for the excellent scenery. There was, however, one amusing moment that should not have been amusing. At the beginning of Act II, Norma, filled with despair at her lover's betrayal, is overcome with a desire to kill her children. But the children were busy hitting each other in a game of tag. It temporarily detracted from the dramatic tension of the opera and reminded one

that Teatro Massimo Bellini is not quite yet of international rank.

PRACTICAL INFORMATION
Tickets

The box office (*biglietteria*) is located at via Perrotta 12, through the wooden doors to the right of the main entrance doors. It is open from 10:00 a.m. to 12:00 noon and 5:00 p.m. to 7:00 p.m. Tuesday through Saturday and a half hour before the performance begins (*dal martedì al sabato dalle ore 10,00 alle ore 12,00 e dalle 17,00 alle 19,00 e una mezza ora prima dell'inzio delle manifestazioni*). You can buy tickets starting seven days before the performance. A monitor in the box office shows the seating plan, with available seats indicated in blue. You have to ask, or point, for a program, since the programs are behind the glass box office window and the personnel speak no English. If you do not speak Italian, you might experience problems.

I suggest writing or faxing ahead for tickets. Fax: (39)(95)321-830. However, do not write to the box office, since they do not read English either. Address your request to Sig. Pino

TICKET TABLE
Prezzi Serali
(Evening Prices in Lit.)

Location	Turni A	B	C	D
Poltrone di platea (orchestra)				
1° sett. (front)	65.000	40.000	40.000	56.000
2° sett. (rear)	50.000	30.000	30.000	40.000
Palco 1°Ordine (box seat 1st tier)				
centrale (center)	56.000	41.000	41.000	50.000
laterale (side)	54.000	39.000	39.000	48.000
Palco 2°Ordine (box seat 2nd tier)				
centrale (center)	62.000	44.000	44.000	53.000
laterale (side)	58.000	42.000	42.000	50.000
Palco 3°Ordine (box seat 3rd tier)				
centrale (center)	51.000	36.000	36.000	48.000
laterale (side)	46.000	34.000	34.000	46.000
Palco 4°Ordine (box seat 4th tier)				
centrale (center)	42.000	30.000	30.000	40.000
laterale (side)	39.000	28.000	28.000	38.000
Galleria (gallery)	15.000	12.000	12.000	13.000

$1 = Lit. 1.200, but can vary due to the fluctuating value of the dollar.
Lit. is an abbreviation for Italian Lire.

Cuccia, who is fluent in English, French, German, and Spanish. You can request tickets for any opera in the season beginning a few weeks before the season opens. Special preference is given to foreigners. Tickets cannot be ordered by telephone. The address is:

Sig. Pino Cuccia
Teatro Massimo Bellini
via G. Perrotta 12
95100 Catania, Italy

Tickets to *Turno* (subscription) A are frequently *tutto esaurito* (sold out). If you have a choice, plan on series B, C, or D for a better selection of seats. *Turno* E/Az means subscription E and is reserved for *aziende* (companies). *Turno*

S is reserved for *scuole* (schools). Both are closed to the public. Evening dress is requested for *Turno* A.

Except for the first row, the *laterale* seats do not offer a good view of the stage. If you have a choice, buy *centrale* seats.

Your ticket might appear confusing, so a translation of a sample ticket appears below.

Turni A and B performances begin at 8:30 p.m. (*ore* 20,30); *Turni* C and D performances begin at 6:00 p.m. (*ore* 18,00). Performances start on time (even in Sicily), and no one is admitted after the curtain has gone up. Check the posters in front of the theater for any change in the starting time.

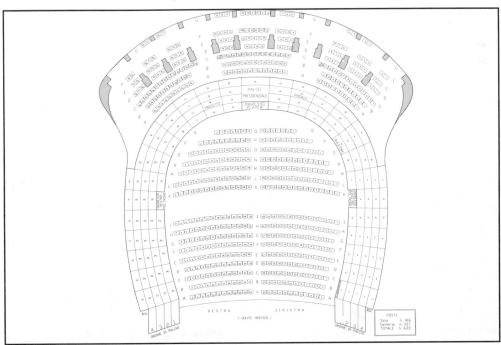

Seating Plan (Courtesy of Teatro Massimo Bellini)

TICKET TRANSLATION

Teatro Massimo Bellini	Greatest Bellini Theater
Stagione Lirica 1990	Opera Season 1990
Turno A	Subscription A
Poltrona di platea	**Orchestra (Section)**
Fila M N. 26	**Row M Seat 26**
Norma	(Opera)

Finding Your Way

The Teatro Bellini faces Piazza Bellini. It is bordered on the north by via G. Perrotta and on the south by via Birreria. The opera house extends over both bordering streets with archways that allow cars to pass through. Via Landolina and via Teatro Massimo lead into the piazza from the east. I would not recommend taking public transportation.

The main entrance to Massimo Bellini, located under the portico, faces Piazza Bellini. Everyone enters through the front doors, even those seated in the *galleria*. You first pass through a red-carpeted entrance hall and then into an egg-shaped foyer. If you hold tickets in the *platea* (rear orchestra), continue straight through the hallway into the auditorium. Even-numbered seats are on the right (*lato destra*); odd-numbered on the left (*lato sinistra*). Seat numbers begin with 1 on the extreme left and 2 on the extreme right, increasing sequentially to the center aisle. Those seated in the *poltrone* (front orchestra) should follow the hallway around to the right for *destra* or left for *sinistra*. The side entrance is between rows I and K. Red and gold seat numbers are on the backs of the seats, and row letters are on the sides of the first chairs in the rows. Signs posted over the stairs in brass letters direct you to the upper tiers: *1° ordine, al 2° ordine, al 3° ordine, al 4° ordine, al 5° ordine* (1st tier, to 2nd tier, to 3rd tier, to 4th tier, to 5th tier). Box numbers begin with 1 next to the stage on the left and continue until 27 on the right. Boxes 13, 14, and 15 are in the center. Ushers are recognizable by their maroon jackets with gold trim.

Programs are sold on the right side of the foyer and cost Lit. 10.000. The program (in Italian) contains the complete libretto, articles, and photographs relating to the opera and composer. Cloakrooms (*guardaroba*) are located through the right and left doors off the foyer and cost Lit. 500. Ladies' rooms (*signore*) and men's rooms (*signori*) are on both sides of the hallway surrounding the *platea* and on each tier. The bar is between the *3° ordine* and *4° ordine* off the Bellini foyer.

Daniel Oren, conductor of centennial *Norma* (Photo by Romano)

Norma, celebrating centennial (Courtesy of Teatro Massimo Bellini)

Planning Your Trip
OPERA PROGRAM

The season runs from the beginning of January to the end of June. The 1990 season opened on January 9 with a new production of Pietro Mascagni's *Guglielmo Ratcliff* and closed on June 30 with Giacomo Puccini's *La bohème*. The season included the *prima esecuzione assoluta* (first performance ever) of Sylvano Bussotti's *Bozzetto Siciliano*. Other new productions were Giuseppe Verdi's *Il trovatore*, Johann Strauß's *Wiener Blut*, and Bellini's *Norma*. The season also included the first performance at Teatro Bellini of Carl Maria von Weber's *Der Freischütz*, Giovanni Battista Pergolesi's *La serva padrona*, and Pyotr Il'yich Tchaikovsky's *Eugene Onegin*. The titles of some non-Italian operas are translated into Italian, so you may have to guess what opera you are seeing.

Massimo Bellini is a *stagione* house, which means only one opera is presented at a time. Operas share the stage with ballet. To be sure your visit coincides with an opera, write for a schedule. Send your request to Sig. Pino Cuccia at the address above.

TRAVEL INFORMATION

I would advise against staying in Catania: the streets are dirty and crowded, filled with purse snatchers and pickpockets. At the Jolly Hotel where I stayed, I found the personnel extremely unpleasant. They would not even give me a detailed map of Catania, although they had many. They reserve them for their "business" clientele. Central Palace Hotel does not bother responding to reservation requests. Instead, combine a trip to Teatro Bellini with a mini-vacation and stay outside Catania at the Sheraton Catania, Via Antonelio da Messina 45, 95020 Cannizzaro (Catania) Italy, telephone (39)(95)271-557, fax (39)(95)271-380; or the Mazzaro Sea Palace, via Nazionale 147, Mazzaro Bay, 98030 Taormina, Sicily, Italy, telephone and fax: (39)(942)24004. Rent or hire a car for your visit to the opera house. Taxi drivers really take advantage of tourists.

The eating establishments around the opera house are not the greatest, nor is the neighborhood. A couple of sandwich shops are on via Michele Rapisardi, and Caffe Mozart is at the corner of Michele Rapisardi and Antonio di Sangiuliano.

You can contact the Italian Government Travel Offices at 630 Fifth Avenue, New York, NY 10011, 212-245-4822, for travel and opera information. They respond promptly.

TURIN
Teatro Regio Torino

The Teatro Regio Torino, originally called Il Regio Teatro di Torino, was inaugurated on December 26, 1740, with Francesco Feo's *Arsace*. Designed by Filippo Juvarra and built by Benedetto Alfieri, the Regio was commissioned by Re Carlo Emanuele III as the new *teatro di corte*. On the night of February 8, 1936, a fire raced through the theater, destroying everything in it path. Thirty-seven years passed before Turin had another opera house. The *nuovo* Teatro Regio Torino, designed by Carlo Mollino and Marcello Zavelani Rossi, was inaugurated on April 10, 1973, with a dazzling production of Giuseppe Verdi's *I vespri siciliani*.

HISTORICAL OVERVIEW
Background

The first theater of note in Turin was the Teatro Carignano, which opened in 1710 as the private theater of the Carignano family. By 1753, the theater had fallen into such a state of disrepair that it had to be rebuilt. Principe Liugi di Carignano commissioned Benedetto Alfieri to do the job. Fire gutted the Teatro Carignano in 1787, but reconstruction immediately followed. Exquisitely decorated in intense red and glittering gold, the intimate theater is still in use today.

The idea of building the Teatro Regio dates back to 1713, when the Duchy of Savoy was transformed into a kingdom. Work on the new opera house began in 1738. Everything proceeded so smoothly that the theater, connected to the palace by a private corridor so the king could go directly from the royal box to his private quarters, opened around two years later. Starting in 1798, the theater suffered a few name changes, reflecting the invading powers. After France invaded, the opera house was known first as Teatro Nazionale. Three years later, it assumed a French name, Grand Théâtre des Arts, and in 1804, Teatro Imperiale. Only when the Savoys returned a decade later did the Teatro Regio regain its birth name. In 1838, Pelagio Palagi was commissioned to increase the theater's capacity. In 1901, the Regio closed for four years to modernize, a task overseen by Ferdinando Cocito. Disaster struck in 1936, when a conflagration left the theater in ruins.

The struggle to rebuild the theater began with a national competition, won by architects Morbelli and Morozzo in 1937. The project was elaborated upon in 1939, 1948, 1955, and 1962, but nothing was ever built. Finally, the hapless architects were released from their contract. Their project was abandoned in favor of a striking modern edifice concealed behind Alfieri's original baroque structure, so the new opera house would not clash with the baroque architecture on the surrounding piazza. The first bulldozers appeared in 1966. Seven years later, a new performing arts complex was born on the original site on the Piazza Castello of the Regio. In 1990, Teatro Regio Torino celebrated its 250th anniversary.

The Theater

Il Regio Teatro di Torino was a palatial structure, designed in the baroque style of Turin. Exquisite French crystal chandeliers lined the elaborately decorated golden foyers. Three box tiers topped by three balconies, including a draped red velvet and gold-trimmed center royal box, formed the auditorium, which accommodated 2,500 people.

A tan concrete roof perforated with fifteen round skylights joins the new Teatro Regio to its baroque shield. The façade of the steel and red brick opera house is glass, crisscrossed with ''green'' metal rods. It accommodates twelve smoked glass entrance doors with white vertical pull bars. Three rows of white glass globe lights in black wrought-iron holders illuminate the entrance. Spacious, modern foyers with red velvet couches, red carpet, and white tables and chairs lead to aerial bridges and gangways that distribute the audience around the theater. The

Façade of Regio Torino (Photo by author)

horseshoe-shaped auditorium, conceived on one plane, holds an ellipsoid, steeply raked seating area. The thirty-seven boxes, suspended outside of the ellipsoid plane, follow the horseshoe's perimeter. The ceiling, executed by the designer Castellano, is covered with vibrating indigo geometric patterns that fade as they approach the boxes. A purple and lavender proscenium arch

Auditorium (Courtesy of Teatro Regio Torino)

frames the stage. Clouds of crystal clear, needle-thin "icicles," suspended from the ceiling, illuminate the auditorium with 1,762 bulbs. The auditorium accommodates 1,788.

Performance History

The first opera performed was Sigismondo d'India's *Zalizura* in 1612. Various operas originally given in Venice and Naples were the fare, such as Domenico Sarri's *Didone abbandonata* offered in 1727. French operas, performed in French, which was unique in Italy during that time, first surfaced in the 1760s with François Philidor's *Le Sorcier* and *Tom Jones*. Operas written specifically for the Regio, like Riccardo Broschi's *Merope* and Christoph Willibald Gluck's *Poro*, also entered the repertory.

Giacomo Meyerbeer's *Semiramide riconosciuta* arrived in 1819, followed by Otto Nicolai's *Il templario* in 1840. Forty years later, the world première of Alfredo Catalani's *Elda* took place. His *Loreley*, actually a revision of *Elda*, was introduced on February 16, 1890. Giacomo Puccini's *Manon Lescaut* saw the stage for the first time on February 1, 1893. Puccini was accorded fifty curtain calls, and *Manon Lescaut* was deemed an unqualified success. Alfredo Keil's *Irene* graced the stage on March 22, 1893, and Gaetano Luporini's *I dispetti amorosi* appeared on February 27, 1894. The première of Arturo Berutti's *Taras Bulba* took place on March 9, 1895, and the following year Puccini's *La bohème* was introduced on February 1 with Arturo Toscanini on the podium. It was a gala occasion, attended by a coterie of Italian nobility, Pietro Mascagni, Alberto Franchetti, and other Italian composers, as well as all the Italian critics. The reception was not good: the audience was apathetic and the critics hostile. Toscanini conducted many unforgettable performances during his tenure as music director, from 1895 to 1898 and 1905-06.

The *prima rappresentazione assoluta* of Italo Montemezzi's *Hellera* took place on March 17, 1909, followed the next year by Giocondo Fino's *La festa del grano* on February 12. Raffaele de Miero's *Morgana* was premiered on February 16, 1911, and Ubaldo Pacchierotti's *Il Santo* on February 15, 1913. Two world premières took place in 1914: Riccardo Zandonai's *Francesca da Rimini* on February 19 and Elmerico Francassi's *Finlandia* on March 25. After World War I, Carlo Adolfo Cantù's *Ettore Fieramosca* graced the stage for the first time on March 5, 1921, followed by Adriano Lualdi's *La figlia del Re* on March 18, 1922. The next year, Giuseppe Blanc's *Il convegno dei martiri* received its world première on November 11 and his *La valle degli eroi* on March 21, 1931.

World premières could be seen also at the Teatro Vittorio Emanuele and Teatro Carignano. These theaters hosted the Regio's opera seasons, along with Teatro della Moda, Teatro Alfieri, and Teatro Nuovo, during the Regio's thirty-seven-year absence.

On April 4, 1976, Sandro Fuga's *L'imperatore Jones* became the first *prima rappresentazione assoluta* in the new Teatro Regio. Sylvano Bussotti's *Phaidra/Heliogabalus* followed on February 13, 1981, and Azio Corghi's *Gargantua* on May 2, 1984. Many of the recent productions at the Regio have been both innovative and naturalistic, including the 1986 launching of Luigi Dallapiccola's *Ulisse* with everything bared, followed by an Italian-accented *Der Ring des Nibelungen* in 1988.

I saw a dazzling double-bill production of Mascagni's *Cavalleria rusticana* and Ruggero Leoncavallo's *Pagliacci*. In the *Cavalleria* cast were Bruna Baglioni as Santuzza and Nicola Martinucci as Turiddu. The singing was *sufficente*. In *Pagliacci*, Leo Nucci sang the role of Silvio and the Prologue quite admirably. The rest of the cast—Giuseppe Giacomini (Canio), Elena Mauti Nunziata (Nedda), and Ettore Nova (Tonio)—was adequate. Yuri Ahronovitch conducted the Franco Zeffirelli production from Teatro alla Scala.

Top: *Cavalleria rusticana* (Courtesy of Teatro Regio
Torino, Photo by Peterle)
Lower left: Elena Mauti Nunziata in *Pagliacci*
(Courtesy of Teatro Regio Torino, Photo by Peterle)
Lower right: *Pagliacci* (Courtesy of Teatro Regio
Torino, Photo by Peterle)

PRACTICAL INFORMATION
Tickets

The box office, identified by *Teatro Regio Torino Biglietteria* (Regio Theater Turin Box Office) in large white letters on top, is located at Piazza Castello 215, to the left of the opera house in a separate building. Posted in the window is *Orario per il pubblico 10-12 ad 15,30-19 dal martedì al sabato, 10-12 ad 14-18,30 domenica, lunedì chiuso* (Hours for the public, 10:00 a.m. to 12:00 noon and 3:30 p.m. to 7:00 p.m. Tuesday through Saturday; 10:00 a.m. to 12:00 noon and 2:00 p.m. to 6:30 p.m. Sunday, closed Monday). On performance days, the box office is also open one hour before curtain time. Tickets can be purchased beginning five days before the performance.

An orderly line waiting for the box office to open forms outside. It turns into a pushing match inside. Each of the three windows has a hand-written sign above indicating which *Turni* are sold at that window. The left window sells tickets for the same-day performance. The only seating plan is in front of the right window. Unfortunately, three of the most unpleasant women in Turin work behind the box office windows.

Tickets can also be reserved through the mail. (No faxes, telegrams, or telexes.) Mail orders are accepted until twenty days before the performance date. Include on your request form

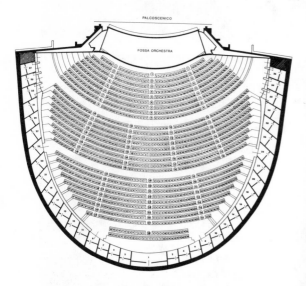

Seating Plan (Courtesy of Teatro Regio Torino)

Poster of 1990/91 season (Courtesy of Teatro Regio Torino)

TICKET TABLE
Prezzi per La Stagione Lirica)
(Prices in Lit. for the Opera Season)

Location	Turno A	Turno B	Turni C/D/E/F	Fuori Abbonamento	Abbonamenti Speciali
Poltrona (orchestra)	150.000	80.000	40.000	40.000	40.000
Posto palco (seat in box)	220.000	110.000	60.000	40.000	40.000

$1 = Lit. 1.200, but can vary due to the fluctuating value of the dollar.
Lit. is an abbreviation for Italian Lire.

your name, address, telephone number, opera, date, section, and number of seats needed. You will receive either a confirmation or a rejection of your request. If you receive a confirmation, send a bank or postal money order in Italian Lire made out to "Teatro Regio." It should arrive at least fifteen days before the performance. Tickets cannot be ordered by phone. Write to:

Biglietteria del Teatro Regio
Piazza Castello, 215
10124 Turin, Italy

The ticket table is very straightforward and does not reflect the fact that the view of the stage from the center orchestra seats is far superior to the view from the side seats.

Your best chance for tickets is for the *fuori abbonamento* (nonsubscription) performances. *Turno A* and *Turno B* are almost always *tutto esaurito* (sold out). The high-priced tickets of *Turno A* and *Turno B* are not only "status" but also reflect the better quality of the singers.

The extreme side seats are bad, which I know from sitting in one during the *Cav/Pag* performance. The situation was especially acute during *Pagliacci*, when all I could see were the spectators sitting on the bench. I never saw Colombina, Pagliaccio, Taddeo, or Arlecchino in the *commedia*.

Understanding your ticket will help you find your seat. Below is a translation of a sample ticket.

Evening performances begin at 8:30 p.m. (*ore* 20.30), except *Turno E*, which begins at 8:00 p.m. (*ore* 20). Matinees start at either 3:00 p.m. or 3:30 p.m. (*ore* 15 *o ore* 15.30). Check the posters in front of the theater for the exact starting time. No one is admitted once the curtain has gone up. If you are late, you will have to wait in an alcove off the entrance foyer where tele-vision monitors are set up. Though the doors are shut to latecomers, there is a lot of seat switching from side seats to any empty center seats.

Finding Your Way

The Teatro Regio Torino is on Piazza Castello. It is bordered on the north by the small square of the Archivio di Stato, on the east by Nuova Piazza, and on the south by via Giuseppe Verdi. Trams 13 and 15 and bus 55 stop by the opera house. It is a twenty-five-minute walk from the central train station. (The first seven minutes are not very pleasant.)

The main entrance to the Regio faces Piazza Castello. After entering the huge foyer turn right for *pari* (even-numbered seats) or left for *dispari* (odd-numbered seats). Six doors lead into the vast auditorium: front pair at rows 9 and 10, middle pair at rows 18 and 19, and rear pair at rows 27 and 28. The auditorium is divided into different *settori* (sectors). Match the *settore* on your ticket with the *settore* posted on the signs. The ushers wear maroon suits with maroon turtlenecks and medallions with an R in the middle. They are not very friendly to foreigners, so try to find your seat on your own.

Programs of the entire season are for sale at tables set up on your right and left. The cost is Lit. 15.000. The programs (in Italian) contain articles, color illustrations, and photographs of the operas as well as comprehensive lists of all the available recordings of the works performed. Be sure to get your "souvenir" program of the opera from either the ladies in white jackets and black skirts or the gentlemen in blue jackets and gray pants who tear your ticket. The cloakroom (*guardaroba*) is straight ahead as you enter the theater. There is no charge. Unmarked ladies'

TICKET TRANSLATION

Teatro Regio Torino	Royal Theater Turin
Settore A	**Sector A**
N° 61 Fila 10	**Seat 61** Row 10

Bruna Baglioni and Nicola Martinucci in *Cavalleria rusticana* (Courtesy of Teatro Regio Torino, Photo by Peterle)

rooms (*signore*) are located on both sides of the entrance foyer down a flight of stairs, which is protected by a gate. Another ladies' room and the men's room (*signori*) are up one flight. Two bars are situated in the wings on the top level, with a huge, marble-floor foyer displaying advertisements located between them. The smoke in both bars and the foyer is very thick. There are special seats for the disabled.

Planning Your Trip

OPERA SCHEDULE

The season runs from mid-November to mid-July. The 1990/91 season opened on November 21 with Verdi's *Don Carlos* (French version) and closes on July 14 with Gioacchino Rossini's *Il barbiere di Siviglia*. Verdi's *Don Carlo* (Italian version), Puccini's *La fanciulla del West*, Karl Goldmark's *Die Königin von Saba*, Zandonai's *Francesca*

da Rimini, and Bussotti's *L'ispirazione* complete the season.

Teatro Regio is a *stagione* house, which means only one opera is performed at a time. Opera shares the stage with ballet. To be sure your trip coincides with an opera, contact the Italian Government Travel Offices (ENIT) at 630 Fifth Avenue, New York, NY 10011, 212-245-4822, for an opera schedule. They respond promptly. It takes a long time to get the schedule from the opera house, but if you are not in a hurry, here is the address:

Biglietteria e Ufficio Informazioni
del Teatro Regio
Piazza Castello 215
10124 Turin, Italy

You can call (39)(11)88151 for ticket information during box office hours. (39) = country code; (11) = city code. In Italy, dial (011)88151. You must speak Italian. You should also inquire about any possible *sciopero* (strike), which translates into canceled performances. Turin is six hours ahead of Eastern Standard Time.

TRAVEL INFORMATION

Turin is an industrial city, with unpleasant taxi drivers and no hotels I would recommend. Especially avoid all hotels within a seven-block radius of the Stazione Porta Nuova. I experienced nasty and rude behavior at several of the "top" hotels around the Central Railroad Station. The worst offender was the Turin Palace, where I witnessed the managing personnel ridiculing guests behind their backs. I would suggest arriving for a matinee performance and then leaving Turin.

There are a couple of cafes near the Regio where you can get a light meal: Caffe Regio and Caffe Roberto, both on via Po. A couple more are on the Piazza Castello.

You can contact the Italian Government Travel Offices (address above) for travel information. They respond promptly.

VENICE
Teatro La Fenice

The most exquisite of Venice's eighteenth-century opera houses, La Fenice was inaugurated on May 16, 1792, with a gala performance of Giovanni Paisiello's *I giuochi d'Agrigento* and the ballet *Amore e Psiche*. Designed by Giannantonio Selva and owned by the Società, La Fenice (The Phoenix) was so named to symbolize the resurrection of the Società by constructing a new building after it was forced to relinquish its ownership in Teatro San Benedetto on June 10, 1787. La Fenice was consumed by a fire on December 13, 1836, but it arose from the ashes to emerge as the world's most beautiful opera house. On December 26, 1837, G. Lillo's *Rosmunda in Ravenna* and a dance by A. Cortesi, *Il ratto delle venete donzelle*, inaugurated the rebuilt opera house. The gala opening night crowd, which included the archduke and Viceroy Ranieri, was dazzled by the magnificent structure. Designed by brothers Tommaso and Giambattista Meduna, the opera house was rebuilt following Selva's original plans.

HISTORICAL OVERVIEW
Background

On March 6, 1637, a momentous occasion occurred in Venice. The world's first public opera house, Teatro San Cassiano, opened its doors. The opera house, named after the parish in which it was located, as was the custom in those days, boasted five tiers of thirty-one boxes each. The opera house was owned by the Tron fam-ily, who rented the boxes annually to Venetian nobility and foreign princes and admitted the general public to the hard, backless bench orchestra seats. This was the second Teatro San Cassiano. The first, a playhouse designed in 1556 by celebrated Italian architect Andrea Palladio, lay in ruins. This theater survived until the 1800s.

The success of Teatro San Cassiano led to the opening of many public opera houses in Venice. On January 20, 1639, the second, Teatro San Giovanni e San Paolo, was born. Considered Venice's best opera house at that time, it closed in 1748. Teatro San Moisè opened in 1640, built by the San Barnaba branch of the Giustinian family. It hosted opera until 1818, when it was converted into a puppet theater, known as Teatro Minerva. Today it has a mundane existence as a shop.

The wooden Teatro Novissimo came into existence on January 14, 1641, but burned to the ground six years later. Teatro SS Apostoli opened in 1649, offering opera for thirty-eight years. Teatro San Apollinare survived only nine years as an opera house. It was demolished in 1690. Teatro San Samuele opened as a comedy house in 1655 but gave operas beginning in 1710 until its demise in 1894.

Teatro San Salvatore, opened in 1661 and built by the Vendramin family, was one of the foremost opera houses in Venice. Its gilded auditorium offered five glorious golden tiers of thirty-three boxes each. The theater experienced a few name changes during its 329-year existence: it became Teatro San Lucca in 1799, Teatro Apollo in 1833, and has been known since 1875 as Teatro Goldini. It is the oldest theater in Venice.

Teatro San Angelo opened in 1676. Built by the families Capello and Marcello on the Canal Grande, it staged operas until the end of the eighteenth century. In 1678, Venice's most magnificent opera house, Teatro San Giovanni Grisostomo, opened. Designed by Tomaso Bezzi for Vincenzo Grimani, the opera house boasted a golden auditorium with five tiers of thirty-nine boxes each, rimmed and trimmed by glorious marble figurines and bas-reliefs. A magnificent chandelier holding four flaming hands of white wax illuminated the room. Renamed Emoroniti, it has been called Teatro Malibran since 1835, when Maria Malibran refused her fee, telling the impresario to use it for the theater. Later the theater was transformed into a cinema, but recently it has become a theater again. Teatro San Fantino opened in 1699 and survived for twenty-one years.

The story of La Fenice begins with the Teatro San Benedetto, erected in 1755 and ravaged by fire eighteen years later. Subsequently rebuilt, it reopened as Teatro Venier in 1784. A short time later, a dispute erupted between the Venier family, who owned the land, and the Società, which owned the theater. The Società went to court and lost, so it decided to construct a new theater. (Teatro Venier was renamed Teatro Rossini in 1868. Today it is a movie house.)

The Società's petition to Consiglio dei Dieci for permission to build La Fenice in the Campo di San Fantin area was approved on August 8, 1787. A competition was held, and twenty-nine projects were submitted, including ones from Cosimo Morelli, Giuseppe Pistocchi, Pietro Bianchi, Andrea Bon, and Selva. The prize was a gold medal worth 300 zecchini. Although Selva's plan was the best, public opinion favored Bianchi. So Bianchi walked off with the prize on May 12, 1790, and Selva built La Fenice. Two years later, an elegantly attired crowd arrived by gondola for opening night and was dazzled by the splendor of the auditorium, decorated by Francesco Fontanesi.

On December 1, 1807, Napoleon was welcomed to Venice by a festive celebration of Lauro Corniani Algarotti's *Il giudizio di Giove* at La Fenice. With Napoleon's arrival, Selva was chosen to construct a new "government" box, and Giuseppe Borsato won the competition to redecorate the opera house in an Imperial style. The result was a neoclassical auditorium, covered with gold intaglio, rich fabrics, mirrors, and a grand escutcheon. It is believed that Giambattista Canal decorated the ceiling with *Il trionfo di Apollo sul cocchio* (The triumph of Apollo on a coach), which was surrounded by medallions and friezes. Pietro Moro probably did the reliefs, and Costantino Cedini painted the new curtain, which replaced the curtain he had executed in 1792. A gala celebration featuring Johann Simon Mayr's *Il ritorno di Ulisse* and Salvatore Viganò's dance *Gli Strelizzi* reopened La Fenice on December 26, 1808.

By 1825, the exquisite decorations had been badly discolored by the thick black smoke from the oil lamps, so the Società entrusted Luigi Locatelli to study a new system of illumination to prevent the decorations from turning black. Soon astral lamps brightened the auditorium, with the grand central chandelier boasting forty-eight flames. Three years later, on July 8, Borsato was commissioned to restore the auditorium's darkened ornamentation. P. Generali's *Francesca da Rimini* celebrated the reopening on December 27, 1828.

At almost nine in the evening on December 12, 1836, rehearsals were in full swing for the Venice première of Gaetano Donizetti's *Lucia di Lammermoor* when a huge fire raced through the theater, devouring everything except the exterior walls and the *sale apollinee*. The cause of the fire: a recently installed Austrian stove, found perfectly intact after the conflagration. A year later, a new theater, like its symbol, had risen from the ashes. In 1844, gas replaced the oil illumination. Four years later, the Venetians rebelled against their Austrian occupiers and destroyed the imperial box. By 1853, building problems had surfaced, the result of hasty reconstruction after the fire. Another competition was held, but none of the fifteen submitted projects was acceptable to the Società. Then Giambattista Meduna presented his proposal, which was approved. When E. Petrella's *Marco Visconti* reopened the opera house on December 26, 1854, La Fenice looked very much like it does today.

Political problems with the Austrians closed La Fenice on September 8, 1859. Later Venice was annexed to Italy, and on October 31, 1866, the doors reopened. The rich season was attended by Vittorio Emanuele II, the royal family, ministers, and new government. The imperial box was transformed to the royal box, and the escutcheon of the House of Savoy was displayed.

During World War I, La Fenice shut its doors. Then in 1936, the descendants of the Società handed over their boxes to the municipality. Soon thereafter, the opera house became a self-governing body, joining the *Ente Autonomo* (autonomous corporation). At the same time, Eugenio Miozzi modernized the building, which included installing a revolving stage. Nino Barbantini brought back some neoclassical aspects to the decorations. La Fenice is looking forward to 1992, when it will celebrate its bicentennial by reviving the most important world premières that have graced its stage.

The Theater

La Fenice is a perfectly proportioned neoclassical building, blending harmoniously with its surroundings. On its façade, a huge slab of white stone from Istria extends up from the Corinthian columns of its tetrastyle portico. Masks of Comedy and Tragedy, probably executed by Domenico Fadiga, gaze over statues of Terpsichore (right) and Melpomene (left), believed to be the work of Giovanni Ferrari. In the middle is a lunette decorated with a relief of a lyre

adorned with the head of Mercury. Flanked by trumpets evoking Apollo, the lyre rests on a background of laurels. In the squares above, the left one boasts a helmet, shield, club, and halberd resting on leafy branches of oak, and the right one holds a thyrsus, vessel, and torch between vine leaves. In the center, "SOCIETAS MDCCXCII" with a phoenix framed in a wreath of laurels reminds all who pass by that the Società built the opera house known as La Fenice in 1792. On the flanking "soft" yolk stucco part of the façade, two tympanums adorn two Empire windows. In the vestibule of the façade, two marble stelae commemorate Carlo Goldini and Selva. "*Risorta dall'incendio*" (resurrected from the fire) was added in 1836.

The façade facing the canal is plain and linear, bordered by a stone entablature with a large semicircular window resting on top. Three Empire windows, crowned by tympanums, allow light

Façade of La Fenice during carnival (Courtesy of Teatro La Fenice, Photo by Arici & Smith)

into the stage area. Five ashlar-formed porticos hold lunettes displaying monochromatic frescoes of *putti* alluding to the theater and the arts. This was added by Sebastini Santi in 1837. On the beveled edge, "MDCCXCII" and a large relief of the phoenix watching those who arrive by water are thought to have been executed by Domenico Fadiga.

In La Fenice, as it was rebuilt after the 1836 fire, five tiers of boxes soared through the pale yellow, green, gold, and white horseshoe-shaped auditorium with each parapet boasting a different decoration. A simple ornamental design of chiaroscuro, the color simulating streaked Greek marble, adorned the first parapet. Groups of bas-reliefs with an array of shields, helmets, arrows, sacrificial knives, oak branches, and masks of Tragedy interposed with pretty reclining nymphs and elves embellished the second. The third was inhabited by dancing *putti* alternating with an assortment of lyres, griffins, and cornucopias, while on the next higher, winged female creatures dwelled alongside candelabra, hand bells with masks of Comedy, and multicolored garlands. A simple pattern covered the top. The imperial box, designed by Borsato, was flanked by a pair of gilded wood caryatids and topped by a large crown. A glittering chandelier illuminated the glorious room. Surrounding the chandelier were concentric circles enclosing twelve egg-shaped compartments inhabited by Muses and lyres, the work of Tranquillo Orsi. The proscenium was decorated with intaglio divided into compartments, with winged maidens inhabiting the lunettes. In the center resided a clock. Two curtains were created, representing *l'Apoteosi della Fenice* by Cosroe Dusi and *Rinuncia di Enrico Dandolo alla corona d'Oriente* by Giovanni Busato.

Today's gold and coral horseshoe-shaped auditorium, redecorated in 1854, dazzles with its unrivaled elegance. The parapets of the three box tiers and two galleries display endless gold filigree encircling painted panels of medallions and *putti* by Leonardo Gavagnin and flowers by

Giuseppe Voltan. The large center box, flanked by a pair of gilded caryatids, is topped by a golden Lion of Venice holding "PAX TIBI MARCE EVANGELISTA MEUS" (Peace to you Marco, my evangelist). Two gilded phoenixes rest underneath. Cherubs support a sky-colored ceiling surrounded by gilded stucco, the work of Osvaldo Mazzoran. Maidens and cherubs swirl around the celestiallike center chandelier with radiant lights secured to its arms. Torchlike electrified candles ring the tiers. A large gilded phoenix stares out from atop the proscenium, and a clock faces down from the proscenium arch. In 1854, Eugenio Moretti Larese created a curtain representing *Doge Domenico Michiel all'assedio di Tiro*, which was replaced by Antonio Ermolao Paoletti's representation of *Onfredo Giustiniani che porta a Venezia l'annuncio della vittoria di Lepanto*. Currently, the curtain is a dark green/gray/black with gold emblems. Crystal chandeliers illuminate the splendid light coral, pink, and sand entrance hall, which is populated by marble columns and pilasters with gold Ionic capitals. On the *primo piano* is a room dedicated in 1866 to commemorate the sixth centenary of Dante Alighieri's birth with frescoes representing episodes from the *Divine Comedy* and probably executed by Giacomo Casa. The room was redecorated in 1976 with bold contemporary works by Virgilio Guidi. Enormous eyes, noses, and mouths in red, yellow, green, and blue, painted on huge white spaces, which are symbolically joined to the surviving 1700s stucco, hint at the coming bicentennial event. The opera house seats 823.

Performance History

Claudio Monteverdi's *Il combattimento di Tancredi e Clorinda*, performed in 1624 at the Palazzo Mocenigo Dandolo, was the first opera heard in Venice. Six years later, his *Proserpina rapita* was staged to celebrate the marriage of Giustiniana Mocenigo to Lorenzo Guistinian. Francesco Manelli's *Andromeda* inaugurated the Teatro San Cassiano, where the première of Mon-

Upper left: *Ernani* (Courtesy of Teatro La Fenice)
Upper right: Bruno Beccaria and Silvia Mosca in *Ernani* (Courtesy of Teatro La Fenice)
Bottom: *Ernani* (Courtesy of Teatro La Fenice)

teverdi's *Il ritorno di Ulisse in patria* was given in February 1641, followed by Francesco Cavalli's *Egisto* in 1643 and his *L'Ormindo* the next year. Francesco Sacrati's *Delia* inaugurated the Teatro San Giovanni e San Paolo, which hosted the première of Monteverdi's *L'incoronazione di Poppea*, among others, in 1642. Monteverdi's *Arianna* inaugurated the Teatro San Moisè. Gioacchino Rossini's *La cambiale di matrimonio* was premiered there on November 3, 1810, his *La scala di seta* on May 9, 1812, and his *Il Signor Bruschino* the next year. Sacrati's *La finta pazza* inaugurated the Teatro Novissimo, while Antonio Cesti's *Orontea* opened the Teatro Apostoli, and Cavalli's *Oristeo* launched the Teatro Apollinare, the site of the première of his *La Calisto* in 1651. Castrovillari's *Pasife* opened the Teatro Salvatore, which was the scene of Donizetti's *Enrico di Borgogna* on November 19, 1818. Freschi's *Elena rapita da Paride* inaugurated the Teatro Angelo, which saw several operas by Antonio Vivaldi. Teatro San Giovanni Grisostomo was inaugurated by Carlo Pallavicino's *Vespasiano*, and Teatro Fantino opened with Pignatta's *Paolo Emilio*. Teatro San Benedetto, inaugurated with Gioacchino Cocchi's *Zoë*, hosted the première of Rossini's *L'italiana in Algeri* on May 22, 1813, his *Eduardo e Cristina* six years later, and Giacomo Meyerbeer's *Emma di Resburgo* the same year. Federico and Luigi Ricci's *Crispino e la Comare* was introduced on February 28, 1850, and La Fenice revived it in 1983 for Carnival.

After La Fenice opened, Mayr's *Sapho* was introduced in 1794, followed two years later by Domenico Cimarosa's *Gli Orazi ed i Curiazi*. The world première of Rossini's *Tancredi* took place on February 6, 1813, and after the première, all Venice was singing "*di tanti palpiti*." The aria, commonly called the "rice aria," was supposedly written while Rossini was waiting for the rice to boil. However, no one was singing after *Sigismondo*, which inaugurated the Carnival season on December 26, 1814: The audience found it boring. Rossini returned on February 3, 1823, with *Semiramide*, one of his finest dramatic pieces.

The Venetians enjoyed the opera so much that Rossini was serenaded by a band as he returned to his hotel.

Two of Vincenzo Bellini's ten operas were introduced at Fenice: *I Capuleti e i Montecchi* on March 11, 1830, and *Beatrice di Tenda* on March 16, 1833. Donizetti's *Belisario* followed three years later, on February 4. After the performance, the Venetians, thrilled by the opera, carried Donizetti on their shoulders back to his hotel. His *Maria di Rudenz* was premiered at the rebuilt Fenice on January 30, 1838, but after this première, Donizetti walked back to his lodgings alone! The opera was canceled after two performances.

Giuseppe Verdi's *Ernani*, introduced on March 9, 1844, was the first world première of a Verdi opera not hosted by La Scala. The opera received a tumultuous reception, with Verdi taking fifty curtain calls. The work extended Verdi's reputation beyond Italy's borders. Austria occupied Venice at this time, so when his *Attila* was premiered on March 17, 1846, Verdi became a hero with "*Avrai tu l'universo, resti l'Italia a me*" (You will have the universe, but leave Italy to me). When Verdi's *Macbeth* was performed, such bedlam followed Malcolm and Macduff's duet, "*La patria tradita*," that the last act was banned entirely. By the time Verdi presented *La maledizione* (*Rigoletto*'s original title) to the Austrian censors, as was required, his name was a "curse." They branded the libretto "revoltingly immoral" and "obscenely trivial." Finally, a compromise was reached, and *Rigoletto* was premiered on May 11, 1851. For months afterward, "*La donna è mobile*" resounded through the streets of Venice.

Verdi's *La traviata* opened on March 6, 1853, and according to some accounts, including Verdi's own, it was a disaster. Operas were not created from contemporary topics in the mid-nineteenth century, so the performers had some problems with this avant-garde work. Besides, Fanny Salvini-Donatelli, who sang Violetta, was a rather large lady, so her dying of consumption appeared ridiculous. Verdi's last world première, *Simon Boccanegra*, took place on March 12, 1857. Although one of Verdi's favorite operas, it was not one of the public's favorites.

On May 6, 1897, Ruggero Leoncavallo's *La bohème* was world premiered, and three years later, on February 22, Ermanno Wolf-Ferrari's *La Cenerentola* was introduced. During this era, some great singers graced the stage: Enrico Caruso, Toti dal Monte, and Beniamino Gigli.

On April 21, 1938, Verdi's *Don Carlo* inaugurated La Fenice's first season managed by the *Ente Autonomo*. La Fenice kept its doors open during World War II. The only interruption was the announcement on April 26, 1945, of Milan's liberation during a performance of Giacomo Puccini's *Madama Butterfly*. Several important contemporary operas have been world premiered during the Contemporary Music Festival that La Fenice hosts: Igor Stravinsky's *The Rake's Progress*, on September 11, 1951; Benjamin Britten's *Turn of the Screw*, on September 14, 1954; the first stage performance of Serge Prokofiev's

Ognenniy angel (The Fiery Angel), sung in Italian as *L'angelo di fuoco*, on September 29, 1955; and Luigi Nono's *Intolleranza 1960* six years later. During this time, prominent artists like Maria Callas, Renata Tebaldi, Marilyn Horne, Mirella Freni, and Luciano Pavarotti periodically delighted La Fenice's audiences.

I saw a powerful new production of one of their bicentennial operas, Verdi's *Ernani*. Renato Bruson (Don Carlos) sang admirably despite a "slight indisposition," as did Roberto Scandiuzzi (Silva). However, Silvia Mosca (Elvira) missed many notes and was loudly booed at the end of the performance. Bruno Beccaria (Ernani) was rigid and stylized in his singing and acting. Dario Lucantoni conducted. Although the opera got off to a shaky start, there were many enjoyable moments during the nearly three-and-a-half-hour performance. However, the previous performance was booed off the stage. That was the first time ever a premature curtain had fallen at Fenice. The opera was a co-production with Parma, and their *intenditori* had traveled to Venice.

Auditorium with view of royal box (Courtesy of Teatro La Fenice, Photo by Arici & Smith)

73

PRACTICAL INFORMATION
Tickets

The box office (*biglietteria*) is located at 1977 San Fantin, through the glass and wood door to the left of the main entrance. The box office is open Monday through Saturday 9:30 a.m. to 12:30 p.m. and 4:00 p.m. to 6 p.m. (*dal lunedì al sabato dalle ore 9.30 alle ore 12.30 e dalle 16 alle 18*). The box office reopens one hour before curtain time (*servizio spettacolo*). If there is a Sunday performance, the box office opens on Sunday and is closed on Monday. The current schedule, with *tutto esaurito* pasted across sold-out performances,

is posted on the right side of the box office. Programs for the season are piled on a shelf underneath. At the window you will find a seating plan with X through the seats already sold. Unfortunately, a couple of the box office ladies are not very pleasant or helpful. You can buy tickets beginning one month before each performance.

Tickets can be ordered through the mail for all operas listed in the printed schedule. Print your name, address, telephone number, opera, date of performance, section, and number of seats desired. List alternate dates and sections to increase your chances. Payment in full in the form of an international telegraphic money order in Italian Lire must accompany your order. You

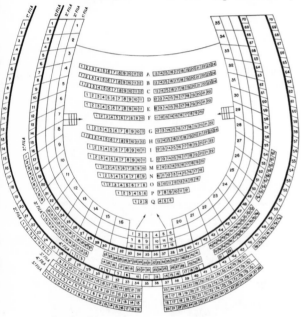

Seating Plan (Courtesy of Teatro La Fenice)

Poster for Bicentennial Celebration (Courtesy of Teatro La Fenice)

Settore (Section)	Prezzi (Prices in Lit.)	
	Turno A (1st Performance)	Repliche (Repeat)
Platea (orchestra)	80.000	60.000
Posto di palco centrale (center box seat)	80.000	60.000
Posto di palco laterale (side box seat)	65.000	50.000
1ª Galleria (1st balcony)	35.000	25.000
2ª Galleria (2nd balcony)	25.000	20.000

TICKET TABLE

$1 = Lit. 1.200, but can vary due to the fluctuating value of the dollar.
Lit. is an abbreviation for Italian Lire.

will receive notification as soon as possible that your request has been confirmed or at least that it has been processed. Your money will be returned if your request cannot be fulfilled. Tickets must be picked up at least one-half hour before the performance begins. Address your requests to:

Biglietteria del Teatro La Fenice
Campo San Fantin
30124 Venezia, Italy

Tickets can be ordered by telephone (521-0161) five days before the performance but only by residents of Venice. Payment must be made immediately by telegraphic money order, and tickets must be picked up at least one-half hour before the performance.

Tickets are extremely difficult to buy because of the limited seating capacity of the theater. Your best chance for tickets is a *fuori abbonamento* (non-subscription) performance, noted as "*f.a.*" on the schedule. Order your tickets as early as possible. *Turno A*, Sunday afternoon, and Carnival performances are always *tutto esaurito* (sold out). Since La Fenice was built when opera houses were social gathering places, except for the first row in the side boxes, your view of the stage might be limited.

Your ticket might appear confusing, so below is a translation of one.

Evening performances can begin anytime between 7:00 p.m. and 8:30 p.m. (*ore 19 e ore 20.30*) depending on the length of the performance. One evening series begins at 6:30 p.m. (*ore 18.30*). Sunday matinees start at 4:00 p.m. (*ore 16.00*). Check the posters outside the theater or pick up a program at the box office for the exact starting time. Do not arrive late. No one is seated once the curtain goes up, and the television monitor is usually out of order.

Finding Your Way

La Fenice faces Campo San Fantin, bordered on the south by Corte San Gaetano, on the west by Rio Menuo de la Verona, and on the north by Calle de la Fenice. Piazza San Marco is a pleasant ten-minute walk from La Fenice on Calle drio la Chiesa. From the *Stazione F.S. San Lucia* (main railroad station), take either the express or local *vaporetto* and exit at Pontite San Marco.

The main entrance at San Fantin 1977 is for those holding tickets in the *platea* (orchestra) and *palchi* (boxes) only. Those seated in the 1^a *galleria* and 2^a *galleria* enter at 968A Calle de la Fenice, by the sign *ingresso alle gallerie* (entrance to the galleries). For *platea* ticket holders, after entering, turn left and then take the second staircase up on the right. You will be in the rear of the orchestra at Row Q. In each row, seat numbering begins with 1 on the left aisle. Numbers are on backs of the salmon-colored velvet seats, and row letters in gold are on the sides. For *palchi* ticket holders, after entering, turn left and take the first twin staircase up on the right. You will be on the *prima fila* (1st tier). Turn right for *destra* and left for *sinistra*. Continue up for the *seconda* and *terza fila* (2nd and 3rd tiers). Box 1 and 35 are stage boxes on the left and right, respectively. Boxes 16 and 20 are in the center, flanking the *Palchettone* (former royal box). The *maschere* (ushers) are recognizable by their blue suits with La Fenice insignia.

Programs are for sale at a table set up in the lobby and cost Lit. 10.000. The program (in Italian) contains a synopsis in English, the complete libretto, and articles and illustrations relating to the opera. A marvelous book that I highly recommend for anyone interested in the architecture and decorations of La Fenice is also for sale:

TICKET TRANSLATION

Teatro La Fenice - Venezia	The Phoenix Theater - Venice
Ente Autonomo	Autonomous Corporation
Poltrona Fila 0 N. 7	**Orchestra Row 0 Seat 7**
16 Mag. 1990	May 16, 1990

Renato Bruson in *Ernani* (Courtesy of Teatro La Fenice)

Il Teatro La Fenice: I progetti-L'architettura-Le decorazioni, published by Albrizzi Editore. It costs Lit. 90.000. The cloakroom (*guardaroba*) is straight across the entrance foyer and down the stairs. The cost is Lit. 1.000. Ladies' (*signore*) and men's (*signori*) rooms are near the cloakroom. The bar is one flight up from the *prima fila*, where you will see a sign *Bar*. It is on the right in the *sala di Dante*. Unfortunately, the air is so laden with smoke that it is impossible to enjoy a drink or Guidi's whimsical paintings decorating the walls.

Planning Your Trip
OPERA SCHEDULE
The opera season runs from November through mid-July. The 1990/91 season opened on November 11 with a *nuovo allestimento* (new production) of Alban Berg's *Lulu* and will close on July 14 with a new production of Verdi's *Simon Boccanegra*. Verdi's *La traviata*, Engelbert Humperdinck's *Hänsel und Gretel*, Georg Friederich Händel's *Semele*, Pyotr Il'yich Tchaikovsky's *Eugene Onegin* (new production), Bellini's *I Capuleti e i Montecchi*, and Francesco Cilèa's *Adriana Lecouvreur* complete the season.

La Fenice is a *stagione* house, which means only one opera is presented at a time. Opera shares the stage with ballet and concerts. To be sure your visit corresponds with an opera, contact the Italian Government Travel Offices (ENIT) at 630 Fifth Avenue, New York, NY 10011, 212-245-4822, for an opera schedule. They respond promptly. It takes a long time to get the schedule from the opera house.

TRAVEL INFORMATION
The best hotel for operagoers in Venice is the Hotel Bauer Grünwald & Grand Hotel, San Marco 1459, 30124, Venice, Italy; telephone (39)(41)520-7022, fax (39)(41)520-7557. For reservations in the United States, call toll-free, 1-800-223-6800 (member of the Leading Hotels of the World). Singles start at $150, doubles at $200 between April 1 and October 31 and at $75 and $130 between November 1 and March 31. A continental breakfast is included. A glorious five-star hotel with 210 rooms and 6 suites, the Bauer Grünwald is ideally located in the heart of Venice only a couple of blocks from Piazza San Marco. With a magnificent view of the Grand Canal, the hotel exudes Italian charm and courtesy, while offering impeccable service. Its modern decor blends beautifully with an Old World elegance, and you can watch and hear the gondoliers serenading their passengers right from your room. The hotel has hosted some of the greatest names in opera: Maria Callas, Renata Tebaldi, Giulietta Simionato, Mario del Monaco, and Igor Stravinsky. The Bauer is only a five-minute walk from La Fenice. Contact the concierge for all your last-minute opera ticket needs.

Restaurants near La Fenice are Taverna La Fenice, 1935 S. Marco, and Antico Martini, 2010 S. Marco. Ristorante al theatro and Cafe Tier flank the opera house. In addition, the Bauer Grünwald offers a panoramic terrace restaurant right on the Grand Canal.

You can also contact the Italian Government Travel Offices (address above) for travel information.

Germany

The World Première of *Lear* on July 9, 1978 at Nationaltheater (Courtesy of Inter Nationes, Photo by Rabanus)

BAYREUTH
Festspielhaus, Bayreuther Festspiele

The Bayreuth Festspielhaus was inaugurated on August 13, 1876, with a gala presentation of Richard Wagner's *Das Rheingold*. This opera launched the first complete production of *Der Ring des Nibelungen*. For the momentous occasion, an illustrious royal and musical crowd descended on Bayreuth, but King Ludwig, Wagner's most loyal and devoted royal patron, was nowhere to be seen. He had attended the dress rehearsal a week earlier.

The Festspielhaus, designed by Otto Brückwald, was built as a shrine to Wagner's art. The purpose of the Bayreuther Festspiele is to carry out this "sacred" function.

HISTORICAL OVERVIEW
Background

In 1864, "mad" King Ludwig II commanded an opera house be built for Richard Wagner in Munich. Noted architect Gottfried Semper was hired to draw plans for Wagner's theater, but this opera house was never built. Wagner's affair with Hans von Bülow's wife, Cosima, was just too much for Catholic, conservative Munich, and Wagner was driven into exile in Switzerland, settling in Triebschen. Cosima, a domineering type, joined him there, where they were married in 1870. Wagner then commenced his search to find the perfect spot to build his "temple." He wanted it located in a small and remote town, so he would have a captive audience that could do nothing else but concentrate on his music.

In April 1870, Wagner and Cosima journeyed to Bayreuth because of the magnificent Markgräfliches Opernhaus. This glorious baroque theater, built by Giuseppe Galli-Bibiena during the reign of Margrave Frederick, was reputed to have the deepest stage in Germany. However, what was not mentioned was that it was also narrow, the auditorium was small, and the technical facilities were nonexistent. Wagner's trip was not futile, however. He decided Bayreuth was the ideal place to build his theater.

On a cold and rainy May 22, 1872, Wagner laid the cornerstone for the Festspielhaus. The festival house, based on Semper's Munich plans and taking four years to erect, was built to Wagner's specifications. The court architect of Leipzig, Otto Brückwald, and mechanical engineer Karl Brandt were in charge of construction. Money was a constant problem until King Ludwig II came to the rescue by arranging a state loan, not only for the completion of the theater but also to build Wagner a villa nearby, known as Wahnfried.

On August 6, 1876, King Ludwig II arrived at the Festspielhaus for the final dress rehearsal. Seven days later, Wagner's lifelong dream of having his own theater was a reality. At the inauguration, Kaiser Wilhelm I, the emperor of Brazil, and fifty-seven other royal personages mingled with Franz Liszt, Pyotr Il'yich Tchaikovsky, Edvard Grieg, Charles Gounod, Camille Saint-Saëns, and Gustav Mahler. The Bayreuther Festspiele was one of the earliest summer music festivals, spawning a tradition that Salzburger Festspiele and Glyndebourne Festival Opera followed.

The Theater

The orange-coral brick and wood Festspielhaus, perched on top of a *grüner Hügel*, was originally planned as a temporary structure. The classic amphitheater-style auditorium, lined with hollow wood pylons, its ceiling covered with canvas, boasted extraordinary acoustics. The covered orchestra pit and the walls of columnar projections presented a monotonous setting. The audience had nowhere to look except the stage. The festival house accommodates 1,925.

Exterior of Festspielhaus (Courtesy of Inter Nationes)

Performance History

The inaugural summer of 1876 saw the production of three complete *Ring Cycles*. *Das Rheingold* opened the first cycle on August 13. *Die Walküre* followed the next day. The world première of *Siegfried* took place on August 16 and the world première of *Götterdämmerung* on August 17. It has been written that *Der Ring des Nibelungen* was not artistically impressive. The orchestra, led by Hans Richter, played too fast and lacked inspiration. The staging did not fare much better. The new gas lighting system proved unreliable, repeatedly plunging the stage into total darkness during the performance. Although most of the performers made the grade, especially Amalia Materna's Brünnhilde, not much enthusiasm could be displayed because Wagner had forbidden curtain calls. The speed with which *Das Rheingold* was performed set a record that held for seventy-six years. In only two hours and thirty-one minutes, Richter was able to have the Rhine gold stolen from the Rhine maidens and given to Fafner and to move the gods across the bridge into Valhalla. In 1952, Joseph Keilberth express mailed the gold, allowing the gods to move into their castle in under two and a half hours.

Although the first cycle sold out (the status cycle), the second and third cycles played to half-empty houses. Bad press, poor reviews, exorbitant ticket prices, and the remote location doomed the festival, especially financially. For the next six years, the Festspielhaus remained dark.

The doors of the Festspielhaus reopened on July 26, 1882, for the world première of *Parsifal*. Sixteen times that year, *Parsifal* was anointed King of the Knights of the Grail. But the road was so tortuous that no other operas were offered that season. Wagner died the following winter in Venice, and his widow, the autocratic Cosima, took over running the festival. She believed her mission was to preserve the festival as a memorial to Wagner. She ruled like a tyrant, transforming the Festspielhaus into the "temple" and the performances into religious rites. The audience believed they were making their pilgrimage to Mecca. Her productions were viewed as rigid and hyperrealistic, and she never deviated from her beliefs in what Wagner would have wanted. It was rumored she even sent notes to the conductor's podium during the performance, if she felt the conductor had erred.

In 1908, Siegfried Wagner, Richard Wagner's only son, took the helm. During his twenty-two-year reign, only ten festivals managed to be anointed. World War I and political unrest in Germany grounded the rest. However, in those ten seasons, he transformed the festival from a "religious rite" to a reexamination and reinterpretation of Wagner's operas. When Siegfried died in 1930, his widow, an Englishwoman named Winifred Williams Wagner, assumed control. A staunch admirer of Adolf Hitler and supporter of his racist theories, she led Bayreuth through a dark and distasteful period, when it received large sums of money from the Third Reich for productions and special dispensation for Jewish artists to perform there. Hitler turned the festival into a forum for Nazi propaganda, making it the cultural mecca of his regime. Every summer, he took up residence at Wahnfried and decorated the festival grounds with swastikas. In 1944, World War II finally caught up with Bayreuth.

After the war, the bad taste of Nazism clung to the festival until Winifred's sons, Wieland and Wolfgang, took over in 1951, reopening it with *Parsifal*. They steered the festival in an entirely new direction, with Wieland introducing a new artistic concept. Abstract imagery replaced the nationalistic symbols and helped dislodge the stigma of Nazism.

Parsifal (Courtesy of Bayreuther Festspiele, Photo by Rauh)

When Wieland died in 1966, Wolfgang took sole control, inviting well-known directors from different countries to Bayreuth. In 1981, the late

Jean-Pierre Ponnelle staged a controversial *Tristan und Isolde*. But the storm surrounding that production was mild compared with the hurricane that Patrice Chéreau created with his centennial *Ring*. He transported the *Ring* to the Age of the Industrial Revolution (or capitalist era), which almost brought on a riot. In 1988, Harry Kupfer forged another controversy by setting the *Ring* in the aftermath of a nuclear holocaust. The audience practically booed it off the stage.

Bayreuth is not the place to go if you are looking for great Wagnerian singing, since the casts are composed of new talent. Unfortunately, some of the singers are discovered prematurely.

My experience at Bayreuth dates back to 1975, when I saw half of a *Ring* (*Das Rheingold*, *Die Walküre*) and a dreadful *Die Meistersinger von Nürnberg*. I could not get tickets to the marvelous *Tristan und Isolde* that season. Since I have not been able to obtain tickets again, I can only report the reactions of some devout Wagnerite friends, who witnessed the *Ring* in 1988 and 1989. Although they were not part of the crowd that booed the production, they registered deep disappointment with the mediocre quality of the singing. They are not returning, but I hope to revisit soon.

PRACTICAL INFORMATION
Tickets

If you do venture to Bayreuth without tickets, the box office (*Kartenbüro*) is located on the left side of the Festspielhaus. It is only open during the Festspiele, every morning from 10:00 a.m. to 12:00 noon and every afternoon beginning one-half hour before the performance (*vormittags 10-12 Uhr und nachmittags eine halbe Stunde vor Beginn der Aufführung*). Usually around fifty people are waiting each morning for the box office to open. Once it does, everyone pushes and shoves for a good position to buy the few available tickets, which are typically side seats with a partial view of the stage.

You can order tickets by mail starting in mid-

November for the following summer festival. Address your requests to:

Festspielhaus
Kartenbüro
Postfach 100262
8580 Bayreuth 1, Germany

Tickets can not be ordered by telephone. However, you can call (49)(921)20221 for ticket information between 11:00 a.m. and 12:00 noon, Monday through Friday. (49) = country code, (921) = city code. You should speak German. Germany is six hours ahead of Eastern Standard Time.

The ticket table for the Bayreuther Festspiele is quite detailed. Prices vary not only by row and section but also according to the position of the seat in the row, accurately reflecting your ability to see the stage.

TICKET TABLE

Seat Locations	Prices in DM
Parkett - Mittel (center orchestra)	
1.-6. Reihe (rows 1-6)	220
7.-12. Reihe (rows 7-12)	200
13.-18. Reihe (rows 13-18)	185
19.-24. Reihe (rows 19-24)	170
25.-30. Reihe (rows 25-30)	155
Parkett - Links und Rechts (orchestra - left and right sides)	
1.-15. Reihe (rows 1-15) (closest to center)	131,50
1.-15. Reihe (rows 1-15) (middle of side)	115,50
1.-15. Reihe (rows 1-15) (extreme side)	95,50
16.-30. Reihe (rows 16-30) (closest to center)	115,50
16.-30. Reihe (rows 16-30) (middle of side)	95,50
16.-30. Reihe (rows 16-30) (extreme side)	76,50
Mitelloge (center box)	
1. Reihe (row 1)	193
2. Reihe (row 2)	178
3. Reihe (row 3)	163
4. Reihe (row 4)	148
Logen - Links und Rechts (side boxes - left and right sides)	
1. Reihe (row 1) (closest to center)	193
1. Reihe (row 1) (middle of side)	178
1. Reihe (row 1) (extreme side)	163
2. Reihe (row 2) (closest to center)	178
2. Reihe (row 2) (middle of side)	163
2. Reihe (row 2) (extreme side)	148
3. Reihe (row 3) (closest to center)	163
3. Reihe (row 3) (middle of side)	148
3. Reihe (row 3) (extreme side)	118
Balkon Mitte (center balcony)	
1. Reihe (row 1)	105
2. Reihe (row 2)	96
3. Reihe (row 3)	87
4. Reihe (row 4)	33
5. Reihe (row 5)	17
Balkon - Links und Rechts (side balcony - left and right sides)	
1. Reihe (row 1) (closest to center)	90
1. Reihe (row 1) (closest to side)	81
2. Reihe (row 2) (closest to center)	81
2. Reihe (row 2) (closest to side)	72
3. Reihe (row 3) (closest to center)	72
3. Reihe (row 3) (closest to side)	62
Galerie - Links und Rechts (left and right sides of gallery)	
1. Reihe (row 1)	39
2.-4. Reihe (rows 2-4)	34
Plätze mit beschränkter Sicht (Seats with limited view)	16
Hörplätze (Seats with no view)	8

**$1 = 1.6 DM, but can vary due to the fluctuating value of the dollar.
DM is an abbreviation for Deutsche Mark.**

Getting tickets for the Bayreuth Festival is more difficult some seasons than others. The odds for the 1988 season of the new *Ring* were one in eight. However, the odds drop substantially after the *Ring* production is a few seasons old, especially if it has been panned by the critics. The seasons with no *Ring Cycle* are the easiest, because *Ring* tickets are only sold for the complete cycle.

If you really want to have tickets in hand before you go, try ordering tickets for a few seasons before your planned trip. Most likely, you will not receive any tickets, even if your request arrives at the beginning of the acceptance period. It is rumored that you need to receive five rejections before they send you tickets! This way, when you really want the tickets, you might have received enough refusals for your order to be filled. If you get tickets before you really wanted them, change your plans and go. You have beaten the odds.

If you arrive in Bayreuth without tickets, immediately make a sign that reads "*Suche Karte*" or "*Karten Gesucht*" (I am looking for a ticket or seeking tickets). Then stand in a prominent position and hope someone has tickets to sell. Sometimes, if you appear every morning at the box office, the clerk will eventually take pity on you and suddenly "find" a ticket. Usually it will not be a good seat, but at least you will get in.

There is also a black market for tickets. The scalper, recognizable by his blue polyester suit, carries a "*Tauschen*" sign. Since it is illegal to buy

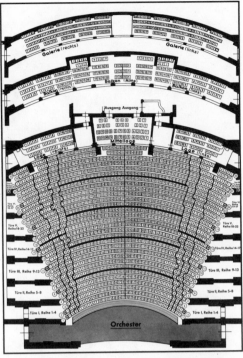

Seating Plan (Courtesy of Bayreuther Festspiele)

or sell tickets on the festival grounds, he skirts the law by "exchanging" the tickets. However, he mainly buys tickets for the hotels in town, where the markup is so large that he earns enough to live on for the rest of the year.

Your ticket gives you all the information you need to find your seat with no problem, once you know the meaning of the words. A translation of a sample ticket appears below.

TICKET TRANSLATION			
Festspiele Bayreuth	1989	Bayreuth Festival	1989
Mittwoch, 16.August 1989	16 Uhr	Wednesday, August 16, 1989	4 p.m.
Parsifal		**(Opera)**	
DM 185.- (A 3)	Parkett **Rechts**	(Price)	Orchestra **Right**
	Türe IV		Door IV
	Reihe 14		Row 14
	Platz **14**		Seat **14**
Nach Beginn der		After the beginning	
Aufzüge kein Einlaß		of the act, no entrance	

Götterdämmerung (Courtesy of Bayreuther Festspiele, Photo by Rauh)

All performances (except *Das Rheingold*) begin at 4:00 p.m. (16 *Uhr*). *Das Rheingold* begins at 6:00 p.m. (18 *Uhr*). You must be punctual, and you must be prepared to sit through the seemingly endless acts on uncomfortably hard, wood-backed, armless seats. The score is always performed uncut, and no one enters once the act begins or leaves before the act ends. The ushers, women in blue uniforms, lock the doors of the auditorium and place their folding chairs by the exits. No one can budge them.

Finding Your Way

The Festspielhaus sits on a hill, around fifteen minutes from town. The road leads to the south entrance. If your tickets says *links*, go around to the left (west); *rechts*, to the right (east). Then match the *Tür* number on your ticket with the number above the door. This will lead you to the correct row. Doors and seats are numbered identically on both the right and left sides, so it is important to be on the correct side. If you enter through the wrong door, you can only correct your mistake by exiting, since there are no aisles. Seat numbers begin at 1 on the extreme right and left sides and increase until they meet in the middle.

The programs (*Programmheft*) are sold by the *blaue Mädchen* who carry them in baskets outside the Festspielhaus. The programs (in German, English, and French) are thick, heavy, and boring. Filled with articles mainly geared to the Wagner aficionado, they contain no synopses and few pictures. The cloakroom (*Garderobe*) is located through the Ludwig entrance on the south side. The ladies' room (*Damen*) and men's room (*Herren*) are located on the north side of the building. Rest rooms are **not** free at Bayreuth: You will need several 10-pfenning coins to use the facilities. Since dinner is usually taken during the hour-long intermissions, you will

Siegfried (Courtesy of Bayreuther Festspiele, Photo by Rauh)

probably eat at one of the restaurants located east of the Festspielhaus. The Steigenburger offers full-course meals, and reservations must be made. There is a menu in German posted outside the restaurant. A menu is also available in English when you book your reservations. Upstairs at the Steigenburger is an espresso bar with ice cream dishes and cones. A cafeteria, located next to the Steigenburger, serves cold dishes. There are other concessions in or near the cafeteria which offer an assortment of food, ranging from bratwurst to desserts, plus soft drinks and *Bier vom Faß* (draught beer). When the next act is about to begin, the orchestra plays a leitmotiv from the south balcony.

Planning Your Trip
OPERA SCHEDULE

The festival season runs from the end of July to the last Monday in August. The 1990 season opened on July 25 with *Der fliegende Holländer* and closed on August 28 with *Götterdämmerung*. *Lohengrin*, *Parsifal*, *Das Rheingold*, *Die Walküre*, and *Siegfried* completed the season. The operas are scheduled so that you can see all seven over a nine-day period.

For schedule and ticket information, write to:

Bayreuther Festspiele
Postfach 100262
8580 Bayreuth 1, Germany

Keep in mind that for dyed-in-the-wool Wagnerites, going to Bayreuth is a "pilgrimage to Mecca," giving the festival a somewhat stuffy atmosphere. However, it also offers a unique opportunity to enjoy Wagnerian operas as the composer envisioned his works to be experienced.

Since this opportunity is available to very few, consider attending one or more of the fabulous *Ring Cycles* currently playing in other European opera houses: Opernhaus Zürich, Nationaltheater, Deutsche Oper Berlin, and Oper der Stadt Köln. In October 1991, La Monnaie will join the crowd in unveiling a new *Ring* as well.

TRAVEL INFORMATION

The weather at Bayreuth is unpredictable, changing from hot and humid to cold and rainy. So be prepared for both. The Festspielhaus is not air-conditioned, so if it is hot, they hose down the roof, which, as might be expected, does little good. In 1983, headlines were made when the men removed their jackets because of the heat inside the auditorium. Today it is a common practice. Many in the audience dress formally.

Hotels will not accept reservations during the festival season unless you first have confirmed festival tickets. If you have to cancel, the hotel will gladly resell your ticket (at a huge profit). Therefore, once you get your ticket confirmation, write to the Visitor Service in Bayreuth for hotel information and reservations:

Gästedienst des Fremdenverkehrsvereins
Luitpoldplatz 9
8580 Bayreuth, Germany
Telephone (49)(921)22011

The German National Tourist Office, 747 Third Avenue, 33rd Floor, New York, NY 10017, 212-308-3300, can send you travel information, but they can not assist you with opera information. Write far in advance, because they take a long time to respond.

BERLIN
Deutsche Oper Berlin

*T*he Deutsche Oper Berlin was inaugurated on September 24, 1961, with a gala performance of Wolfgang Amadeus Mozart's *Don Giovanni*. The glittering occasion, attended by an illustrious array of dignitaries, including Mayor Willy Brandt, President Heinrich Lübke, and twenty-one ambassadors, was marred by the building of the Berlin Wall just six weeks earlier. Thousands of East Berliners who had planned to join the festivities were forbidden to cross into West Berlin. The new opera house, located on the site of the original Deutsches Opernhaus Charlottenburg, was designed by Fritz Bornemann.

HISTORICAL OVERVIEW
Background

It was not until 1910 that opera activity entered into what, until recently, was known as West Berlin. Leading citizens of the then-independent city of Charlottenburg raised the money to build the Deutsches Opernhaus Charlottenburg. Construction began in the summer of 1911, and on November 7, 1912, the new opera house opened. Designed by Heinrich Seeling, the Deutsches Opernhaus Charlottenburg was at the corner of Bismarckstraße and Richard-Wagner-Straße on land donated by the city. Charlottenburger Oper, as the Berliners called it, was conceived as a *Volksoper*, financed by the Friends of the Charlottenburger Oper and catering to the tastes of middle-class Berliners. Offering good performances and innovative produc-

tions of repertory favorites, the new opera had attracted 11,000 subscribers by its second year of operation.

Its glory was short-lived, however. World War I and the defeat of Germany forced Kaiser Wilhelm II's abdication in 1918. Chaos reigned instead. Germany became a republic with Friedrich Ebert as president, and political parties sprouted like weeds. One such party was the Kommunistische Partei Deutschlands (KPD), founded by Karl Liebknecht and Rosa Luxemburg in Berlin. A year later, counterrevolutionary German *Freikorps* officers murdered the KPD founders. Inflation raced through the economy, ushering in the rapid fall of the deutsche mark, which continued unabated until one dollar bought four million deutsche marks. The revolution and economic crisis brought great hardship on the Charlottenburger Oper, with many subscribers deserting because of economic problems. Its founding concept could no longer attract large enough audiences. In addition, Charlottenburg lost its independent city status in 1920 and became the seventh district in the huge city of Berlin. Five years later, the city of Berlin took over the Deutsches Opernhaus, redecorating it and renaming it Städtische Oper.

In 1933, Adolf Hitler's rise to power and the formation of the Third Reich profoundly affected the Städtische Oper. Its original name, Deutsches Opernhaus, was returned, and its appearance was transformed into a miniature Reich's Chancellory. The opera house, under the command of Paul Joseph Goebbels and the Ministry of Propaganda, was used as a mouthpiece for *Nationalsozialismus* until Allied bombers scored a direct hit on the night of November 23, 1943. Only a skeleton of the grand Deutsches Opernhaus remained.

After the war, the Theater des Westens, one of the few theaters still standing in Berlin, became the temporary home of West Berlin's opera, rechristened the Städtische Oper. Finally in 1957, the burned-out ruins were carefully demolished, leaving the small unscathed section of the building. This was integrated into the new opera house, which took five years to complete. The Städtische Oper, now called Deutsche Oper Berlin, moved into its new domicile in 1961. One of its old props, the Commendatore from *Don Giovanni*, emerged from the ashes to appear in the inaugural opera.

The Theater

The majestic but somber Deutsches Opernhaus Charlottenburg represented the canon of theater architecture at the turn of the century. The façade boasted six pairs of Ionic columns flanking decorative reliefs, with a cornice populated by six domineering allegorical figures. Classically adorned foyers led into an unpretentious *Jugendstil* rectangular-shaped auditorium, which claimed the largest stage in the world in 1912. Three horseshoe-shaped balconies rose around the slightly graded orchestra. The theater accommodated 2,300. When the Deutsches Opernhaus became the Städtische Oper in 1925, it shed its somber appearance when the auditorium was painted Bordeaux red.

A decade later, under the careful eye of *das dritte* Reich-approved architect Paul Baumgarten, the Städtische Oper was transformed into a *Reichsoper*. Glittering chandeliers illuminated the foyers, which were swathed with mirrors and marble. The auditorium, enhanced by a new gold, ivory, and red color scheme, saw mahogany paneling replace the reliefs trimming the balcony.

Top: Façade of Deutsche Oper with sculpture by Hans Uhlmann (Courtesy of Inter Nationes) Bottom: Auditorium, Deutsche Oper (Courtesy of Inter Nationes)

A new curtain by Paul Scheurich showing allegorical figures in *Triumph der Oper* covered the stage. But it was the construction of the *Führerloge* in the middle of the first balcony that permanently transformed the ambience of the room and gave the opera house the indelible stamp of Nazism.

The Deutsche Oper Berlin is a starkly modern and austere building, bearing no resemblance to the opera house it replaced. The concrete, glass, and steel structure boasts an enormous solid stone façade finished in colored mosaic. Facing south and dubbed the "wailing wall" by irreverent Berliners, the solid front serves as a barrier between the auditorium and the sun and traffic noise from Bismarckstraße. A soaring steel sculpture by Hans Uhlmann, imbedded in the sidewalk, distracts from the dull façade. The east and west walls are of glass, allowing panoramic views of the city to infiltrate the opera house. The unadorned, two-tier auditorium, paneled with cebrano wood and illuminated by saucerlike fixtures, directs the viewers' concentration to the stage. There are no bad seats, a feat accomplished by zigzagging the balcony into discrete boxlike forms. The auditorium seats 1,885.

Performance History

The first operas performed in Berlin took place in 1688, during the reign of Frederick I of Prussia. The first opera house, Hofoper, opened on December 7, 1742, with Carl Heinrich Graun's *Cleopatra e Cesare*. In fact, all of Berlin's opera activity, until the opening of the Deutsches Opernhaus Charlottenburg, took place in what was formerly called East Berlin (to be discussed in the forthcoming guide, *Opera! The Guide to the Great Houses of Eastern Europe and the U.S.S.R.*).

The Deutsches Opernhaus Charlottenburg was inaugurated on November 7, 1912, with Ludwig van Beethoven's *Fidelio*. An illustrious opening night crowd attended the festivities. Under the leadership of Georg Hartmann, the opera house wasted no time in hosting world premières. The first was Kurt Hösel's *Wieland der Schmied* on January 11, 1913. Giacomo Puccini came to direct the German première of his *La fanciulla del West* on March 28, 1913. Ignatz Waghalter's *Mandragola* was introduced on January 21, 1914, followed by his *Jugend* on February 17, 1917, the same year Leopold Schmidt's *Die glückliche Insel* was staged on April 26. Friedrich E. Koch's *Die Hügelmühle* was premiered on May 10, 1918, followed by Frantisek Neumann's *Herbststurm* on April 9, 1919. Gustav Scheinpflug's *Das Hofkonzert*, on February 3, 1922, was the last world première before the Charlottenburger Oper closed.

On September 18, 1925, the Städtische Oper reopened with Richard Wagner's *Die Meistersinger von Nürnberg*, conducted by Bruno

Dietrich Fischer-Dieskau in *Mathis der Maler*, February 1959 (Courtesy of Inter Nationes)

Walter. Walter held the post of *Generalmusikdirektor* until 1929, and Heinz Tietjen was the new *Intendant*. The pair caused a scandal in 1927 when they produced Ernest Křenek's jazz opera, *Jonny spielt auf*. The leading character, Jonny, was a black jazz band leader who stole a violin from the virtuoso Daniello and conquered the world. Not the stuff Berliners were ready for. On November 13, 1928, Julius Bittner's *Mondnacht* saw the light.

Carl Ebert took the reins in 1931 and, along with Fritz Busch and Fritz Stiedry, elevated drama to equal status with music. The team created a sensation with their first production of Giuseppe Verdi's *Macbeth*. Suddenly, lovers of spoken drama flocked to the Städtische Oper. Kurt Weill's *Die Bürgschaft* received its world première on March 10, 1932, followed the same year by Franz Schreker's *Der Schmied von Gent* on October 29. But dark clouds were on the horizon, and by February 1933, the Nazis had seized power. Two weeks later, Ebert staged his last new production, Wagner's *Der fliegende Holländer*. In the middle of March, an *SA-Trupp*

Upper left: Städtische Oper's world première of *Rosamunde Floris*, September 21, 1960 (Courtesy of Inter Nationes)
Upper right: Luciano Pavarotti in *L'elisir d'amore* (Courtesy of Deutsche Oper, Photo by Kranichphoto)
Bottom: *La bohème* (Courtesy of Deutsche Oper, Photo by Kranichphoto)

stormed the Städtische Oper, and Goebbels took control. (Hermann Wilhelm Göring controlled the other Berlin opera house, Staatsoper/Unter den Linden.) Ebert, Busch, and Stiedry, along with Paul Breisach, Rudolf Bing, Alexander Kipnis, and other Berlin artists, fled Germany.

The Wagnerian baritone Wilhelm Rode, not bothered by being the *Intendant* of the Nazi propaganda opera house, remained at the helm until 1944, as the newly named Deutsches Opernhaus slowly sank into mediocrity. Hitler was a frequent visitor, attending performances of Wagner's *Die Meistersinger von Nürnberg* and Otto Nicolai's *Die lustigen Weiber von Windsor.*

Four months after the war, Wagnerian bass Michael Bohnen organized a provincial opera company and moved into the Theater des Westens, where he staged Beethoven's *Fidelio*. Against the backdrop of denazification, scandals, and "tainted" artists, seven operas were produced that year. The next year, Nazi-banned contemporary operas were revived. Then Frida Leider tried to produce Wagner's *Die Walküre*. A vociferous debate ensued in the German press about the wisdom of staging "Nazi Wagner operas" so soon after the capitulation. But Heinz Tietjen, who was reappointed *Intendant* in 1948, had no qualms about "Nazi Wagner operas" and proceeded to stage all of them, as well as the world premières of Werner Egk's *Circe* on December 18, 1948, Arthur Honegger's *Totentanz* on March 13, 1949, and Fritz Behrend's *Die lächerlichen Preziösen/Der schwangere Bauer* on May 22 of the same year.

In 1951, the Theater des Westens hosted the world premières of Robert Oboussier's *Amphitryon* on March 13 and Winfried Zillig's *Troilus und Cressida* on November 27. Boris Blacher's *Preußisches Märchen* was introduced the next year on September 23. Ebert, Busch, and Bing returned to the Städtische Oper in 1954, making Verdi and Mozart operas the predominant fare. Jean-Pierre Ponnelle designed the "scandalous" world première of Hans Werner Henze's *König Hirsch*, performed on September 23, 1956.

Blacher's *Rosamunde Floris* graced the stage for the first time on September 21, 1960. The Städtische Oper introduced Dietrich Fischer-Dieskau and Elizabeth Grümmer to the opera world.

The first *Uraufführung* (world première) in the new opera house took place on September 25, 1961, Giselher Klebe's *Alkmene*. With Gustav Rudolf Sellner at the helm for the next eleven years, modern opera played an important role in the repertory. Several operas were commissioned by the Deutsche Oper: Roger Sessions's *Montezuma*, premiered on April 19, 1964; Henze's *Der junge Lord*, on April 7, 1965; Roman Haubenstock-Ramati's *Amerika* on October 8, 1966; Luigi Dallapiccola's *Ulisse (Odysseus)*, on September 29, 1968; and Blacher's *200 000 Taler*, on September 25, 1969.

In 1972, Egon Seefehlner took the reins, and the emphasis turned toward glorious voices. Although the Deutsche Oper is a highly subsidized house, carrying an obligation to offer avant-garde works, few appeared during Seefehlner's tenure. The two commissioned world premières were Wolfgang Fortner's *Elizabeth Tudor*, on October 23, 1972, and Toshiro Mayuzumi's *Kinkakuyi*, on June 23, 1976.

Next came Siegfried Palm, under whose tenure Plácido Domingo and Luciano Pavarotti made guest appearances, and the world premières of Wilhelm Dieter Siebert's *Untergang der Titanic* took place on September 6, 1979, and Mauricio Kagel's *Aus Deutschland* on May 9, 1981.

In 1981, Götz Friedrich took over as *Intendant*, bringing contemporary works once again to the forefront, along with avant-garde productions. His view of opera as music theater has stimulated international interest in the happenings on Bismarckstraße. The world première of Henze's *Das verratene Meer* took place on May 4, 1990.

I was fortunate to see Friedrich's controversial "time tunnel" *Der Ring des Nibelungen*, where the beginning takes place at the end and the end at the beginning. Although I found the production one of the most satisfying *Ring Cycles* I have attended, more conservative Wagner types might not agree. The Valkyries donned black leather outfits, and the dead heroes, wrapped in blood-stained sheets, were shoved unceremoniously into morgue shelves. Loge was a pimp, and Fafner's monster dragon took the form of a high-tech machine.

PRACTICAL INFORMATION
Tickets

The box office (*Kasse*) is located at Bismarckstraße 35, inside the main entrance to the opera house. It is open Monday through Friday 2:00 p.m. to 8:00 p.m. and Saturday and Sunday from 10:00 a.m to 2:00 p.m. (*Montag bis Freitag:* *14.00-20.00 Uhr, Sonnabend und Sonntag: 10.00-14.00 Uhr*). The box office reopens one hour before curtain time (*Abendkasse*). Tickets go on sale on Sunday for the next ten days.

Tickets can be ordered by mail by all non-residents of Berlin. Write to:

Kartenbüro der Deutschen Oper Berlin
Richard-Wagner-Straße 10
1000 Berlin 10, Germany

You can order tickets by telephoning (49) (30)34381 beginning the Monday after tickets go on sale at the box office. For ticket information, telephone (49)(30)341-0249. (49) = country code; (30) = city code. If calling, you should speak German. Berlin is six hours ahead of Eastern Standard Time.

The ticket table for Deutsche Oper Berlin

TICKET TABLE			
Platzarten (Type of Seat)	**Eintrittspreise (Ticket Prices in DM)**		
Parkett (orchestra)	A	B	C
1.-2. Reihe (rows 1,2)	54	68	95
3.-6. Reihe (rows 3-6)	54	68	95
7.-12. Reihe (rows 7-12)	42	52	75
13.-19. Reihe (rows 13-19)	35	42	60
20.-22. Reihe (rows 20-22)	25	30	42
Hochparkett (rear orchestra)			
23.-26. Reihe (rows 23-26)	25	30	42
Loge Mitte rechts (middle box right)	19	23	30
**Loge Mitte links (middle box left)	19	23	30
Logen A, B, C (boxes A, B, C)			
1. Reihe (row 1)	54	68	95
2.-3. Reihe (rows 2,3)	42	52	75
4. Reihe (row 4)	25	30	42
I. Rang (1st balcony)			
1. Reihe (row 1)	70	91	125
2. Reihe (row 2)	54	68	95
3.-5. Reihe (rows 3-5)	35	42	60
6.-9. Reihe (rows 6-9)	19	23	30
Logen A, B, C (boxes A, B, C, all rows)	35	42	60
Loge D (box D)			
1. Reihe (row 1)	54	68	95
2.-3. Reihe (rows 2,3)	42	52	75
4. Reihe (row 4)	25	30	42
II. Rang (2nd balcony)			
1. Reihe (row 1)	19	23	30
2.-3. Reihe (rows 2,3)	15	20	25
4.-5. Reihe (rows 4,5)	15	20	25
6.-9. Reihe (rows 6-9)	10	12	16
Loge A (box A)	19	23	30

** Versehrtenloge is reserved for disabled patrons.
$1 = 1.6 DM, but can vary due to the fluctuating value of the dollar.
DM is an abbreviation for Deutsche Mark.

is quite detailed. The price depends not only on the section and row but also on the caliber of the singers. If someone of Pavarotti's stature is singing, the Category is C. If a relatively unknown repertory singer is performing, Category A prevails.

Tickets for Berliner Festwochen, *Premieren*, and especially the occasional *Uraufführung* (world première) are the most difficult to come by. Tickets for repertory revivals with A or B casts are usually available. *Freier Verkauf* (nonsubscription) performances have the most tickets available. If you see *Ausverkauft* (sold out) or *geschlossene Vorstellung* (closed performance), think of another date. If you want tickets for one of the "difficult to get" categories, either write far in advance or arrive in Berlin ten days before the

performance, when the tickets go on sale, and stand in line.

Your ticket is relatively easy to understand once you know the meaning of the German words, so below is a translation of a sample ticket.

The starting time is not printed on your ticket. Although operas usually begin at 8:00 p.m. (*20 Uhr*), there are enough exceptions to make it necessary to confirm the time. No one is admitted after the performance has begun. Starting times are listed in the monthly *Berlin Programm Magazin*, the weekly newspaper *Die Zeit*, and the Wednesday edition of the daily newspaper *Die Welt*. These two newspapers also list the weekly performance schedules and starting times for all the major opera houses in Germany.

TICKET TRANSLATION

Deutsche Oper Berlin Berlin-Charlottenburg, Bismarckstraße			German Opera Berlin Berlin-Charlottenburg, Bismarckstreet		
Reihe	**Parkett**	Sitz Nr.	Row	**Orchestra**	Seat Number
6	Links	16	6	Left	16
Montag, 8. Januar 90			Monday, January 8, 1990		

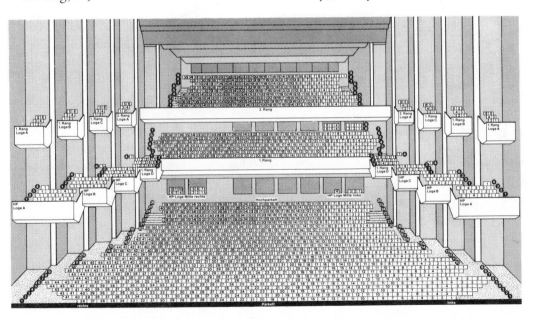

Seating Plan (Courtesy of Deutsche Oper)

Finding Your Way

The Deutsche Oper Berlin faces Bismarckstraße. It is bordered on the west by Richard-Wagner-Straße and on the east by Krumme Straße. You can reach the theater by public transportation: U-Bahn U1 or U7, exit Deutsche Oper, or bus 1, exit Deutsche Oper.

The main entrance is at 35 Bismarckstraße. Take the stairs at either end of the hall up to the *Parkett*, *1.Rang* and *2.Rang*. Since the seats stretch across the auditorium in unbroken rows, it is crucial that you enter on the correct side. Enter on the right side for *rechts* and on the left side for *links*. Several doors lead into the auditorium on both the right and left sides. Seats begin with 1 on the left aisle and increase sequentially until the right aisle. The center seats are roughly 15 through 25, depending on the row. Seat numbers in the *1.Rang* and *2.Rang* are numbered similarly to the *Parkett*. For the boxes, *Loge A* is closest to the stage and *Loge D* nearest to the middle.

Programs are for sale in the entrance foyer and from the program sellers next to the doors. The program (in German) contains a synopsis in English and photographs and articles pertaining to the opera and costs 5 DM. The cloakroom (*Garderobe*) is located at the front end of the entrance foyer. It is divided into sections according to where you are seated. The ladies' room (*Damen*) and men's room (*Herren*) are located opposite the cloakroom and on both sides of *1.Rang* and *2.Rang*. Bar and refreshments are available on the side foyers. The *Parkett* level foyer brims over with sculpture and paintings in rotating exhibits. There are seats reserved for disabled patrons (*Versehrtenloge*) located in the *Loge mitte links* (middle box left). Call 34-381 to make the appropriate arrangements. Radio amplifiers are available for hearing-impaired patrons.

Planning Your Trip

OPERA SCHEDULE

The season runs from the end of August until the beginning of July. The 1990/91 season opened on August 21 with Johann Strauß's *Die Fledermaus* and will close on July 6 with Carl Maria von Weber's *Der Freischütz*. Mozart's *Die Entführung aus dem Serail* and *La clemenza di Tito*, Richard Strauss's *Salome*, Paul Hindemith's *Mathis der Maler*, and Verdi's *Otello* are new productions. Wagner's *Tristan und Isolde*, *Der fliegende Holländer*, *Lohengrin*, *Das Rheingold*, *Die Walküre*, *Siegfried*, and *Götterdämmerung*; Puccini's *Turandot*, *Madama Butterfly*, and *Manon Lescaut*; Verdi's *Macbeth*, *Aida*, *Rigoletto*, and *Il trovatore*; Beethoven's *Fidelio*; Mozart's *Così fan tutte*, *Die Zauberflöte*, *Don Giovanni*, and *Le nozze di Figaro*; Strauss's *Arabella*; Nicolai's *Die lustigen Weiber von Windsor*; Charles Gounod's *Faust*; and Camille Saint-Saëns's *Samson et Dalila* complete the season. Although almost all operas are sung in their original language, some of the titles are translated into German, so you might have to do some guessing with a few of the non-German operas to figure out what the opera is.

Deutsche Oper Berlin operates on a repertory system with a different opera every night. Opera shares the stage with ballet. To be sure your visit coincides with an opera, write ahead for a schedule:

Kartenbüro der Deutsche Oper Berlin
Richard-Wagner-Straße 10
1000 Berlin 10, Germany

TRAVEL INFORMATION

A few minutes' walk from the U-Bahn U7, which stops right in front of the opera house, is the five-star Bristol Hotel Kempinski Berlin, Kurfürstendamm 27; telephone (49)(30)884-340. Singles start at $175, doubles at $225.

There are a couple of restaurants near the opera house, but for a better selection, go to Kurfürstendamm.

The German National Tourist Office, 747 Third Avenue, 33rd Floor, New York, NY 10017, 212-308-3300, can help you with travel information, but they cannot help you with opera information. Write far ahead. They take a long time to respond.

COLOGNE
Oper der Stadt Köln

*T*he Großes Haus of the Oper der Stadt Köln was inaugurated on May 18, 1957, with Carl Maria von Weber's *Oberon*. The gala production regaled a distinguished opening night crowd. Designed by Wilhelm Riphahn, the concrete, brick, and glass opera building is one of the most distinctive opera houses constructed during the 1950s.

HISTORICAL OVERVIEW
Background

The *alte Kölner Opernhaus*, located on Barbarossaplatz, opened in 1902. Designed by Carl Moritz and constructed in fin-de-siècle style, the building was an architectural curiosity until it succumbed to bombs during World War II. After the war, a competition was held for the best design of a new opera house complex, but architect Hermann von Berg submitted such spectacular plans for the rebuilding of the old opera house, with a streamlined façade, that his rebuilding idea was considered as well. Seven locations were contemplated for the new building: Rudolfplatz, Volksgarten, Stadtgarten, Sachsenring, Theodor Heuss-Ring, Cäcilienstraße, and Glockengasse. The currency reform of 1948, which lifted the restriction on the type of building materials that could be employed, influenced the choice, as did the opinion that the new opera house should be on its own property and take a dominant role in the new image of the city. On

June 17, 1951, the decision was made to lay the old opera house to rest and build the new opera complex in the Glockengasse area. New drawings were needed, so a second competition was held on March 4, 1952. Although it was a difficult choice between Werner Kallmorgen's and Riphahn's plans, Wilhelm Riphahn's designs were selected on September 17.

With the sound of a whistle, building began on September 13, 1954. The opera house, more than two and a half years under construction, created quite a fuss. Its unusual form was ridiculed as looking like everything from a monument to Ramses III to a bunker for prelates. But the opera house has stood the test of time, and now, more than thirty years later, it is recognized as an outstanding architectural feat of its era.

The Theater

The Oper der Stadt Köln, set on its own plaza, is a striking concrete, brick, and glass trapeze-shaped building with five jutting balconies. The functional style is typical of that period. The blue and gray foyers, illuminated with crystal droplet chandeliers and Murano glass globe lamps, lead into an auditorium swathed in warm Persian walnut wood. Two tiers of black pear wood and silver gray drawer-shaped boxes rise above the gray velvet orchestra seats. Numerous butterfly-shaped lights glow from the ceiling. The auditorium accommodates 1,346.

Top: Façade of Oper der Stadt (Photo by author)
Bottom: Auditorium with view of drawer-shaped boxes (Courtesy of Oper der Stadt Köln, Photo by Leclaire)

Performance History

Richard Wagner's *Die Meistersinger von Nürnberg* inaugurated Cologne's old *Opernhaus* on September 6, 1902. Between 1917 and 1924, Cologne experienced some of its greatest opera years under *Dirigent* Otto Klemperer. The world première of Erich Korngold's *Die tote Stadt* was given on December 4, 1920, Alexander von Zemlinsky's *Der Zwerg* on May 29, 1922, and Franz Schreker's *Irrelohe* two years later.

After World War II, with 95 percent of Cologne in ruins, opera performances continued in the Great Hall of the University of Köln, where a new version of Rolf Liebermann's *Leonore 40/45* was staged in 1952.

Following the inauguration of the new opera house in 1957, the world première of Wolfgang Fortner's *Bluthochzeit* took place on June 8, 1957, and of Bernd Alois Zimmermann's *Die Soldaten* on February 15, 1965. *Die Soldaten*, a

"total theater experience," encompassed jazz, electronic music, ballet, film, circus, and spoken dialogue. In 1980, to commemorate the 100th anniversary of Jacques Offenbach's death, *Intendant* Michael Hampe staged a gala performance of *Les Contes d'Hoffmann*, with John Pritchard on the podium and Plácido Domingo in the title role.

I was fortunate to have seen that marvelous production of *Les Contes d'Hoffmann*. Cologne is best known for its innovative and sometimes controversial staging, which makes its performances a unique theater experience. In 1987, Oper der Stadt Köln became the first German opera house to offer surtitles for all operas not sung in German.

PRACTICAL INFORMATION
Tickets

The box office (*Vorverkaufskasse*) is located at Offenbachplatz, on the right side of the opera house. Enter through the glass door on the Glockengasse side of the plaza. The box office is open Monday through Friday from 11:00 a.m. to 2:00 p.m. and 4:00 p.m. to 6:00 p.m. and Saturday from 11:00 a.m. to 2:00 p.m. (*Montag bis Freitag von 11-14 und 16-18 Uhr, Sonnabend von 11-14 Uhr*). In addition, the box office opens one hour before curtain time (*Abendkasse*). A price list is posted between the two box office windows, and monthly schedules are on a shelf opposite the windows. Tickets go on sale fourteen days before the performance.

Tickets can be ordered by mail. The only problem is that mail orders are not processed until the tickets for the performance go on sale at the box office. Write to:

Oper der Stadt Köln
Postfach 18 02 41
5000 Köln 1, Germany

You can order tickets by telephoning (49) (221)221-8400 beginning fourteen days before the performance, between 9:00 a.m. and 12:00 noon and 2:00 p.m. and 4:00 p.m. Monday

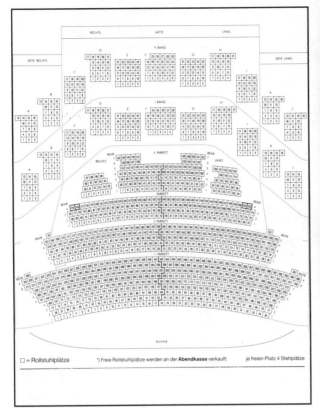

Seating Plan (Courtesy of Oper der Stadt Köln)

Foyer of Oper der Stadt (Courtesy of
Inter Nationes)

TICKET TABLE

Platzgruppe (Seat Location)	Preisgruppe (Ticket Price in DM)		
	1	2	3
1. Parkett Mitte (front orchestra center)	53	71	95
1. Parkett Seite (front orchestra side)	51	66	81
2. Parkett Mitte (middle orchestra center)	51	66	81
I. Rang Mitte (1st tier center)	51	66	81
2. Parkett Seite (middle orchestra side)	49	53	67
3. Parkett (rear orchestra)	49	53	67
I. Rang Seite (1st tier side)	42	49	53
4. Parkett (last 7 rows in orchestra)	31	41	47
II. Rang Mitte (2nd tier center)	27	29	31
II. Rang Seite (2nd tier side)	16	17	19

$1 = 1.6 DM, but can vary due to the fluctuating value of the dollar.
DM is an abbreviation for Deutsche Mark.

Top: *L'italiana in Algeri* (Courtesy of Oper der Stadt Köln, Photo by Leclaire)
Bottom: *Oberon*, inaugural opera on May 18, 1957 (Courtesy of Inter Nationes)

TICKET TRANSLATION

Bühnen der Stadt Köln		Stages of the City of Cologne	
Opernhaus		Opera House	
Mittwoch	11. April 1990	Wednesday	April 11, 1990
19.30		7:30 P.M.	
Die verkaufte Braut		(Opera)	
2. Parkett	**Mitte rechts**	**2nd Section Orchestra**	**Center Right**
Reihe 3	**Platz Nr. 89**	**Row 3**	**Seat Number 89**

through Friday and 9:00 a.m. and 12:00 noon on Saturday. (49) = country code; (221) = city code. In Germany, dial (0221)221-8400. (Note the hours are different from the box office hours.) If calling, you should speak German. Cologne is six hours ahead of Eastern Standard Time. For ticket availability beginning one hour before the performance, call 221-8248.

The problem with ordering tickets by mail or by telephone is that the Oper der Stadt Köln is only set up to receive payment by eurocheques or through money transfer (*Überweisung*) to their bank account. They do not accept credit cards.

The *Preisgruppe* depends on the caliber of the singers (expensive guest artists or "house" singers) and whether the production is new (*Neuinszenierung*) or a repertory revival. Non-subscription performances (*Vorstellungen im freien Verkauf*) have the most tickets available. When star singers appear, tickets are impossible to purchase, because these singers do not visit Cologne very often. There are no bad seats.

It is important to understand your ticket since there are no ushers. Your ticket contains all the information you need to find your seat with no problem.

Most operas begin at 7:30 p.m. (19.30 *Uhr*) except on Sundays, when they begin at 5:00 p.m. (17.00 *Uhr*). However, the never-ending Wagner sagas begin much earlier, and short operas begin later. Starting times of all the operas are listed in the monthly programs and the *Theater in Köln* newspaper found in the box office. The weekly German-language newspaper *Die Zeit* and the Wednesday edition of the daily newspaper *Die Welt* list the performance schedules and starting times for the week of all the major opera houses in Germany.

Finding Your Way

The Oper der Stadt Köln faces Offenbachplatz with Tunis Straße running in front. Bordered on the north by Glockengasse and on the south by Brüderstraße, the opera house is a pleasant fifteen-minute walk from the *Hauptbahnhof* along the *Fußgängerzone* (pedestrian zone).

The main entrance to the opera house is off Offenbachplatz. After passing through the box office foyer, you will find stairs leading up to the auditorium on both sides of the entrance foyer. The elevator (*Aufzug*) is on the left. On the *Parkett* (orchestra) level, all the doors going into the auditorium are clearly marked with signs corresponding to the information on your ticket: *1.Parkett rechts*, *2.Parkett rechts*, *3.Parkett links*, *4.Parkett links*, and so on. Each door leads to a specific section in the orchestra. Since seat and row numbers repeat in each section and the seats stretch across the auditorium in unbroken rows, it is crucial that you enter through the correct door on the correct side. In every section of the *Parkett*, each seat begins with 1 on the right side and increases sequentially to the end of the section on the left side, and each row begins with 1.

If you are seated in *1.Rang* (1st tier) or *2.Rang* (2nd tier), continue up the staircase. Again all the entrance doors are clearly marked according to the information on your ticket. *Loge* (box) A is on the extreme right and *Loge* L on the extreme left. Every box has identically numbered seats, so make sure the *Loge* letter corresponds with your ticket.

Programs are sold at a desk in the center of the entrance hall and cost 3.50 DM. The program (in German) includes illustrations and articles relevant to the opera. The cloakroom (*Garderobe*), down a few stairs toward the back of the hall, is divided into sections according to your seating location. The men's room (*Herren*) and ladies' room (*Damen*) are located on both the right and left sides behind the cloakrooms and on the sides of each tier. Small tables are set up in the *Parkett* foyer during intermission where you can buy champagne. No smoking is permitted. A bar and buffet are on the Brüderstraße end of the foyer, and smoking is permitted here. There is also a *Raucherraum* (smoking room) on the Glockengasse end of the foyer. There are accommodations for the disabled. Four seats numbered 115, 116, 151, and 152 in *3.Parkett, 4.Reihe* (3rd section orchestra, 4th row) are designated *Rollstuhlplätze* (wheelchair seats).

Planning Your Trip
OPERA SCHEDULE
The season runs from September until the beginning of July, changing somewhat each year depending on the school vacation. The 1990/91 opera season opened on September 9 with a new production of Wagner's *Siegfried* and will close on July 7 with a *Musical-Gastspiele*. The new productions are Wolfgang Amadeus Mozart's *Don Giovanni* and *Die Entführung aus dem Serail*, Wagner's *Götterdämmerung*, Offenbach's *Barbe-Bleue*, and Leoš Janáček's *Z mrtvého domu* (From the House of the Dead). Mozart's *La finta giardiniera* and *Die Zauberflöte*, Giuseppe Verdi's *Simon Boccanegra* and *La traviata*, Wagner's *Das Rheingold* and *Die Walküre*, Richard Strauss's *Elektra*, Ludwig van Beethoven's *Fidelio*, Engelbert Humperdinck's *Hänsel und Gretel*, Bedřich Smetana's *Prodaná nevesta* (The Bartered Bride), Giacomo Puccini's *Madama Butterfly* and *La bohème*, Benjamin Britten's *Turn of the Screw*,

Gaetano Donizetti's *L'elisir d'amore*, Reinhard Febel's *Nacht mit Gästen*, and Christoph Willibald Gluck's *Orfeo ed Euridice* complete the season.

Oper der Stadt Köln operates on a repertory system with a different opera every night. Opera shares the stage with ballet and other musical events. To be sure your visit coincides with the opera, write for a schedule:

Vorverkaufskasse-Oper der Stadt Köln
Offenbachplatz
5000 Köln 1, Germany

TRAVEL INFORMATION
The best hotel in Cologne is the Excelsior Hotel Ernst, Domplatz, 5 Cologne 1, Germany; telephone (49)(221)2701, fax (49)(221)135-150. For reservations in the United States, call toll-free, 1-800-223-6800 (member of the Leading Hotels of the World). Singles begin at $170, doubles at $240. A continental breakfast is included. The hotel is a magnificent five-star establishment with 155 rooms and 20 suites. Conveniently located opposite the *Dom* in the best section of Cologne and offering a glorious view, the Excelsior Hotel Ernst exudes Old World elegance and class. It is especially delightful if you like to be pampered, and who does not? The hotel is only steps from the main railroad station and a delightful ten-minute walk along the pedestrian zone to the opera house. It is safe to walk back after the performance. See the concierge about all your last-minute opera tickets needs.

There are two restaurants next to the opera house on Offenbachplatz: Opern Terrassen and Offenbach's. In addition, the Hanse-Stube (expensive) is located in the hotel and a McDonald's is next to the hotel. Several restaurants are in the pedestrian zone.

The German National Tourist Office, 747 Third Avenue, 33rd Floor, New York, NY 10017, 212-308-3300, can send you travel information only. Write far ahead. They take a long time to respond.

FRANKFURT
Städtische Bühnen, Oper Frankfurt
Alte Oper

ie Alte Oper, originally known as Frankfurter Opernhaus, was inaugurated on October 20, 1880, with a dazzling production of Wolfgang Amadeus Mozart's *Don Giovanni*. The gala performance regaled an illustrious opening night audience that included Kaiser Wilhelm I, Crown Prince Friedrich Wilhelm, Prince Heinrich, and Prince Bernhard von Weimer. Silk programs were printed with gold lettering for the royal guests. Designed by Richard Lucae, the opera house survived sixty-four years, until bombs demolished it during World War II. After the war, opera found a new home in the Städtische Bühnen. Inaugurated on December 23, 1951, with Richard Wagner's *Die Meistersinger von Nürnberg*, the performing arts complex was designed by Otto Apel and Hannsgeorg Beckert. Meanwhile, the Alte Oper was transformed into a *Musik- und Kongreßzentrum*, reopening on August 28, 1981.

HISTORICAL OVERVIEW
Background

In 1782, Frankfurt's first theater, the Städtisches Comödienhaus, opened in the Paradeplatz. By 1855, the city had outgrown its theater, so the Senate decided to enlarge the house, hiring architect Rudolf Heinrich Burnitz to oversee the work. But the population kept growing, so the idea of building a new opera house was considered in 1862. However, the Senate procrastinated until Prussian troops marched on Frank-furt on July 16, 1866. Three years later, on December 14, another proposal for a new theater was submitted by Oberbürgermeister Dr. Daniel Heinrich Mumm von Schwarzenstein. Meanwhile, several wealthy people grew impatient and offered the municipality of Frankfurt a great deal of money to build the Frankfurter Opernhaus. All they asked in return was to be guaranteed their choice of boxes, for which they would pay the subscription. The municipality accepted, not only donating land at Rahmhof but contributing additional money as well. There was a limited competition with architects Otto Brückwald of Altenburg, Gédéon Bordiau of Brussels, Johann Heinrich Strack of Berlin, Rudolf Heinrich Burnitz of Frankfurt, and Gustav Gugitz of Vienna invited to submit drawings. Gugitz was forced to withdraw for health reasons, and Richard Lucae of Berlin took his place. Lucae won the competition and was commissioned on October 27, 1871, to build the opera house. In 1873, the site was moved from Rahmhof to the area near Bockenheimer Warte, so Lucae had to draw new plans. Finally the project got under way, but then Lucae died unexpectedly on November 26, 1877. The task of completing the building fell to Albrecht Becker and Eduard Giesenberg. When the Alte Oper opened, it was managed by a directorate elected by the subscribers.

On the night of March 22, 1944, the Alte Oper almost disappeared in a bombing raid and raging fire. Only its façade and magnificent grand foyer survived as evidence of its former glory. The rebuilding of the Frankfurter Opernhaus did not begin until 1971. Taking almost ten years to complete, the façade was rebuilt following Lucae's original plans. The inside was redesigned as a music and convention center by the architectural group of Braun, Schlockermann, and Professeur Keilholz. This multifunction interior better justified the enormous rebuilding expense.

Meanwhile in 1951, the reborn Oper Frankfurt found a new home in the Städtische Bühnen. Erected on the site of a ruined playhouse, the performing arts complex gained a *Schauspielhaus* (playhouse) and *Kammerspiel* (experimental theater) twelve years later. Catastrophe struck on the night of November 12, 1987. An unemployed East German, frustrated at not finding a job, thought the building was a bank (as so many glass buildings in Frankfurt are) and set it on fire. He was put behind bars, and the Oper Frankfurt moved into the Schauspielhaus. Oper Frankfurt should be back in its own home by April 1991.

The Theaters

The Alte Oper was a magnificent neoclassical building. Covered with *Savonnières* stone, the façade oozed elegance and grandeur. Rounded arches and Corinthian columns and pilasters complemented by lavish adornments revealed the builder's taste for Florentine Renaissance. Above each of the twenty-four arches were relief portraits of poets and composers. The main pediment, by Emil Hundrieser, displayed the allegorical figures Rhein and Main, below which DEM WAHREN SCHOENEN GUTEN (To the true, beautiful, and good) was carved. Above those figures, four statues by Gustav Herold representing Poetry, Dance, Comedy, and Tragedy looked out from lofty niches.

A magnificent double-sided grand staircase greeted all who passed through the portals. Illuminated by numerous bronze candelabra, the yellow marble staircase was ringed by Corinthian

Detail of façade of Alte Oper (Photo by author)

columns and pilasters and complemented by dark red marble walls. Poetry, Truth, Art, and Nature, in larger-than-life sculptures by Franz Krüger, stood in the columned hallway. The ceiling was embellished with a painting by Eduard von Steinle, depicting the personification of Poetry surrounded by the Genii of Inspiration, Truth, Harmony, and Knowledge and flanked by Hate and Love. A frieze with the allegorical figures of Architecture, Music, Painting, and Sculpture encircled the ceiling.

The grand staircase led up to the grand foyer, where scenes from William Shakespeare's *As You Like It* and *King Lear* were depicted. The walls dissolved into shafts of yellow marble with gold bases and capitals. Six-sided panels filled with Apollo and the nine Muses encompassed the ceiling. Four star-shaped paintings of Triton, Pan, a shepherd boy blowing a shawm, and a maiden playing a lyre covered the ceiling, while dark red silk velour drapery adorned the windows. Above the transoms on both sides of the foyer were scenes from Mozart's *Le nozze di Figaro*, *Die Entführung aus dem Serail*, *Die Zauberflöte*, and *Don Giovanni*. The grand foyer is the only room of the Frankfurter Opernhaus incorporated into the new building.

The gold, white, and red auditorium, with three tiers and two galleries sweeping around an unbroken horseshoe, was constructed of iron covered with wood to give it superb acoustics.

Angels playing various musical instruments gazed down from the ceiling, where a gold-plated bronze chandelier hung, boasting three hundred lights. The ceiling was drawn by Eduard von Steinle and painted by J. Welsch. Yellow marble Corinthian columns flanked the proscenium boxes. The proscenium arch, painted by Otto Philipp Donner von Richter, showed the union of the Rhein and the Main through the power of music. The walls, seats, and drapery of the boxes were purple. The Alte Oper seated 1,800.

The "new" Alte Oper kept its neoclassical façade, but behind the nineteenth-century exterior resides a state-of-the-art *Musik- und Kongreßzentrum*. Modern exhibition halls are interspersed among three auditoriums: Großer Saal (2,012 seats), Mozart Saal (676 seats), and Hindemith Saal (304 seats).

The Städtische Bühnen is a large, modern, glass, concrete, and steel complex. Its block-long glass façade allows the historic outside to integrate with the contemporary interior. Inside the glass doors of the Städtische Bühnen are modern, functional theaters. Opera is housed in the Großes Haus, which is joined to the rest of the complex by a long foyer, furnished with square leather seats and dynamic metallic sculptures by Zoltan Kemeny. Before the fire, the auditorium was red and black. The restored auditorium, designed by architect Toyo Ito, boasts light blue walls with dark blue seats. A star-filled sky covers the ceiling. The Großes Haus seats 1,375.

Performance History

The first opera performed in Frankfurt was Johann Theile's *Adam und Eva* or *Der erschaffene, gefallene und aufgerichtete Mensch* on June 4, 1698. During the eighteenth century, Singspiel, opera

Façade of Alte Oper (Courtesy of Inter Nationes)

buffa, and opéra comique were the primary fare. After the Städtisches Comödienhaus opened in 1782, Mozart operas dominated the repertory. Other works like Peter von Winter's *Das unterbrochene Opferfest*, Joseph Weigl's *Corsar*, and Ferdinando Paër's *Camilla* surfaced from time to time. In 1810, Carl Maria von Weber's *Silvana* was premiered, followed by Ludwig Spohr's *Zémire und Azor* in 1819.

Shortly after the Frankfurter Opernhaus opened, the world première of Karl Reinthaler's *Das Käthchen von Heilbronn* took place on December 8, 1881. Engelbert Humperdinck's *Dornröschen* was introduced on November 12, 1902, in a stunning, critically acclaimed production. The Alte Oper became a showplace for introducing contemporary operas until its demise in 1944.

Julius Bittner's *Die rote Gred* was world premiered on October 26, 1907. Five years later, Franz Schreker's *Der ferne Klang*, staged for the first time on August 18, made a powerful impression. His *Die Gezeichneten* followed on April 25, 1918, and *Der Schatzgräber* on January 21, 1920. Frederick Delius's *Fennimore und Gerda*, an opera suffused with pastoral impressionism, appeared on October 21, 1919, with the composer present. Rudi Stephan's *Die ersten Menschen* first saw the stage on July 1, 1920. Two years later, Paul Hindemith's controversial opera about nuns and sexuality, *Sancta Susanna*, was premiered on March 26. Ernst Křenek, who used jazz parlance in an atonal style, saw his *Der Sprung über dem Schatten* introduced on July 9, 1924.

On September 1, 1924, Clemens Krauss became *Intendant*. The first novelty under his reign, Simon Bucharoff's *Sakahra*, offered on November 8, 1924, was not received kindly by the press. Bernhard Sekles's *Die zehn Küsse*, under Krauss's direction, received its world première on February 25, 1926. Eugen d'Albert's *Der Golem* followed on November 14, 1926. There were three world premières in 1930: Arnold Schönberg's *Von heute auf morgen* on February 1, Wilhelm Grosz's *Achtung Aufnahme* on March

23, and George Antheil's *Transatlantik* on May 25, with the composer present.

Even Adolf Hitler's rise to power did not stop the flow of world premières: Hannsheinrich Dransmann's *Münchhausens letzte Lüge* emerged on May 18, 1934, only to disappear soon thereafter. Werner Egk's *Zaubergeige* arrived on May 22, 1935, and his *Columbus* on January 13, 1942. A *Sing-Oper* by Hermann Reutter, *Doktor Johannes Faust*, was introduced on May 26, 1936, followed by his opera oratorio, *Odysseus*, on September 7, 1942. Carl Orff's *Carmina burana* received its world première on June 8, 1937. Not quite opera or oratorio, sung in a mixture of Latin, middle high German, and old French, *Carmina burana* caused a sensation. His scenic cantata *Die Kluge* followed on February 20, 1943. Then came the bombs.

Now the Alte Oper hosts only one opera a year. All other opera performances are staged at the Städtische Bühnen, where each operatic ingredient—voices, music, scenery, and drama—receives equal weight. The productions are original and creative, especially the lesser-known operas.

I witnessed a delightful performance of Antonín Dvořák's *Rusalka* with Clarry Bartha as Rusalka, Manfred Schenk as the Wassermann, Eva Randova as the Hexe, and Allan Glassman as the Prinz. Imre Palló conducted. Considering the cramped stage of the Schauspielhaus, Oper Frankfurt did an admirable job of conveying the fairy tale quality of the opera. Rusalka even periodically splashed in a water-filled pond in the middle of the stage. The Schauspielhaus has only 855 seats, so it was easy for the fine voices to fill the theater.

PRACTICAL INFORMATION
Tickets

STÄDTISCHE BÜHNEN
The box office (*Vorverkaufskasse*) is located at Theaterplatz 3 by the main entrance to the complex. The box office is open Monday through

Friday 10:00 a.m. to 6:00 p.m. and Saturday from 10:00 a.m. to 2:00 p.m. (*Montag bis Freitag 10-18 Uhr; Samstag 10-14 Uhr*). On performance days, the box office opens one hour before curtain time (*Vorstellungskasse*). Tickets can be purchased beginning twenty days before a performance.

You can order tickets through the mail between four and six weeks before a performance. Send your requests to:

Städtische Bühnen-Oper
Untermainanlage 11
6000 Frankfurt 1, Germany
Tickets can be reserved by calling (49)

TICKET TABLE

Group 1

Parkett Reihe 1-12 (orchestra, rows 1-12)

1.Rang Reihe 1-3 (1st tier, rows 1-3)

1.Rang 1. Reihe Prosz.-Plätze (1st tier 1st row stage seats)

Group II

Parkett Reihe 13-16 (orchestra, rows 13-16)

1.Rang Mitte Reihe 4-5 (1st tier center, rows 4-5)

1.Rang Seite 1.Reihe (1st tier side, row 1)

1.Rang Seite 2.Reihe (1st tier side, row 2)

2.Rang Mitte 1.Reihe (2nd tier center, row 1)

Group III

Parkett Reihe 17-20 (orchestra, rows 17-20)

1.Rang Mitte Reihe 6 (1st tier center, row 6)

1.Rang Seite Reihe 2-4 (1st tier side, rows 2-4)

2.Rang Mitte Reihe 2-3 (2nd tier center, rows 2-3)

Group IV

Parkett Reihe 21-22 (orchestra, rows 21-22)

2.Rang Mitte Reihe 4 (2nd tier center, row 4)

2.Rang Seite 1.Reihe (2nd tier side, row 1)

2.Rang 1.Reihe Prosz. Plätze (2nd tier, row 1 stage seats)

Group V

2.Rang Mitte Reihe 5 (2nd tier center, row 5)

2.Rang Seite 1.Reihe (2nd tier side, row 1)

2.Rang Seite Reihe 2-4 (2nd tier side, rows 2-4)

3.Rang Mitte Reihe 1-3 (3rd tier center, rows 1-3)

3.Rang 1.Reihe Prosz. Plätze (3rd tier, row 1 stage seats)

Group VI

3.Rang Mitte Reihe 4-7 (3rd tier center, rows 4-7)

3.Rang Seite Reihe 1 (3rd tier side, row 1)

Group VII

3.Rang Halbmitte (3rd tier partial side)

3.Rang Seite Reihe 2 Prosz. Plätze (3rd tier side, row 2 stage seats)

(69)236-061 during box office hours, beginning twenty days before the performance. (49) = country code; (69) = city code. In Germany, dial (069) 236-061. Tickets ordered by phone must be picked up or paid for at least one day before the performance. Germany is six hours ahead of Eastern Standard Time. For ticket availability on the day of the performance, telephone 256-2434.

Ticket prices have not yet been set for the restored opera house. Therefore, only the locations grouped by price are listed, beginning with the most expensive.

Tickets are not difficult to buy for Oper Frankfurt, except for the international star cast and repertory favorites.

Even though the opera house has not recovered from its burns, the ticket should look similar to the ticket for Oper Frankfurt's temporary home, Schauspielhaus.

Frankfurt, like most other German cities, tries to have all its operas end at the same time, instead of beginning at the same time. Since operas come in varying lengths, curtain time varies. The usual starting time is 7:30 p.m. (19.30). Shorter operas begin at 8:00 p.m. (20.00), and lengthy operas begin at 7:00 p.m., 6:30 p.m., or 6:00 p.m. (19.00, 18.30, or 18.00), depending on how interminable they are. Starting times are listed in the monthly program at the box office and in the *Frankfurter Woche*, available at tourist offices. In addition, both the weekly German-language newspaper *Die Zeit* and the Wednesday edition of the daily newspaper *Die Welt* list the operas and their start-

ing times for the week for all the opera houses in Germany.

Alte Oper

The box office is normally located by the Alte Oper on the Opernplatz. Because of reconstruction, it is currently located in a building opposite the right side of the Alte Oper. There is an awning in front, white marble with glass globe lighting inside, and long lines. The box office is open Monday through Friday 10:00 a.m. to 6:00 p.m., Saturday 10:00 a.m. to 2:00 p.m. (*Mo bis Fr 10-18 Uhr, Sa 10-14 Uhr*). It opens again one hour before the performance begins (*Abendkasse: 1 Stunde vor Vorstellungsbeginn*). Tickets go on sale one month before the performance.

Tickets can be ordered by mail until one month before the performance. Write to:

Alte Oper Frankfurt
Vorverkaufskasse
Opernplatz
6000 Frankfurt 1, Germany

STÄDTISCHE BÜHNEN FRANKFURT AM MAIN

OPER | SCHAUSPIEL | BALLETT

GROSSES HAUS
RUSALKA   DM   9,00
FR 08.06.90, 19.30 UHR

REIHE   5   Links
PLATZ   21

Für verfallene Eintrittskarten kein Ersatz. Umtausch oder Rücknahme nur bei Vorstellungsänderung. Karte bitte bis Vorstellungsschluß aufbewahren. Bei Verspätung Einlaß nur bei Aktschluß.   034/01

163901019734

Ticket to *Rusalka* (Courtesy of Oper Frankfurt)

TICKET TRANSLATION

Städtische Bühnen		Frankfurt am Main	City Stages		Frankfurt on the Main
Oper	Schauspiel	Ballet	Opera	Drama	Ballet
Grosses Haus			Large Theater		
Rusalka		DM48	(Opera)		(Price)
FR	08.06.90	19,30 Uhr	Friday	June 8, 1990	7:30 P.M.
Reihe 5		**Links**	**Row 5**		**Left (Side)**
Platz 21			**Seat 21**		

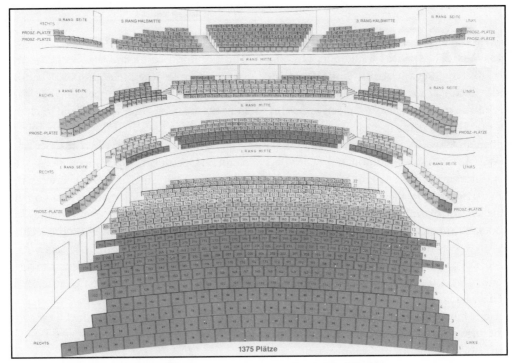

Seating Plan of Großes Haus, Städtische Bühnen (Courtesy of Oper Frankfurt)

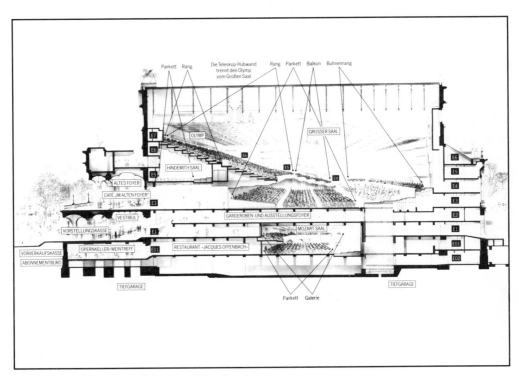

Cross section of Alte Oper (Courtesy of Alte Oper)

You can reserve tickets by calling (49)(69) 134-0400 or (49)(69)134-0401 during box office hours. For ticket availability on the day of performance, call 134-0405 or 134-0406.

Since there are only a couple of operas performed in the Alte Oper each year, your trip might not coincide with a performance. However, you can take a tour through the Alte Oper on Saturdays at 3:00 p.m. or Sundays at 9:30 a.m. The cost is 5 DM. The starting point is on the left side of the building about halfway up. Look for the sign *Führungen*.

Finding Your Way

STÄDTISCHE BÜHNEN

The Städtische Bühnen complex faces Theaterplatz. Untermainanlage borders the complex on the west, Neue Mainzer Straße on the east, and Hofstraße on the south. The theater is a ten-minute walk from the *Hauptbahnhof* (main railroad station). You can take the following public transportation to the opera house: U-Bahn U1, U2, U3, or U4, exit Theaterplatz, and Straßenbahn 11, exit Theaterplatz. It is rumored that the Straßenbahn will soon disappear.

The main entrance to the opera house is on Theaterplatz, near the Untermainanlage side. After going up some stairs, you will be in the entrance foyer. If you are seated in the *Parkett* continue straight ahead, turning left if your ticket reads *links* and right if your ticket says *rechts*. Take the staircase up if you are seated in *1.Rang*, *2.Rang*, or *3.Rang*. Seat numbers begin with 1 on the left and increase sequentially with no repetition until *3.Rang*. Do not be surprised to see armed police. They are present at every performance.

Programs are for sale in the foyers and from the program sellers near the doors. They cost 3.50 DM. The program (in German) contains articles and illustrations relating to the opera. The cloakroom (*Garderobe*) is located in the entrance foyer. The ladies' room (*Damen*) and men's room (*Herren*) are nearby. You will find the bar in the "grand glass" foyer.

ALTE OPER

The Alte Oper faces Opernplatz. Bockenheimer Landstraße passes in front of the plaza. The old opera house is around a fifteen-minute walk from the Städtische Bühnen. You can reach the Alte Oper with U-Bahn U1, exit Opernplatz.

The main entrance to the Alte Oper faces south on Opernplatz. Operas are performed in the Großer Saal, which is located between the third and sixth *étage*. There are elevators on the first *étage*. You will find the men's room (*Herren*) and ladies' room (*Damen*) on the second *étage*, where the check rooms (*Garderoben*) are located. Refreshments are available on the third *étage* in the Café "Im alten Foyer." A wheelchair ramp is located where the tours (*Führungen*) begin, on the left side of the Alte Oper.

Planning Your Trip

OPERA SCHEDULE— STÄDTISCHE BÜHNEN

The opera season varies, depending on the school vacation. The 1989/90 season opened on October 22 with a new production of Mozart's *La finta giardiniera* and closed on July 7 with Giuseppe Verdi's *Macbeth*. The repertory of the Frankfurter Oper ranges from baroque to contemporary, with special emphasis given to the baroque period and classical modern works. Christoph Willibald Gluck's *Iphigénie in Aulide*, Henry Purcell's *Dido and Aeneas*, Mozart's *Così fan tutte* and *La clemenza di Tito*, Dvořák's *Rusalka*, Leoš Janáček's *Jenůfa*, Benjamin Britten's *A Midsummer Night's Dream*, John Cage's *Europeras 1 & 2*, Dmitri Shostakovich's *Nos* (The Nose), Johann Strauß's *Der Zigeunerbaron*, Gioacchino Rossini's *Il barbiere di Siviglia*, Vincenzo Bellini's *Il pirata* (new production), Verdi's *Rigoletto*, *Un ballo in maschera*, and *Otello*, Giacomo Puccini's *Tosca* and *La bohème*, and Wagner's *Der fliegende Holländer* completed the season.

Oper Frankfurt operates on a repertory system with a different opera every night. Opera shares the stage with ballets and recitals. To be sure your visit coincides with an opera, write ahead for a schedule, but be sure to specify when you plan to visit Frankfurt since you will address your request to the Tourist Board. The Oper Frankfurt does not reply to schedule requests.

Stadt Frankfurt Am Main
Verkehrsamt
Kaiserstraße 52
6000 Frankfurt am Main, Germany
Telephone (49)(69)212-35873

ALTE OPER

One or two operas are performed each year by the Oper Frankfurt at the Alte Oper. In 1990, the opera was Schönberg's *Moses und Aron*, which received five performances.

TRAVEL INFORMATION

HOTELS

The best hotel for operagoers in Frankfurt is the Frankfurt Intercontinental, Wilhelm-Leuschner Straße 43, 6000 Frankfurt/am Main, Germany; telephone (49)(69)26050, fax (49)(69)252-467. For reservations, call toll-free in the United States, 1-800-327-0200. Singles start at $140, doubles at $170. However, the hotel offers opera packages in conjunction with the Oper Frankfurt, and the room rates are substantially re-duced. Contact the hotel directly for these great packages, which I highly recommend. The Intercontinental is a modern five-star hotel with 800 rooms and a fantastic view of the River Main. Offering all the comforts of home in luxurious surroundings, the hotel is conveniently near the *Hauptbahnhof* in the best part of Frankfurt. For a special treat, order a bottle of their Privat-Cuvée Sekt (German champagne) while you relax watching the river traffic. The opera house is only an eight-minute walk from the hotel, and it is safe to walk back after the performance. Contact the concierge about last-minute opera ticket needs.

There are several places to dine around the theater complex: Theater Cafe on the Neue Mainzer Straße side of the Theaterplatz, Restaurant Binding Bräu on the corner of Weißfrauenstraße and Friedenstraße, and Zur Müllerin on Weißfrauenstraße next to Binding Bräu.

The Alte Oper offers many eating possibilities on the basement level of the building. Use the staircase to the right.

You can request travel information from the German National Tourist Office, 747 Third Avenue, 33rd Floor, New York, NY 10017, 212-308-3300. Do not even bother to ask about opera schedules or tickets. Write far ahead. They take a long time to respond.

HAMBURG
Hamburgische Staatsoper

*T*he starkly modern Hamburgische Staatsoper was inaugurated on October 15, 1955, with a gala performance of Wolfgang Amadeus Mozart's *Die Zauberflöte*. Günther Rennert's production dazzled the opening night crowd, which included Germany's President Theodor Heuß. Gerhard Weber designed the glass and concrete opera house, which has been praised as one of the best conceived theaters in postwar Europe.

HISTORICAL OVERVIEW
Background

In the seventeenth century, Hamburg was a major seaport and center of world trade, filled with noblemen, aristocrats, and diplomats fleeing the ravages of the Thirty Years War. Three of these people, lawyer Peter Lütjens, organist Johann Adam Reinke, and alderman Gerhard Schott, joined together to establish Germany's first public opera house, Opern-Theatrum, which opened on January 2, 1678. Constructed by the Italian builder Sartorio, the opera theater was an oblong and gabled wooden structure, located between Jungfernstieg and the corner of Gänsemarkt and the Colonnaden, near the present Hamburgische Staatsoper. The theater was run as a self-supporting operation. But by 1738, the combination of financial mismanagement, constant attacks from the clergy, who found opera sinful, and waning interest of the public led to the disbanding of the resident company. Traveling comedy troupes occupied the stage until the Opern-Theatrum was demolished in 1763.

On July 31, 1765, the Ackermannsche Commödienhaus opened on the site of the former Opern-Theatrum. Named after its founder Konrad Ernst Ackermann, the new theater offered a mixture of musical theater and plays. The company's director, Friedrich Ludwig Schröder, was far-sighted, introducing one of the first ticket subscription systems in theater and establishing a pension fund for his artists. Two years later, its name was changed to Deutsches Nationaltheater. The theater's name was changed again in 1809 to Hamburgisches Stadttheater, and then to Hamburgisches Deutsches Stadttheater in 1811. During Napoleon's occupation of Hamburg, it was known as Théâtre du Gänsemarkt. Accommodating 1,600, the former comedy house survived more than half a century before the wooden structure had outlived its usefulness and plans for a new theater were drawn.

The foundation stone for the Neue Stadt-Theater was laid on May 16, 1826. Located on Dammtorstraße, the site of today's Staatsoper, and designed by Carl Friedrich Schinkel, the brick theater opened on May 3, 1827. Although the exterior of the Neue Stadt-Theater was ridiculed as looking like a factory where pleasure was produced, the interior was richly decorated. The immense auditorium boasted three tiers of free-standing boxes and a gallery. It was illuminated by a chandelier holding sixty-four oil lamps. The theater accommodated 2,800. Though the acoustics were reported to be excellent, the technical facilities were anything but, so in 1873-74, under the careful eye of Hamburg's architect, Martin Haller, the opera house was remodeled. One thousand electric lights were introduced in 1891, and modern technical facilities were installed during 1925-26.

Around the same time, political turmoil reigned in Germany. A precipitous fall in value of the deutsche mark in 1923, meant that four million DM were worth only one U.S. dollar. Tickets to the opera that had cost 170 DM now cost 3,000 DM, and those costing 1,500 DM now cost 20,000 DM. To compensate, foreigners paid a 400 percent surcharge. A decade later, Adolf Hitler seized power. Fortunately for the Hamburg Oper, the Nazis believed a first-rate opera house in Hamburg was good propaganda, so they practiced a hands-off policy and bestowed on it the status of Staatsoper.

World War II finally caught up with the Staatsoper during the night of August 3, 1942, when bombs ignited an inferno that leveled the auditorium. Miraculously, the stage area remained unscathed. After the war, the surviving stage was divided in two: half remained the stage, and the other half was converted into an auditorium with 606 seats. In 1949, the seating capacity was increased to 1,226, and in the early 1950s, a new opera house was erected around the existing stage. Then another calamity struck. On November 1, 1975, fire broke out in the Staatsoper's warehouse, wiping out almost the entire stock of sets and costumes, worth 25 million DM. It took three seasons to recover from the conflagration, just in time to celebrate the 300th anniversary of *Oper in Hamburg* on January 2, 1978.

The Theater

The Hamburgische Staatsoper is a rigidly austere structure of glass and concrete. Its glass façade, trimmed with turquoise and embellished with

Top: Banners announcing performance of *Aufstieg und Fall der Stadt Mahagonny* (Photo by author)
Bottom: Auditorium viewed from stage (Courtesy of Hamburg Oper Archive)

flower boxes, rests on narrow, gold-colored poles. STAATSOPER in gold letters is affixed to the building's concrete sides.

Although the new opera house was built around the existing stage, it bears no resemblance to the previous Staatsoper. The multicolored auditorium of red seats, beige tiers, warm woods, and green *Loge* walls includes an orchestra section and four balconies. It is a marvel: there are no bad seats. This was accomplished by dividing the balconies into shoeboxlike segments, with everyone sitting close to and facing the stage. The room is unembellished, directing the audience's attention to the stage. The auditorium seats 1,675.

Performance History

On January 2, 1678, Johann Theile's *Adam und Eva* or *Der erschaffene, gefallene und aufgerichtete*

Elisabeth Steiner and Ria Urban in *Der Rosenkavalier* (Courtesy of Inter Nationes)

Mensch opened the Opern-Theatrum. The first Singspiele performed were based on biblical and allegorical themes written by local composers like Johann Wolfgang Franck, Nikolaus Adam Strungk, and Theile. However, the audience's predilection for gross and vulgar topical references, combined with their insatiable appetite for animal blood, which oozed over the stage by the gallon whenever performers were murdered, resulted in the Protestant clergy's condemnation of the Singspiel. Two outstanding universities then came to the rescue of this new art form by declaring, through lengthy, erudite papers, that Singspiel was not sinful.

In 1694, a brilliant operatic era was ushered in by Reinhard Keiser, who composed 116 operas during the next forty years, of which thirty-five have been preserved. Because of his choice of popular subjects, his works were well liked. Some of his most successful pieces were *Mahmuth II* (1696), *Ismene* (1699), *Störtebecker und Gödje Michel* (1701), *Ottavia* (1705), *Die Leipziger Messe* (1710), *L'inganno fedele* (1714), and *Der Hamburger Jahrmarkt* (1725). When he became *Intendant* in 1703, he began mounting extravagant productions. Eventually his lavishness caught

up with him, forcing him into hiding to escape his nagging creditors. Then he married a wealthy woman, who helped rehabilitate his fortunes. Keiser's operas departed from the stage shortly after he departed this world in 1739. Neither has been resurrected.

During Keiser's tenure, Georg Friederich Händel joined the orchestra, playing the violin and harpsichord. Händel's musical genius soon surfaced with the première of his first opera, *Almira*, on January 8, 1705. *Nero* followed the same year, and *Rodrigo* graced the stage two years later. During the same time, composer, conductor, and singer Johann Mattheson saw his operas staged but not without some real-life excitement. It was December 5, 1704, during a performance of his *Cleopatra*, which he conducted while playing the harpsichord. Händel played second violin. In one act Mattheson sang, giving Händel the conducting chores. However, when Mattheson returned, Händel refused to step down. A duel ensued. Händel's life was saved when Mattheson's sword broke on a big button on his garment. The audience's behavior was just as uncivilized. The spectators brawled among themselves, while outside their waiting coachmen feuded.

When the Ackermannsche Commödienhaus opened in 1765, Singspiel by Johann Adam Hiller, Christian Weiße, and in 1787, Mozart, appeared on stage. Two years later, Mozart operas followed.

In 1827, Ludwig Spohr's *Jessonda* surfaced in the recently opened Neue Stadt-Theater, where Friedrich von Flotow conducted the world première of his *Alessandro Stradella* on December 30, 1844. Eighteen years later, Charles Gounod traveled to Hamburg to conduct his *Faust*. The remodeled opera house was opened on September 16, 1874, with Richard Wagner's *Lohengrin*. That same year, Bernhard Pollini took the reins as *Intendant*. When Gustav Mahler became *Kapellmeister* in 1891, the opera was led to the highest *niveau*. Mahler's parting gift was thirteen new productions in the 1896/97 season

Top: *Intolleranza* (Courtesy of Inter Nationes)
Bottom: *Der Freischütz* (Courtesy of Inter Nationes)

before he said *auf Wiedersehen* with Ludwig van Beethoven's *Fidelio* and left for Vienna. In November that same year, Pollini went to sleep and never woke up, bringing an end to Hamburg's most glorious opera era.

The world première of Leo Blech's *Versiegelt* took place on November 4, 1908. A decade later, the political turmoil from the streets spilled into the opera house. It was November 6, 1918, during the third act of Wagner's *Tannhäuser*. The chorus of returning pilgrims passed by and Elisabeth, dressed in white, realized that Tannhäuser was not among them. She fell on her knees before a crucifix, praying that Tannhäuser's sins be forgiven: *Allmächtige Jungfrau*. Suddenly, armed revolutionary workers and soldiers stormed the theater, ordering the smartly dressed audience to exit. In this *Tannhäuser*, Elisabeth never died. On December 4, 1920, Erich Korngold's *Die tote Stadt* was world premiered, and seven years later on November 18, Ottorino Respighi's *La campana Sommersa* graced the stage for the first time ever. Some of opera's greatest voices, such as Enrico Caruso and Lotte Lehmann, were heard there.

During the Nazi era, Karl Böhm and Oscar Fritz Schuh exercised artistic control minus all the talented Jewish artists and other able people who were forced to flee Germany. For the 260th anniversary of the Hamburg Oper on June 23, 1938, Hitler, Paul Joseph Goebbels, and Joachim von Ribbentrop attended the performance of Wagner's *Die Meistersinger von Nürnberg*. Four years later, the opera house lay in ruins, a victim of Hitler's ambitions.

Mozart's *Le nozze di Figaro* opened the provisional opera house on January 9, 1946. Doubled in size three years later, the theater reopened with Richard Strauss's *Der Rosenkavalier* on October 15, 1949. The first *Intendant* was Günther Rennert, who made contemporary works the focal point of the repertory and introduced the concept of "*Musiktheater*": opera that is experienced both emotionally and intellectually. When Rolf Liebermann took the reins, he captured the attention of the international opera world by his numerous opera commissions. The world première of Hans Werner Henze's *Prinz von Homburg* followed on May 22, 1960. Walter Goehr's *Arden muß sterben* was introduced in 1967, and Humphrey Searle's *Hamlet* was performed for the first time the next year. The world première of Krzysztof Penderecki's *Diably z Loudun* (The Devils of Loudun), under its German title, *Die Teufel von Loudun*, took place on June 20, 1969. Three seasons later, Mauricio Kagel's *Staatstheater* was staged, with Walter Steffens's *Unter dem Milchwald* gracing the stage the following year. Many of the world's greatest opera singers were heard in Hamburg: Birgit Nilsson, Leonie Rysanek, Montserrat Caballé, Plácido Domingo, and Luciano Pavarotti.

I saw a delightfully outrageous production of Kurt Weill's *Aufstieg und Fall der Stadt Mahagonny*. The creative and amusing interpretation was the first *Mahagonny* I have enjoyed. Set on a mostly bare stage and performed without intermission, this performance had all the inhabitants dressed uniformly in white ties, black tails, white gloves, and top hats. While periodically rocking in perfect unison in white wicker rocking chairs under a monstrous, atrocious chandelier, they donned Mickey Mouse masks. The audience loved it. Bravos resounded through the auditorium when the curtain fell. (Heavily subsidized opera companies can afford to be audacious.) Andreas Reinhardt was responsible for the costumes and scenery, while Günter Krämer staged the work. Trudeliese Schmidt and William Pell were Jenny and Jim Mahoney, respectively. Bruno Weill kept everything moving along nicely.

PRACTICAL INFORMATION
Tickets

The box office (*Kasse*) is located at 35 Große Theaterstraße, the street that borders the north of the Staatsoper. It is open Monday through Friday from 10:00 a.m. to 2:00 p.m. and from

TICKET TABLE

Platzgattung (Seat Location)	Kassenpreise in DM (Prices in DM)				
	C	B	A	S	P
1. Preisgruppe (price group)	80	100	110	150	180

Parkett 1.-5.Reihe, Platz 5-Mitte (orchestra rows 1-5, seats 5-middle)
1.Rang Balkon, 1.,2.Reihe (1st tier balcony, rows 1,2)
1.Rang, Loge 2-5, Platz 3,4 (1st tier, boxes 2-5, seats 3,4)

	C	B	A	S	P
2. Preisgruppe (price group)	75	85	100	135	165

Parkett 6.,7.Reihe, Platz 5-Mitte (orchestra rows 6,7, seats 5-middle)
Parkett 11.Reihe, Platz 5-Mitte (orchestra row 11, seats 5-middle)
Parkett 12.Reihe, Platz 4-Mitte (orchestra row 12, seats 4-middle)
Parkett 13.Reihe, Platz 3-Mitte (orchestra row 13, seats 3-middle)
Parkett 14.Reihe, Platz 2-Mitte (orchestra row 14, seats 2-middle)
Parkett 15.Reihe (orchestra, row 15)
1.Rang Balkon, 3.,4.Reihe (1st tier balcony, rows 3,4)
1.Rang, Loge 2-5, Platz 1,2 (1st tier, boxes 2-5, seats 1,2)

	C	B	A	S	P
3. Preisgruppe (price group)	65	75	95	120	150

Parkett 8.,9.Reihe, Platz 7-Mitte (orchestra, rows 8,9, seats 7-middle)
Parkett 10.Reihe, Platz 6-Mitte (orchestra, row 10, seats 6-middle)
1.Rang Balkon, 5.Reihe (1st tier balcony, row 5)
1.Rang, Loge 1, Platz 3,4 (1st tier, box 1, seats 3,4)

	C	B	A	S	P
4. Preisgruppe (price group)	55	70	85	110	135

Parkett 4.-7.Reihe Platz 1-4 (orchestra rows 4-7, seats 1-4)
Parkett 8.-9.Reihe Platz 1-6 (orchestra rows 8,9, seats 1-6)
Parkett 10.Reihe Platz 1-5 (orchestra row 10, seats 1-5)
Parkett 11.Reihe Platz 1-4 (orchestra row 11, seats 1-4)
Parkett 12.Reihe Platz 1-3 (orchestra row 12, seats 1-3)
Parkett 13.Reihe Platz 1/2 (orchestra row 13, seats 1,2)
Parkett 14.Reihe Platz 1 (orchestra row 14, seat 1)
Parkett 16.-21.Reihe (orchestra rows 16-21)
1.Rang, Loge 1, Platz 1,2 (1st tier, box 1 seats 1,2)
2.Rang Balcon, 1.Reihe (2nd tier balcony, row 1)

	C	B	A	S	P
5. Preisgruppe (price group)	50	60	75	100	120

Parkett 22.-25.Reihe (orchestra rows 22-25)
2.Rang Balkon, 2.Reihe (2nd tier balcony, row 2)
2.Rang, Loge 2-5, Platz 2-4 (2nd tier, boxes 2-5, seats 2-4)

	C	B	A	S	P
6. Preisgruppe (price group)	45	50	65	85	105

2.Rang Balkon, 3.Reihe (2nd tier balcony, row 3)
2.Rang Balkon, 4.Reihe Platz 1-6 (2nd tier balcony, row 4, seats 1-6)
2.Rang, Loge 1, Platz 2-4 (2nd tier, box 1, seats 2-4)

	C	B	A	S	P
7. Preisgruppe (price group)	35	35	50	65	85

2.Rang Balkon 4.Reihe, Platz 7-Mitte (2nd tier balcony, row 4 seats 7-middle)
2.Rang, Loge 1-5 Platz 1 (2nd tier, boxes 1-5, seat 1)

	C	B	A	S	P
8. Preisgruppe (price group)	15	15	15	15	15

3.Rang Alle Plätze (3rd tier, all seats)

	C	B	A	S	P
9. Preisgruppe (price group)	10	10	10	10	10

4.Rang Alle Sitzplätze (4th tier, all seats)

	C	B	A	S	P
10. Preisgruppe (price group)	4	4	4	4	4

4.Rang Steh- und Hörplätze (4th tier, standing and listening places)

Hörplätze have no view of the stage.
$1 = 1.6 DM, but can vary due to the fluctuating value of the dollar.
DM is an abbreviation for Deutsche Mark.

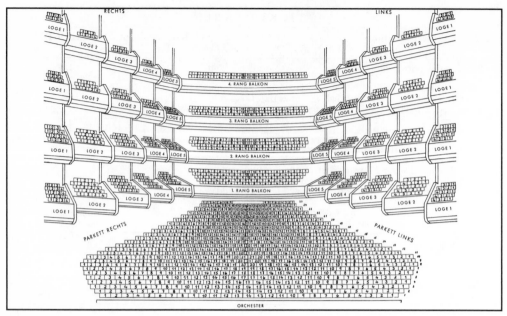

Seating Plan (Courtesy of Hamburg Oper)

4:00 p.m. to 6:30 p.m., Saturday from 10:00 a.m. to 2:00 p.m. (*Öffnungszeiten Montag bis Freitag 10.00 Uhr-14.00 Uhr und 16.00 Uhr-18.30 Uhr, Sonnabend 10.00 Uhr-14.00 Uhr*). The box office reopens one and a half hours before the performance (*Abendkasse*). A seating plan is posted between two of the box office windows, and there are usually long lines. In my experience, the box office clerks were not friendly or helpful, even when one spoke German. Tickets go on sale fourteen days before the performance.

Tickets can also be ordered by mail until four weeks before the performance, but only for tickets costing more than 15 DM. Indicate with your order the maximum price ticket you will accept. You will receive a written response before tickets go on sale at the box office. Then send your money. Your tickets will be sent after payment has been received. Write to:

Hamburgische Staatsoper-Vorverkauf
35 Große Theaterstraße
2000 Hamburg 36, Germany

You can order tickets by calling (49)(40) 351-721 beginning at 11:00 a.m. during box office hours. (49) = country code; (40) = city

code. In Germany, dial (040)351-721. Tickets will be held at the box office until thirty minutes before the performance. You should speak *hochdeutsch*. Hamburg is six hours ahead of Eastern Standard Time.

Ticket prices for the Hamburg Oper vary not only with section and series but also with row and seat, accurately reflecting the desirability of the seat and the performance.

Your best chance for tickets is *freier Verkauf* (nonsubscription) performances and contemporary operas. Tickets to new productions (*Premieren*), except contemporary operas, are the most difficult to obtain. If you see *Ausverkauft* (sold out) or *geschlossene Vorstellung* (closed performance), think of another date.

Many of the German contemporary operas, like Alexander von Zemlinsky's *Der Kreiderkreis*, Weill's *Aufstieg und Fall der Stadt Mahagonny*, and Alban Berg's *Lulu* and *Wozzeck*, have much spoken dialogue, similar to the early Singspiel. If you understand German, sit close to the stage. Otherwise, it will be difficult to understand the dialogue.

Understanding your ticket will enable you to find your seat with no problem. This is impor-

Old and new computerized ticket (Courtesy of Hamburg Oper)

tant since there are no ushers. A translation of a sample ticket appears below.

Operas usually begin at 7:30 p.m. (19.30). However, the starting times vary considerably according to the length of the opera: *Carmen* began at 7:00 p.m., *Lohengrin* at 6:00 p.m., and *Wozzeck* at 8:00 p.m. (Germans like having all their operas end at the same time.) Starting times are listed in the monthly *Hamburg Führer*, the weekly newspaper *Die Zeit*, and the Wednesday edition of the daily newspaper *Die Welt*. The newspapers also list the performance schedule for the week for all the opera houses in Germany. If you arrive late, plan on waiting in the foyer where there is a television monitor.

Finding Your Way

The Hamburgische Staatsoper faces Dammtorstraße, bordered on the north by Große Theaterstraße and on the south by Kleine Theaterstraße. The following buses stop by the Staatsoper: 36, 100, 102, 109, 603, 604, and 605, exit Stephansplatz. You can reach the theater by U-Bahn, exit Gänsemarkt, and S-Bahn, exit Dammtor. If you

are arriving from another city by train, get off at Hamburg-Dammtor, which is one stop from Hamburg-Hauptbahnhof. An elevated walkway leads directly from Dammtor station to the Colonnaden, the street behind the Staatsoper.

There are entrances on Große Theaterstraße and Kleine Theaterstraße. Signs posted on both sides of the entrance foyer direct you upstairs: *Aufgang zum Parkett und 1.2.3.4. Rang links* (Staircase to orchestra and 1st, 2nd, 3rd, and 4th tiers left); *Aufgang zum Parkett und 1.2.3.4. Rang rechts* (Staircase to orchestra and 1st, 2nd, 3rd, and 4th tiers, right). It is two flights up to the *Parkett* level. Seats are numbered identically on both the right and left sides of every row, beginning with 1 on the extreme right and left side of each row. The numbers increase sequentially until they meet in the teens or twenties in the center of the row. Since the rows stretch unbroken across the auditorium and the numbering is identical, it is crucial to enter the auditorium on the correct side.

The seat numbering in *1.Rang Balkon, 2.Rang Balkon, 3.Rang Balkon*, and *4.Rang Balkon* is simi-

TICKET TRANSLATION			
Hamburg Oper		Hamburg Opera	
Grosses Haus		Large Theater	
Mahagonny		(Opera)	
09.06.90	19.30	June 9, 1990	7:30 P.M.
1. Rg.	**Balkon Lks**	**1st Tier**	**Balcony Left**
Reihe 3	**Platz 7**	**Row 3**	**Seat 7**

lar to the *Parkett*. *Logen* are located on the sides of the *Ränge*, with *Loge* 5 nearest the center and Box 1 closest to the stage. There are no ushers per se, but the ladies selling programs, recognized by their red blouses, black skirts, and red and black checkered jackets, can direct you if you are lost. Do not be surprised to see armed police. They are present at every performance.

Programs are for sale in the entrance foyer and from the program sellers stationed next to the doors leading into the auditorium. The program (in German) contains photographs and articles pertaining to the opera and costs 4.90 DM. A one-page synopsis in English is available, gratis, in the entrance foyer. The cloakroom (*Garderobe*) is located one flight down from the entrance foyer and costs 1.90 DM. The cloakroom is divided into sections according to where you are seated. The ladies' room (*Damen*) and men's room (*Herren*) are located in the yellow hallways on both sides of each tier. Bar and refreshments are in the large olive-green carpeted, gold-columned foyer on the *Parkett* level. If you are in a wheelchair, go to the information desk on the north side of the entrance foyer for assistance.

Planning Your Trip
OPERA SCHEDULE
The season runs from the end of August to the beginning of June. Some seasons include Broadway musicals, sung in German, on the schedule. The 1990/91 season opened on August 29 with Wagner's *Der fliegende Holländer* and will close on May 20 with a new production of Karlheinz Stockhausen's *Montag aus Licht*. Other new productions are Mozart's *Le nozze di Figaro*, Jules Massenet's *Werther*, Wagner's *Parsifal*, and Vincenzo Bellini's *I Capuleti e i Montecchi* (concert form). Other operas on the schedule are Mozart's *Idomeneo* and *Die Zauberflöte*, Beethoven's *Fidelio*, Engelbert Humperdinck's *Hänsel und Gretel*, Albert Lortzing's *Zar und Zimmermann*, Strauss's *Elektra*, Wagner's *Tannhäuser*, Gaetano Donizetti's *L'elisir d'amore*, Giacomo

Puccini's *Tosca* and *Madama Butterfly*, Giuseppe Verdi's *Il trovatore* and *Don Carlo*, Pyotr Il'yich Tchaikovsky's *Eugene Onegin*, Dmitri Shostakovich's *Ledi Makbet Mtsenskovo uyezda* (Lady Macbeth of the Mtsensk District), and Georges Bizet's *Carmen*.

The Hamburg Oper is a repertory house with more than one opera performed at a time. Opera shares the stage with ballet. To be sure your visit coincides with an opera, write ahead for a schedule (*Spielplan Vorschau*):

Hamburgische Staatsoper-Tageskasse
Große Theaterstraße 35
2000 Hamburg 36, Germany

TRAVEL INFORMATION
The best hotel for operagoers in Hamburg is the Hotel Vier Jahreszeiten, Neuer Jungfernstieg 9-14, 2000 Hamburg 36, Germany; telephone (49)(40)34-940, fax (49)(40)349-4602. Reservations can be made in the United States by calling toll-free, 1-800-223-6800 (member of the Leading Hotels of the World). Singles begin at $150 and doubles at $200. This elegant, five-star hotel with 139 rooms and 36 suites radiates luxury and charm. Located in the best section of Hamburg, with a magnificent view of the *Binnen-Alster*, the hotel offers impeccable service along with elegant decor. In fact, the view is so glorious that you might not want to leave your room, except, of course, to attend the Hamburgische Staatsoper, which is only two blocks away. Contact the concierge for all your last-minute opera ticket needs.

Numerous restaurants are within a couple of blocks of the Staatsoper: Fellini on Dammtorstraße, Queen's Pub, Spaghetti Factory, and McDonald's on Gänsemarkt, and many on Colonnaden, the *Fußgängerzone* or pedestrian street behind the Staatsoper.

You can contact the German National Tourist Office, 747 Third Avenue, 33rd Floor, New York, NY, 10017, 212-308-3300, for travel information only. Write early because they take a long time to respond.

MUNICH
Nationaltheater
Cuvilliéstheater

The magnificent Hof- und Nationaltheater was inaugurated on October 12, 1818, with a gala performance of Albert Klebe and Ferdinand Fränzl's *Die Weihe*. Designed by Karl von Fischer and modeled after the Théâtre de l'Odéon in Paris, the theater stood a scant four years before fire consumed it on January 14, 1823. Since the architect had died in 1820, the task of rebuilding fell to Leo von Klenze. Although von Fischer's original plans were to be followed exactly, Klenze managed to incorporate some of his own ideas. The rebuilt Nationaltheater opened on January 2, 1825. This theater was more fortunate. It stood for more than a century before joining the ranks of World War II casualties on October 4, 1943. Gerhard Graubner and Karl Fischer undertook the task of rebuilding. The Nationaltheater reopened on November 21, 1963, with Richard Strauss's *Die Frau ohne Schatten*.

HISTORICAL OVERVIEW
Background

The first operas in Munich were performed in the Herkulessaal of the Residenz until the city's first opera house, Opernhaus am Salvatorplatz, was opened in 1656. Almost a century later, the Altes Residenztheater, better known as the Cuvilliéstheater after its architect François Cuvilliés, was inaugurated. Discussion about building an opera house to replace the aging Opernhaus am Salvatorplatz began in 1792, but nothing was done. By 1799, the old Opernhaus was termi-

nally ill, and the need for a new opera house became overwhelming.

Finally, the first Hof- und Nationaltheater came into being. Duke Max Joseph, dazzled by the beauty of the Théâtre de l'Odéon on a trip to Paris, commanded a replica be constructed on the palace grounds at a cost of 800,000 gold ducats. When fire destroyed the building a short time later, tears streamed down the duke's face as the opera house crumbled. The calamity inspired King Ludwig I to provide most of the rebuilding funds. His subjects provided the rest by paying a 1 pfenning beer tax. A little less than a century later, after World War I, the recognition of royal patronage was eliminated when *Hof* was dropped from the theater's name.

Calamity struck again during World War II, when firebombs scored a direct hit. The crystal chandeliers melted, the bas-reliefs and frescoes turned black, and ivory chairs vanished. Only weeds and trees appeared on stage for twenty years. A decade after the bombing, the citizens of Munich took some action to ensure the rebuilding of the theater. In 1953, the Friends of the Nationaltheater was formed and began an annual lottery to raise money for reconstruction. After a few years, they had collected $5 million but were still far short of the $20 million needed. So 200,000 Bavarians signed a petition asking the *Freistaat Bayern* for the remaining $15 million. The Free State of Bavaria obliged, and reconstruction began in 1958. Five years later, on November 21, the Nationaltheater reopened.

Altes Residenztheater met a fate similar to that of the Nationaltheater during World War II. However, it was luckier. Foreseeing the likelihood of damages, the Bavarians dismantled its magnificent gold and white interior and stored it during the war. When the theater reopened in 1958, all the original ornaments and trappings were back in place.

The Theaters

NATIONALTHEATER

The Nationaltheater is a stately neoclassical building with eight majestic Corinthian columns supporting its massive portico. Built of light stone, the opera house opens into a marble columned, terrazzo-floor entrance hall. The gray marble inner foyer hosts busts of Richard Wagner, Wolfgang Amadeus Mozart, and Strauss. Upstairs the sky-blue, ivory, and gold *Königsallee* is filled with busts of Bruno Walter, Carl Maria von Weber, Carl Orff, and Hans Knappertsbusch. Diamondlike crystal chandeliers illuminate the marble and mirror space, which joins a pink and gold room prominently displaying a bust of von Fischer. Karl Böhm, Clemens Krauss, Giuseppe Verdi, Giacomo Puccini, and Vincenzo Bellini inhabit the end area.

In the auditorium, five ivory and gold tiers soar majestically around deep pink orchestra seats. The rose pink decor of the auditorium contrasts with the sky blue ceiling, proscenium, and royal boxes. Heavy Corinthian columns flank the proscenium boxes, while massive caryatids guard the royal box. A three-ton double-tier crystal chandelier, made from seventy thousand bits of polished glass and holding one hundred eighty glittering light bulbs, complements the delicate electric candles rimming the tiers. The Nationaltheater seats 2,120.

Top: Façade of Nationaltheater with statue of Max Joseph in foreground (Courtesy of Inter Nationes)
Middle: Tiers in Nationaltheater (Courtesy of Inter Nationes)
Bottom: Auditorium with view of royal box, Cuvilliéstheater (Courtesy of Inter Nationes)

CUVILLIÉSTHEATER

Portraits of *Hofdamen* cover the octagonal marble entrance hall, which is lined with coral velvet benches. A raspberry-silk-covered "transition cubicle" separates the outside world from the gold, ivory, and raspberry auditorium. Four intricately carved tiers soar in rococo splendor around the orchestra. In the center, a red- and gold-crowned royal box is surrounded by cherubs and goddesses. Electrified crystal chandeliers, which rise to the ceiling when the performance begins,

Top: *Rienzi* (Courtesy of Inter Nationes, Photo by Rabanus)
Bottom: World Première of *Lou Salome* on May 10, 1981 (Courtesy of Inter Nationes, Photo by Rabanus)

Madama Butterfly, 1939 performance (Courtesy of Bayerische Staatsoper archives)

brighten the cozy silk-lined auditorium. Horn-blowing cherubs embellish the marble gray proscenium. The Cuvilliéstheater seats 442.

Performance History

The first opera heard in Munich was Giovanni Battista Maccioni's *L'arpa festante*, performed in 1651. Five years later, Johann Kaspar von Kerll's *Oronte* inaugurated the Opernhaus am Salvatorplatz. Giovanni Battista Ferrandini's *Catone in Utica* opened the Altes Residenztheater on October 12, 1753, where the world première of Mozart's *Idomeneo* took place on January 29, 1781. Meanwhile, opera buffa found a home in the Redoutenhaus where Mozart's *La finta giardiniera* was premiered on January 13, 1775, and Carl Maria von Weber's *Abu Hassan* on June 4, 1811.

When the Hof- und Nationaltheater opened in 1818, most operatic events shifted there. Composer Franz Lachner became *Generalmusikdirektor* in 1836, bringing many new works to Munich. His own opera, *Catharina Cornaro*, was presented in 1841. Although his works were extremely popular then, today the scores collect only dust, as Wagner overshadowed his accomplishments.

Wagner's arrival in Munich in 1864 coincided with the ascent of King Ludwig II to the throne. Under Ludwig's patronage, the world première of *Tristan und Isolde* took place on June 10, 1865; its extravagance and grandeur purportedly caused the defeat of the Royal Bavarian Army by the Prussians the following year. The première was so expensive that no money was left in the treasury to buy weapons. *Die Meistersinger von Nürnberg* was introduced on June 21, 1868, in the presence of King Ludwig himself, but within four years, Ludwig II had such a paranoid fear of crowds that he no longer visited the opera house when his subjects were also in attendance. Instead, he commanded 209 opera performances where he was the only spectator.

Hans von Bülow conducted both the *Tristan*

und Isolde and *Die Meistersinger von Nürnberg* premières. Von Bülow's admiration of Wagner and his involvement with Wagner's works led to a love triangle, the consequence of which was that von Bülow's wife, Cosima, left him two years later and eventually married Wagner. Meanwhile, Wagner was working on what was to be his greatest triumph, *Der Ring des Nibelungen*, and he did not want any "sneak previews." He tried to delay the première until the entire cycle was completed, but his patron was insistent. Since Ludwig held the purse strings, Ludwig got his way. *Das Rheingold* was premiered on September 22, 1869, and *Die Walküre* on June 26, 1870. Although *Siegfried* and *Götterdämmerung* were premiered at Bayreuth, the entire *Ring* was presented at the Nationaltheater in November 1878. Five years after Wagner's death, on June 29, 1888, *Die Feen*, the first opera he wrote, was finally staged.

Ticket to Nationaltheater (Courtesy of Bayerische Staatsoper)

Nationaltheater in ruins, 1943 (Courtesy of Bayerische Staatsoper)

Ermanno Wolf-Ferrari's *Le donne curiose*, *I quattro rusteghi*, and *Il segreto di Susanna* were introduced in German as *Die neugierigen Frauen*, *Die vier Grobiane*, and *Susannens Geheimnis* on November 27, 1903, March 19, 1906, and December 4, 1909, respectively. Then Hans Pfitzner conducted the world première of his *Das Christelflein* on December 11, 1906, and directed the first performance ever of his *Palestrina* on June 12, 1917, which Bruno Walter conducted. Walter was also on the podium for the world premières of Erich Korngold's *Violanta* and *Der Ring des Polykrates* on March 28, 1916, Paul von Klenau's *Sulamit* on November 16, 1913, Walter Courvoisier's *Lanzelot und Elaine* on November 3, 1917, Franz Schreker's *Das Spielwerk* on October 30, 1920, and Walter Braunfels's *Die Vögel* a month later. In 1927, the *Uraufführungen* of Hugo Röhr's *Coeur Dame* took place on January 15, Wolf-Ferrari's *Sly* (under the German title, *Das Himmelskleid*) on April 21, and Ernst Křenek's *Mammon* on October 1. Four years later,

Jaromir Weinberger's *Die geliebte Stimme* was introduced on February 28, Gian Francesco Malipiero's *Torneo notturno* (under the German title, *Komödie des Todes*) was staged for the first time on May 15, and Pfitzner's *Das Herz* saw the light on November 12. The world premières continued almost annually despite the arrival of the Nazis. By 1934, they had hung an iron noose firmly around Germany's neck and squeezed out anyone who disagreed with them as well as all Jewish artists. Both *Intendant* Clemens von Franckenstein and *Generalmusikdirektor* Hans Knappertsbusch had to flee, leaving the National-theater an orphan.

Then Krauss, more to the Nazis' taste, assumed the roles of both *Intendant* and *Generalmusikdirektor*, overseeing the world premières of Strauss's *Der Friedenstag* on July 24, 1938, Orff's *Der Mond* on February 5, 1939, and Strauss's *Capriccio* on October 28, 1942.

After the war, opera resumed with Beethoven's *Fidelio* on November 1945 at the Prinz-regententheater. The world première of Paul Hindemith's *Die Harmonie der Welt* took place there on August 11, 1957. Mozart's *Le nozze di Figaro* reopened the Cuvilliéstheater the following year on June 12. Eleven years later, the Cuvilliéstheater witnessed the first presentation ever of Günter Bialas's *Die Geschichte von Aucassin* on December 12.

The Nationaltheater was finally resurrected on November 21, 1963. Strauss's *Die Frau ohne Schatten* regaled the opening night audience, which was filled with the rich and the royal: former King Umberto of Italy, former Queen Soraya, and Begum Aga Khan, along with Thyssens, Mellons, Krupps, Rothchilds, and droves of princes, dukes, counts, and barons too numerous to name. Werner Egk's *Die Verlobung in San Domingo* was world premiered six days later. Several world premières followed, among them Aribert Reimann's *Lear* on July 9, 1978, Giuseppe Sinopoli's *Lou Salomé* on May 10, 1981, and Heinrich Sutermeister's *Le Roi Bérenger* on July 22, 1985. The following year saw Volker

Giuseppe Sinopoli, composer of *Lou Salome* (Courtesy of Deutsche Grammophon/Deutsche Oper, Photo by Barda)

David Kirchner's *Belshazar* introduced on January 25 and Reimann's *Troades* on July 7.

I saw a delightful production at the Nationaltheater of Strauss's *Die Liebe der Danae*, which had opened the Strauss Festival in 1988. Filled with gold, special effects, and neat tricks, the opera offered an enjoyable evening, although I must confess this is not one of my favorite Strauss operas. Sabine Hass was splendid as Danae, and there were praiseworthy performances by John Bröcheler as Jupiter and Paul Frey as Midas. The conducting by Wolfgang Sawallisch was impeccable.

The following evening, I witnessed an amusing performance at the Cuvilliéstheater of Strauss's *Intermezzo*, described as (loosely translated) "a bourgeois comedy with symphonic interludes." The production was hilarious, due in no small part to the superb singing and acting of the cast, especially Felicity Lott as Christine. The staging by Kurt Wilhelm and sets by Jörg Zimmermann, especially the tobogganing scene, contributed to the fun. Gustav Kuhn held everything together marvelously.

PRACTICAL INFORMATION
Tickets

NATIONALTHEATER

The box office (*Vorverkaufskasse*) is located at Maximilianstraße 11, one block from the theater at the corner of Marstallplatz and Maximilianstraße. It is open Monday through Friday from 10:00 a.m. to 1:00 p.m. and 3:30 p.m. to 5:30 p.m., Saturday from 10:00 a.m. to 12:30 p.m. (*Montag bis Freitag 10.00 bis 13.00 Uhr und 15.30 bis 17.30 Uhr, Samstag 10 bis 12.30 Uhr*). On performance days, the box office opens one hour before curtain time (*Abendkasse*). However, the *Abendkasse* is at a different location, around the corner from the main entrance of the Nationaltheater on Maximilianstraße. The long line you see in the box office by Window III is for reduced student tickets. Do not wait in that line (unless you are a student with a valid identification). Go to Window I or II. You can buy tickets beginning seven days before the performance.

Ticket availability is posted on the door of the *Vorverkaufskasse* under the following heading: *Information über den Stand der im Verkauf befindlichen Eintrittskarten Nationaltheater (Staatsoper)*. Next to the date and opera, you will see one or more of the following words: *billige Seitenplätze vorhanden* (cheap side seats available), *Stehplätze vorhanden* (standing room available), *Karten vorhanden* (tickets available), *Ausverkauft* (sold out), *geschlossene Vorstellung* (closed performance). *Schalter* indicates the box office window where those particular tickets are sold.

Tickets can also be reserved through the mail but only four weeks before the performance. The box office will hold the tickets for your arrival. Address your requests to:

Eintrittskartenkasse der Bayerischen Staatsoper
Maximilianstraße 11
8000 Munich 22, Germany

You can order tickets by calling (49)(89) 221-316 during box office hours but only seven days before the performance. (49) = country

Plätze (Seats)		Preise in DM (Prices in DM)						
(Row)	(Seat #)	H	S	E	F	FP	PH	SP
Parkett (orchestra)								
Reihe 1-2	R-69	74	86	102,5	126,5	145,5	193,5	241
Reihe 3-13	70-539	66,5	77	92	113,5	130,5	173,5	216
Reihe 14-18 Reihe 19 Reihe 20	540-755} 776-788} 803-808}	56	65	77,5	95	109,5	145,5	181
Reihe 19 Reihe 20 Reihe 21-22	756-775} 789-802} 809-828}	44	51	60,5	74,5	85,5	113,5	141
Balkon (first tier)								
Reihe 1	1-52	74	86	102,5	126,5	145,5	193,5	241
Reihe 2 Reihe 3 Reihe 3	1-25} 1-12} 15-26}	66,5	77	92	113,5	130,5	173,5	216
Reihe 2 Reihe 4 Reihe 5 Sessel	26-41} 1-23} 1-16} 1-8}	56	65	77,5	95	109,5	145,5	181
Reihe 2 Reihe 3 Reihe 4	42-57} 27-38} 24-31}	44	51	60,5	74,5	85,5	113,5	141
Reihe 2 Reihe 3 Reihe 4	58-69} 39-46} 32-39}	32	37	44	53,5	61,5	81,5	101
Reihe 3 Reihe 4	47-58} 40-51}	20,5	22,5	24	33,5	38	46	61
Reihe 3	59-70	11,5	13	14	16	18	20,5	23
1.Rang (second tier)								
Reihe 1	1-28	66,5	77	92	113,5	130,5	173,5	216
Reihe 1 Reihe 2 Reihe 2	29-40} 1-6} 9-20}	56	65	77,5	95	109,5	145,5	181
Reihe 1 Reihe 2 Reihe 3 Reihe 4 Sessel	41-52} 21-32} 1-20} 1-16} 1-8}	44	51	60,5	74,5	85,5	113,5	141
Reihe 1 Reihe 2 Reihe 2 Reihe 3	53-64} 7-8} 33-40} 21-32}	32	37	44	53,5	61,5	81,5	101
Reihe 2 Reihe 3	41-52} 33-48}	20,5	22,5	24	33,5	38	46	61
Reihe 2	53-64	11,5	13	14	16	18	20,5	23
2.Rang (third tier)								
Reihe 1	1-28	56	65	77,5	95	109,5	145,5	181
Reihe 1 Reihe 2	29-36} 1-20}	44	51	60,5	74,5	85,5	113,5	141
Reihe 1 Reihe 2 Reihe 3 Sessel	37-48} 21-30} 1-20} 1-8}	32	37	44	53,5	61,5	81,5	101

continued

continued

Reihe 1 Reihe 2 Reihe 3	49-64} 31-40} 21-30}	20,5	22,5	24	33,5	38	46	61
Reihe 3	31-36}	11,5	13	14	16	18	20,5	23
Stehplätze (standing places)								
Reihe 4 Steh.	1-28}	11,5	13	14	16	18	20,5	23
Reihe 2 Steh. Reihe 3 Steh.	29-58} 59-86}	7,5	8	9	11,5	13	16,5	18

3.Rang (fourth tier)

Reihe 1	1-29	44	51	60,5	74,5	85,5	113,5	141
Reihe 1 Reihe 2	30-41} 1-30}	32	37	44	53,5	61,5	81,5	101
Reihe 1 Reihe 3 Sessel	42-57} 1-31} 1-8}	20,5	22,5	24	33,5	38	46	61
Reihe 1	58-73}	11,5	13	14	16	18	20,5	23
Stehplätze (standing places) Reihe 4 Steh.	1-37}	11,5	13	14	16	18	20,5	23
Reihe 2 Steh. Reihe 3 Steh.	38-87} 88-133}	7,5	8	9	11,5	13	16,5	18

Galerie (top tier)

Reihe 1	1-32	32	37	44	53,5	61,5	81,5	101
Reihe 1 Reihe 2	33-48} 1-31}	20,5	22,5	24	33,5	38	46	61
Reihe 1 Sessel	49-76} 1-8}	11,5	13	14	16	18	20,5	23
Stehplätze (standing places) Reihe 3 Steh. Reihe 4 Steh.	1-35} 36-66}	11,5	13	14	16	18	20,5	23
Reihe 2 Steh. Partiturplatz Hörerplatz	67-102} 1-28} 29-48}	7,5	8	9	11,5	13	16,5	18

Sessel (chair), Partiturplatz (restricted view of stage), Hörerplatz (no view of stage)
$1 = 1.6 DM, but can vary due to the fluctuating value of the dollar.
DM is an abbreviation for Deutsche Mark.

code; (89) = city code. In Germany, dial (089) 221-316. You should speak German. Munich is six hours ahead of Eastern Standard Time.

The ticket table for the Nationaltheater is very detailed, with the ticket prices accurately reflecting your ability to see and hear the performance. Ticket prices vary not only with section, row, and seat but with each series. The "letter code" price is printed after the opera in the monthly schedule.

Tickets for the Nationaltheater are difficult, but not impossible, to get. Your best chance for tickets is *freier Verkauf* (nonsubscription) operas, or *Wiederaufnahmen* (repertory) operas with not so spectacular casts, and contemporary operas. The most difficult tickets to obtain are for *Neuinszenierungen* (new productions), world-renowned artists, opening nights of each opera, and the *Münchner Opernfestspiele* (Summer Festival). If you must see an opera in one of these categories, either write for tickets as soon as reservations are accepted or arrive in Munich seven days ahead and get in line very early in the morning.

Your ticket might appear confusing, but understanding it will help you find your seat with no problem. This is important since there are no ushers, only door guards, a collection of dark blue-suited men who guard the doors into the auditorium in a manner that appears almost menacing. They will let you pass if you are going through the correct door but will forcibly bar your way if you are wrong and will not show you how to correct your mistake. They are more interested in selling programs than helping you. Especially avoid the door guards on left side of the *Parkett*. They are the worst.

Understanding your ticket will enable you to find your seat with no problem. A translation of a sample ticket appears below.

The starting time of the opera is not on the ticket and varies considerably, depending on the length of the opera. Since operas come in varying lengths, curtain time varies. Here is a small sampling: *Der Rosenkavalier* began at 6:00 p.m., *Salome* at 8:00 p.m., *Don Giovanni* at 7:00 p.m., and *La bohème* at 7:30 p.m. Therefore, check the starting times on the posters outside the box office, or in the *Offizielles Monatsprogramm des Fremdenverkehrsamtes*, the weekly *Die Zeit*, or the Wednesday edition of the daily *Die Welt*. (These two newspapers list the operas and starting times for all the opera houses in Germany.)

TICKET TRANSLATION

BAYERISCHE STAATSOPER	BAVARIAN STATE OPERA
Nationaltheater	National Theater
MÜNCHEN	MUNICH
3. VI. 1990	June 3, 1990
2	**Seat 2**
1.Rang Rechts	**1st Tier Right**
2.Reihe - Türe I	**2nd Row—Door 1 (enter through)**
DM 56.00	**(Price)**

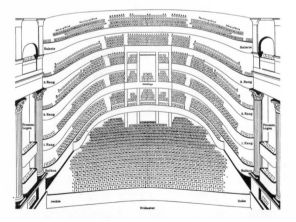

Seating Plan Nationaltheater (Courtesy of Bayerische Staatsoper)

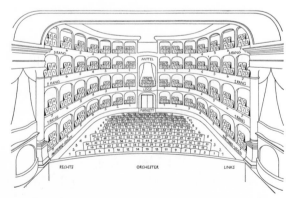

Seating Plan Cuvilliéstheater (Courtesy of Bayerische Staatsoper)

CUVILLIÉSTHEATER

Tickets for the Cuvilliéstheater are sold at the Nationaltheater box office, Maximilianstraße 11. (See Nationaltheater for details.) However, the *Abendkasse* is located at Residenzstraße 1, through the *Brunnenhof* ("fountain" courtyard) of the Residenz to the left of the main entrance to the theater. The box office opens a half hour before curtain time. The long line next to the wall is for reduced student tickets. Go to the short line in front of the box office window, unless you are a student.

Tickets are available by mail and telephone from the Nationaltheater's box office. (See Nationaltheater for details). Unfortunately, the ticket table for the Cuvilliéstheater is almost as complicated as for the one for the Nationaltheater.

Tickets are difficult to get for the Cuvilliéstheater, because the theater is small. Again, the *freier Verkauf* performances are the easiest, and arriving in Munich seven days before the performance might help as well.

Understanding your ticket will enable you to find your seat with no problem. A translation of a sample ticket appears below.

The starting time is not on the ticket, although most operas begin at 7:30 p.m. There are exceptions, however, so check the starting times on the posters in front of the box office, in the *Offizielles Monatsprogramm des Fremdenverkehrsamtes*, *Die Zeit*, or the Wednesday edition *Die Welt*.

Finding Your Way
NATIONALTHEATER

The Nationaltheater faces Max-Joseph-Platz, with Residenzstraße passing in front, bordered on the south by Maximilianstraße and on the east by Marstallplatz. You can reach the opera house from the *Hauptbahnhof* (main railroad station) by *Straßenbahn* 17, exit Nationaltheater. You can also take *Straßenbahn* 19, exit Theaterstraße, Omnibus 53, exit Odeonsplatz; U-Bahn 3, 4, 5, or 6, exit Odeonsplatz, and the S-Bahn, exit Marienplatz.

The main entrance to the Nationaltheater is located at Max-Joseph-Platz 2, where an enormous statue of Max Joseph sits in the middle of the square. You can also enter the opera house from the *Abendkasse* or *Erfrischungsraum* (restaurant) on Maximilianstraße. The first staircase in the entrance foyer leads up to the *Königsallee* on *1.Rang*. The next staircase leads to the tiers (*Balkon* und *Ränge*). If you are seated in the *Parkett*, continue straight ahead. Above each door, you will see *Tür* followed by a Roman numeral. Match the *Tür* number on your ticket with the number appearing above the door. If you try to go through an incorrect door, the door guard will physically stop you. (At least you do not have to worry about being in the wrong seat.) The seat numbers are brass plates affixed to the bottoms of the seats. Odd-numbered seats are on the left and even numbers on the right.

Unfortunately, the programs are sold by these door guards on each *Rang*. They cost 5 DM. The program (in German) contains a few

TICKET TRANSLATION

Bayerische Staatsoper	Bavarian State Opera
Altes Residenztheater	Old Residence Theater
Cuvilliéstheater	Cuvilliés Theater
Eingang Residenzstr. 1	Entrance Residenz Street 1
Parkett rechts	**Orchestra Right**
Reihe 3	**Row 3**
Montag, 4. Juni 1990 42	**Monday, June 4, 1990 (Seat) 42**

Cuvilliéstheater

TICKET TABLE

Plätze (Seats)		Preise in DM (Prices in DM)				
		G	S	F	FP	PH
Parkett (orchestra)						
Reihe 1-6 (rows 1-6)		55,5	77	113,5	130,5	173,5
Reihe 7-12 (rows 7-12)		49,5	68,5	100,5	115,5	153,5
Parterre-Logen (orchestra boxes)						
Vorderplätze (front seats)	Loge 1-6	55,5	77	113,5	130,5	173,5
	Loge 7	49,5	68,5	100,5	115,5	153,5
Rückenplätze (rear seats)	Loge 1-2	49,5	68,5	100,5	115,5	153,5
	Loge 3-5	38	52,5	77	88,5	117,5
	Loge 6	27	37	53,5	61,5	81,5
	Loge 7	10,5	14	19,5	22,5	29
1.Rang Logen (1st tier boxes)						
Vorderplätze (front seats)	Loge 1-6	55,5	77	113,5	130,5	173,5
	Loge 7	49,5	68,5	100,5	115,5	153,5
Rückenplätze (rear seats)	Loge 1-2	49,5	68,5	100,5	115,5	153,5
	Loge 3-6	16,5	23,5	33,5	38	51,5
	Loge 7	10,5	14	19,5	22,5	29
2.Rang Logen (2nd tier boxes)						
Vorderplätze (front seats)	Loge 1-5	44	60,5	89	102	135,5
	Loge 6-7	38	52,5	77	88,5	117,5
Rückenplätze (rear seats)	Loge 1-2	38	52,5	77	88,5	117,5
	Loge 3	16,5	23,5	33,5	38	51,5
	Loge 4-7	10,5	14	19,5	22,5	29
3.Rang Logen (3rd tier boxes)						
Vorderplätze (front seats)	Loge 1-2	38	52,5	77	88,5	117,5
	Loge 3-5	32	44	64	73,5	97,5
	Loge 6	27	37	53,5	61,5	81,5
	Loge 7	16,5	23,5	33,5	38	51,5
Rückenplätze (rear seats)	Loge 1	32	44	64	73,5	97,5
	Loge 2	16,5	23,5	33,5	38	51,5
	Loge 3-7	10,5	14	19,5	22,5	29

$1 = 1.6 DM, but can vary due to the fluctuating value of the dollar.

articles and illustrations pertaining to the opera. The cloakroom for those seated in the orchestra (*Parkett Garderobe*) is located off the entrance hallway. The *Garderobe* for each tier is located on both sides of the hallway surrounding the tier. There is no charge. The ladies' room (*Damen*) and men's room (*Herren*) are also on the hallway around each tier. Bars are located near the cloakrooms on each tier (no smoking) and on the entrance level in the inner foyer (smoking). Fortunately, smoking is prohibited in the mar-velous *1.Rang Königsallee*, making it possible to enjoy the rooms and breathe at the same time. During intermissions, everyone promenades around the *Königsallee* counterclockwise. With military types guarding the doors to the auditorium and armed *Polizei* roaming the building, do not even think of promenading around clockwise. (*Das ist Deutschland*.) Also, at the performance I attended, someone yelled "bravo" before the music had finished, and most of the audience gasped in horror.

Falstaff (Courtesy of Théâtre Royal de la Monnaie archives)

Parsifal (Courtesy of Gran Teatre del Liceu, Photo by Català)

Festa Teatrale celebrating the 250th anniversary of Teatro di San Carlo (Courtesy of Teatro di San Carlo, Photo by Romano)

Salome (Courtesy of Gran Teatre del Liceu, Photo by Bofill)

Plácido Domingo and Mirella Freni in *Adriana Lecouvreur* (Courtesy of Gran Teatre del Liceu, Photo by Català)

Luciano Pavarotti in *Il trovatore* (Courtesy of Teatro Comunale)

Peter Seller's production of *Die Zauberflöte* (Courtesy of Glyndebourne Festival Opera, Photo by Gravett)

Left: Ceiling of auditorium, Teatro di San Carlo (Courtesy of Teatro di San Carlo, Photo by Romano)
Right: Auditorium with view of royal box and ceiling, Teatro Massimo Bellini (Courtesy of Teatro Massimo Bellini, Photo by Angelo)

Auditorium, Teatro Comunale (Courtesy of Teatro Comunale, Photo by Marchiori)

Salon Royal, Théâtre Royal de la Monnaie (Courtesy of Belgian Tourist Office, Photo by Roland)

Grand Foyer with statue of Vincenzo Bellini, Teatro Massimo Bellini (Courtesy of Teatro Massimo Bellini, Photo by Angelo)

Façade of Teatro Massimo Bellini (Courtesy of Teatro Massimo Bellini, Photo by Angelo)

Façade of Teatro della Pergola (Photo by author)

Façade of Théâtre Royal de la Monnaie (Courtesy of Belgian Tourist Office)

Staircase to all levels, Opéra Bastille (Courtesy of NORR, Photo by Ferré)

Aerial view of Opéra Bastille during construction (Courtesy of NORR, Photo by Ferré)

L'italiana in Algeri (Courtesy of Société des Bains de Mer/Opera de Monte-Carlo)

Ognenniy angel (The Fiery Angel) (Courtesy of De Nederlandse Oper, Photo by Pieper)

If you cannot get tickets, all is not lost. Tours (*Führungen*) through the Nationaltheater are offered every Friday at 2:00 p.m. and cost 5 DM. Ask at the information window in the *Tageskasse* (box office).

CUVILLIÉSTHEATER

The Cuvilliéstheater faces Residenzstraße, located inside the royal complex around the corner from the Nationaltheater. You enter the complex at Residenzstraße 1. Walk through the courtyard to reach the theater. The entrance foyer, a long arched room, leads into an octagonal hallway before reaching the *Parkett* foyer. The stairs on the left of the *Parkett* foyer lead up to the *I.Rang*. The entrance straight ahead goes into the *Parkett*, and the entrances immediately to the right and left of the orchestra bring you to the *Parterre Logen rechts* and *Parterre Logen links*, respectively. Stairs to the *II.-, III.Ränge* are in the rear on the right and left sides. They are marked *Aufgang*. In the *Parkett*, even-numbered seats are on the right (*rechts*) and odd-numbered are on the left (*links*). Seat numbers, beginning with 1 on the left side and 2 on the right side, increase sequentially with no repetition. *Logen* 1 are the center boxes on all tiers, and boxes 7 are closest to the stage.

Programs are for sale in the *Parkett* foyer and cost 4,50 DM. The program (in German) contains a few articles and illustrations pertaining to the opera. Cloakrooms (*Kleiderabgabe*) are located on the right and left side of the entrance hallway. There is no cost. Drinks are available in the front entrance foyer on the left as you walk out during intermission. The ladies' (*Damen*) and men's (*Herren*) rooms are located on the sides of the *Parkett* foyer.

If you cannot get tickets, you can still visit the Cuvilliéstheater Monday through Saturday from 2:00 p.m. to 5:00 p.m. and Sunday from 10:00 a.m. to 5 p.m. at a cost of 2 DM.

Planning Your Trip
OPERA SCHEDULE

The regular season runs from mid-September through June, with the *Münchener Opernfestspiele* (Munich Opera Festival) taking place during July. The repertory ranges from baroque to contemporary, with emphasis given to works by Wagner and Strauss. The 1990/91 season opened on September 18 with Leoš Janáček's *Věc Makropulos* (The Makropoulos Affair) and will close on June 25 with a ballet. The last opera will be a new production of Sergei Prokofiev's *Lyubov' k tryom apel'sinam* (The Love for Three Oranges) on June 24. Other *Neuinszenierungen* at the Nationaltheater are Wagner's *Die fliegende Holländer*, Gioacchino Rossini's *L'italiana in Algeri*, and Modest Mussorgsky's *Boris Godunov*. The *Opernfestspiele* will open on July 6 with the world première of Krzysztof's Penderecki's *Ubu rex* and will close on July 31 with Wagner's *Die Meistersinger*. *Wiederaufnahmen und Neueinstudierungen* are Pfitzner's *Palestrina*, Strauss's *Die Ägyptische Helena* and *Die schweigsame Frau*, Hindemith's *Mathis der Maler* and *Cardillac*, Engelbert Humperdinck's *Hänsel und Gretel*, Johann Strauß's *Die Fledermaus*, Wagner's *Der Ring des Nibelungen* and *Parsifal*, Alban Berg's *Wozzeck*, Mozart's *Die Entführung aus dem Serail*, Wolf-Ferrari's *I quattro rusteghi*, Rossini's *Mosè*, Pietro Mascagni's *Cavalleria rusticana* and Leoncavallo's *Pagliacci*, Francesco Cilèa's *Adriana Lecouvreur*, Verdi's *Un ballo in maschera* and *Otello*, Giacomo Puccini's *Manon Lescaut*, Jules Massenet's *Werther*, and Pyotr Il'yich Tchaikovsky's *Orleanskaya deva* (The Maid of Orleans). The Cuvilliéstheater offers a new production of Mozart's *Apollo et Hyacinthus/Il sogno di Scipione* and during the festival, the Munich première (*Erstaufführung*) of Manfred Trojahn's *Enrico*. Other operas on the schedule: Strauss's *Capriccio* and Wolf-Ferrari's *Le donne curiose*.

The Nationaltheater is a repertory house, which means a different opera is performed every night. Opera shares the stage with ballet. To be sure your visit coincides with an opera, write for schedule and ticket information. Specify the month you plan on visiting, because they only send schedules covering a two-month period. For 14 DM you can receive the bimonthly programs for a year. Write to:

Tageskasse der Bayerischen Staatsoper
Maximilianstraße 11
8000 Munich 22, Germany

TRAVEL INFORMATION

The best hotel for operagoers in Munich is Hotel Vier Jahreszeiten Kempinski, Maximilianstraße 17, 8000 Munich 22, Germany; telephone (49)(89)230-390, fax (49)(89)230-39693. In the United States, call toll-free, 1-800-426-3135. Singles start at $160 and doubles at $250. The Vier Jahreszeiten is a luxurious five-star hotel with 395 rooms and 45 suites, conveniently located in the best part of Munich. A rooftop swimming pool, sauna, massage, and solarium help turn an opera holiday into a vacation. You will be in good company, for all the opera stars stay at the hotel, which is only three blocks from the opera house. Contact the chief concierge, David Langartner, for all your last-minute opera ticket needs.

There is a restaurant in the opera house. Entrance is on Maximilianstraße around the right side of the opera house. Look for *Erfrischungsraum*. There is also a restaurant in the main entrance hall of the Cuvilliéstheater. A few of the many nearby restaurants are Spatenhaus an der Oper on Max-Joseph-Platz, Max 2 Espresso on Maximilianstraße, and Bistro Eck in the Hotel Vier Jahreszeiten.

The German National Tourist Bureau, 747 Third Avenue, 33rd Floor, New York, NY 10017, 212-308-3300, can send you travel information only. Write early; they take a long time to respond.

Austria

Die Zauberflöte in Felsenreitschule (Courtesy of AP&IS/PSF, Photo by Weber)

SALZBURG

Großes Festspielhaus, Kleines Festspielhaus, Felsenreitschule
Salzburger Festspiele

The Salzburg Festival officially opened on August 22, 1920, with Hugo von Hofmannsthal's *Jedermann*. Directed by Max Reinhardt, the play was performed on an open-air platform in the Cathedral Square. Two years later, operas by Wolfgang Amadeus Mozart joined the repertory. The first festival hall, reshaped by Eduard Hütter as a provisional theater from its original role as a seventeenth-century winter riding school, opened in 1925. Subsequent restructuring and rebuilding resulted in the Kleines Festspielhaus. Meanwhile, Johann Bernhard Fischer von Erlach's seventeenth-century baroque summer riding school was converted into a second theater, known as the Felsenreitschule. The third theater in the festival complex, the Großes Festspielhaus, designed by Clemens Holzmeister, was inaugurated on July 26, 1960, with Richard Strauss's *Der Rosenkavalier*.

Salzburger Festspiele was originally established as a festival to celebrate Mozart operas. Since its inception, the program has expanded to include works of many composers.

HISTORICAL OVERVIEW
Background

The idea of holding a regular Mozart festival was born in 1842 when a statue of Mozart by sculptor Ludwig Schwanthaler was unveiled in the presence of his two surviving sons. Thirty-five years later, the first Mozart festival took place. It was celebrated periodically until 1910. The

formation of the *Festspielhausgemeinde* by Hugo von Hofmannsthal, Max Reinhardt, Franz Schalk, and Strauss in 1917 laid the foundation for a regular celebration of Mozart's works. It is ironic that the city where Mozart spent several impoverished years reaps wealth and world recognition from a festival his memory.

The focal point for the new festival was the seventeenth-century royal stables, which had been converted into cavalry barracks in the nineteenth century. A year after the provisional theater opened in 1925, it was redesigned by Clemens Holzmeister, who added a foyer covered with frescoes. In the 1930s, the theater acquired the name Kleines Festspielhaus and received new technical equipment and more seats. The audience orientation was also reversed. The building continued to be refashioned after the Anschluß by Benno von Arend. The outcome was not satisfactory, so additional work was performed in 1962-63 by Erich Engels and Hans Hoffmann, resulting in the house's present appearance.

Meanwhile, the Felsenreitschule gained a convertible roof, stage, and orchestra pit and began hosting plays. The first opera graced its stage in 1948. Remodeled in 1968-69 by Holzmeister, the Rock Riding School acquired a lower stage area, a "removable" auditorium, and a waterproof awning. Holzmeister was also responsible for construction of the Großes Festspielhaus, which was begun in 1956 and finished four years later at a cost of 210 million Austrian shillings. Fifty-five thousand cubic yards of rock were blasted from the face of the mountain to accommodate the stage, reputed to be the largest in Europe.

Theater

The three festival halls are under one roof, sandwiched between splendid baroque façades. Five bronze doors, with ornamental handles by Toni Schneider-Manzell, lead into the largest of the three, the Großes Festspielhaus. The steel and concrete building boasts a Latin-inscribed façade: *Sacra Camenae Domus / Concitis Carmine Patet / Quo Nos Attonitos / Numen Ad Auras Ferrat* (The holy house of the Muse is open for lovers of the arts, may heavenly power inspire us and raise us to the heights). The Adnet marble floor entrance hall, illuminated by Murano glass wall lights, presents two Carrara marble sculptures by Wander Bertoni, ''Music'' and ''Theater.'' Adjoining the hall are the former stables of Prince-Archbishop Wolf Dietrich, converted into a foyer with stone columns, arched ceiling, and green serpentine floor containing mosaic horses by Kurt Fischer. On the wall hangs a steel relief, ''Homage to Anton Webern,'' by Rudolf Hoflehner. A bust of Holzmeister watches over the *Parterre*-level foyer. This area is decorated with the tapestries ''Fire/Water/Air'' by Fischer and ''Struggle

between Good and Evil'' by Giselbert Hoke and divided by marble pillars sporting relief masks by Heinz Leinfellner. There you can also view a model of the entire *Festspielbezirk* (Salzburg Festival District). Busts of Max Reinhardt, Karl Böhm, Alexander Moissi, Strauss, Bernhard Paumgartner, and Josef Kaut and a tapestry by Oskar Kokoschka entitled ''Amor and Psyche'' inhabit an adjoining corridor. The side foyers leading to the boxes boast a huge wall painting entitled *From Night to Day* by Wolfgang Hutter on the left and a wood-paneled motif, ''Salzburg, Its Architects, and Its Music,'' designed by Karl Plattner on the right. The strikingly modern auditorium, shaped like a pinched, sloping-sided rectangle, accommodates rows of narrow raked wooden seats and a stage extending deep into the old Mönchsberg. Convex and concave wood elements panel the side walls; light and dark woods cover the tier and the orchestra level. The theater seats 2,170.

Massive wrought-iron gates protect the Kleines Festspielhaus and Felsenreitschule from the outside world. A horse fountain, created by baroque sculptor Andreas Götzinger, greets you. Next, frescoes of allegoric figures, ancient saga characters, theatrical scenes, and religious images, executed in 1926 by Anton Faistauer, surround you in the red marble floor square hall. The frescoes, a victim of Adolf Hitler's displeasure, were

View of Festival Quarter with Hohensalzburg Fortress in the background (Courtesy of PSF)

Auditorium, Großes Festspielhaus (Courtesy of AP&IS)

Tapestry by Giselbert Hoke, *Struggle between Good and Evil*, in Großes Festspielhaus (Courtesy of AP&IS)

backdrop and rows of wooden benches to accommodate the twentieth-century spectator. A waterproof awning, which can be opened or closed according to the weather's fickleness, protects its 1,549 spectators.

The Karl Böhm Hall, built in 1660 by Archbishop Johann Ernst Thun as a winter riding school, was transformed in 1926 to its present form. Built into the Mönchsberg, which is visible as the back wall, the hall is paneled in wood, above which tapestries from the Dutch school of the late seventeenth century hang. The fresco-covered ceiling, painted in 1690 by Johann Michael Rottmayr and Christoph Lederwasch and restored in 1926 and 1976, depicts ''attacks against dummies dressed as Turks,'' as described in the Salzburg catalog.

Top: View toward stage, Felsenreitschule (Courtesy of PSF, Photo by Schaffler)
Bottom: View toward stage, Kleines Festspielhaus (Courtesy of PSF, Photo by Steinmetz)

restored in 1956 by Alberto Susat. However, they suffered some permanent damage and outlines suggest the lost frescoes. Along the corridor to the right of the Kleines Festspielhaus auditorium, busts of von Hofmannsthal, Bruno Walter, Clemens Krauss, and Wilhelm Furtwängler share space with Kay Krasnitzky's twelve bronze tablets, based on subjects from Ovid's *Metamorphoses*. A tapestry by Oskar Kokoschka in a motif of the sun and the moon hangs nearby. A bust of Arturo Toscanini watches over the box foyer, where tapestries designed by Anton Kolig can be seen. The rectangular auditorium is wood paneled, with inlay work and matching tapestry designed by Slavi Soucek. The Kleines Festspielhaus accommodates 1,384.

The Felsenreitschule boasts an arcade of spectator boxes that were cut into the Mönchsberg during the seventeenth century as its stage

Performance History

The first opera performed in Salzburg was Rodolfo Campeggi's *Andromeda* in 1618. Heinrich Biber's *Arminius* and Georg Muffat's *Le fatali felicità di Plutone* were performed in 1687 and Biber's *Alessandro in Pietra* two years later. In 1719, the Heckentheater in the gardens of Schloß Mirabell was inaugurated with Antonio Caldara's *Dafne*. Mozart's *Apollo et Hyacinthus* (1767), *Il sogno di Scipione* (1772), and *Il Re Pastore* (1775) were performed there. Intermittent Mozart festivals began at the end of the 1800s. In 1901, Lilli Lehmann sang a marvelous Donna Anna in Mozart's *Don Giovanni*. Nine years later, Gustav Mahler conducted a memorable *Le nozze di Figaro*.

At the newly created Salzburger Festspiele, Mozart operas were first seen in 1922 at the Stadttheater. The first opera inside the new Festspielhaus, Ludwig van Beethoven's *Fidelio* with Lotte Lehmann, was performed on August 13, 1927. During the initial seasons, Mozart and Strauss operas filled the repertory, with the occasional Christoph Willibald Gluck piece. Strauss conducted his *Der Rosenkavalier* in 1929, and Giuseppe Verdi operas joined the repertory in the 1930s.

The era of great conductors began in 1933. Walter conducted *Tristan und Isolde* to commemorate the fiftieth anniversary of Richard Wagner's death, and Toscanini led Verdi's *Falstaff*, Beethoven's *Fidelio*, Mozart's *Die Zauberflöte*, and Wagner's *Die Meistersinger von Nürnberg* with electrifying results. But when the Nazis came, both great conductors fled, along with Reinhardt, Stefan Zweig, and other talented Jews associated with the festival. Those happy to serve the Nazis were richly rewarded by the Third Reich. Krauss was appointed artistic director, and Fürtwangler, Böhm, Vittorio Gui, and Herbert von Karajan were frequent conductors. "Aryan" work replaced "degenerate modern art," and the festival hit bottom.

In May 1945, the Americans occupied Salzburg and revived the festival with Mozart's *Die Entführung aus dem Serail*. The audience consisted primarily of the Occupation Forces. By the next year, three more operas returned to the stage, and tourists were sprinkled in the audience.

Feeling competition from other festivals, Salzburg began hosting world premières and staging contemporary works beginning with the 1947 season. The first world première, Gottfried von Einem's *Dantons Tod*, appeared on stage on August 6, 1947, followed by his *Der Prozess* on August 17, 1953. Carl Orff's *Antigone* was introduced on August 9, 1949, and Boris Blacher's *Romeo und Julia* surfaced the next year. Werner Egk's *Irische Legende* was introduced in 1956, and Erbse's *Julietta* three years later. The world première of Strauss's *Die Liebe der Danae*, postponed from 1944, took place on August 14, 1952, and Rolf Liebermann's *Penelope* was performed for the first time on August 17, 1954.

Von Karajan took over leadership of the festival in 1964, remaining at the helm until his recent death. Great voices were heard on stage: Franco Corelli, Leontyne Price, Giulietta Simionato, and Nicolai Ghiaurov. Hans Werner Henze's *Bassariden* was world premiered on August 6, 1966, followed seven years later by Orff's *De Temporum Fine Comoedia*, under its German title, *Das Spiel vom Ende der Zeiten*. The 1980s saw a renewed emphasis on modern works, with the world premières of Friedrich Cerha's *Baal* in 1981, Luciano Berio's *Un Re in ascolto* in 1984, and Krysztof's Penderecki's *Die schwarze Maske* in 1986.

During the last couple of decades, almost as many stars as shine in the skies have appeared on the festival stages. Although the ticket prices are astronomical, red ink flows every year. The Austrian government and Salzburg residents eliminate the deficit, but they are not delighted with their obligation. There is speculation that, with von Karajan dead, the festival may not see as many stars.

Top: *Capriccio* (Courtesy of Austrian Press & Information Service/PSF, Photo by Weber)
Lower left: Christian Boesch in *Die Zauberflöte* (Courtesy of AP&IS/PSF, Photo by Weber)
Lower right: Max Reinhardt, director of first *Jedermann* (Courtesy of AP&IS)

139

PRACTICAL INFORMATION
Tickets

If you venture to the Salzburger Festspiele without tickets, the festival box office (*Vorverkaufskasse*) is located at Hofstallgasse 1. The box office opens daily from 9:30 a.m. to 5:00 p.m. (*täglich 9.30 bis 17.00 Uhr*) during the festival. All tickets to the opera performances are usually sold out long before the festival opens, with only an occasional returned ticket available.

You can order tickets by mail starting in December for the next festival season. However, your ticket order form should arrive no later than January 5 for the coming festival season. Reservations by telegram, telexes, faxes, and telephone are not accepted. Indicate the performance(s), date(s), price(s), seat location, and number of tickets desired. Give alternative prices, dates, and seat locations to increase your chance of success. You will receive a response by April. Only when you have received a bill do you send in payment. Mail your request to:

Kartenbüro der Salzburger Festspiele
Postfach 140
5010 Salzburg, Austria

Tickets can also be ordered in the United States for the Salzburger Festspiele from the Austrian Music Festivals. However, they will not accept ticket orders for opera performances exclu-

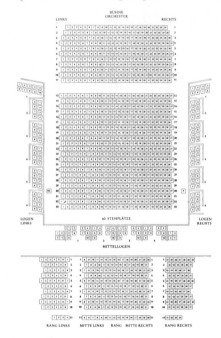

Seating Plan Kleines Festspielhaus (Courtesy of PSF)

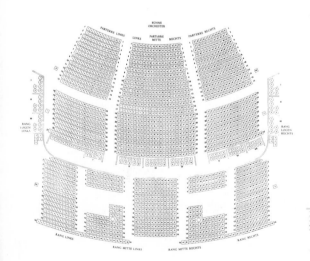

Seating Plan Großes Festspielhaus (Courtesy of PSF)

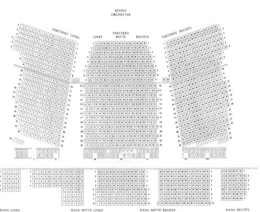

Seating Plan Felsenreitschule (Courtesy of PSF)

GROßES FESTSPIELHAUS

Location	Entrittspreise (Prices in ÖS)
Parterre (orchestra):	
Reihe 1-12 (rows 1-12)	3.300
Reihe 13-20 (rows 13-20)	2.800
Reihe 21-25 (rows 21-25)	2.200
Reihe 26-27 (rows 26-27)	1.700
Logen-Vordersitze (boxes-front seats)	2.800
Logen-Rücksitze (boxes-rear seats)	1.700
Rang (balcony):	
Reihe 1 (row 1)	2.800
Reihe 2-3 (rows 2,3)	2.200
Reihe 4-7 (rows 4-7)	1.700
Reihe 8-10 (rows 8-10)	1.300
Reihe 11-13 (rows 11-13)	1.000
Reihe 14-16 (rows 14-16)	700
Säulensitze (seats behind the columns)	300

KLEINES FESTSPIELHAUS

Parterre (orchestra):	
Reihe 1-12 (rows 1-12)	3.300
Reihe 13-15 (rows 13-15)	2.800
Reihe 16-20 (rows 16-20)	2.200
Reihe 21-26 (rows 21-26)	1.700
Reihe 27-29 (rows 27-29)	1.300
Reihe 30-31 (rows 30, 31)	1.000
Reihe 32-33 (rows 32,33)	700
Mittellogen-Vordersitze (center boxes - front seats)	2.800
Mittellogen-Rücksitze (center boxes - rear seats)	2.200
Seitenlogen (side boxes):	
Vordersitze 2-4 (front seats in boxes 2-4)	2.200
Vordersitze 5-6 (front seats in boxes 5,6)	1.700
Rücksitze 2-4 (rear seats in boxes 2-4)	1.000
Rücksitze 5-6 (rear seats in boxes 5,6)	700
Rang (balcony):	
Reihe 1 (row 1)	2.800
Reihe 2-3 (rows 2,3)	2.200
Reihe 4-5 (rows 4,5)	1.700
Reihe 6-7 (rows 6,7)	1.300
Reihe 8-9 (rows 8,9)	1.000
Reihe 10 (row 10)	700
Stehplätze (standing room)	150

FELSENREITSCHULE

Parterre (orchestra)	
Reihe 1-9 (rows 1-9)	3.300
Reihe 10-12 (rows 10-12)	2.800
Reihe 13-16 (rows 13-16)	2.200
Reihe 17-20 (rows 17-20)	1.700
Reihe 21-22 (rows 21,22)	1.300
Reihe 23 (row 23)	1.000
Logen-Vordersitze (boxes-front seats)	2.200
Logen-Rücksitze (boxes-rear seats)	1.700
Rang (balcony):	
Reihe 1 (row 1)	2.200
Reihe 2-4 (rows 2-4)	1.700
Reihe 5 (row 5)	1.300
Reihe 6 (row 6)	1.000
Reihe 7-8 (rows 7,8)	700

Prices are for opera performances only. Orchestral concert, recital, ballet, chamber music tickets are less expensive.
$1 = 10 ÖS, but can change due to the fluctuating value of the dollar.
ÖS is an abbreviation for Austrian Shilling. It is also abbreviated S.

sively. In addition, your choice of ticket categories is limited. Write to:

Austrian Music Festivals
342 Madison Avenue, Suite 948
New York, NY 10173

The ticket table is detailed. Ticket prices change every couple of rows, directly relating the desirability of the seat to its cost.

Tickets to the opera performances are a bit difficult to come by. But first, before you even think of tickets, think money. You will need plenty of it. Most opera tickets cost between $170 and $300, and that is per ticket. Then I would recommend you do the following: order tickets by mail as soon as reservations are accepted and order tickets to a variety of performances, since preference is given to patrons requesting tickets to different events. If you still come up empty handed and are set on going, take lots of money with you and plan on spending it, so you have the option of paying scalper's prices at the festival if all else fails. A black market exists, with ticket prices up to six times face value. You can find out who has tickets for sale through the grapevine by letting it be known that you are in the market for tickets and are prepared to pay accordingly. The concierges at the better hotels can also help.

The tickets are easy to understand, once you know the meaning of the German words, so below is a translation of a sample ticket.

Most operas begin at 6:00 p.m. (18.00), but as you can see from the sample ticket, there are exceptions. To check the starting times, look in the *Spielplan* in the festival brochure.

Finding Your Way

The festival complex faces Hofstallgasse, bordered by Siegmundsplatz on the north, Toscaninihof on the south, and the Mönchsberg on the west. From the *Hauptbahnhof* (main train station), you can reach the festival theaters by bus/trolley 1 or 2.

The entrance to the Großes Festspielhaus is on Hofstallgasse. The two staircases on the right and left lead up to the auditorium (*Parterre*, *Rang* and *Logen*). Use the right side if your ticket reads *rechts* and the left side if your ticket reads *links*. Seat 1 is located on the extreme left aisle, with the numbers increasing sequentially to the extreme right aisle. Seat numbers in the twenties are in the middle, except in rows 16 and 17. You will find similar seat numbering in the *Rang*.

Programs to the individual operas are sold in the foyer. The price varies. The program (in German) contains a synopsis in English, articles, and illustrations relating to the opera and composer. (The program to the complete festival is superfluous.) The cloakroom (*Garderobe*) is on the entrance level in the rear. You will find the rest rooms (*WC*) on the right and left sides on

---

TICKET TRANSLATION

Salzburger Festspiele 1989	Salzburg Festival 1989
Kleines	Small
Festspielhaus	Festival House
Rang Rechts	Balcony Right
Reihe 4	**Row 4**
Sitznr. 25	**Seat 25**
Juli 1989	July 1989
29	29
19.00 Uhr	7:00 p.m.
La Cenerentola	(Opera)

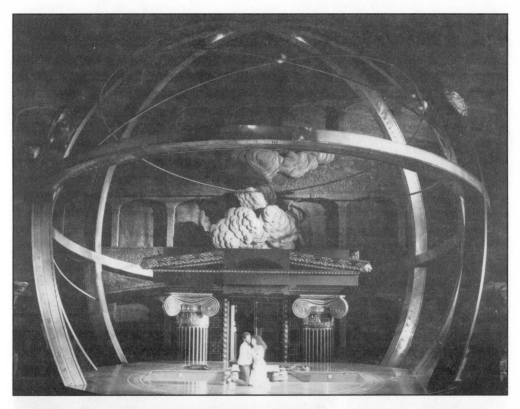

Herbert von Karajan, director of
the Festival until his death
(Courtesy of AP&IS)

Top: *Il ritorno di Ulisse in patria* (Courtesy of AP&IS/PSF, Photo by
Weber)
Lower left: *Le nozze di Figaro* (Courtesy of AP&IS/PSF, Photo by
Weber)

each floor. Refreshments and drinks for non-smokers are offered on the *Parterre* level. Refreshments and drinks for smokers are offered on the entrance level.

For the Felsenreitschule and Kleines Festspielhaus, enter through the massive wrought-iron gate on Hofstallgasse. In the Kleines Festspielhaus, the seats stretch in unbroken rows across the *Parterre*, so it is important to enter the auditorium on the correct side. Although this is not the case in the Felsenreitschule, it is still inconvenient (and embarrassing) to enter on the wrong side. Seat numbering in both theaters is similar to the Großes Festspielhaus.

Programs to individual operas are sold in the foyer. The price varies. The program (in German) contains a synopsis in English, articles, and illustrations relating to the opera and composer. (The program to the complete festival is superfluous.) The cloakrooms (*Garderoben*) are on the right at the entrance, and the rest rooms (*WC*) are on the left. Refreshments and drinks are served in the Karl Böhm Hall. There are special seats for disabled patrons. Specify that you are in a wheelchair when requesting tickets.

Planning Your Trip
OPERA SCHEDULE

The Salzburg Festival runs from the end of July to the end of August. The 1990 festival season opened on July 26 with a special *Festabend* program and closed on August 31 with a concert. The first opera was Mozart's *Idomeneo* on July 27, and the last opera was Mozart's *Don Giovanni* on August 30. Mozart's *Così fan tutte*, Verdi's *Un ballo in maschera*, Richard Strauss's *Capriccio*, and Beethoven's *Fidelio* completed the schedule. In addition, there were concert performances of the *Orpheus* cycle: Claudio Monteverdi's *L'Orfeo*, Gluck's *Orfeo ed Euridice*, Joseph Haydn's *L'anima del filosofo ossia Orfeo ed Euridice*, and Ernst Křenek's *Orpheus und Eurydike*. The operas are scheduled on a rotating basis, so it is possible to attend a different opera almost every evening.

Top: James Morris and Kathleen Battle in *Le nozze di Figaro* (Courtesy of AP&IS/PSF, Photo by Weber) Bottom: Plácido Domingo and Josephine Barstow in *Un ballo in maschera* (Courtesy of PSF, Photo by Weber)

Josephine Barstow and Günter Reich in *Die schwarze Maske*, World Première 1986 (Courtesy of AP&IS/PSF , Photo by Weber)

The 1991 program, in honor of the bicentennial of Mozart's death, is offering eight Mozart operas. The schedule begins with *Die Zauberflöte* on July 27 and ends with *Idomeneo, Re di Creta* on August 29. In addition, the *Uraufführung* (world première) of Helmut Eder and Herbert Rosendorfer's *Mozart in New York* will take place on August 15.

Since the festival fare ranges from operas, ballets, dramas, and orchestral concerts to instrumental and song recitals, church concerts, serenades, and chamber music, write to the above address for a complete schedule to be sure your visit coincides with the opera.

If you plan to attend the festival on a regular basis, you might be interested in the Association of the Friends of the Salzburg Festival, Mönchsberg 1, 5020 Salzburg, Austria; telephone (43)(662)842-541, ext. 222 or 284, between 10:00 a. m. and 12:00 noon Monday through Friday (Austrian time). They send out information bulletins concerning festival productions and artists three times a year. Currently, there is a waiting list of one to two years to join the association.

TRAVEL INFORMATION

The founding members of the *Festspielhausgemeinde* envisioned the festival to be the best and the most exclusive. They invited the rich and famous, encouraging them to rent castles and give parties, which led to the assertion that the festival's true function was social. That claim never was denied and still rings true today. Every year, festival goers don black ties, evening gowns, and jewels for the opera performances, so keep that in mind when you pack. Also remember that the weather can be hot and humid or cold and rainy, so prepare for both.

Since Salzburg is very popular during the festival season, I would recommended that you make hotel reservations as early as possible. The closest and most luxurious hotel is the Goldener Hirsch, Getreidegasse 37, 5020 Salzburg; telephone (43)(662)848-511. During the festival, singles start at $200 and doubles at $350. For additional hotel information, write to:

Fremdenverkehrsbetriebe
Auerspergstraße 7
5024 Salzburg, Austria

The Austrian National Tourist Office, 500 Fifth Avenue, New York, NY 10110, (212) 944-6880, can send you travel information as well as Festspiele information. They respond promptly.

VIENNA
Staatsoper Wien

gala performance of Wolfgang Amadeus Mozart's *Don Giovanni* inaugurated the Staatsoper Wien, originally known as the Hofoper, on May 25, 1869, in the presence of Kaiser Franz Joseph I. Designed by August Siccard von Siccardsburg and Eduard van der Nüll, the Hofoper was regarded not only as a monument to Vienna's position in the operatic world but also as a place for the royal court to entertain. During the final months of World War II, bombs heavily damaged Vienna's crown jewel of opera, leaving only the façade and part of the foyer. In 1949, Erich Boltenstern, Otto Prossinger, and Ceno Kosak undertook the rebuilding effort. The Staatsoper reopened on November 5, 1955. with Ludwig van Beethoven's *Fidelio*.

HISTORICAL OVERVIEW
Background

During the reign of Leopold I, court architect Johann Burnacini erected a three-floor wooden opera house on the site where the Nationalbibliothek stands today. When Leopold I died in 1705, his eldest son, Joseph I, became emperor and ordered court architect Giuseppe Galli-Bibiena to build two theaters. Since these theaters were not open to the public, the Kärntnertortheater was constructed for them in 1708. When Maria Theresa ascended the throne in 1740, she erected the Theater bei der Hofburg (better known as the Burgtheater on the Michaelerplatz), which opened in 1742. Built by Sel-

lier, the Burgtheater served as a home for opera for slightly more than a decade. Meanwhile, Schönbrunner Schloßtheater, designed by Ferdinand Hetzendorf von Hohenberg, opened on August 28, 1749.

The Kärntnertortheater burned down in 1761 during a performance of Christoph Willibald Gluck's ballet, *Don Juan in Hell*. The theater recovered from Don Juan's burning in hell the following year and reopened as the Hofopernhaus. This was the Staatsoper's predecessor. Two more theaters were conceived before the birth of the Hofoper: the short-lived Theater auf der Wieden, also known as the Freyhaustheater (1787-1801), and the Theater an der Wien, opened in 1801, renovated in 1961, and still in use today.

In the middle of the nineteenth century, Emperor Franz Joseph I decreed that the inner city fortifications be torn down, including the Hofopernhaus, and the city center be reconstructed. A competition was held for the best design of a new opera house. Architects van der Nüll and von Siccardsburg won from among thirty-five submissions. Von Siccardsburg was responsible for the building, and van der Nüll was responsible for the interior decoration. Construction began in late 1861 and continued for more than eight years, but neither architect lived to witness its completion. As soon as the construction began, their opera house was derided as a sunken box because of the depth of the foundation. The petty Viennese architects who lost the competition played a leading role in the ridicule. Newspapers ran campaigns against the two men, and all Vienna made jokes at their expense. The architects could endure no more. Depressed and suffering from eye trouble, van der Null hanged himself in April 1863. Two months later, von Siccardsburg, convalescing from an operation, had a relapse and died of a stroke and heartbreak. He was only thirty-two years old. G. Gugitz and J. Stork, hired to see the building completed, faithfully executed van der Null's and von Siccardsburg's remaining plans. The ultra-conservative Viennese were shocked and outraged at the finished product, dubbing it "the Waterloo of architecture."

When the Hapsburg Empire collapsed in 1918, Hofoper was renamed the Staatsoper, no longer recognizing nearly three hundred years of royal patronage. Twenty years later, swastika flags flew from the opera house and German troops marched on the city. The Nazis lost no time in smashing the bust of Gustav Mahler displayed in the vestibule of the opera house. On March 12, 1945, incendiary bombs set fires that raged for two days, leaving the auditorium and stage facilities in rubble. After the war, two competitions were held for the reconstruction of the opera house, with Erich Boltenstern and Otto Prossinger the winners. Boltenstern was responsible for reconstructing the auditorium and the cloakrooms. Prossinger, along with Felix Cevela, designed the old Imperial Hall and Smoking Room, while Ceno Kosak fashioned a new hall off the grand foyer. By 1955, the Staatsoper was back in all its glory.

The Theater

The Renaissance-style Hofoper, flanked by Josef Gasser's fountains of Music, Dance, Joy, Frivolity on the left and Lorelei, Sorrow, Love, Vengeance on the right, is an imposing whitish-gray stone building. Bronze statues by Ernst Julius Hähnel of Love, Imagination, Heroism, Comedy, and Tragedy gaze from between the loggia arches,

Top: Exterior, Staatsoper (Courtesy of Wiener Fremdenverkehrsband)
Middle: Auditorium, Staatsoper (Courtesy of Wiener Fremdenverkehrsband)
Bottom: Auditorium before World War II destruction (Courtesy of Austrian National Tourist Office)

where frescoes by Moritz von Schwind entitled *Zyklus der Zauberflöte* are displayed. The names **Mozart, Beethoven, Rossini, Weber, Spontini, Spohr,** and **Humperdinck** are inscribed on the façade, which bears the plaque **Kaiser Franz Joseph I 1868**, topped by two eagles and a crown.

Marble medallions of architects von Siccardsburg and von der Null, by Josef Cesar, guard the grand staircase, while allegorical statues representing Painting, Sculpture, Architecture, Music, Dance, Poetry, and Tragedy by Gasser watch over it. Franz Dobiaschofsky's paintings portraying Ballet, Comic Opera, and Tragic Opera and Johann Preleuthner's reliefs depicting Ballet and Opera adorn the walls. Dobiaschofsky also designed the ceiling painting, *Fortuna Distributing Her Gifts*, which was executed by Michael Rieser.

The ornateness of the original red, cream, and gold horseshoe-shaped auditorium was a war casualty. The caryatids, nudes, garlands, and gallery arches that embellished the auditorium lie entombed beneath the opera house floor. The decor of the present ivory and gold auditorium, with its burgundy corduroy seats and huge doughnut-shaped crystal chandelier, is austere and somber. The iron curtain showing Orpheus

leading Eurydice was created by Rudolf Eisenmenger. The Hofoper accommodated 2,880 (1,720 seated and 1,160 standing). The Staatsoper seats 1,709, with 567 standing.

Performance History

The first opera heard in Vienna was Ludovico Bartolaia's *Il Sidonio* in 1633. Francesco Bonacossi's *Ariadna abbandonata* followed in 1641, with Francesco Cavalli's *Egisto* and Claudio Monteverdi's *Il ritorno di Ulisse in patria* appearing two years later. Leopold I, who ascended the throne in 1658, propelled opera to the primary spot in court entertainment. A composer and poet in his own right, Leopold composed some of the music for Pietro Antonio Cesti's *Il pomo d'oro*, which was written for his marriage to Princess Margaret Theresa of Spain and performed in 1668. A thousand people were needed to mount and perform this most spectacular of baroque court operas, which included twenty-four different stage settings.

Iron curtain by Rudolf Eisenmenger (Courtesy of Wiener Fremdenverkehrsband)

Allegorical statues around the grand staircase (Courtesy of Wiener Fremdenverkehrsband)

Top: *Fidelio*, 1970 production (Courtesy of AP&IS)
Lower left: Christa Ludwig and Wilma Lipp in *Der Rosenkavalier*, 1967 (Courtesy of AP&IS)
Lower right: *Danton's Tod* in Theater an der Wien, 1963 (Courtesy of AP&IS)

Giuseppe Carcano's *Amleto* inaugurated the Theater bei der Hofburg on February 5, 1742. The theater was so poorly attended, it was turned into an exhibition hall for sporting events and closed in 1747. It reopened on May 14, 1748, with Gluck's *Semiramide riconosciuta*, written to celebrate Empress Maria Theresa's birthday. In 1754, Gluck was appointed *Kapellmeister*, and ten of his operas received world premières over the next sixteen years, including *Orfeo ed Euridice* on October 5, 1762, *Alceste* on December 26, 1767, and *Paride ed Elena* on November 3, 1770. The Burgtheater played a role in Mozart's musical career as well, hosting the *Uraufführungen* (world premières) of *Die Entführung aus dem Serail* on July 16, 1782, *Le nozze di Figaro* on May 1, 1786, and *Così fan tutte* on January 26, 1790. Vincente Martín y Soler's *Una cosa rara* and Domenico Cimarosa's *Il matrimonio segreto* were introduced on November 17, 1786, and February 7, 1792, respectively. Mozart's *Der Schauspieldirektor* graced the stage for the first time at the Schönbrunner Schloßtheater on February 7, 1786, and his *Die Zauberflöte* at the Theater auf der Wieden on September 30, 1791.

Theater an der Wien, which opened on June 13, 1801, with a play by theater founder Emmanuel Schikaneder and music by Franz Teyber, was the site of the world première of Beethoven's *Fidelio* on November 20, 1805. Later the theater became a home for operetta, introducing Franz Schubert's *Die Zauberharfe* in 1820, Albert Lortzing's *Der Waffenschmied* twenty-six years later, Johann Strauß's *Die Fledermaus* on April 5, 1874, and his *Der Zigeunerbaron* on October 24, 1885. The Kärntnertortheater was also busy hosting premières: Carl Maria von Weber's *Euryanthe* on October 25, 1823, Gaetano Donizetti's *Linda di Chamounix* on May 19, 1842, and Friedrich von Flotow's *Martha* on November 25, 1847.

A Mozart work was chosen to open Vienna's new opera house, because the Kärntnertortheater had ruffled many feathers by virtually ignoring Mozart's death in 1792. The inaugu-ration of the Hofoper with *Don Giovanni* was intended to soothe the ruffled feathers. From its inception, the Hofoper was an *Intendants* (director's) house that was plagued with problems. The first *Intendant*, Franz von Dingelstedt, served less than a year, departing with the comment, "Concerts are superfluous, opera at best a necessary evil!" Johann von Herbeck followed, introducing Karl Goldmark's *Die Königin von Saba* on March 10, 1875. That same year, Franz von Jauner took the reins and mounted the entire *Ring Cycle*. Although Jauner's successes were numerous, such as engaging Giuseppe Verdi to conduct his *Aida* and *Messa da Requiem*, he amassed huge debts and was forced out after only five years. A short time later, he committed suicide.

In 1880, the Hofoper was under Wilhelm Jahn's guidance. Karl Goldmark's *Merlin* was world premiered on November 19, 1886. His *Das Heimchen am Herd* followed on March 21, 1896. Antonio Smareglia's *Vassallo di Szigeth* was introduced on October 4, 1889, and Jules Massenet's *Werther* was staged for the first time ever on February 16, 1892.

Mahler's legendary reign began in 1897. He immediately conquered Vienna with his 1897 production of Richard Wagner's *Lohengrin*. The critics wrote, "It was at once both tender and fiery." Mahler's crowning glory came in 1903 with Wagner's *Tristan und Isolde*, followed a year later by Beethoven's *Fidelio*. But in 1906, his radical production of Mozart's *Don Giovanni*, part of the 150th anniversary celebration of Mozart's birth, caused such a tremendous uproar that it triggered his downfall. By 1907, Mahler's uncompromising standards, his attacks on tradition (which he called "a blend of convenience and slovenliness"), combined with the revolutionary stage designs of Alfred Roller, the first designer to bring impressionistic techniques to the opera stage, resulted in his resignation. He said he was forced out by a "revolt of the mediocrities," which was true.

In 1919, Richard Strauss and Franz Schalk

shared the *Intendant* duties. Strauss's *Die Frau ohne Schatten* was premiered on October 10, 1919, with brilliant singing by Maria Jeritza and Lotte Lehmann. Despite several marvelous productions of his operas, the honeymoon was over after five years, and Strauss was out. Clemens Krauss took the helm in 1929, introducing contemporary opera. He left for Berlin in 1934 to become Hitler's favorite director.

With the arrival of the Nazis, Field Marshall Hermann Wilhelm Göring essentially took control of the Staatsoper, wasting no time in turning it into an Aryan and fascist domain, its quality reduced to that of a provincial theater. On June 30, 1944, war forced the Staatsoper to close its doors after Valhalla crumbled in flames in the final act of Wagner's *Götterdämmerung*. On March 12, 1945, bombs leveled the building.

After the war, opera continued at Theater an der Wien and Volksoper until the Staatsoper reopened with seven new productions the first season. In 1956, Herbert von Karajan started his eight-year tenure, which proved to be the most controversial and turbulent in Staatsoper history. He concluded an agreement with La Scala for joint productions, thereby bringing many great Italian singers to the Staatsoper, along with Birgit Nilsson, Leonie Rysanek, and Christa Ludwig.

On May 23, 1971, the world première of Gottfried von Einem's *Der Besuch der alten Dame* took place. In 1982, the first non-German *Intendant*, Lorin Maazel, took the helm. Not only was he non-German, he was an American. His contract ran for four years, but he lasted only two.

I saw an interesting performance of Mozart's *Così fan tutte*, adequately sung by Roberta Alexander as Fiordiligi, Margareta Hintermeier as Dorabella, Lucio Gallo as Gugliemo, and Deon van der Walt as Ferrando. The attractive production was staged by Johannes Schaaf and designed by Hans Schavernoch, with costumes by Lore Haas. Nikolaus Harnoncourt conducted.

Since the Staatsoper puts on seven operas a week, the quality of the performances varies

considerably. I have heard that the great nights are heavenly, but the bad nights are nothing short of disaster. Mahler used to say, "One great performance a week is pretty good," and that was during the Staatsoper's greatest era.

Top: Paul Schöffler in *Fidelio* (Courtesy of AP&IS)
Bottom: Leonie Rysanek in *Der Rosenkavalier*, 1967 (Courtesy of AP&IS)

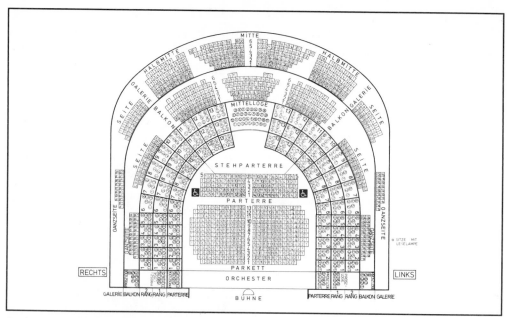

Seating Plan (Courtesy of Staatsoper Wien)

TICKET TABLE

Kategorie (Category)	Preise der Plätze (Prices of Seats in ÖS)			
	IV	V	VI	S
Parkett 1.-6. Reihe (front orchestra rows 1-6)	1400	1600	1800	2500
Parkett 7.-13. Reihe (front orchestra rows 7-13)	1120	1280	1440	2000
Parterre 1. Reihe (rear orchestra row 1)	1120	1280	1440	2000
Parterre 2.—5. Reihe (rear orchestra rows 2-5)	840	960	1080	1500
Parterre Prosc. Loge 1. Reihe (orch. stage box row 1)	1120	1280	1440	2000
Parterre Prosc. Loge 2. Reihe (orch. stage box row 2)	460	460	460	460
Parterre Loge 1-6, 1. Reihe (orch. boxes 1-6, row 1)	1120	1280	1440	2000
Parterre Loge 1-6, 2. Reihe (orch. boxes 1-6, row 2)	460	460	460	460
Parterre Loge 1-6, 3. Reihe (orch. boxes 1-6, row 3)	210	210	210	210
Parterre Loge 7-13, 1. Reihe (orch. boxes 7-13, row 1)	1400	1600	1800	2500
Parterre Loge 7-13, 2. Reihe (orch. boxes 7-13, row 2)	840	840	840	840
Parterre Loge 7-13, 3. Reihe (orch. boxes 7-13, row 3)	460	460	460	460
Mittelloge 1.-4. Reihe (center box, rows 1-4)	1400	1600	1800	2500
1. Rang Prosc. Loge 1. Reihe (tier 1 stage box row 1)	1120	1280	1440	2000
1. Rang Prosc. Loge 2. Reihe (tier 1 stage box row 2)	460	460	460	460
1. Rang Loge 1-6, 1. Reihe (tier 1 boxes 1-6, row 1)	1120	1280	1440	2000
1. Rang Loge 1-6, 2. Reihe (tier 1 boxes 1-6, row 2)	460	460	460	460
1. Rang Loge 1-6, 3. Reihe (tier 1 boxes 1-6, row 3)	210	210	210	210
1. Rang Loge 7-13, 1. Reihe (tier 1 boxes 7-13, row 1)	1400	1600	1800	2500
1. Rang Loge 7-13, 2. Reihe (tier 1 boxes 7-13, row 2)	840	840	840	840
1. Rang Loge 7-13, 3. Reihe (tier 1 boxes 7-13, row 3)	460	460	460	460

continued

continued

2. Rang Loge 1-6, 1. Reihe (tier 2 boxes 1-6, row 1)	840	960	1080	1500
2. Rang Loge 1-6, 2. Reihe (tier 2 boxes 1-6, row 2)	210	210	210	210
2. Rang Loge 1-6, 3. Reihe (tier 2 boxes 1-6, row 3)	90	90	90	90
2. Rang Loge 7-13, 1. Reihe (tier 2 boxes 7-13, row 1)	1120	1280	1440	2000
2. Rang Loge 7-13, 2. Reihe (tier 2 boxes 7-13, row 2)	460	460	460	460
2. Rang Loge 7-13, 3. Reihe (tier 2 boxes 7-13, row 3)	210	210	210	210
Balkon Prosc. Loge 1. Reihe (balcony stage box row)	280	280	280	280
Balkon Prosc. Loge 2.-3. Reihe (bal. stage box rows 2-3)	90	90	90	90
Balkon Mitte 1. Reihe (balcony center row 1)	840	840	840	840
Balkon Mitte. 2.-6. Reihe (balcony center rows 2-6)	560	560	560	560
Balkon Seite 1. Reihe (balcony side row 1)	560	560	560	560
Balkon Seite 2. Reihe (balcony side row 2)	280	280	280	280
Balkon ganz Seite 1. Reihe (bal. total side row 1)	280	280	280	280
Balkon ganz Seite 2. Reihe (bal. total side row 2)	140	140	140	140
Galerie Mitte 1. Reihe (gallery center row 1)	560	560	560	560
Galerie Mitte 2.—6. Reihe (gallery center rows 2-6)	350	350	350	350
Galerie Halbmitte 1. Reihe (gal. off-center row 1)	460	460	460	460
Galerie Halbmitte 2-6. Reihe (gal. off-center rows 2-6)	280	280	280	280
Galerie Seite 1. Reihe (gallery side row 1)	280	280	280	280
Galerie Seite 2.-3. Reihe (gallery side rows 2-3)	140	140	140	140
Galerie ganz Seite 1. Reihe (gal. end-side row 1)	140	140	140	140
Galerie ganz Seite 2. Reihe (gal. end-side row 2)	90	90	90	90
Parterre Stehplätze (standing behind orchestra)	20	20	20	20
Balkon Stehplätze (standing behind balcony)	15	15	15	15
Galerie Stehplätze (standing behind gallery)	15	15	15	15
Rollstuhl-/ Begleitersitze (wheelchair/companion seat)	150	150	150	150

$1 = 10 ÖS, but can vary due to the fluctuating value of the dollar.
ÖS is an abbreviation for Austrian Shilling. It is also abbreviated S.

PRACTICAL INFORMATION
Tickets

The box office (*Tageskasse*) is located at Hanusch-gasse 3, the street behind and to the west of the opera house. Go through the archway into the courtyard. The box office is on the left side. Box office hours are Monday through Friday from 8:00 a.m. to 6:00 p.m., Saturday from 9:00 a.m. to 2:00 p.m., and Sunday from 9:00 a.m. to 12 noon (*Montag bis Freitag 8 bis 18 Uhr, Samstag 9 bis 14 Uhr, an Sonntag 9 bis 12 Uhr*). Tickets go on sale seven days before the performance.

Ticket availability is posted in the entrance foyer in German, English, French, and Italian. There are eight *Schalter* (windows). Window 1 is the *Blitzschalter* (express window), for people who know exactly what they want. Everyone else should go to windows 2, 3, 4, 5, 6, or 8. *Schalter 7* is for picking up reservations. The evening box office (*Abendkassa*) is located inside the main entrance of the opera house on both the right and left sides (enter *Zugang*, exit *Abgang*). It opens one hour before curtain time.

You can reserve tickets through the mail. They begin processing ticket orders one month before the performance. The latest your ticket order can reach the box office is fourteen days before the performance. Do not send any money with your request. You pay for your tickets when you pick them up. Tickets must be claimed at Hanuschgasse 3, *Schalter 7*, no later than one day before the performance. Otherwise they will be released. Write to:

Bundestheaterverband-Kassen
Hanuschgasse 3
1010 Vienna, Austria

Tickets can be ordered by calling (43)(1) 513-1513, starting six days before the performance during the following time periods: Monday through Friday from 9:00 a.m. to 5:00 p.m., Saturday between 9:00 a.m. and 2:00 p.m., and Sunday and holidays between 9:00 a.m. and 12:00 noon. (43) = country code; (1) = city code. In Austria, dial (01)513-1513. You can also order by fax: (43)(1)51444-2969. Austria is six hours ahead of Eastern Standard Time. Prepaid tickets can be picked up at the opera house box office on the day of the performance.

However, I would not recommend telephoning or faxing. For either method you first go through a central switchboard, where the *Bundestheaterverband* (Federal Theater Associ-

ation) puts you on hold for a long time, though they know you are telephoning from overseas. Usually, after patiently waiting for fifteen minutes or so, while you watch your phone bill climb, there is a good chance you will be disconnected. That is exactly what happened to me, three times, when I tried to send a fax. The *Bundestheaterverband* is a huge bureaucracy, and the less contact you have with them, the happier you will be. You can call 527-636 in Vienna to inquire about ticket availability, but be prepared to wait or be disconnected.

The ticket table for the Staatsoper is very detailed, with the price of tickets varying considerably not only in each section but also in each row. The cost of the ticket accurately reflects your ability to see the stage. The different price categories indicate the quality of the cast.

The most difficult times to get tickets are September through mid-October and *Wiener Festwochen* (mid-May to the end of June). Most of those performances are *Ausverkauft* (sold out) or have *sehr eingeschränkter Kartenverkauf* (very limited number of tickets available). Also, *Vorstellungen im Abonnement* (subscription performances) have only a small number of tickets. Tickets are not available for *geschlossene Vorstellung* (closed performances). Otherwise, tickets are not difficult to purchase. Keep in mind that many seats, especially in the second and third rows of the side boxes, offer terrible views or no views of the stage.

Understanding your ticket should help orient you in the confusing maze of the Staatsoper, so below is a translation of a sample ticket.

Most operas begin at 7:00 p.m. (19.00 Uhr).

TICKET TRANSLATION

Staatsoper	State Opera
Così Fan Tutte	(Opera)
Parterre Loge 2 Reihe Platz	**Orchestra Box 2 Row Seat**
Links 1	**Left 1**
Dienstag, 5. Juni 90 19.00 Uhr	Tuesday June 5, 1990 7 p.m.
Preis ÖS	(Price)

You can confirm the time by checking the posters by the opera house. No one is admitted after the curtain has gone up.

Finding Your Way

The Staatsoper faces Opernring, bordered on the west by Operngasse, on the east by Kärntnerstraße, and on the north by Philharmonikerstraße. You can reach the opera house by *Straßenbahn* 52, or 58 from the *Hauptbahnhof*, changing at Opernring (the end of the line) to 2, exit Oper. U-Bahn U1, U2, and U4 stop by the Staatsoper, exit Oper.

The main entrance is at Opernring 2. The grand staircase leads up to the *Parterre Logen*. Continue for the *1.Rang* and *2.Rang*. Box 1 is closest to the stage, and box 13 is closest to the middle. Entrance to the *Parkett/Parterre* is to the right (*rechts*) and left (*links*) of the grand staircase. Seat numbering begins with 1 on both the extreme right and left aisles, increasing to the center aisle, so it is important to be on the correct side. Seat numbers in red and gold are on the bottoms of the chairs. Stairs on the extreme left and right ends of the entrance foyer lead to the *Balkon/Galerie*, where seat numbering is similar to that of the orchestra. The ushers are recognizable by their chocolate brown jackets. Unfortunately, some of them in the *Parkett/Parterre* are nasty old men. However, the younger ushers are quite pleasant. Do not be surprised to see armed policemen patrolling the halls. They are present at every performance.

The programs are sold by the ushers and cost 23 ÖS. The program (in German) contains a synopsis in English and articles and illustrations relevant to the opera. The cloakroom (*Garderobe*) is on the right side of the entrance foyer, down a flight of stairs. There is no charge, but a tip is expected. Ladies' rooms (*Damen*) are located on the Operngasse side on each level, and men's rooms (*Herren*) are located on the Kärntnerstraße side on each level. You will find the bars in the grand foyer on *1.Rang* (no smoking) and one

flight down from the *Parkett* level on the Operngasse side (smoking). There are special places for wheelchair patrons on either side of the *Parterre*.

Tours (*Führungen*) are offered through the opera house from the Operngasse side daily at 1:00 p.m., 2:00 p.m., and 3:00 p.m. For various reasons, however, there are no tours on many days, so check the notice posted under the *Führungen* sign.

Planning Your Trip
OPERA SCHEDULE

The opera season runs from the beginning of September to the end of June. The 1989/90 season opened on September 1 with Strauss's *Elektra* and closed on June 30 with Puccini's *Turandot*. Forty-five operas from twenty-two composers were in the repertory, ranging from eighteenth- and nineteenth-century Italian operas and romantic and classical German works to twentieth-century classical modern pieces.

The Staatsoper is a repertory house, which means a different opera is performed each night. Except for rehearsals, special events, and certain holidays, there are performances every night during the season.

TRAVEL INFORMATION

Formal evening clothes are required for attending a première or gala if you are seated in the orchestra or boxes. Otherwise, dark suits for the men and "after 5" dresses or suits for the ladies are requested. Since the Staatsoper is one of the major tourist attractions of Vienna, the suggested dress code is to discourage those in the usual tourist attire from entering the opera house.

The best hotel for operagoers in Vienna is the Hotel Bristol, Kärntnerring 1, 1015 Vienna, Austria; telephone (43)(1)515-160, fax (43)(1) 5151-6550. For reservations in the United States, call toll-free, 1-800-223-6800 (member of the Leading Hotels of the World). Singles start at $200, doubles at $300. This is an elegant five-star hotel with 136 rooms and 11 suites. It is across the street from the opera house. The hotel

Loggia with statues by Ernst Julius Hahnel
(Courtesy of AP&IS)

transports you back to Imperial Vienna, with its luxury and impeccable service. The rooms are furnished with original pieces from the baroque, Regency, and Biedermeier periods, and the walls are covered with silk. To complete the experience, order a box of mouth-watering Imperial Tortes. They are scrumptious. Located in the best section of Vienna, the Bristol offers all the conveniences of the twentieth century. No hotel is closer to the main entrance of the opera house. In addition, the concierge can arrange tickets for you, so you do not have to deal with the Staatsoper bureaucracy. He also performs miracles in finding hard-to-get tickets. And if you are arriving on the day of the opera, he will pick up and pay for the tickets you have reserved through the mail.

A few recommended restaurants across from the Staatsoper are the Restaurant Korso bei der Oper (expensive), Rotisserie Sirk, and Restaurant zu den 3 Husaren. In addition, restaurants ranging from McDonald's to gourmet are located on the *Fußgängerzone* (pedestrian section) of Kärntnerstraße, starting behind the Staatsoper.

The Austrian National Tourist Office, 500 Fifth Avenue, New York, NY 10110, 212-944-6880, can send you travel information and the opera schedule.

Belgium

Jenůfa (Courtesy of La Monnaie archives)

BRUSSELS
Théâtre Royal de la Monnaie

The Théâtre Royal de la Monnaie opened its doors on March 24, 1856, with a delightful performance of Jacques François Halévy's *Jaguarita l'Indienne*. The splendidly attired opening night crowd, dazzled by the magnificence of the new opera house, shouted repeatedly for the architect, Joseph Poelaert, and showered him with thundering applause. La Monnaie found its niche by becoming a leading avant-garde center. The theater added *Opéra National* to its name in 1963.

HISTORICAL OVERVIEW
Background

The first Théâtre de la Monnaie opened in 1700 with the entire royal court celebrating the festive occasion. Designed by Paolo and Pietro Bezzi and built by the Italian Gio-Paolo Bombarda, treasurer to Maximilien-Emmanuel of Bavaria, the theater was located on the site of the former Hôtel Ostrevent, where coins were minted. Hence the name, *la monnaie* (the mint). *Grand théâtre* was added to reflect its greatness. In 1717, the Brussels banker Jean-Baptiste Meeus procured La Monnaie, which he and his daughters supervised until 1763.

In 1810, Napoleon, accompanied by Empress Marie-Louise, visited the Grand Théâtre. Aghast at its terrible state of disrepair, he promised to build a new opera house. Nine years later, the promise was fulfilled. The second La Monnaie, designed by Damesne and constructed just

behind the first, opened in 1819 with much pageantry and splendor. A newspaper of the time described the scene as follows: "At 7 o'clock, S.A.R. the prince of Orange, and S.A.I. his esteemed spouse entered their magnificent box; S.M. the king appeared soon thereafter with S.M. the queen, and S.A.R. prince Frédéric des Pays-Bas. The audience expressed its satisfaction by repeated applause and called loudly for the architect, M. Damesne, in order to pay him a well-deserved tribute for his accomplishment. They honored the royal family by proclaiming *vive le roi! vive la reine! vivent le prince et la princesse! vive le prince grand-maître!* Couplets were dedicated to Grétry and Damesne."

Thirty-six years later, disaster struck while stagehands were erecting scenery for a performance of Giacomo Meyerbeer's *Le Prophète*. It was nine o'clock in the morning on January 21, 1855, when flames bellowed through the roof and black smoke shot toward the sky. By eleven o'clock the theater was gone, gutted by fire. Only the walls and the recently erected peristyle escaped destruction. The city agreed to rebuild the theater immediately. The third La Monnaie, located on the same site as the second, opened in 1856. Thirty-one years later, the orchestra pit was lowered for a performance of Richard Wagner's *Die Walküre*, and, for the first time, the auditorium darkened. In 1897, the theater was electrified.

Two years after its 100th birthday, the theater was condemned as a fire risk. The management appealed for "special dispensation" since they did not have any money for renovation. In 1985, their "special dispensation" expired, and after a performance of Richard Wagner's *Die Meistersinger von Nürnberg*, La Monnaie was closed. The renovation, costing more than $25 million and taking sixteen months, was accomplished by a group of young architects working under the amusing name of Architecture et Construction entre Rêve et Réalité (Architecture and Construction between Dream and Reality). When the theater reopened on November 12, 1986, with Ludwig van Beethoven's *Ninth Symphony*, it looked splendid. Richard Strauss's *Der Rosenkavalier* inaugurated the new opera season seven days later.

The Theaters

The first La Monnaie possessed a sumptuously decorated, elliptical, five-tier, unheated auditorium seating 1,200. Although some of the box holders basked in the warmth of their own private small stoves, the majority shivered from act to act, thawing out only during intermission in the heated foyer. The second La Monnaie, dazzling in white and gold, offered four tiers of boxes.

The third La Monnaie boasts a stately appearance accomplished by its Grecian peristyle. The relief pediment, designed by Eugène Simonis and supported by eight massive Ionic columns, is carved from French stone. The sculpture represents *L'Harmonie des Passions Humaines*. Harmony herself is in the center, with Lyric Poetry and Heroic Poetry to her immediate right. Next to them, Love, Discord, Remorse, and Murder are gathered. Pastoral Poetry and Satirical Poetry are seated on Harmony's left, with Sensual Delight, Desire, Deceit, Hope, Pain, and Consolation nearby. Underneath this magnificent pediment, THEATRE ROYAL DE LA MONNAIE-KONINKLIJKE MUNTSCHOUWBURG is proclaimed in gold letters. Gold roman numerals MDCCCXIX and MDCCCLVI flank

Top: Façade of La Monnaie at night (Courtesy of Belgian National Tourist Office)
Bottom: Auditorium, La Monnaie (Courtesy of La Monnaie archives)

the façade and mark the important construction dates. Caryatids of Polymnia and Euterpe by Victor Poelaert, brother of the architect, are on the left side and Thalia and Melpomène, by Melot, are on the right side.

The modest surroundings of the Place heightens the contrast with the magnificent interior. The former red and gold entrance hall is now sparkling white, its ceiling embellished with a striking abstract triptych painted by Sam Francis. Splashes of yellow, red, green, blue, and purple on a white background face a bold black and white geometric patterned marble floor, sculpted by Sol Lewitt. The burgundy and gold horseshoe-shaped auditorium, populated with

Entrance foyer—ceiling by Sam Francis, floor by Sol Lewitt (Courtesy of Belgian National Tourist Office, Photo by Roland)

top of the proscenium are the gold letters S.P.Q.B. on a burgundy background. A glittering crystal chandelier assisted by pairs of elegant candelabra illuminates the glorious auditorium. The *Salon Royal* (not open to the public) was designed by Charles Vandenhove and is a blend of modern and classical styles. Walls of white carrara marble and a floor of red- and white-striped Belgian marble enclose brass-topped white marble obelisks, nude white Greek statues on brass pedestals, and sculpted fragments of arms, legs, hands, and feet. Giulio Paolini executed the statues, and Daniel Buren created the floor. La Monnaie seats 1,140.

Performance History

Jean-Baptiste Lully's *Atys* inaugurated the first Théâtre de la Monnaie on November 19, 1700. During the initial seasons, Lully's *Persée*, *Bellérephon*, *Armide*, and *Amadis*, along with André Destouches's *Omphale*, André Campra's *Tancrède*, and works by Jean-Philippe Rameau filled the repertory. A three-year interlude of Italian opera began in 1727, under the artistic direction of Antoine-Marie Peruzzi, with Domenico Sarri's *Arsace* and Giuseppe Maria Orlandini's *Griselda* taking center stage. In 1746, Maurice de Saxe (Princess de Bouillon murders Adriana for Maurice de Saxe in Francesco Cilèa's *Adriana Lecouvreur*) occupied Belgium, ushering in opéra comique. The French exited in 1749, taking opéra comique with them. A decade later, the first Belgian opera was staged—Pierre van Maldere's *Le Déguisement pastoral*. The French revolution caused major difficulties at La Monnaie, and although its doors remained open, the only entertainment came from the circus: tightrope walkers, ventriloquists, acrobats, and jugglers.

The second Théâtre de la Monnaie was inaugurated on May 25, 1819, with André Grétry's *La caravane du Caire*. A prologue, with song and dance entitled *Momus à la nouvelle salle* by M. Bernard, preceded the opera. Then the course of Belgian history was changed by a performance

cherubs and nymphs, boasts four tiers. The names Mozart, Rossini, Grétry, Meyerbeer, Boieldieu, and Offenbach circle the room, while allegorical figures of Belgium protecting the arts, executed in Louis XIV style, stare down from a sky-background ceiling of painted columns and arches. Hendrickx's monumental figure of Belgium is seated on the throne, and the Belgian lion, spreading his majestic colors, is at her feet. "Painting" by M. Verheyden is to her right and "Music" by Hamman is to her left. "Sculpture" and "Architecture" by Wauters complete the scene. Winged genies and allegorical figures by Nolot and Rubé dwell nearby. Large sculpture reliefs embellish the first parapet and a tableau representing Tragedy, Music, and Dance enhances the second. Two gold genies holding clusters of lights flank the royal stage box. At the

Così fan tutte (Courtesy of La Monnaie archives)

of Daniel François Auber's *La Muette de Portici* on August 24, 1830. The opera, based on events that occurred in 1647, dealt with the uprising of the Neapolitans against their Spanish oppressors. Belgium, ruled by King William I of Orange, was in the throes of political unrest. Although William attended the Belgian première of *La Muette de Portici* on February 12, 1829, without incident, subsequent performances were banned. Suddenly, King William lifted the ban on August 24, 1830, and a performance was scheduled for that evening. The opera sold out immediately, with hundreds more, unable to get tickets, gathered in front of the theater. Act I played without disturbance. Act II ran smoothly until Masaniello, the Neapolitan fisherman who led the revolt, and Pietro, his friend, swore revenge on their Spanish oppressors in the duet, "*Amour sacré de la patrie*" (Sacred love of the fatherland). The audience shouted for an encore. Masaniello and Pietro obliged. Masaniello then learned that the Spanish viceroy's son had seduced his helpless mute sister. He swore vengeance, crying out to his followers, "*Aux armes*." The audience jumped to its feet, storming out of the theater onto the Place de la Monnaie,

where mobs of hungry and jobless workers joined them. The revolution that would give Belgium its independence had begun, inspired by a duet. La Monnaie was closed for two weeks. When it reopened on September 12, 1830, for a benefit performance for the wounded, the Belgian national anthem, "Brabançonne," was on the program. Two weeks later, the constitutional monarchy of Belgium was born, and Prince Leopold of Saxe-Coburg ascended the throne as Leopold I, King of Belgium. When La Monnaie was gutted by fire in 1855, performances continued at the Théâtre du Cirque, where one of the first Flemish operas, Benoit's *Isa*, was performed in 1867.

After La Monnaie was rebuilt, the world première of Charles Lecocq's *La Fille de Madame Angot* took place on December 4, 1872, followed by his *Giroflé-Girofla* two years later. La Monnaie's most glorious period began in 1875. Jules Massenet's *Hérodiade* was world premiered on December 19, 1881, Ernest Reyer's *Sigurd* on January 7, 1884, and his *Salammbô* on February 10, 1890, with Maurice Renaud. Meanwhile Emmanuel Chabrier's *Gwendoline* graced the stage for the first time on April 10, 1886, followed by Benjamin Godard's *Jocelyn* two years later and Xavier Leroux's *Evangéline* in 1895. Vincent d'Indy's *Fervaal* was introduced on March 12, 1897, and his *L'Étranger* four years later. In 1887, Nellie Melba dazzled the audience with her Gilda in Giuseppe Verdi's *Rigoletto*, and Enrico Caruso followed with Rodolfo in Giacomo Puccini's *La bohème* in 1910.

When the Germans occupied Belgium during World War I, Belgian artists refused to perform. After the war, a new company, formed by Maurice Kufferath and Corneil de Thoran, reopened the theater on December 21, 1918. Although Kufferath died the following year, de Thoran led La Monnaie until his death in 1953. During his reign, the world première of Darius Milhaud's *Les Malheurs d'Orphée* took place on May 7, 1926, Arthur Honegger's *Antigone* on

José van Dam in *Don Carlos* (Courtesy of Belgian National Tourist Office)

Wozzeck (Courtesy of La Monnaie archives)

December 28, 1927, and Sergei Prokofiev's *Igrok* (The Gambler) on April 29, 1929.

In 1981, Gerard Mortier took the helm and changed La Monnaie's fame from the role it played in Belgium's fight for freedom to the operas that played behind its doors. With a strong commitment to introducing new works, La Monnaie has commissioned several operas: the world première of Philippe Boesmans's *La Passion de Gilles* took place on October 18, 1983, followed by André Laporte's *Das Schloß* on December 16, 1986. March 19, 1991, witnesses another *création mondiale/wereldcreatie*, John Adams's *The Death of Klinghoffer.*

I saw a riveting new production of Leoš Janáček's *Z Mrtvého Domu* (From the House of the Dead). Against a stage almost empty except for a huge broken wing of the tormented eagle, which appeared lifeless until it healed and flew to freedom, the grim mosaic of life in a Siberian prison was reenacted by a large, splendid cast. Sylvain Cambreling kept the dramatic tension with his incisive conducting. The opera was performed without intermission, which heightened the emotionally devastating work. It was greeted with well-deserved bravos and cheers. Surtitles, in both French and Flemish, appeared sporadically.

L'incoronazione di Poppea (Courtesy of La Monnaie archives)

PRACTICAL INFORMATION
Tickets

The box office (*bureau de location/bespreekbureau*) is located at rue de la Reine, on the right side of the opera house. The box office is open Monday through Saturday from 11:00 a.m. to 6:00 p.m. (*du lundi au samedi inclus de 11 à 18 h*) and one hour before the performance. Tickets go on sale approximately one month before the first performance of each opera for all performances of that opera. The exact date is listed in the season's program. There is a large color-coded seating plan on the left wall with corresponding prices.

The box office personnel understand little English.

Tickets can be reserved by mail at the same time they go on sale at the box office. Reserved tickets must be picked up at least thirty minutes before curtain time, otherwise they will be released. Write to:

Bureau de location
Théâtre Royal de la Monnaie
rue Léopold 4
1000 Brussels, Belgium

Tickets can also be reserved by telephone. Call (32)(2)218-1211, 218-1202, or 219-6341 during box office hours. (32) = country code; (2) = city code. In Belgium, dial (02)218-1211.

TICKET TABLE

Seat Location	Prix des Places (Price of Seats in fb)		
	II	IV Première	III Ring
Categorie 1	2.800	4.600	3.200
fauteuils d'orchestre (front/center orchestra) 1er balcon face (1st balcony center) 1ères loges face (1st balcony center box seat)			
Categorie 2	1.900	3.200	2.200
fauteuils d'orchestre côté (side orchestra) fauteuils de fond (rear orchestra) 1er balcon côté (1st balcony side) 1ères loges côté devant (1st balcony side box seat front)			
Categorie 3	1.500	2.000	1.600
2e balcon face (2nd balcony center) baignoires devant (boxs surrounding orchestra seats front)			
Categorie 4	950	1.200	1.000
3e balcon face (3rd balcony center) 2èmes loges côté devant (2nd balcony side box seat front)			
Categorie 5	500	600	500
4e balcon face (4th balcony center) 3èmes loges côté devant (3rd balcony side box seat front)			
Categorie 6	250	350	250
4èmes loges côté (4th balcony side box seat)			
Fonds de Loges (rear of boxes)			
1ères loges côté (1st balcony side seat)	950	1.600	1.100
baignoires (surrounding orchestra)	750	1.000	800
2èmes loges côté (2nd balcony side seat)	500	600	500
3èmes loges côté (3rd balcony side seat)	250	300	250

All tickets remaining five minutes before curtain time are sold for 150 fb to those under 25 and over 60 years of age. (Proof of age required.)
Category III are special prices for the Ring Cycle being performed in October 1991.
$1 = 35 fb, but can vary due to the fluctuating value of the dollar.
Fb is an abbreviation for Belgian franc. It is also abbreviated F.

Tickets reserved by telephone must be paid for within ten days in Belgian francs sent by international postal money order. You should be able to speak French or Flemish. Belgium is six hours ahead of Eastern Standard Time.

The ticket table is fairly detailed, with the prices accurately reflecting how well you can see the stage. Belgium has two official languages, Flemish and French. For simplicity, Flemish has been omitted from the ticket table.

Your best chance for tickets is *vente libre/vrije verkoop* (nonsubscription) performances and con-

temporary operas. Tickets to new productions (*nouvelle production/nieuwe produktie*) and premières are the most difficult to find. If you see *complet/uitverkocht* (sold out) or *à bureaux fermés/ besloten voorstelling* (closed performance), think of another date.

Your ticket will look quite different from what you are accustomed to seeing. From left to right, the first number is the section, the letter is either the row or box, and the second number is your seat. Below is a translation of a sample ticket.

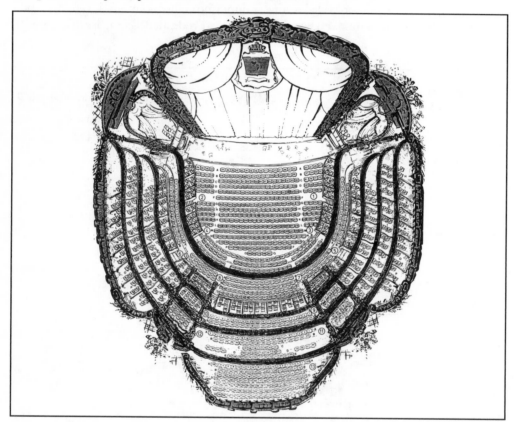

Seating Plan (Courtesy of Théâtre Royal de la Monnaie)

TICKET TRANSLATION

Nationale Opéra National	National Opera
Koninklijke Muntschouwburg	Royal Theater at the Mint (Flemish)
Theatre Royal de la Monnaie	Royal Theater at the Mint (French)
1 C **N° 99**	**Orchestra** **Row C** **Seat 99**
11 05 1990 * 20	May 11, 1990 8 P.M.

Most operas begin at 8:00 p.m. (20 *h/uur*), although the longer operas can start any time between 6:00 p.m. (18 *h/uur*) and 7:30 p.m. (19.30 *h/uur*), depending on their length. Starting times are listed in the season's schedule available at the box office and in the English language guide *What's On*. The doors are locked once the performance begins and can only be opened from the inside. Latecomers can watch the opera from television monitors on each tier.

Finding Your Way

Théâtre Royal de la Monnaie faces Place de la Monnaie, bordered by rue du Princes to the north, rue Léopold to the east, and rue de la Reine to the south. It is a twelve-minute walk from the Gare Centrale and ten minutes from the Grand Place. You can reach La Monnaie by the following public transportation: Métro line 1, exit De Brouckere; Pré-métro line 3, exit De Brouckere; Tram 52, 55, 58, 62, or 81, exit De Brouckere.

The main entrance is on Place de la Monnaie. After passing through the entrance hall, you will be in the foyer in front of the cloakrooms (*vestiaire*). Take the stairs on the right for *impair/oneven* (odd-numbered) sections/seats and the left for *pairs/even* (even-numbered) sections/seats. (Section numbers are orchestra 1-4, 1st tier 5-8, 2nd tier 9-10, 3rd tier 11-12, 4th tier 13.) Match the number on your ticket with the number over the door. In the orchestra, seat numbers increase sequentially beginning with 26 on the left aisle and 27 on the right aisle, meeting in the center. Numbers do not repeat. The numbering system, except beginning with 1, is similar on the *balcon* levels. Ushers are recognized by their black skirts and white blouses.

Programs are for sale in the entrance foyer and cost 200 fb. Programs (in French or Flemish) contain the complete libretto and articles about the opera and composer. A synopsis in English is available. Request one when you buy your program. To the left of the entrance foyer is a book-

Così fan tutte (Courtesy of Belgian National Tourist Office)

store where a marvelous book on La Monnaie, *Un Théâtre d'Opera: L'Équipe de Gerard Mortier à la Monnaie*, is for sale. The book is filled with magnificent color photographs and covers everything from the history of La Monnaie to its current operating philosophy. The book is in French with an English summary entitled *Opera as Theater* included.

The cloakrooms (*vestiaire*) are on the ground floor foyer. There is no charge. You must check your coat, umbrella, and anything else you may have with you. The ladies' room (*dames*) is located on the left side down the flight of stairs by the *vestiaire*. The men's room (*messieurs*) is to the right of the ladies' room. There are more rest rooms on the tiers. You will find a bar toward the front on the parterre level (no smoking) and another facing the Place de la Monnaie on the first tier level (smoking). There are elevators to the right of the *vestiaire*.

Planning Your Trip
OPERA SCHEDULE

The season runs from the beginning of September through June. The 1990/91 season opened on September 2 with a concert. The first opera was a new production of Verdi's *Simon Boccanegra* on September 9. The season closes on June 25 with Claudio Monteverdi's *L'incoronazione di Poppea*. Other new productions are Hans Zender's *Stephen Climax*, Adams's *The Death of Klinghoffer* (world première), and Mozart's *Die Zauberflöte*. Arrigo Boïto's *Mefistofele* and Janáček's *Jenůfa* complete the schedule. In October 1991, four complete cycles of Wagner's *Der Ring des Nibelungen* (new production) will be presented, beginning on October 8.

La Monnaie is a *stagione* house, which means only one opera is presented at a time. Opera shares the stage with ballets and concerts. To be sure your visit coincides with an opera performance, contact the Belgian Tourist Office, 745 Fifth Avenue, New York, NY 10151, 212-758-8130, for a schedule.

If you visit Brussels often and can read French or Flemish, you might be interested in joining *Amis de la Monnaie*, which costs 2,000 fb. You will receive the monthly *La Monnaie Magazine*, which describes the current productions, including color photographs and program information. For more information, write or call:

Amis de la Monnaie asbl
4 rue Léopold
1000 Brussels, Belgium
(32)(2)217-5680

TRAVEL INFORMATION

The best hotel for operagoers in Brussels is Hotel Royal Windsor, rue Dusquesnoy 5, 1000 Brussels, Belgium; telephone (32)(2)511-4215, fax (32)(2)511-6004. Singles start at $260, doubles at $305. Price includes a continental breakfast. For reservations in the United States, call toll-free, 1-800-223-6800 (member of the Leading Hotels of the World). It is a deluxe five-star hotel with 285 rooms and 15 suites located in the heart of Brussels. Only five minutes from the Gare Centrale and the Grand Place, the Royal Windsor offers all the comforts you desire in delightfully furnished rooms. It is a pleasant twelve-minute walk to the opera house, and it is safe to walk back after the opera. Contact the concierge for all your last-minute opera ticket needs.

There are a few restaurants on rue du Princes directly opposite the opera house and several more on rue de l'Ecuyer. In addition, Les Quatre Saisons is located in the hotel (very expensive). I would not recommend the quaint restaurants on rue Boucher: they are tourist traps that employ high-pressure techniques, practically forcing you to leave a tip, even though service (15 percent) is included. Do not tip. I would especially avoid Le Lautrec.

You can also contact the Belgian Tourist Office (address above) for travel information. They respond promptly.

Denmark

Stage curtain by Aagaard and Bache (Courtesy of Det Kongelige Teater archives)

COPENHAGEN
*Det Kongelige Teater * Gamle Scene, Nye Scene*

$\mathcal{D}$et Kongelige Teater, now known as the Gamle Scene, was inaugurated on October 15, 1874, with a potpourri of entertainment. The overture to Frederik Kuhlau's *Elverhøj*, a prologue by Carl Ploug with music by J. P. E. Hartmann, a tableau in honor of Ludvig Holberg, Holberg's *Det lykkelige Skibbrud*, and another tableau in honor of Adam Oehlenschläger delighted the illustrious opening night audience. Designed by Vilhelm Dahlerup and Ove Petersen, the Royal Theater was unique as the home to three art forms: opera, ballet, and drama. On August 28, 1931, a much needed annex (popularly called *Stærekassen* or Nesting Box but officially known as the Nye Scene) was inaugurated with the overture to *Elverhøj*, Julius Magnussen's *Fra Fiolstræde til Kongens Nytorv*, and Holberg's *Den Vægelsindede*. Designed by Holger Jacobsen, the Nye Scene became drama's primary home.

HISTORICAL OVERVIEW
Background

When Frederick V ascended the throne in 1746, plans were made for the first Kongelige Teater. Frederick donated land in the Kongens Nytorv and hired Niels Eigtved, his court builder, to oversee the theater's construction. An 800-seat rococo theater, built somewhat flimsily and in great haste, opened on December 18, 1748. After two years, the city of Copenhagen took over its administration. In 1770, Giuseppe Sarti, an Italian composer, decided to try his hand at the theater business only to realize he should keep to directing and composing. In 1772, King Christian VII placed the theater under royal control with Sarti as director. Two years later, Christian commissioned C. F. Harsdorff to enlarge the structure. The result was a spacious, well-constructed 1,375-seat house that survived 100 years.

In 1785, a curious proviso was introduced by the theater's management: curtain calls were prohibited and performers could not bow or curtsy to acknowledge applause, even royal applause. The Kongelige Teater became a state institution, with its director accountable to the Minister of Culture, when King Frederick VII renounced his autocracy in 1849.

Soon a second Kongelige Teater was built next to the first. This Royal Theater ranked with Europe's classical theaters such as the Burgtheater in Vienna and Théâtre Français in Paris. Little has changed since the theater opened in 1874, except for the addition of a revolving stage in 1930. Five years later, a special law known as *Lov om Kulturel Fond* (Cultural Fund Act) was passed, designating the theater as Denmark's national theater and turning it into a heavily subsidized government institution.

Around the same time, the annex was built across the street in the Radio House and connected by a bridge to Det Kongelige Teater. Unfortunately, operating two stages did not work out, and the Radio House reclaimed its stage. It was not until 1957, after much rebuilding, that the right formula was found for both stages to operate successfully. However, this resulted in great name confusion, so new names were given to both houses: the original Kongelige Teater was called Gamle Scene (Old Stage), and the annex was called Nye Scene (New Stage).

ble pilasters topped by gold capitals, is encircled by white marble busts of the theater's artists on black marble pedestals. In the center spot stands a larger-than-life white marble statue of the actress Johanne Luise Heiberg. The Gamle Scene seats 1,536. The Nye Scene, looking like a poor relative next to the Gamle Scene, seats 1,091.

The Theater

Statues of Holberg and Adam Oehlenschläger guard the entrance to the Gamle Scene, which faces a small park where there is a statue of Frederick V astride his horse. On gala occasions, torches are placed on the roof, where they blaze into the nighttime sky. The auditorium, decorated in gold, white, and red velvet, boasts four horseshoe-shaped tiers, a canopied royal box, and busts of composers, poets, and philosophers as adornment. Over the proscenium the words "*Ei Blot Til Lyst*" (Not Only for Pleasure) are etched, and Muses gaze down on the audience from overhead. The curtain, painted by C. F. Aagaard and Otto Bache in 1874, shows an idealized Acropolis landscape, which becomes visible as several cherubs pull the curtain aside. The gold grand foyer, adorned with copper-colored mar-

Performance History

Operas first saw the stage in Copenhagen in the mid-1600s: Caspar Förster's *Il Cadmo* was performed in 1663. Twenty-six years later, Paul C. Schindler's *Der vereinigte Götterstreit* took place. The wooden theater in which it was playing caught fire, killing 180 people. Amalienborg Palace sits on the site today. Reinhard Keiser's *Ulysses* was premiered in 1722 to commemorate Frederick IV's birthday, and the birth of Prince Christian in 1749 was celebrated with the première of Christoph Willibald Gluck's *La contesa dei numi*.

One of the first operas to grace the stage at the Kongelige Teater was Scalabrini's *L'amor premiato* (under the Danish title, *Den belønnede Kærlighed*) in 1758. The opera fare was mainly French (Jean-Baptiste Lully, Jean-Philippe

Façade of Gamle Scene at night (Courtesy of Det Kongelige Teater, Photo by Mydtskov)

Auditorium, Gamle Scene (Courtesy of Det Kongelige Teater Informationsafdelingen)

Die Zauberflöte (Courtesy of Det Kongelige Teater, Photo by Mydtskov)

Rameau, François-André Philidor, Pierre-Alexandre Monsigny, and André Grétry) and Italian (Giovanni Battista Pergolesi and Niccolò Piccinni). But many Danes did not embrace the artificial style of the performances. One in particular, Johan Herman Wessel, presented his sentiments in the burlesque *Kærlighed uden Strømper* (Love without Stockings) in 1773. Six years later, the première of Hartmann's Singspiel, *Balders Død*, took place, followed by *Fiskerne* in 1780.

Danish opera was officially born in 1786, when Johann Gottlieb Naumann's *Orpheus og Euridice* was staged. The world première of F. L. A. Kunzen's *Holger Danske* followed on March 31, 1789. Kunzen became the theater's director in 1795, introducing Wolfgang Amadeus Mozart operas, followed with operas by Gaetano Donizetti, Vincenzo Bellini, and Gioacchino Rossini. By the nineteenth century,

Singspiel was firmly rooted in the repertory, and several of Christoph Ernst Weyse's works were premiered: *Sovedrikken* in 1809; *Faruk* in 1812; *Ludlams Hule* in 1816, and *Et Eventyr i Rosenborg Have* in 1827. November 6, 1828, saw the world première of Kuhlau's *Elverhøj*, a "national musical comedy," and Jenny Lind first sang at the Royal Theater in 1843, causing a sensation. Three years later, the world première of Hartmann's *Liden Kirsten* appeared on May 12.

Shortly after the new Kongelige Teater opened, Peter Heise's *Drot og Marsk* was world premiered on September 25, 1878. Ten years later, C. F. E. Horneman's *Alladdin* graced the stage. In 1892, August Enna's *Heksen* was mounted, followed by *Den lille Pige med Svolvstikkerne* in 1897.

Danish opera achieved greater prominence in the beginning of the twentieth century with the world premières of Carl Nielsen's *Saul og*

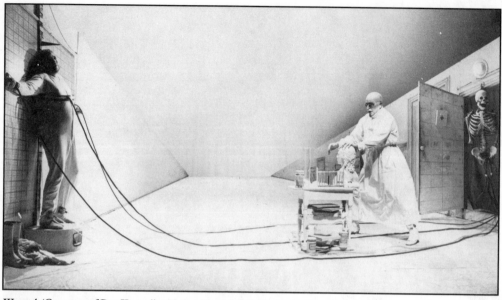

Wozzeck (Courtesy of Det Kongelige Teater, Photo by Mydtskov)

David on November 28, 1902, and his *Maskarade* on November 11, 1906. *Saul og David*, based on the Old Testament and rich with oratorio-like music, was a grand opera in the true sense of the word. *Maskarade* was of a totally different genre: an eighteenth-century Danish-style opera buffa set to a Holberg comedy. It has been said that Nielsen composed both operas (except the third act of *Maskarade*) while he played second violin in the Royal Orchestra between 1889 and 1905. Three years later he was appointed *chef d'orchestre*, a position he held until 1914. During his tenure, on March 6, 1909, the world première of Georg Høeberg's *Et Bryllup i Katakomberne* took place. Høeberg succeeded Nielsen and conducted the first complete *Der Ring des Nibelungen* given at the theater.

Lauritz Melchior, unquestionably the greatest Wagnerian tenor of the twentieth century, made his debut on April 2, 1913, as a baritone singing Silvio in Ruggero Leoncavallo's *Pagliacci*. He appeared as a baritone in many performances before touring Sweden with Mme. Charles Cahier. She persuaded him to retrain his voice as a tenor, so Melchior studied with Wilhelm

Herold, the reigning tenor at Det Kongelige Teater from 1893 to 1915, and made his second debut on October 8, 1918, as a tenor singing the title role in *Tannhäuser*.

In 1931, Johan Hye-Knudsen took the helm. Four years later, he reset Giuseppe Verdi's *Un ballo in maschera* in eighteenth-century Sweden, almost two decades before Stockholm's Kungliga Teater relocated the opera. Then on April 9, 1940, the Nazis occupied Denmark and a dark chapter in Danish history unfolded. To boost morale, Danish national operas were revitalized, and contemporary operas, many of which were banned by the Nazis, were performed during the late afternoon, because of wartime curfews.

Since the war, an impressive variety of operas has been staged, with comic operas leading the list of most frequently performed works. International stars like Birgit Nilsson, Giuseppe di Stefano, and Victoria de los Angeles have delighted the audience with their guest appearances. However, most productions are performed by repertory singers.

I saw an amusing production of Mozart's

Figaros Bryllup (*Le nozze di Figaro*), with Sten Byriel as Figaro, Grith Fjeldmose as Susanna, and Tadeusz Wojciechowski conducting. Although the singing was adequate, it was in Danish and took some getting used to before I could enjoy the performance.

PRACTICAL INFORMATION
Tickets

The box offices (*billetkontor*) for both Gamle Scene and Nye Scene are located inside the lobby of the Gamle Scene, Kongens Nytorv 9. The box office on the right side of the lobby sells tickets for Gamle Scene and on the left side for Nye Scene. The box offices are open Monday through Saturday from 12:00 noon to 5:00 p.m. and on performance days from 12:00 noon to 8:00 p.m. Box offices are closed Sundays. (*Åbningstid: mandag-lørdag kl. 12.00-17.00; dagens forestilling: kl. 12.00-20.00. Billetkontorerne er lukket på søndage.*) Next to the box office windows are brochures that contain detailed seating plans of both Gamle Scene and Nye Scene, enabling you to point to the exact seat you want. There is also a list of operas scheduled for the next two months. You can buy tickets for performances beginning three weeks ahead.

Tickets can be reserved by mail. The box office accepts reservations for the entire season from anyone living outside Copenhagen. Payment must be sent with your order. Include either a bank draft for the amount in Danish krone or the number and expiration date of your credit card. If the ticket price is more (premières, galas, and guest soloist performances are more

expensive), you will be notified. You will receive acknowledgment of your reservation. One month before the performance, your seat will be assigned. Tickets must be picked up one hour before the performance. Send your requests for both Gamle Scene and Nye Scene to:

Det Kongelige Teater
Billetkontoret
Postboks 2185
1017 Copenhagen, Denmark

Tickets can be ordered by phone at (45) 3314-1002 up to three weeks in advance. (45) = country code. Denmark does not use city codes. Call Monday through Saturday from 12:00 noon to 5:00 p.m. Denmark is six hours ahead of Eastern Standard Time.

The ticket table is quite detailed, as several different seating sections fall under similar price groups.

If you avoid the guest soloist performances, premières, and galas, you will not have any trouble buying tickets. If you want to attend one of the most desirable performances, write for tickets as early as possible. If a performance has *lukket forestilling* (closed performance) or *udsolgt* (sold out) next to it, think of another date.

To help you understand your ticket, a translation of one appears below. There are no ushers.

Operas usually begin at 8:00 p.m. (*kl. 20,00*), although longer operas start earlier. Unfortunately, people are still allowed to enter during the performances. The opera schedule for the month, with starting times, is listed in the English-language brochure *Copenhagen This Week*.

TICKET TRANSLATION

Det. Kgl. Teater		The Royal Theater	
Nye Scene		New Stage	
1. Parket		**1st Section Orchestra**	
9 Rk.	**Nr. 13**	**Row 9**	**Seat 13**
4. Febr. 1987	Kl. 20,00	February 4, 1987	8 P.M.
Pris: 130 Kr.		(Price)	

175

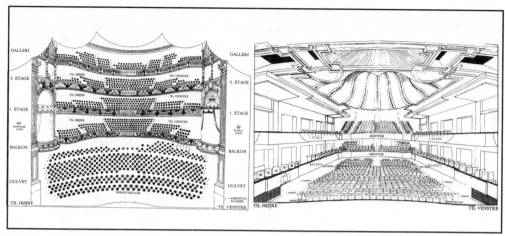

Seating Plan Gamle Scene (Courtesy of Det Kongelige Teater)

Seating Plan Nye Scene (Courtesy of Det Kongelige Teater)

TICKET TABLES
Gamle Scene

Seating Locations	Prices in Dkr.
Prisgruppe A	170

Gulvet 1.-2. ork.rk. (orchestra center seats 1,2)
Gulvet 1.-8. rk. (orchestra rows 1-8)
Balkon 1.-4. rk. midtfor (tier 1 rows 1-4 center)
Balkon 1.-2. rk. th. og tv. (tier 1 rows 1,2 both sides)

Prisgruppe B	140

Gulvet 9.-13. rk. (orchestra rows 9-13)
Balkon 5.-6. rk. midtfor (tier 1 rows 5,6 center)
Balkon 3.-4. rk.th.og tv. (tier 1 rows 3,4 both sides)
1.Etage 1.-2. rk. midtfor (tier 2 rows 1.2 center)
1.Etage 1. rk. th. og tv. (tier 2 row 1 both sides)

Prisgruppe C	80

Gulvet 14.-17. rk. (orchestra rows 14-17)
Balkon 3. rk. nr. 42-54 (tier 1 row 3 seats 42-54 ex.side) (even)
Balkon 3. rk. nr. 41-49 (tier 1 row 3 seats 41-49 ex.side) (odd)
1.Etage 3.-5 rk. midtfor (tier 2 rows 3-5 center)
1.Etage 2.-3. rk.th.og tv (tier 2 rows 2-3 both sides)
2.Etage 1.-2. rk. midtfor (tier 3 rows 1,2 center)
2.Etage 2. rk.th.og tv (tier 3 row 2 both sides)

Prisgruppe D	40

1.Etage 2. rk. nr. 42-54 (tier 2 row 2 seats 42-54) (even)
1.Etage 2. rk. nr. 41-53 (tier 2 row 2 seats 41-53) (odd)
2.Etage 3.-5. rk. midtfor (tier 3 rows 3-5 center)
2.Etage 2.-3. rk.th.og tv (tier 3 rows 2,3 both sides)
Galleri 1.-3. rk. midtfor (gallery rows 1-3 center)
Galleri 1. rk.th.og tv (gallery row 1 both sides)

Prisgruppe E	30

2.Etage 2.rk. nr. 42-46/56-58 (tier 3 row 2 seats 42-46/56-58) (even)
2.Etage 2.rk. nr. 43-47/57-59 (tier 3 row 2 seats 43-47/57-59) (odd)
Galleri 2.-5. rk.th.og tv (gallery rows 2-5 both sides)

continued

Nye Scene

Seating Locations	Prices in Dkr.
Prisgruppe A	130

1. Parket 1.-3. ork.rk. (front orchestra center seats 1-3)
1. Parket 1.-9. rk. (orchestra rows 1-9)
Balkon 1.-9. rk. tv. (tier 1 rows 1-9 left side)
Balkon 9.-18. rk. th. (tier 1 rows 9-18 right side)
Balkon 1.-3. rk. midtfor (tier 1 rows 1-3 center)

Prisgruppe B	100

2. Parket 1.-7. rk. (mid-orchestra rows 1-7)
Balkon 4.-6. rk. th. og tv. (tier 1 rows 4-6 both sides)

Prisgruppe C	70

1. Etage 10.-18. rk. th. og tv. (tier 2 rows 10-18 both sides)
1. Etage 1.-4. rk. midtfor (tier 2 rows 1-4 center)

Prisgruppe D	30

1. Etage 5.-8 rk. midtfor (tier 2 rows 5-8 center)

Prisgruppe E	20

1. Etage 9. rk. midtfor (tier 2 row 9 [last row] center)

$1 = 7 Dkr., but can vary due to the fluctuating value of the dollar.
Dkr. is an abbreviation for Danish krone. It is also abbreviated kr.

Finding Your Way

Gamle Scene faces Kongens Nytorv (a huge, busy traffic circle surrounding a small park), bordered by Tordenskjoldsgade on the east and Holmens Kanal on the west. Nye Scene is joined to Gamle Scene by a bridge over Tordenskjoldsgade. Heibergsgade borders Nye Scene on the south. You can reach both theaters on the following buses: 1, 6, 7, 9, 10, 17, 28, 29, 31, and 41.

The main entrance to the Gamle Scene is at Kongens Nytorv 9. The main entrance to Nye Scene is at Tordenskjoldsgade 3. It is difficult to miss the entrance to the Gamle Scene, but the entrance to the Nye Scene is so unpretentious that it is easy to walk right past.

Enter the Gamle Scene through one of the three arched doorways. If you are seated in the *gulvet* (orchestra), *balkon* (1st tier), *1.etage* (2nd tier), or *2.etage* (3rd tier), continue through the entrance foyer and up the stairs. Even numbers (*lige*) are on the right side (*til højre*), and odd numbers (*ulige*) are on the left side (*til venstre*). In the *gulvet*, the rows stretch unbroken across the auditorium. Therefore it is crucial to enter on the correct side. Seats 1, 2 are in the center

of each row with the numbers increasing sequentially to the aisles. Doors lead into the *gulvet* between rows 3 and 4 and rows 11 and 12. Continue up the stairs for the *balkon*, *1.etage*, and *2.etage*. The seat numbering is similar to the *gulvet*.

Programs are for sale in the entrance foyer and cost kr. 12.00. Programs (in Danish) contain pictures of the production and articles about the opera. Cloakrooms (*garderobe*) are on the *1.etage*, as are the men's room (*herrer*), ladies' room (*damer*), and bar. The restaurant is on the *2.etage*. *Smørrebrød* (open sandwiches) must be ordered ahead.

The Gamle Scene has a wheelchair ramp from the street level to the entrance hall, where there are elevators that go to all levels except the *galleri*. There are four places for wheelchairs (*kørestolsplad*) in the *gulvet*. Ask for those tickets at the box office.

The entrance to the Nye Scene is through glass doors. Straight ahead are the stairs leading up to the mezzanine, where you will find exhibitions relating to the theater. Unfortunately, the explanations are only in Danish, so it is difficult to comprehend what the exhibition is about. Continue up a second flight to the *parkett/parterre*. Even numbers (*lige*) are on the right (*til højre*), and odd numbers (*ulige*) are on the left (*til venstre*). The seats stretch in unbroken rows across the auditorium. Seats 1, 2 are in the center, with seat numbers increasing sequentially from the center out to the aisles. If you are seated in the *balkon* or *1.etage* continue up the stairs. The first six seats on the extreme right side of the *balkon* are reserved for royalty.

Finding your way in the Nye Scene can be confusing, and there are no ushers. But persevere, and sooner or later a kindly opera patron will notice your bewilderment and show you where your seat is (which is exactly what happened to me).

Programs are for sale in the entrance foyer and cost kr. 12.00. The program (in Danish) contains pictures of the production and articles about the opera. A huge coat check operation (*garderobe*) is on the left in the entrance hall. Since the rows are very narrow, you should check your coat and packages. Some people do not, which presents an obstacle course to those seated farther on in the row. The men's room (*herrer*) and ladies' (*damer*) room are on the mezzanine level to the right and left of the staircase, where you will also find a bar. Coffee service is available in the entrance foyer. For visually impaired patrons, both theaters offer an audiocassette of the printed program (kr. 12.00) in Danish.

Planning Your Trip
OPERA SCHEDULE
The season runs from the beginning of September through the end of May. The 1990/91 season opened on September 1 with a ballet. Mozart's *Die Zauberflöte* followed four days later. The season closes on May 31 with Mozart's *Le nozze di Figaro*. The repertory ranges from very early baroque opera to contemporary pieces with special emphasis on Danish composers. Niel-

sen's *Maskarade*, Richard Wagner's *Parsifal* and *Der fliegende Holländer*, Mozart's *Così fan tutte* and *Don Giovanni*, Verdi's *Otello* and *I vespri siciliani*, Jacques Offenbach's *Les contes d'Hoffmann*, Giacomo Puccini's *La bohème* and *Tosca*, Alban Berg's *Wozzeck*, Rossini's *Il barbiere di Siviglia*, and Dimitri Shostakovich's *Ledi Makbet Mtsenskovo uyezda* (Lady Macbeth of the Mtsensk District) complete the season.

The Gamle Scene and Nye Scene are repertory houses with different works performed each evening. There are performances every day except Sunday. Opera shares the stage with ballet, musicals, comedy, and drama. If you have a choice, see your opera at the Gamle Scene.

To be sure your visit coincides with an opera, write ahead for the season's schedule. (A ticket order form with instructions in English is attached to the schedule.) Write to:

Det Kongelige Teater
Billetkontoret
Postboks 2185
1017 Copenhagen, Denmark

TRAVEL INFORMATION
Two good hotels are within a five-minute walk of the theaters. At the five-star Hotel d'Angleterre, 34 Kgs. Nytorv, 1050 Copenhagen, singles start at $250 and doubles at $300. At the appropriately named Hotel Opera, Tordenskjoldsgade 15, 1055 Copenhagen, singles are $150, doubles $180.

There is a restaurant at the Gamle Scene, but you must telephone ahead for reservations. You have a wide choice of eating places a few blocks away on the *fodgængerzone* (walking street).

The Scandinavian National Tourist Offices, 655 Third Avenue, New York, NY 10017, 212-949-2333, can send you travel information and opera schedules, but write very far ahead. They take more than two months to respond, even to faxed requests.

France

Allegorical sculpture in front of façade, Opéra Garnier (Photo by author)

PARIS
Opéra de Paris Garnier
Opéra de Paris Bastille

The majestic Théatre National de l'Opéra, now called Opéra de Paris Garnier, was inaugurated on January 5, 1875, with a glorious program. Excerpts from Daniel François Auber's *La Muette de Portici*, Jacques-François Halévy's *La Juive*, Gioacchino Rossini's *Guillaume Tell*, Giacomo Meyerbeer's *Les Huguenots*, and Léo Delibes's ballet *La Source* regaled the gala opening night crowd, which included the newly elected president of the Third Republic, Maréchal de MacMahon, and his wife, Madame la Maréchal. The president and his wife arrived in a state coach drawn by four black horses and accompanied by two hundred cavalrymen wearing cuirasses. Although the architect, Charles Garnier, had designed the opera house in the style of and for the Second Empire, by the time the Théatre National de l'Opéra, also known as Palais Garnier, opened, France was the Third Republic.

More than one hundred years later, a new opera house, Opéra de Paris Bastille, opened. Surrounded by controversy and personnel upheavals, the Opéra Bastille was inaugurated on the eve of Bastille Day 1989. President François Mitterand invited his fellow chiefs of state from around the world for a private inaugural concert. The opera house, designed by Canadian architect Carlos Ott, has been criticized by some for looking like a "beached ocean liner" but praised by others as embodying opera for the twenty-first century.

HISTORICAL OVERVIEW
Background

It was a chilly evening on January 14, 1858, when Emperor Napoleon III and the empress were riding to l'Opéra on rue le Peletier to attend a gala performance. The theater's façade was brilliantly lit by hundreds of gas lights. Suddenly three thunderous bomb explosions pierced the air—the work of Italian anarchist Felice Orsini, who was not happy with the revival of the Second Empire or Napoleon III. Although Napoleon escaped any physical harm, he was severely shaken by the attempt and ordered a new opera house built, even though there were three other opera houses in Paris at the time: Théâtre Italien, Théâtre Lyrique, and Opéra-Comique.

An open competition for the best design attracted 175 submissions, from which Charles Garnier's drawings were chosen. Fortunately, he was only thirty-five years old at the time, since fourteen years elapsed before the opera house was completed. Problems cropped up almost immediately after the foundation stone was laid in 1861. First, a subterranean lake was discovered which took eight months to drain. Then soft ground required the construction of a double concrete foundation. Finally, the façade was unveiled on August 15, 1867. Three years later, construction was halted when France declared war on Prussia. France was defeated, and the Second Empire crumbled and was replaced by the Third Republic. While all this was going on, the unfinished opera house served successively as a hospital, a military storage place, and a prison.

Twenty-one years after the theater opened in 1875, calamity struck during the first act of *Thétis et Pelée*. A dreadful crash drowned out Rose Caron's voice: the massive crystal chandelier had broken loose, plummeting into the orchestra and crushing the unfortunate woman seated beneath it.

After the armistice on November 11, 1918, many VIPs and members of the royalty visited l'Opéra: Woodrow Wilson, General John Joseph Pershing, Henri Philippe Pétain, King Albert I of Belgium, and the Queen of Romania. Then the glory of l'Opéra faded. Although the Palais Garnier kept its doors open during World War II, due partly to France's collaboration with the Nazis and the Nazis' desire for some high-brow culture, air raid sirens turned many a marathon opera into a short story.

Since World War II, the prestige of l'Opéra has had its share of ups and downs (mainly downs). On the eve of July 14, 1989, the Palais Garnier relinquished the role it had played for more than a century, that of prima donna of the Paris opera, to the Opéra Bastille. Conceived at the end of the Second Empire when opera was for the rich and privileged, Palais Garnier could not adequately serve as a popular opera house for the next century. However, Palais Garnier, which the Paris Ballet now calls home, remains a shrine to Napoleon III and a witness to both the prosperity and extravagance of his regime.

The first proposal for a new, state-of-the-art opera house surfaced in 1968. Nine years later, the proposal was reaffirmed, and near the end of 1981, a study was commissioned to investigate the feasibility of the project. Finally on March 8, 1982, President François Mitterand announced the building of a new opera house on the Place de la Bastille. In November 1982, an international architectural competition was launched, attracting 1,650 entrants. By the deadline on May 13, 1983, 756 projects were received and submitted to the jury. On July 5, the jury sub-mitted six projects to Mitterand, who on November 17 selected the *Lauréat du concours* (winner of the competition): Carlos Ott. The budget was set at the equivalent of $400 million, and the bicentennial of the storming of the Bastille was chosen as the target opening date.

That turned out to be only the prologue to a tale filled with more treachery than *Götterdämmerung* and more drama than *Le Prophète*:

September 1985: Gérard Mortier, head of the Théâtre de la Monnaie in Brussels was appointed director of the Opéra-Bastille project. He planned a season of 200 to 250 performances in the Grande Salle. January 1986: Mortier quit after the brewing French political intrigues grew too hot for him. April 1986: new Prime Minister Jacques Chirac wanted to abandon the project completely, but Culture Minister François Léotard saved it. Summer 1986: Finance Minister Edouard Balladur suspended construction during the latter half of July, causing losses of 750,000 francs a day until the work resumed. August 1987: Daniel Barenboïm was appointed artistic and musical director, and Pierre Vozlinsky was named general director. March 1988: Barenboïm and Vozlinsky announced the first season would open on January 10, 1990, with a Barenboïm/Chéreau production of Wolfgang Amadeus Mozart's *Don Giovanni*. A total of 72 productions in 1990 and 120 in 1991 were planned. May 1988: Barenboïm signed a contract for $1.1 million and Vozlinsky was dismissed. August 31, 1988: Pierre Bergé (of Yves Saint Laurent fashion fame) was put in charge. January 13, 1989: Bergé fired Barenboïm. A short time later, conductor Pierre Boulez quit, commenting, "I cannot work with nonprofessionals." Patrice Chéreau followed suit, adding, "The whole thing makes me want to throw up." Their actions set off numerous lawsuits. May 1989: Myung-Whun Chung was appointed the new music director. July 13, 1989: the Opéra Bastille opened. August 1989: General Director René Gonzalèz resigned. March 17, 1990: Opéra Bastille staged its first opera. Stay tuned.

Façade of Opéra Garnier (Photo by author)

The Theaters

The Palais Garnier, with **Académie Nationale de Musique, Poésie Lyrique**, and **Chorégraphie** carved in its façade, is covered with pigeon droppings that detract from its grandeur. The neoclassical exterior, with busts of Auber, Ludwig van Beethoven, Mozart, Gasparo Spontini, Meyerbeer, Halévy, and Rossini looking out from between pairs of Corinthian columns and medallions of Giovanni Battista Pergolesi, Joseph Haydn, Johann Bach, and Domenico Cimarosa guarding the entrances, hints at the lavishness inside. Saturated with marble, onyx, bronze, gold, and precious woods, the interior boasts vestibules, salons, and foyers draped with velvet brocades and lined with mirrors, columns, and sculptures. Crystal chandeliers, hung from exquisitely embellished ceilings, illuminate the spaces. The crimson and gold auditorium, originally brightened by a 9,000-gaslight crystal chandelier, boasted a stage so large that the entire Comédie-Française could fit on it. The auditorium ceiling, originally painted by Jules-Eugène Lenepveu, was repainted in 1962 by Marc Chagall. It was a formidable task for the seventy-five-year-old Russian painter, because the ceiling covered more than 2,100 square feet. The result was his famous *Bouquet de rêves*. The theater seats 2,156.

Detail of façade (Photo by author)

183

Façade with "grand staircase," Opéra Bastille
(Photo by author)

Performance History

Italian opera was performed as early as 1604 in Paris, when Giulio Caccini's *Euridice* had its French première. With the marriage of Louis XIII to the Spanish Infanta in 1612, ballet took center stage until Francesco Sacrati's *La finta pazza* was given in 1645 at the Salle du Petit Bourbon. The next year, Francesco Cavalli's *Egisto* appeared, followed by Luigi Rossi's *Orfeo* in 1647. Three years later, the first French work, Dassoucy's *Andromède*, was staged.

On June 28, 1669, Louis XIV granted Robert Cambert, Abbé Pierre Perrin, and Marquis de Sourdéac the right to establish the Académie de Musique, which was opened at the Salle du Jeu de Paume de la Bouteille with Robert Cambert's *Pomone* on March 3, 1671. The following year, Jean-Baptiste Lully bought the license from Perrin, who was thrown into debtors' prison, and ushered in the first great period in French opera. His pastoral pastiche *Les Fêtes de l'Amour et de Bacchus* was premiered in 1672, followed by his first *tragédie lyrique*, *Cadmus et Hermione*, in 1673, the same year the Académie moved into the Grand Salle du Palais Royale. Lully's operas appeared almost annually until his death: *Alceste*, *Thésée*, *Atys*, *Isis*, *Psyché*, *Bellérophon*, *Proserpine*, *Persée*, *Phaëton*, *Amadis de Gaule*, *Roland*, *Armide et Renaud*, *Acis et Galatée*, and *Achille et Polyxène* (completed by Collasse). On December 4, 1693, M. A. Charpentier's *Médée* was introduced.

On October 1, 1733, the second great period in French opera arrived with the première of Jean-Phillipe Rameau's *Hippolyte et Aricie*. By 1760, twenty-four of his operas had been produced, including *Les Indes galantes* on August 23, 1735, *Castor et Pollux* in 1737, *Dardanus* on November 19, 1739, *Platée* in 1745, *Les Fêtes de l'Hymen et de l'Amour* in 1747, *Zoroastre* in 1749, *Acante et Céphise* in 1751, *Zephire* and *Anacréon* in 1754, and *Les Paladins* in 1760. Rameau's works were complex and cerebral, totally unappreciated by the followers of the Italian school. This resulted in a great controversy known as the

The Opéra Bastille is an immense conglomeration of granite, stainless steel, and glass meshed together in a striking configuration, which is unfortunately already marred by graffiti and garbage. Ott chose those materials because they blended with the Paris color scheme. A huge square arch soars above the entrance, through which the outside "grand staircase" passes. The glass façade allows the glorious Paris skyline to fuse with the interior ambience, lending a majestic feeling to the semicircular colonnade foyers. A small transition room, similar to Det Muziektheater in Amsterdam, and sandwiched between two heavy pearwood doors, conveys you from the sights and sounds of Paris to the world of *Les Troyens* or *Samson et Dalila*, which you journey to in curved, black steel, velvet, and pearwood seats. The burgundy and white auditorium offers two steeply raked balconies, served by precipitous staircases. The walls, covered with Breton granite, are complemented by oak floors traversed with smooth granite gangways. The ceiling, looking like undulating waves of light, is a collection of glass pieces with differing diffraction and diffusion characteristics. The blue Cy Twombly-designed curtain with winding white trails covers a stage equipped with the most advanced technical facilities available. The Grande Salle accommodates 2,700.

1st balcony foyer and staircase, Opéra Bastille (Courtesy of NORR, Photo by Ferré)

Top: Opéra Bastille facing Rue de Lyon (Courtesy of NORR, Photo by Ferré)
Bottom: Auditorium (Grand Salle), Opéra Bastille (Courtesy of NORR, Photo by Ferré)

querelle des bouffons (quarrel of the clowns). More than a decade later, Christoph Willibald Gluck came to Paris, where he experienced similar antagonism from the adherents of the Italian school when he tried to produce his *Iphigénie en Aulide*. The première, which took place on April 19, 1774, might never have occurred without the personal intervention of Marie Antoinette. His *Armide* was introduced on September 23, 1777. But Gluck's enemies did not give up. They invited the celebrated Italian composer Niccolò Piccinni to Paris for a contest of sorts. The director of l'Opéra commissioned both Gluck and Piccinni to write an opera based on the same libretto. Gluck's opera *Iphigénie en Tauride* was premiered on May 18, 1779. It was such a smashing success that Piccinni tried to withdraw his opera but was prevented from doing so. His *Iphigénie en Tauride*, introduced a short time later, achieved only a fraction of the popularity of Gluck's version. Finally, the opera war was over, with Gluck's and Rameau's styles vindicated. Ironically, Gluck's last opera for Paris, *Echo et Narcisse*, introduced in 1779, was considered a failure.

During the Revolution, l'Opéra was closed. When it reopened, Louis XVI and Marie Antoinette had lost their heads and Maria Luigi Cherubini and Gasparo Spontini were beginning to set the grand opera style. Cherubini's *Anacréon* was premiered in 1803, and Spontini's *La Vestale* followed four years later on December 15. His *Fernand Cortez* was introduced on November 28, 1809. Rossini's *Le Siège de Corinthe* graced the stage for the first time on October 9, 1826, followed by his *Le Comte Ory* on August 20, 1828. Auber's *La Muette de Portici*, the opera that sparked the Belgian revolt against Dutch rule, was introduced on February 29, 1828, and Rossini's *Guillaume Tell* on August 3, 1829.

French grand opera blossomed on November 21, 1831, with the world première of Meyerbeer's *Robert le Diable*. Halévy's *La Juive* followed on February 23, 1835, Meyerbeer's *Les Huguenots* on February 29, 1836, Hector Berlioz's *Benvenuto Cellini* on September 10, 1838, and Gaetano Donizetti's *La favorite* on December 2, 1840. *Le Prophète*, one of Meyerbeer's most spectacular operas, graced the stage for the first time on April 16, 1849, followed by the première of Charles Gounod's *Sapho* on April 16, 1851. Giuseppe Verdi was commissioned by l'Opéra to compose *Les Vêpres Siciliennes*, which turned into an unpalatable burden. He tried unsuccessfully to be released from his contract, and the première took place on June 13, 1855. Meyerbeer's last spectacular opera, *L'Africaine*, was staged posthumously on April 28, 1865, followed by Verdi's magnificent *Don Carlos* on March 11, 1867, composed for the Exposition of 1867. *Don Carlos* was Verdi's last work for Paris. He refused to compose again for *La Grande Boutique*, as he sarcastically called l'Opéra. Amboise Thomas's grandiose *Hamlet* saw its first light on March 9, 1868.

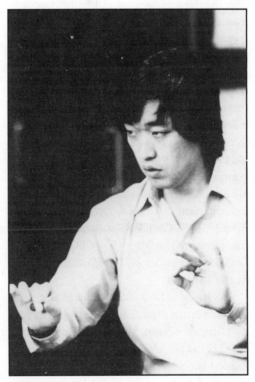

Myung-Whun Chung, music director Opéra Bastille (Courtesy of Teatro Comunale di Firenze archives)

During the Second Empire, the pomp and grandeur of the regime was reflected in the continuing tradition of grand opera, which required five spectacular acts, huge choruses, and a ballet. However, the *abonnés* (subscribers) practically ran the show, their mistresses and lovers influencing the casting and choice of repertory and the Jockey Club members booing any performance they did not like. Ballets could not be performed before the second act and "balletless" operas acquired a ballet. (Several members supported ballerinas and wanted to see them perform.) Richard Wagner experienced their wrath firsthand when he refused to move the erotic Venusberg ballet to the second act of *Tannhäuser*. When the Jockey Club members arrived, all the seductive spells of Venusberg had been cast, and the virginal valley of the Wartburg had taken center stage. They were furious and caterwauled it off the stage. Wagner had to withdraw his opera after the third performance. The 1891 performance of his *Lohengrin* did not fare much better. It was greeted with stink bombs, both inside and outside the theater. The Shah of Persia benefited from the *abonnés'* regulations, however. He visited the opera house in 1889, and, although he slept through the singing, he intently watched the ballet, inviting a couple of ballerinas to join him afterward in his private quarters.

On April 5, 1876, at the newly opened Palais Garnier, Mermet's *Jeanne d'Arc* was the first complete opera performed. The world première of Jules Massenet's *Le Roi de Lahore* followed on April 27, 1877. Camille Saint-Saëns's *Henri VIII* was introduced on March 5, 1883, Massenet's *Le Cid* on November 30, 1885, and his *Thaïs* on March 16, 1894.

Beginning in 1905, the *chef d'orchestre*'s name was listed on the poster and in the program. Two years later, a conductor's stand found its way into the orchestra pit. Until that time, the conductor had led the performance sitting next to the prompter's box, with his back to the orchestra. He only faced the musicians during the overture and intermezzo.

On January 13, 1909, the world première of Henri Février's *Monna Vanna* took place, followed by Igor Stravinsky's *The Nightingale* (under the French title *Le Rossignol*) on May 26, 1914, his *Mavra* on June 3, 1922, and his *Persephone* on April 30, 1934. Darius Milhaud's *Maximilien* was premiered on January 5, 1932. In 1939, all theaters were placed under state supervision, in a nebulous organization called Réunion des Théâtres Lyriques Nationaux. Eventually, the bureaucratic red tape took its toll, and by 1968, the need for drastic change was indisputable as the international circuit singers deserted in droves, resulting in erratic casting and poor attendance. René Nicoly was appointed to reverse this alarming trend, but the task was overwhelming and he died a short time later. Then Rolf Liebermann was lured from the Staatsoper Hamburg in 1973 to restore l'Opéra to its former glory. With a huge budget, he set about accomplishing the task by staging lavish productions of outstanding repertory works with world-renowned artists. The glory was short-lived. Problems reappeared as soon as Bernard Lefort succeeded Liebermann. Lefort resigned before his contract expired, claiming the position was a "thankless and burdensome task."

The bureaucratic methods that helped bring down the old house will remain at the Palais Garnier, and only time will tell if Opéra Bastille can place Paris once again in a prominent position in the operatic world. However, if the inauspicious beginnings at Opéra Bastille are any indication, it could take a long time. The opera originally scheduled to inaugurate the season, Mozart's *Don Giovanni*, was scrubbed. The first season was finally inaugurated on March 17, 1990, with Berlioz's *Les Troyens*. Leoš Janáček's *Kát'a Kabanová* was the only other opera performed, and it ended the season two months later. There were surtitles in both French and English.

PRACTICAL INFORMATION
Tickets

The box office (*bureau de location*), at 120 rue de Lyon, the street bordering the west side of the opera house, is actually two glossy black rectangular boxes with silver-crossed windows that sit on either side of the curved entrance foyer. The box office windows (*guichets*) are open Monday through Saturday from 11:00 a.m. to 6:00 p.m. (*lundi-samedi de 11 h. à 18 h.*). Next to the window, a monitor displays a color-coded seating plan with corresponding color-coded ticket prices. Tickets can be purchased beginning fourteen days before each performance.

Unfortunately, the French are not very polite when waiting in line to buy tickets to an opera with a star-studded cast. If you want to keep your place in line, be prepared to push and shove. Otherwise every French person behind you will be standing in front of you before you get to the *guichet*.

Tickets can be ordered through the mail beginning two months before the first performance of the opera. Send your *bulletin de commande* (ticket order) to:

Opéra de Paris-Bastille
120 Rue de Lyon
75012 Paris, France

You can order tickets by telephoning (33)(1) 4001-1616 beginning one month before the first performance of the opera until five days before the specific performance. (33) = country code, (1) = city code. In France, dial (01)4001-1616. You should speak *en parfait français*. (Although the French massacre English, you know how they are with Americans speaking their language!) Paris is six hours ahead of Eastern Standard Time.

The different seating sections in the Grande Salle are: *parterre* (orchestra), 1er *balcon* (1st balcony), 2ème *balcon* (2nd balcony), and *galeries* (a few seats located on the right and left walls of the theater). The *parterre* offers seats in price Category I-VI; 1er *balcon* offers seats in Category I-V; 2ème *balcon* offers seats in Category III-V and the *galeries* in Category VI. The price categories accurately reflect the desirability of the row and seat.

Tickets are difficult to buy now, since everyone wants to visit the new opera house. Therefore, your best chance will be to the contemporary operas, which almost never sell out. Nearly every seat in the auditorium has a good view of the stage.

Your ticket will give you all the information you need to find your seat with no problem, so below is a translation of a sample ticket.

TICKET TRANSLATION

Opéra de Paris - Bastille	Opera of Paris - Bastille
Kát'a Kabanová	(Opera)
07/05/90 Porte 09 Allee H	May 7, 1990 Door 9 Aisle H
Lundi **19H30** **Rang** **Place**	**Monday** **7:30 P.M.** **Row** **Seat**
370 F **02** **21**	**(Price)** 2 21
Premier Balcon	First Balcony

TICKET TABLE

Cat I	Cat II	Cat III	Cat IV	Cat V	Cat VI
520 Fr.	470 Fr.	370 Fr.	190 Fr.	100 Fr.	40 Fr.

The prices are considerably higher for the premières of each opera.
$1 = 6 Fr., but may vary due to the fluctuating value of the dollar.
Fr. is an abbreviation for French franc.

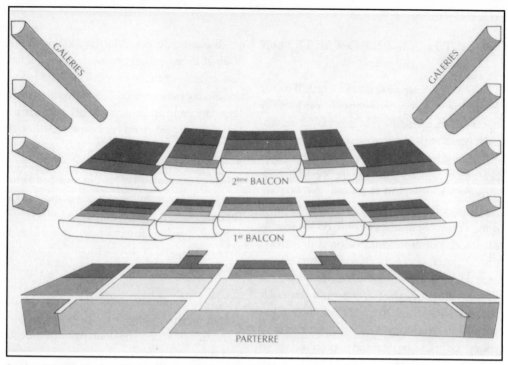

Seating Plan, Opéra Bastille (Courtesy of Opéra de Paris Bastille)

Seating Plan, Opéra Garnier (Courtesy of Opéra de Paris Garnier)

For the 1990/91 season, all the operas are scheduled to begin at 7:30 p.m. (19h30). However, in case of a last-minute change, check the *Paris-Sélection Loisirs*, because no one is admitted after the performance has started.

Opera can also be found at the Chatelet Théâtre Musical de Paris, 2 rue Edouard Colonne, 75001, telephone 4233-0000, located around a mile from Bastille.

Finding Your Way

Opéra de Paris Bastille faces the Place de la Bastille, bordered by rue de Lyon on the west and rue de Charenton on the east. It is located in the 12ᵉ arrondissement. You can reach the opera house with buses 20, 29, 65, 69, 76, 86, 87, and 91, exit Bastille, and by metro 1, 5, and 8, exit Bastille. A red, white, and blue corridor leads directly from the metro into the opera house on the rue de Lyon side.

The main entrance to the Opéra Bastille is at 2 bis, Place de la Bastille. The outside "grand staircase" leads into the grand foyer, *parterre* level. You will be at *porte* 2 on the right or *pair* (even) side. Match the *porte* number on your ticket with the number over the door, which will lead you to the correct *allée* (aisle). Doors 4, 6, and 8 are to the right, and doors 1, 3, 5, and 7 are on the left, or *impair* (odd), side. Seats 1 and 2 are in the center of the row with the numbers increasing sequentially (odd/even) to the side aisles. Seat numbers are underneath the seats so they disappear when the seats, which are thinly padded, are occupied. Staircases leading up to the 1ᵉʳ *balcon* (1st balcony) and 2ᵉᵐᵉ *balcon* are located on the right and left sides of the grand foyer. *Ascenseur* (elevators) are located at the extreme end. Every staircase, level, elevator, and door is clearly marked with signs and arrows.

You will find the *vestiaires* (cloakrooms) on both sides of the grand foyer. *Toilettes* for *dames* (ladies) and *messieurs* (men) are located at the right and left ends of the grand, 1st, and 2nd balcony foyers. Bars are located on the right and left

sides of the 1st balcony and the right side of the 2nd balcony. The entrance for disabled patrons is on the rue de Lyon side. Seats are reserved on both sides of the *parterre* for people in wheelchairs. Call ahead, 4001-1886, to inform them of your visit.

The Opéra de Paris Garnier, Place de l'Opéra, 75009, telephone (33)(1)4742-5371, is now the home for ballet. It overlooks the Place de l'Opéra with Boulevard des Italiens/Boulevard des Capucines passing in front. You can reach the opera house with metro 3, 7, and 8, exit Opéra, and buses 20, 21, 27, 29, 42, 52, 53, 66, 68, 81, and 95, exit Opéra. Tours are offered through the Palais Garnier. Call 4742-5750 for more information.

Planning Your Trip
OPERA SCHEDULE

The first full season, 1990/91, offers eight operas. The season opened on October 5 with a concert. The first opera, Verdi's *Otello* (new production), took place on November 13. The season closes on July 19 with Mozart's *Die Zauberflöte* (new production). Other new productions are Pyotr Il'yich Tchaikovsky's *Pikovaya dama* (The Queen of Spades), Giacomo Puccini's *Manon Lescaut*, and Saint-Saëns's *Samson et Dalila*. Mozart's *Le nozze di Figaro*, Luciano Berio's *Un Re in ascolto*, and Janáček's *Kát'a Kabanová* complete the schedule. Many titles are translated into French, so you might have to guess what opera you are going to see.

The Opéra de Paris Bastille operates as a *stagione* house, which means only one opera appears at a time. The opera shares the stage with concerts and recitals. To be sure your visit coincides with an opera, write ahead for a schedule, but do not be surprised if you do not get a response. Write to:

Opéra Bastille
120 rue de Lyon
75012 Paris, France

You can telephone (33)(1)4720-8898, twenty-four hours a day, for information about the Opéra Bastille in English. If you call from overseas, plan on a high telephone bill and expect to be disconnected, because you will be put on hold for a long time.

TRAVEL INFORMATION

The best hotel for operagoers is the Holiday Inn République, 10 Place de la République, 75541 Paris-Cedex 11, France; telephone (33)(1)4355-4434, fax (33)(1)4700-3234. Reservations can be made in the United States, toll-free, 1-800-465-4329. Singles start at $160, doubles at $210. A huge, delicious buffet breakfast is included. It is a delightful hotel with 333 rooms, ensconced in a fabulous Second Empire building boasting an ornamental Haussmann façade. For a special treat, request a room facing the courtyard. Over-looking the Place de la République in an interesting section of Paris, the hotel offers all the comforts of home. Only a few steps from the Metro République where line 8 runs directly to the Opéra Bastille, the Holiday Inn is thus only five minutes from the opera house. The concierge can assist you with tickets and information, which is a big advantage considering the unresponsiveness of the Opéra Bastille.

Many eating places have cropped up around the new opera house: on rue de Lyon, Fouquet's (expensive), and on Place de la Bastille, La Tour d'Argent (expensive), as well as several moderately priced pizza places and cafés.

Do not waste your time contacting the French Government Tourist Office, because they do not respond. I would suggest you ask your travel agent for travel information.

Façade and "grand staircase" of Opéra Bastille from Place de la Bastille (Courtesy of NORR, Photo by Ferré)

Great Britain

Falstaff with Yvonne Kenny and Claudio Desderi (Courtesy of Glyndebourne Festival Opera, Photo by Gravett)

LONDON
Royal Opera House, Covent Garden

The majestic Royal Opera House, originally known as the Royal Italian Opera House, was inaugurated on May 15, 1858, with a performance of Giacomo Meyerbeer's *Les Huguenots*, sung in Italian under its Italian title, *Gli Ugonotti*. The opening night gala, unlike the festive occasions of most opera house openings, was a disaster. First, the performance started very late because the operagoers could not find their seats. Second, the opera chosen to inaugurate the theater boasted five acts. Combining these two situations resulted in Sunday morning arriving before Act V, so the management canceled the last act "out of respect for the day of rest." Infuriated, the elegantly attired crowd stormed out of the theater. And Queen Victoria had not even bothered to attend. Designed by Edward Middleton Barry, the Royal Opera House was designated the national home for opera and ballet in 1946.

HISTORICAL OVERVIEW
Background

The Drury Lane Theater could be considered London's first opera house. Designed by Sir Christopher Wren, it opened in 1674. The opera house was joined in 1705 by the King's Theater, otherwise known as Haymarket Opera House. The King's Theater, destroyed by fire in 1789, was rebuilt and renamed Her Majesty's Theater when Queen Victoria ascended the throne in 1837.

Meanwhile John Gay's *The Beggar's Opera* opened on January 29, 1728, at the Lincoln Inn's Fields Theater. It was such a smashing hit that it enabled John Rich to pay the £5,650 price tag the first Theatre Royal at Covent Garden carried. William Congreve's *The Way of the World*, a comedy, inaugurated the theater on December 7, 1732. Designed by Edward Shepherd, it survived seventy-six years before fire gutted it on the morning of September 20, 1808. Twenty-five people along with Georg Friedrich Händel's organ perished in the blaze, believed to be caused by hot wadding lodged in the scenery from the previous night's performance. Within nine days, the management had resolved to rebuild the theater. The second Theatre Royal, designed by Robert Smirke and costing the astronomical sum of £187,888, opened in 1809. When the management tried to recoup its enormous monetary outlay by raising ticket prices, the public rebelled. Violent protests, known as the Old Price Riots, ensued. With the protesters ultimately victorious, the management was forced to roll back its ticket prices.

The first signs of Covent Garden's future as England's leading opera house surfaced in 1843, when Michael Costa, the opera music director at Her Majesty's Theater, moved his Royal Italian Opera Company to the Royal Theatre. The theater was reshaped into a form more compatible with grand opera and reopened in 1847 as the Royal Italian Opera House. The opera house lost lots of money during the first few years because of stiff competition from Her Majesty's Theater. Then calamity struck during the early morning hours of March 5, 1856. A masked ball, attended by a distinctly low-class crowd, was drawing to a close. As the orchestra was about to play "God Save the Queen," flames leaped across the room, sending the revelers fleeing in all directions. When dawn broke, only the outer walls were still standing.

Architect Edward Middleton Barry and builders Charles and Thomas Lucas of Lowestoft were hired almost immediately, but lack of money delayed the construction for more than a year. When building finally began, it proceeded in record time, with as many as 1,200 workers on the site during the last few months. The bill totaled £80,000, less than half the cost of building the second Covent Garden. Electricity was installed in 1891, and Edwin O. Sachs altered the theater between 1899 and 1901. The Royal Opera House closed its 1914 season on July 28, the same day Austria declared war on Serbia, starting World War I. The theater did not reopen until 1919. During World War II, the opera house saw duty as a dance hall for the troops.

In 1950-51, more remodeling took place. Around two decades later, a huge expansion program was initiated to extend the opera house west to James Street and south to Russell Street. Designed by GMW Partnerships, the first phase was completed in 1982, the same year the Royal Opera House celebrated its 250th anniversary. The final phase of the expansion will take place between 1993 and 1996, when the stage will be rebuilt. The opera house will be closed.

The Theater

The first Theatre Royal was approached through an alley. The plain fan-shaped auditorium, which was "straightened out" in 1782 and shaped into a horseshoe a decade later, held three tiers of boxes with two galleries in the rear and twenty rows of hard, backless benches in the orchestra. The nine spacious boxes behind the orchestra,

Façade of Royal Opera House (Photo by author)

along with two proscenium boxes, were reserved for royalty, with the massive center box for the king. The steeply raked ceiling, which was flattened in 1782, boasted a painting over the apron by Jacopo Amiconi: *Apollo and the Muses bestowing a laurel on Shakespeare*. For the première of Händel's opera, an organ was installed on stage.

The second Royal Theatre was a majestic Greek Revival building with an imposing Doric tetrastyle portico. Two long friezes and two statues, Comic Muse and Tragic Muse, created by John Flaxman and J.C. Rossi, flanked the portico. In the auditorium, which was decorated in vibrant red and gold with mahogany woodwork, three box tiers topped by two galleries soared up from the orchestra level. The opera house was the first centrally heated theater in Great Britain. Architect Benedetto Albano, responsible for converting the Royal Theatre to the Royal Italian Opera House, refashioned the entrances so they appeared more majestic, doubled the number of tiers to six, and enlarged the proscenium. He added opulent ornamentation to the auditorium and draped velvet hangings around the boxes. Domenico Ferri painted colorful frescoes on the ceiling. The theater accommodated around 2,800.

The current Royal Opera House is a mixture of French and Italian classicism. The portico, flanked by the Flaxman and Rossi statues and friezes salvaged from its predecessor and supported by six Corinthian columns, presents a stately façade. Behind the exterior, an authentic Victorian opera house dwells. The original horse-shoe-shaped auditorium, decorated in crimson, gold, and ivory, boasted three box tiers topped by a gallery. The proscenium displayed a cameo of Queen Victoria and a deep maroon curtain, embroidered with the royal monogram and a fleur-de-lis pattern, hung across the apron. A sparkling central chandelier illuminated the room.

After several renovations, most of the boxes have been eliminated. The decorations have gone through several color changes, even sporting forest green at one point. They were restored to the familiar red, ivory, and gold in 1911. The chandelier has given way to individual pendant lights, complemented by electrified candelabra affixed to the parapets. The parapets are embellished with mermaids, who stare down at the deep rose velvet orchestra chairs. The dome, in an effort to re-create the ambience of an open-air theater, was repainted turquoise and adorned with gold-filigreed spokes in a celestial pattern. The opera house seats 2,098 with 58 standees.

Performance History

The first opera in London, *The Siege of Rhodes*, was performed in 1656, with several composers writing the music. John Blow's *Venus and Adonis* appeared in 1684, and five years later, Henry Purcell's *Dido and Aeneas* was introduced at Josias Priest's boarding school for girls. In April 1692, Dorset Garden was the setting for the first performance of Purcell's *The Fairy Queen*.

Greber's *Gli amori d'Ergasto*, the first Italian opera performed in London, inaugurated the King's Theater on April 9, 1705. The King's Theater was the site of many of Händel's earlier premières: *Rinaldo* on February 24, 1711, *Il Pastor Fido* on November 22, 1712, *Tesco* on January 10, 1713, *Giulio Cesare in Egitto* on Febuary 20, 1724, *Tamerlano* on October 31, 1724, *Rodelinda* on February 13, 1725, *Sosarme, Rè di Media* on Feb. 15, 1732, *Orlando* on January 27, 1733, and

ROYAL OPERA HOUSE
Covent Garden

The Royal Ballet

The Royal Opera

General Director: Jeremy Isaacs

The Royal Opera schedule cover (Courtesy of The Royal Opera)

Serse on April 15, 1738. More than one hundred years later, on July 22, 1847, Her Majesty's Theater was in the limelight again, when the world première of Giuseppe Verdi's *I masnadieri* took place. Queen Victoria, Prince Albert, the Queen Mother, the Duke of Cambridge, and the Prince of Wales along with dukes and lords, were dazzled by the opening night cast that included Jenny Lind.

A few years later, Händel, tired of the machination by impresarios, composers, and even the *castrati*, moved over to the newly opened Royal Theater. Several more of his operas were premiered: *Ariodante* on January 8, 1735, *Alcina* on April 16, 1735, *Atalanta* on May 23, 1736, and both *Arminio* and *Berenice* the following year, on January 12 and May 18, respectively. His

Semele was introduced on February 10, 1744. The premières were such a financial drain that owner Rich returned to mainly offering plays. However, Thomas Arne's *Artaxerxes* was world premiered on February 2, 1762, with the two famous *castrati*, Giusto Ferdinando Tenducci and Nicolo Peretti, dazzling the opening night crowd. His *Love in a Village* was introduced that same year on December 8. Afterward, opera performances again dwindled until the theater was gutted by fire.

The second Theatre Royal was inaugurated on September 18, 1809, with Shakespeare's *Macbeth*. In 1825, Carl Maria von Weber was commissioned to write a new work for the theater. The result, *Oberon*, was premiered on April 12, 1826, with Weber himself conducting. *Oberon* was such a triumph that Weber described it as the "greatest success of my life." Weber did not live to experience any more. He died on June 5, 1826, a short time before his planned trip back to Germany.

On April 6, 1847, the Theatre Royal reopened as the Royal Italian Opera House with Gioacchino Rossini's *Semiramide*. Although non-Italian operas were performed at the opera house, all operas were sung in Italian. Weber's *Die Freischütz* became *Il franco arciero*, and Wolfgang Amadeus Mozart's *Die Zauberflöte* was heard as *Il flauto magico*. Frederick Gye, a manager possessing a unique talent of presenting first-rate opera without going into bankruptcy, took over in 1850. However, he was not immune to disasters, one of which occurred in 1853 when Hector Berlioz came to conduct his *Benvenuto Cellini*. Unfathomable and unappreciated by the audience, *Benvenuto Cellini*, with Berlioz in tow, departed after only one performance.

Three years after Meyerbeer's *Les Huguenots* opened the new opera house in 1858, Adelina Patti, the most celebrated coloratura soprano of all time, made her Covent Garden debut as Amina in Vincenzo Bellini's *La sonnambula*. For twenty-four years she was the reigning diva. Nellie Melba took over the *prima donna assoluta* role

in 1888, a part she played for thirty-eight years, until her farewell concert in 1926. Busts of both these divas rest in the foyer of the opera house. Enrico Caruso thrilled the Covent Garden audience for seven seasons between 1902 and 1914, and other acclaimed artists like Lotte Lehmann, Lauritz Melchior, and Rosa Ponselle delighted the opera crowd between the two world wars.

In 1888, Augustus Harris took the helm at Covent Garden and internationalized the Royal Italian Opera House by having most operas performed in their original language. But not until Gustav Mahler conducted Richard Wagner's *Der Ring des Nibelungen* (sung in German) was Italian eliminated from the opera house's name. Herman Bemberg's *Elaine* was world premiered on July 5, 1892, followed by Jules Massenet's *La Navarraise* on June 20, 1894, and Franco Leoni's *L'oracolo* on June 28, 1905. When the opera house reopened after World War I on May 12, 1919, the Grand Opera Syndicate was in charge of operations, offering a three-month season. The remaining nine months saw rather plebeian fare: the circus, a cabaret, and films. During World War II, soldiers danced on the stage.

Pyotr Il'yich Tchaikovsky's ballet *Sleeping Beauty* reopened Covent Garden on February 20, 1946. Since then, only operas and ballets have graced its stage. In 1947, the Covent Garden Opera Company, renamed The Royal Opera in October 1968, gave its first performance: Georges Bizet's *Carmen* on January 14, 1947. Two years later, the world première of Arthur Bliss's *The Olympians* took place on September 29. Ralph Vaughan Williams's *The Pilgrim's Progress* was introduced on April 26, 1951, and Benjamin Britten's *Billy Budd* on December 1 of the same year. For Queen Elizabeth II's coronation on June 8, 1953, Covent Garden commissioned Britten's *Gloriana*. Michael Tippett's *The Midsummer Marriage* was world premiered on January 27, 1955, and his *Knot Garden* on December 2, 1970. Two years later, Peter Maxwell Davies's *Taverner* was introduced on July 12, followed by Tippett's *Ice Break* on July 7, 1977.

I saw a delightful new production of Rossini's *La Cenerentola*. Cleverly designed and staged, the opera was admirably sung by Alison Browner in the title role, Deon van der Walt as Don Ramiro, Peter Coleman-Wright as Dandini, and Claudio Desderi as Don Magnifico. Carlo Rizzi did a praiseworthy job of conducting. Surtitles helped clarify the fun.

PRACTICAL INFORMATION
Tickets

The box office is at 48 Floral Street, the street that borders the north side of the opera house. It is open Monday through Saturday from 10:00 a.m. to 8:00 p.m. The season is divided into ten "booking periods," each covering a one-month period. Tickets are available for purchase starting the first of the month, a month before the performance. A list of all operas with tickets still available is posted inside the entrance.

Tickets can be reserved by mail three weeks before they can be bought at the box office. For example, tickets for all September performances can be reserved beginning July 10. To increase the likelihood that your ticket order can be fulfilled, list as many different prices, dates, and seat locations as possible. Payment, either by credit card or check in British pounds, must be included with your order. Send your ticket order to:

Royal Opera House
P.O. Box No. 6
London WC2E 7QA, England

Tickets can also be ordered by calling (44) (71)240-1066 or 240-1911 starting the first of the month, a month before the performance. (44) = country code, (71) = city code. In England, dial (071)240-1066. You can charge the tickets to your credit card. Otherwise, payment must be received within three working days. If you telephone, London is five hours ahead of Eastern Standard Time.

Ticket prices for the Royal Opera vary according to the opera and your ability to see the stage. New productions, long operas, and operas with superstars in the cast are the most expensive. The price category of each opera is noted on the schedule.

The ease of getting tickets to the Royal Opera depends entirely on the production and the cast: superstar casts are impossible and new productions are difficult, but repertory revivals usually have tickets available. Remember when you purchase tickets that 25 percent of the available seats are classified as either restricted view or semi-restricted view.

When I first attended the Royal Opera House in February 1974, my ticket for Modest Mussorgsky's *Boris Godunov* in the orchestra stalls cost £8. In 1990, that same ticket cost £79, an increase of almost 900 percent in sixteen years.

Although the tickets are in English, they still can be confusing, so below is an explanation of a sample ticket.

Most operas begin at 7:30 p.m. However, operas can start as early as 5:30 p.m. or as late as 8:00 p.m., so pick up a copy of *Keith Prowse Entertainment Guide* to double check the time. Latecomers wait in the Crush Bar on the grand tier, where television monitors are located.

TICKET TRANSLATION

La Cenerentola	(Opera)
The Royal Opera	The Royal Opera
Tuesday 8 May	Tuesday May 8
7:30 P.M.	7:30 P.M.
Orch. Stalls	**Orchestra Seat**
£70.00 **L5**	(Price) **Row L** **Seat 5**

TICKET TABLE

Location		Price in £		
Orchestra (front orchestra)	56	70	79	89
Stalls (rear orchestra)	47	55	63	74
Stalls Circle (seats surrounding orchestra)				
A Center & A Sides	56	70	79	89
B Center	52	65	73	83
C-D Center, B Sides	43	55	63	74
C Sides, Stage A (Semi-Restricted)	33	43	49	57
Restricted View Seats	9.5	11	12.5	17
Grand Tier (1st tier)				
A-C	64	82	93	101
Semi-Restricted View Seats	43	54	61	68
Boxes (4 seats)				
Grand Tier	256	328	372	404
Balcony Stalls (Semi-Restricted)	92	140	160	192
Balcony Stalls (2nd tier)				
A-C Center	42	54	63	74
A-C Sides	23	35	40	48
Restricted View Seats	9.5	11	12.5	14
Amphitheater (3rd tier center)				
A-K Front	19	19	29	34
A-K Sides (Semi-Restricted)	12	12	17.5	20
L-Q Rear	12	12	17.5	20
Restricted View Seats	2.5	2.5	3	4.5
Lower Slips (3rd tier side, front)				
Semi-Restricted View	12	12	17.5	20
Restricted View	2.5	2.5	3	4.5
Upper Slips (3rd tier side, rear)				
Restricted View Seats	2.5	2.5	3	4.5
Day Seats (3rd tier center, rear)	12	12	17.5	20

$1.80 = £1, but can vary due to the fluctuating value of the dollar.
£ is an abbreviation for British pound.

Seating Plan (Courtesy of The Royal Opera)

Finding Your Way

The Royal Opera House faces Bow Street, bordered on the north by Floral Street, on the west by James Street, and on the south by Russell Street. You can reach the opera house by the Underground, Piccadilly Line, exit Covent Garden. Be prepared to wait at the station for the elevator to the street level. Buses 1, 4, 5, 6, 9, 11, 13, 15, 68, 77, 77A, 170, 171, 171A, 176, 188, 502, and 513 stop near the opera house, exit Aldwych.

The main entrance to Covent Garden is located on Bow Street. If you hold tickets in the orchestra stalls, stalls circle, grand tier, or balcony, enter through the doors on Bow Street. If you hold tickets in the amphitheater, use the Floral Street entrance. If you are seated in the orchestra stalls, walk between the busts of Adelina Patti (left) and Nellie Melba (right). For the stalls circle, leave Patti on your right if you are seated in the left side or Melba on your left if you are seated

in the right side. For those with tickets in the grand tier or balcony tier, turn left after entering the main vestibule and walk up the grand staircase. The first level is the grand tier. Ushers are recognizable by their black dresses and red scarfs.

The ushers sell the programs. They cost £2.50. The program contains a synopsis, articles, illustrations, and photographs about the opera and performers. Ladies' rooms and men's rooms are located on the right side of the entrance foyer, and a ladies' room is at the left end of the pit lobby. More rest rooms are on the tiers. Cloakrooms are on the left of the entrance foyer and in the pit lobby. There is no charge, but a tip is expected. Drinks and a cold buffet are available on all levels. Smoking is not allowed in the pit bar but is permitted in the main lobby bar. The Crush Bar and Long Bar on the Grand Tier are the most interesting places to spend the "interval."

Two wheelchair spaces are available at every performance in the stalls circle; contact Camilla Whitworth-Jones, Royal Opera House Covent Garden, London WC2E 9DD, England, for more information. An infrared-assisted hearing system is available for the hearing impaired, and certain box seats are reserved for patrons with guide dogs.

Planning Your Trip

OPERA PROGRAM

The season runs from mid-September through July. The 1990/91 season opened on September 10 with Giacomo Puccini's *Turandot* and closes on July 24 with Puccini's *La fanciulla del West*. The world première of Harrison Birtwistle's *Gawain* takes place on May 30. The new productions are Christoph Willibald Gluck's *Orfeo ed Euridice* and *Iphigénie en Tauride*, Wagner's *Siegfried* and *Götterdämmerung*, Giuseppe Verdi's *Attila*, Ludwig van Beethoven's *Fidelio*, Richard Strauss's *Capriccio*, and Bizet's *Carmen*. Puccini's *Tosca*, Mozart's *Die Zauberflöte*, Johann Strauß's *Die Fledermaus*, Rossini's *Il barbiere di Siviglia* and *La Cenerentola*, Camille Saint-Saëns's *Samson et Dalila*, Mussorgsky's *Boris Godunov*, and Jacques Offenbach's *Les Contes d'Hoffmann* complete the season.

Covent Garden is a repertory house, which means different operas are performed on consecutive nights. Opera shares the stage with ballet. To be sure your visit coincides with an opera, write ahead for a schedule. However, the schedule will only cover the next booking period. Write to:

Royal Opera House
London, WC2E 9DD, England

If you would like to receive the opera schedule on a regular basis, subscribe to the Mailing List. The cost is £15 a year, which includes overseas airmail postage. Send a bank draft in British pounds, made out to ROH Mailing List, to:

Mailing List
Royal Opera House
Covent Garden
London WC2E 9DD, England

You can also receive regular program information and have priority booking for tickets by joining the Friends of Covent Garden. If you are interested in further information, write to:

The Friends of Covent Garden
Royal Opera House
Covent Garden
London WC2E 9DD, England

TRAVEL INFORMATION

The best hotel in London is the Four Seasons Inn on the Park, Hamilton Place, Park Lane, London W1A 1AZ, England; telephone (44)-(71)499-0888, fax (44)(71)493-1895. Reservations can be made in the United States, toll-free, by calling 1-800-223-6800 (member of the Leading Hotels of the World). Singles start at $290, doubles at $360. It is the best five-star hotel in London, offering 202 rooms and 26 suites. Ideally located in London's finest section, the Four Seasons Inn offers unequaled service amid luxurious surroundings. You will find every amenity you ever wished for in your room, from a private safe to a large umbrella. Only a few minutes' walk to the Piccadilly Line, the hotel is very convenient to the opera house. Contact the concierge for all your last-minute opera ticket needs.

Cold suppers are available at the opera house on the grand tier level, one and a half hours before the performance, by advance reservation. Telephone (071) 836-9453, Monday through Friday 10:00 a.m. to 1:00 p.m. and 2:00 p.m. to 4:00 p.m. and Saturday 10:00 a.m. to 1:00 p.m. There are several restaurants near the opera house, including two pubs, Nags Head and White Lion. Many more eating places are located in the Covent Garden market. In addition, the Inn on the Park has a marvelous restaurant called the Four Seasons. Recently awarded three Michelin stars, it is a true dining experience not to be missed. Lanes is also in the hotel, offering dinner service after the opera.

The British Tourist Authority, 40 West 57th Street, New York, NY 10019, 212-581-4700, can send you travel information.

GLYNDEBOURNE
Festival Opera

Glyndebourne Festival Opera opened on May 28, 1934, with a gala production of Wolfgang Amadeus Mozart's *Le nozze di Figaro*. Founded by Sir John Christie, the festival was set at Christie's country estate. Audrey Mildmay, Christie's wife, sang in the inaugural performance, delighting the opening night crowd.

It was quite a sight for anyone who happened to be in London's Victoria Station that May afternoon. Formally dressed ladies and gentlemen swept through the station toward a special train that transported them fifty-four miles south to Lewes, where a bus conveyed them to Christie's Glyndebourne estate and intimate opera house. Strolling through the expansive gardens surrounding the house and theater, enjoying the flowers, grazing sheep, and acres of trees, the inaugural crowd relived the grandeur and glory of the opera experience during the zenith of princely patronage.

HISTORICAL OVERVIEW
Background

Christie was a frequent visitor to the Salzburger and Bayreuther Festspiele, where he got the idea to present a miniature Festspiele himself. He had dreams of building a small opera house on his Glyndebourne country estate to offer opera in idyllic and tranquil surroundings. His marriage to Canadian soprano Audrey Mildmay in 1931 transformed his dreams to reality.

In the beginning, the project proceeded rather haphazardly, which led to his wife's admonition, "If you're going to spend all that money, John, for God's sake do the thing properly!" And he did. The theater, completed in 1933, boasted up-to-date technical and lighting equipment and an orchestra pit large enough for a symphony orchestra. He even arranged complete performances of three one-act operas to test the acoustics. Although Christie's dream was a Richard Wagner festival à la Bayreuth, it opened as a Mozart opera festival à la Salzburg. Producing Wagner operas in the small, intimate festival theater proved impractical and prohibitively expensive. Besides, Audrey Mildmay, the "house artist," was no Wagnerian soprano but more of the Mozart type.

The first year's festival cost a lot more than it earned. Christie happily paid the difference and continued to improve his private opera house. By the time World War II closed the festival in 1939, Christie had spent more than £100,000 of his own money.

During the war, the house played a different role. Christie converted it into an evacuation center for nursery-age children from London. More than one hundred of them descended on the mansion, accompanied by thirty-five adults, tons of baby food, and miles of diapers.

After the war, the festival slowly trickled back. Money was a big problem. Taxes and inflation put Glyndebourne's expenses beyond what Christie could personally afford, so in 1950, John Lewis Partnership came to the rescue. The following year the Glyndebourne Festival Society was formed, and in 1954, the Glyndebourne Arts Trust was founded. This solid support ensured Glyndebourne's financial future. In 1953, the theater was enlarged to seat 600. Five years later, the seating capacity was increased again, lighting was modernized, and a new rehearsal stage was built.

When Christie died in 1962, his son George took over, leading the Festival Opera along the same road as his father had done, offering world-class opera amid a unique "old court theater" atmosphere. However, the stigma of elitism coupled with ticket demands consistently outstripping the supply prompted serious thoughts by Sir George Christie about increasing the seating capacity once again. However, unlike past expansions, in which the theater was enlarged in a piecemeal fashion, the current plans call for a totally new theater to be built on the same location, turned 180°. In other words, the new stage will sit where the walled garden is now located, and the rear of the auditorium will be placed on the current stage. It will seat 1,150. The architectural firm of Michael Hopkins & Partners was chosen in 1989 to execute the new theater, and although a final decision has not been reached, it is fairly certain that construction will begin in October 1992. The new theater should be ready for the 1994 season.

The Theater

The original Festival Opera auditorium, built as an annex to Christie's 700-year-old Glyndebourne manor house, was constructed of mixed colored bricks and covered by a large tiled roof. It accommodated 300. The current auditorium, rustic in appearance, boasts dark oak-paneled walls, a plank floor, yellow vaulted ceiling, and a chocolate brown proscenium. One small wooden balcony emerges above the light brown velvet orchestra seats. Spiderlike electric candelabra clutch the walls. The theater accommodates 830.

Gardens and Festival Auditorium (Courtesy of Glyndebourne Festival Opera, Photo by Gravett)

Oak columns line a slate "covered way," where a bronze bust of Fritz Busch and a white marble relief of Carl Ebert are displayed. A bust of Sir John Christie sits in the walled garden. The organ room, scene of the first opera performances at Glyndebourne, still houses the magnificent organ along with a painting of young Mozart, the score from *Die Zauberflöte*, and photographs of Sir John and Audrey, among other memorabilia. The organ room leads out to the expansive gardens.

Performance History

The first opera performances at Glyndebourne took place in the early 1920s in the organ room, with the orchestral scores reduced for an organ. By the early 1930s, after his marriage to Mildmay, Christie grew more ambitious, so he and his wife set about finding first-rate leadership for his newly created festival theater. In the winter of 1934, they met Busch, who had been music director of the Dresden Oper until Adolf Hitler came to power, and offered him the post of musical director. Busch, forced to leave Germany by the Nazis, readily accepted. Next they approached Carl Ebert, *Intendant* of the Städtische Oper in Berlin. He needed to escape Germany as well, so he agreed to become artistic director. The singers, none of them international circuit per-

Le nozze di Figaro (Courtesy of Glyndebourne Festival Opera, Photo by Gravett)

formers, were put through endless rehearsals with every detail scrutinized. The result was critically acclaimed performances.

The inaugural season lasted two weeks with six performances of Mozart's *Le nozze di Figaro* and six of *Così fan tutte*. However, after the sold-out inaugural performance, only fifty-four people attended the second performance and fifty-five the third. The festival seemed doomed, but by then word began to spread that the Glyndebourne Festival was more than a "formal gathering" (Christie had recommended black tie): it was also a place to hear great opera. Tickets to the remaining nine performances went quickly. And there has not been an empty seat since.

In 1935, two more Mozart operas were added to the repertory: *Die Zauberflöte* and *Die Entführung aus dem Serail*. Rudolf Bing, better known to U.S. operagoers as the former general manager of the Metropolitan Opera in New York, was put in charge of administration. In 1936, Don Giovanni invited the Commendatore to dinner several times, and four other Mozart gems appeared also. By 1938, the season lasted six weeks and the first non-Mozart operas graced the stage: Gaetano Donizetti's *Don Pasquale* and Giuseppe Verdi's *Macbeth*. The *Macbeth* performance was the first in England. Then World War II put a stop to everything.

The world première of Benjamin Britten's *The Rape of Lucretia* on July 12, 1946, reopened the festival after the war. It was the only opera performed that year. The following year, Britten's *Albert Herring* was world premiered on June 20 and Christoph Willibald Gluck's *Orfeo* shared the festival stage. However, it was not until 1950 brought the infusion of outside money that the seasons got back into full swing. Each season more and more contemporary works are performed, with the 1990 season offering one Mozart work, one Verdi opera, and four twentieth-century pieces. Only at Glyndebourne could such a repertory sell out every performance.

During the 1990 festival, Peter Sellers's production of Mozart's opera *Die Zauberflöte* induced the first boos ever heard at Glyndebourne. Relocated to twentieth-century California with photographs of beaches, freeways, residential neighborhoods, and gas stations as background, Mozart's Singspiel was performed without spoken dialogue. Instead the words were flashed on a screen. Tamino and Sarastro were metamorphosed to a twentieth-century junkie and post-hippie cult guru, respectively. Sounds more like a production at a heavily subsidized European opera house than what you might expect to see at Glyndebourne.

I saw a superb, if more conventional, production of Leoš Janáček's *Kát'a Kabanová* with Nancy Gustafson in the title role. Not only was her voice ideal for the part but her acting and physical characteristics made her eminently believable as the tortured Kát'a. Felicity Palmer exuded appropriate hate as Kabanicha. Ryland Davies and Kim Begley sang admirably in the roles of Tichon and Boris, respectively. Andrew Davis did an excellent job from the podium.

PRACTICAL INFORMATION
Tickets

If you venture to Glyndebourne without tickets, first pass through a brick archway, then look for the sign **Opera House** and **Box Office**. The box office is located on the right side of the slate entrance hall. It opens at the end of April for the entire season; the exact date varies from year to year. On performance days, the hours are Monday through Saturday from 10:00 a.m. to 7:30 p.m. and Sunday from 10:00 a.m. to 6:30 p.m. On nonperformance days, hours are 10:00 a.m. to 5:00 p.m. There are usually very few tickets left when the box office opens. However, the box office accepts tickets back for resale during the festival (deducting £5 for handling), so your chances of finding tickets improve closer to the

performance date. In addition, any available tickets are advertised in the classified section of the *London Times*.

Mail orders are accepted at the beginning of April; the exact day varies from year to year. Payment by international money order in British pounds must be included with your order. Your best chance for tickets is to have your request arrive at the beginning of April. Earlier postmarks will not increase your chances for success. Send your ticket orders to:

Glyndebourne Festival Opera Box Office
Glyndebourne Lewes
East Sussex BN8 5UU, England

The box office accepts telephone reservations from the end of April (exact date changes from year to year) between Monday and Friday, from 10:00 a.m. to 5:00 p.m. However, few tickets are left when telephone orders open. Your chances increase closer to the performance date due to last-minute returns. Telephone reservations will only be held for three days without written confirmation and payment. Call (44)(273)541-111. Glyndebourne is five hours ahead of Eastern Standard Time. (44) = country code, (273) = city code. In England, dial (0273)541-111.

Tickets for Glyndebourne are extremely difficult but not impossible to purchase. Here is how the system works: there is a two-month pri-

TICKET TABLE	
Location	Prices in £
Stalls (orchestra) Rows A-O Center	75
Stalls (orchestra) Rows A-O Sides	54
Stalls (orchestra) Rows P-T	54
Balcony - Rows A-D	75
Balcony - Rows E-G	54
Upper Balcony - All Seats	30
Box A Seats 6@ £75/Seat	450
Box B Seats 8 @ £75/Seat	600
Box C All Seats	54
Box D Seats 6 @ £75/Seat	450

$1.80 = £1, but may vary due to the fluctuating value of the dollar.
£ is an abbreviation for British pound.

ority booking period when corporate sponsors and the 5,000 members of the Glyndebourne Festival Society can purchase their tickets. They reserve all the tickets to the repertory favorites. However, tickets to the lesser-known contemporary operas are usually not sold out when the general booking period opens, so plan on attending one of those operas.

There are no bad seats at Glyndebourne, but the surtitles are not visible from the £30 balcony seats.

Although the tickets are in English, they can still be confusing, so below is an explanation of a ticket.

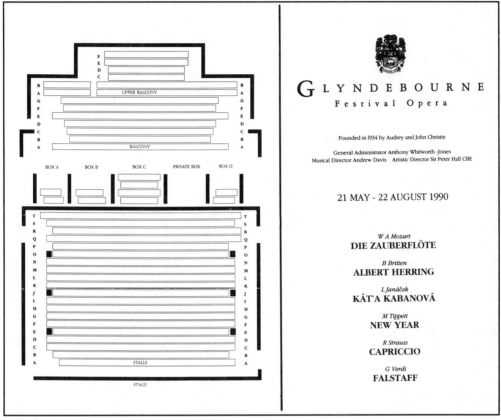

Seating Plan (Courtesy of Glyndebourne Festival Opera)

Poster of 1990 Festival Season (Courtesy of Glyndebourne Festival Opera)

TICKET TRANSLATION

Glyndebourne	Glyndebourne
Kát'a Kabanová	(Opera)
Friday	Friday
June 15 at 6-20 p.m.	June 15 6:20 p.m.
1990	1990
Red Stalls	**Orchestra (enter thru Red Foyer)**
£54.00 Incl. VAT	**(Price including value added tax)**
M2	**Row M Seat 2**

Starting times of the operas range from 5:20 p.m. to 6:20 p.m., depending on the length of the opera. On Sunday, the opera begins one hour earlier. The starting times are printed in the information pamphlet sent with your ticket. All operas have one "long interval," which is a seventy-five-minute dinner intermission. Bells that you can hear in all parts of the garden, but not in a closed car, are rung ten minutes, five minutes, and three minutes before the curtain goes up. All operas are over by 10:00 p.m., except on Sunday when the final curtain falls by 9:00 p.m. Latecomers are not admitted to the auditorium. You can watch the performance on television from the organ room.

Finding Your Way

Glyndebourne is fifty-four miles south of London. If you plan on driving, allow at least three hours. Specific driving instructions are included with your tickets. There is plenty of parking, which costs £1. You can also reach Glyndebourne by train and bus from London. A list of recommended trains from London's Victoria Station is also included with your tickets. Round-trip train fare, including the bus from Lewes to Glyndebourne and return, costs £13 (2nd class) and £26 (1st class). Only "recommended trains" leaving Victoria Station for Lewes (around four miles away) will be met by the bus. The situation at Victoria Station is chaotic: the track is announced only five minutes before the train departs. Just follow the tuxedo-clad crowd, and you will be on the right train. The drawback to the train is that the performances are not delayed if the train runs late or is canceled.

The tickets are color coded to tell you which foyer to use. Red stalls ticket holders (right side) enter through the red foyer. The first door leads to the rear of the stalls, and the second door leads to Rows A-J. Big brass numbers identify the seats. The row letters are on the floor. Blue stalls ticket holders (left side) enter through the blue foyer. Doors to the boxes and red and blue balconies are off the covered way. The entrance to the upper green balcony is near the walled garden. Ushers are distinguished by the Glyndebourne medallion hung from a red ribbon around their necks, since they are also formally attired.

Programs are sold in the covered way, between the blue foyer and the Mildmay Tea Room, and cost £6. The program is filled with articles and pictures on all the operas offered during the season. A detailed map of the festival grounds and building is also included. You will find the cloakroom in Mildmay Hall, which is to the left after entering the covered way. It costs 50p. The men's room and ladies' room are located in the red foyers on the right side. Drinks are sold at the Long Bar, which is located at the far end of the covered way. Arrangements must be made ahead of time for patrons in wheelchairs.

Dinner is eaten during the "long interval." Two expensive gourmet restaurants are on the festival grounds: the Middle and Over Wallop Restaurant and the Nether Wallop Restaurant. You will receive a "Restaurant Arrangement" brochure with your tickets, which will include a menu and reservation form. You can also buy sandwiches, coffee, and cake in Mildmay Hall.

However, the most popular form of dining at Glyndebourne is to picnic on the magnificent grounds. You must bring your picnic, as no picnic foods are available at Glyndebourne. But Glyndebourne picnics are not hamburger, hot dog, and beer affairs. Most include smoked salmon and caviar served on china and iced champagne drunk from crystal glasses. Many picnickers bring folding tables and chairs, white table cloths, sterling place settings, and occasionally a butler. If you prefer picnicking inside, stake out a picnic spot in the picnic pavilion next to the car park or in Mildmay Hall as soon as you arrive.

Planning Your Trip
OPERA SCHEDULE

The festival season runs from mid-May to mid-August. The 1990 season opened on May 21 with Mozart's *Die Zauberflöte* and closed on August 22 with Verdi's *Falstaff*. Britten's *Albert*

Top: Front curtain for *The Rake's Progress* (Courtesy of Glyndebourne Festival Opera, Photo by Gravett)
Bottom: *A Midsummer Night's Dream* (Courtesy of Glyndebourne Festival Opera, Photo by Gravett)

Left: John Christie, Founder (Courtesy of Glyndebourne Festival Opera, Photo by Gravett)
Right: Audrey Mildmay (Courtesy of Glyndebourse Festival Opera, Photo by Gravett)

Herring, Janáček's *Kát'a Kabanová*, Michael Tippett's *New Year*, and Richard Strauss's *Capriccio* completed the season. Operas are scheduled on a rotating basis, so it is possible to see a different opera every evening. The 1991 Festival, to mark the bicentennial of Mozart's death, will offer six Mozart operas. The season opens on May 21, 1991, and closes on August 23, 1991.

If you would like to be informed about Glyndebourne activities, you can join a general mailing list for £2.50. Enclose a money order in British pounds with your letter and send it to:

Mailing List Secretary
Glyndebourne
Lewes, East Sussex BN8 5UU, England

If you plan to attend the festival on a regular basis, you might be interested in putting your name on the waiting list for the Glyndebourne Festival Society. Individual members pay around $100 a year for the privilege of buying tickets before they go on sale to the general public. Corporations pay $5,000 a year or more for the privilege. There is also a Glyndebourne Association America, Inc., that was established in 1976. This is a charitable organization that is looking strictly for donations. You do not get anything tangible in return, only the intangible good feeling that you are promoting opera. For more information, contact Glyndebourne Association America, Inc., c/o Haythe & Curley, 437 Madison Avenue, New York, NY 10022.

TRAVEL INFORMATION

A visit to Glyndebourne is a trip back in time. Witnessing the elegantly dressed ladies and gentlemen sprawled on blankets with paté and champagne takes you back to a bygone era when formal evening wear was de rigueur. And at Glyndebourne it still is. Black tie for the men and short or long dresses for the ladies are the custom at Glyndebourne, so do not forget to pack your formal wear.

The town closest to Glyndebourne is Lewes, where two hotels are located. White Hart Hotel, 55 High Street, Lewes, East Sussex BN7 2LN; telephone (44)(273)474-676, has rooms starting at $140, including a breakfast buffet. The hotel has charm, old furnishings, and ancient plumbing. At Shelleys, High Street (St. Annes Hill), Lewes, East Sussex BN7 2NL; telephone (44) (273)472-361, rooms start at $130. For a list of other hotels in the area, call the information office at Glyndebourne: (44)(273)812-321. The Lewes District Council Information Office can also help you with hotels as well as travel information to the area. Write to:

Lewes District Council Information Office
32 High Street
Lewes, East Sussex BN7 2NL
England
(44)(273) 471-600

Monaco

La bohème (Courtesy of Société des Bains de Mer/Opéra de Monte-Carlo, Photo by Burnie)

MONTE CARLO
Salle Garnier, Opéra de Monte-Carlo

One usually does not associate Monte Carlo with culture but with high-class gambling. So all you opera-loving gamblers and nongamblers alike will be pleasantly surprised: Monte Carlo boasts a small but magnificent opera house, Salle Garnier. The theater was inaugurated on January 25, 1879, with a potpourri of entertainment. Actress Sarah Bernhardt, who was dressed as a nymph, baritone Jules Diaz de Soria, soprano Marie Miolan-Carvalho, and tenor Joseph Victor Capoul regaled the opening night crowd with verse and song. The Duchess of Urach-Württemberg, Prince Charles's sister, her lady-in waiting, and two aides-de-camp of Prince Charles occupied the royal box. Charles was too ill to attend. The architect, Charles Garnier, who also designed the Opéra de Paris, attended the celebration. He graciously acknowledged the applause of the audience from his corner box. Since its inauguration, Salle Garnier has hosted forty-five world premières, an impressive number for such a *petit théâtre*.

HISTORICAL OVERVIEW
Background

During the 1870s, Monte Carlo had become a fashionable winter resort, but the only cultural diversion available took place in a small concert hall. So in April 1878, Prince Charles and the Société des Bains de Mer concluded that an opera house was just what was needed to offer the perfect distraction for Monaco's wealthy pleasure seekers and well-heeled gamblers. A magnificent spot, high on the casino grounds overlooking the Mediterranean, was chosen. Four hundred skilled laborers were imported from Italy and construction began on May 9, 1878. Eight months and sixteen days later, Salle Garnier was completed. The exterior of Salle Garnier was an exact replica, in miniature, of the Palais Garnier. Its interior exuded the splendor of the *Belle Époque*.

The Theater

Salle Garnier is a lavishly ornamented building. Three, enormous, twenty-seven-foot-high arcaded windows dominate the façade. Two sculptures, *Le Chant* by Sarah Bernhardt and *La Danse* by Gustave Doré, stand on either side of the balcony. Lyres woven with antique masks, in a frieze of blue, red, green, purple, and gold mosaic, glisten in the Riviera sunlight. Three *oeils-de-boeuf* stare from under the eaves of the crowned copper roof and two fenestrated pilasters soar into minarets more than one hundred fifteen feet high. The opposite façade boasts massive statues representing Seine and Mediterranean. Added in the summer of 1889, these statues are recessed in turrets.

Salle Garnier was constructed as Prince Charles's private theater. The façade entrance is reserved for Monaco's royalty. Two great statues representing Sculpture and Industry guard the portico, and allegorical figures bearing the shield

Façade of Salle Garnier (Courtesy of Société des Bains de Mer)

of Monaco dwell on the tall arched doorway. A private staircase whisks them up to their exquisite royal box, which is adorned with crimson, gold, silks, and velvet. Four sculptured columns support a canopy dripping with garlands, leafy patterns, and topped by the sovereign crown. In addition, two large state boxes, reserved for members of the government and the administration, and two *loges bénitières*, inhabit the balcony. The prince's guests enter the theater via the casino's vestibule, which leads into a marble-covered atrium surrounded by onyx Ionic columns. Crimson, yellow ocher, gold, and bronze flood the rococo auditorium. Finely carved moldings, caryatids, garlands, sculptures, and paintings bathe in the hue. The names of Mozart, Rossini, Gounod, Verdi, Glinka, and Hérold circle the room. Four allegorical paintings embellish the high-vaulted ceiling. *Comédie*, painted by Lix, shows the Muse, the Poet, Intrigue (with a velvet mask), and Avarice (with sacks of coins). *Musique*, the work of Boulanger, shows the Genius of music, with his wings extended, conducting young women playing violins and men blowing wind instruments. *Danse*, executed by Clairin, offers wild bacchants em-

bodying ancient dance and a Harlequin, a buffoon, a Spaniard, and celestial ballerinas symboling modern dance. *Chant et l'Eloquence*, created by Feyen-Perrin, presents Homer spouting verses and the Poet, the Old, the Outcast, and the Vagrant uttering poignant lamentations. Each piece is separated by huge gold *Renommées* waving palms, sculpted by Jules Thomas. Over the proscenium, two winged beings float on top of "Anno—1878." The auditorium accommodates 524.

Performance History

On February 8, 1879, the first opera, Jean-Robert Planquette's *Le Chevalier Gaston*, was mounted at Salle Garnier. Three additional operas graced the stage the first season, which was under the directorship of Jules Cohen. In 1881, Cohen used his connections to attract great coloratura soprano Adelina Patti to Monaco. She thrilled Monaco with her voice, bringing international recognition to Salle Garnier. She sang in all five operas scheduled that season. The Greek tenor Ernest Nicolini sang with her in all the operas except *Il barbiere di Siviglia*. Eventually they were married. In 1885, the renowned conductor Jules Étienne Pasdeloup was imported from Paris. Expectations ran high, but he presented opera excerpts in costume instead of full-length operas. A tremendous outcry ensued. The following year, full-length operas were back in the repertory, and Pasdeloup was back in Paris.

Four years later, Charles III died, and his son, Albert I, took over. Albert's second wife, American Alice Heine, was an opera lover. Her involvement with the opera in conjunction with Raoul Gunsbourg's appointment as director that year helped propel Salle Garnier into the upper echelons of the opera world. For sixty years, Gunsbourg remained at the helm, leading Salle Garnier through an extraordinary period.

On February 18, 1893, Hector Berlioz's *La Damnation de Faust* was staged for the first time, followed by the world première of de Montgomery's *Aréthuse* on February 10, 1894. Two premières were presented posthumously: César Franck's *Hulda* on March 4, 1894, and *Ghisèle* (finished by Franck's colleagues) on April 6, 1896. Isidore de Lara's *Messaline* was introduced on March 21, 1899, with Francesco Tamagno creating the role of Hélion. Tamagno first appeared at Salle Garnier on January 20, 1894, in the title role of Verdi's *Otello*. Tamagno was Princess Alice's favorite singer, so in 1896, when he raised his fees so high that he almost was not reengaged, Alice intervened. After all, he was Salle Garnier's leading attraction. His fees eventually exacted 20 percent of the entire opera budget. But despite his lavish fees, a rumor persisted that he resold his house seats at scalper's prices. As Tamagno was nearing the end of his career, another golden-voiced tenor emerged— Enrico Caruso. Caruso sang Rodolfo opposite Nellie Melba's Mimi in Giacomo Puccini's *La bohème* on February 1, 4, and 8, 1902, and the

role of the Duke of Mantua opposite Melba's Gilda in Verdi's *Rigoletto* on February 12. The audience and critics went wild at all four performances.

That same year Jules Massenet's association with Salle Garnier was launched with the world première of *Le Jongleur de Notre Dame* on February 18. Three years later, his *Chérubin* was introduced on February 14, followed by his *Thérèse* on February 7, 1907. *Don Quichotte* graced the stage for the first time on February 19, 1910, with Feodor Chaliapin in the title role, and his *Roma* appeared a couple of years later. After Massenet's death, *Cléopâtre* and *Amadis* were premiered in 1914 and 1924, respectively, and Chaliapin sang his last role at Salle Garnier, Boris Godunov, in 1937.

Meanwhile, Camille Saint-Saëns's *Hélène* was world premiered on February 18, 1904, with Melba as Hélène. A year later, Pietro Mascagni conducted the world première of his *Amica* on

Auditorium, Salle Garnier (Courtesy of Société des Bains de Mer)

March 16, with Geraldine Farrar creating the title role. On February 24, 1906, Farrar sang Margarita in the world première of Saint-Saëns' *Ancêtre*. That same season, the posthumous world première of Georges Bizet's *Don Procopio* took place on March 10. The opera was not well received. The next year, Xavier Leroux's *Théodora* was performed for the first time anywhere on March 19. Beginning in 1908 for several seasons, Titta Ruffo captivated the audience with his interpretations. The year 1909 was a glorious season. Not only was Richard Wagner's entire *Der Ring des Nibelungen* mounted on Salle Garnier's toy-sized stage but Gunsbourg also presented fourteen additional operas, which included the première of his own *Le vieil Aigle*, Gabrielle Ferrari's *Le Cobzar*, and Philippe Bellenot's *Naristé*. The world première of Saint-Saëns's *Déjanire* took place in 1910, and three years later, Gabriel Fauré's *Pénélope* graced the stage on March 4. André Messager's *Béatrice* appeared for the first time in 1914 with Puccini's *La Rondine* following on March 27, 1917. Maurice Ravel's *L'Enfant et les Sortilèges* was introduced on March 21, 1925, and Arthur Honegger and Jacques Ibert's *L'Aiglon* on March 11, 1937.

The golden era of opera during Gunsbourg's reign is gone forever: the prohibitive cost of staging world premières and the five-digit fees of today's international circuit stars have placed Gunsbourg-style productions beyond the reach of such a small house. But Opéra de Monte-Carlo celebrated its centennial in 1979 in style with Puccini's *Turandot*, Saint Saëns's *Samson et Dalila*, Wagner's *Die Walküre*, Verdi's *Don Carlos*, and Massenet's *Don Quichotte*.

PRACTICAL INFORMATION
Tickets

The box office (*bureau de location*) is located in the casino atrium at the Place du Casino. The box office window (*guichet*) opens for the season on December 16. It is open Tuesday through Sunday from 10:00 a.m. to 12:30 p.m. and from 2:00 p.m. to 5:00 p.m. (*du mardi au dimanche de 10 heures à 12 h.30 et de 14 heures à 17 heures*).

You can order tickets by mail beginning January 6. Include your name, address, telephone number, the opera(s), date(s), location(s), price(s) and number of seats. Send an international money order payable in French francs to Opéra de Monte-Carlo along with your *bulletin de reservation par correspondance* (order form) to:

Service Location
Opéra de Monte-Carlo
B.P. 139
Monte-Carlo 98007, Monaco Cedex

You can also reserve tickets by telephone beginning January 6. Call (33)(93)507-654 during box office hours. (33) = country code, (93) = city code. You should speak French. Monaco is six hours ahead of Eastern Standard Time.

TICKET TABLE			
Location	Prices in F.Fr.		
	Soirée	Gala	Matinée
Orchestre Centre (center front orchestra, rows 1-9)	400	450	400
Orchestre I (off center, rows 1-9 + row 10)	300	350	300
Orchestre II (side front orchestra, rows 1-9)	150	200	150
Orchestre III (extreme side, front orchestra rows 1-5)	100	100	100
Corbeille I (rear orchestra rows 1-3)	300	350	300
Corbeille II (rear orchestra rows 4-7)	250	300	250

$1 = 6 F.Fr., but can vary due to the fluctuating value of the dollar.
F.Fr. is an abbreviation for French franc. It is also abbreviated F.

Tickets ordered by phone must be paid for within forty-eight hours.

The seats in the orchestra are divided into six price categories, accurately reflecting your ability to see the stage.

Because of the small theater, tickets are difficult to purchase. Your best chance is to write as soon as the box office accepts mail reservations.

Understanding your ticket will help you locate your seat with no problem. A sample ticket is translated below.

Evening performances begin at 8:30 p.m. (20 *h*. 30), and afternoon performances begin at 3:00 p.m. (15 *h*.). No one is admitted to the auditorium once the curtain has gone up. The schedule and starting times are listed in the monthly *Bienvenue a Monte-Carlo*.

Der Freischütz with Gessendorf and Robert Shunk (Courtesy of SBM/Opéra de Monte-Carlo, Photo by Heyligers)

Seating Plan (Courtesy of SBM/Opéra de Monte-Carlo)

TICKET TRANSLATION

Opera de Monte-Carlo	Monte Carlo Opera
Salle Garnier	Salle Garnier
Soirée	Evening Performance
du Vendredi 17 Mars 1989 à 20 H 30	Friday March 17, 1989 at 8:30 P.M.
Représentation de Gala	**Gala Performance**
(Tenue de soirée)	**(Black tie)**
Centre Prix: 450F	**Center (Price)**
Orchestre	**Orchestra**
Place Nº 180	**Seat 180**

Finding Your Way

Salle Garnier is on the Place du Casino and is surrounded by gardens. Avenue de Monte-Carlo leads into the opera house. You can reach the theater with buses 1 and 4, exit Place du Casino.

Salle Garnier faces the Mediterranean. You enter the auditorium through the casino atrium. Only the ruling royalty and VIPs use the façade entrance. Odd-numbered seats are on the left, and even-numbered seats are on the right side. Seats begin with 1 on the left aisle and 2 on the right aisle, meeting in the center of the row. The numbers do not repeat. Seats in the *corbeille* (rear orchestra) begin with 1, 2, in the center of row 1 and increase sequentially to the side aisles.

Programs are sold at the entrance to Salle Garnier and cost 100 F.Fr. The program (in French) contains all the operas of the season, with a short article and a couple of illustrations on each work. The cloakroom (*vestiaire*), ladies' room (*dames*), men's room (*messieurs*), and bar are all located in the casino atrium.

If you visit Monte Carlo regularly and read French, you might be interested in joining Association des Amis de l'Opéra de Monte-Carlo. You can reserve your tickets before they go on sale to the public. For more information, contact:

Le Millefiori
1, rue des Genêts
98000 Monte Carlo, Monaco

Planning Your Trip
OPERA SCHEDULE

The season runs from mid-January to the end of March. The 1991 season opened on January 17 with Bizet's *Carmen* and closed on March 24 with Puccini's *La Rondine*. Igor Stravinsky's *The Rake's Progress* and Wolfgang Amadeus Mozart's *Die Zauberflöte* completed the season.

Salle Garnier is a *stagione* house, which means only one opera is presented at a time. To be sure your visit coincides with an opera, write or call for a schedule, but do not waste your time contacting Salle Garnier. They do not respond. Instead, contact:

Société des Bains de Mer
450 Park Avenue
New York, NY 10022
1-800-221-4708

TRAVEL INFORMATION

Monaco is a gambling town with a strict dress code for attending the opera. Black tie for the men and evening dress for the ladies is required for galas; jacket and tie for the men and dress or fancy skirt for the ladies is required at all other performances.

Two luxury hotels are convenient to Salle Garnier. At the Hotel de Paris, Place du Casino, telephone (33)(93)508-080, singles begin at $200 and doubles at $230. At Loews Monte-Carlo, 12 avenue des Spélugues, telephone (33)(93)506-500, singles start at $170 and doubles at $200.

Several eating places, from inexpensive snack bars to costly haute cuisine restaurants are located very near Salle Garnier, offering a wide choice of food.

For travel information, contact Société des Bains de Mer (address above) as well. The Monaco Government Tourist and Convention Bureau does not respond to requests.

The Netherlands

Die Entführung aus dem Serail (Courtesy of De Nederlandse Oper, Photo by Pieper)

AMSTERDAM
Het Muziektheater, De Nederlandse Opera

The world première of Otto Ketting's *Ithaka* and the ballet *Zoals Orpheus* inaugurated Het Muziektheater on September 23, 1986. The gala production, commemorating the historic occasion of the opening of the first opera house in Amsterdam, enthralled an illustrious opening night audience. Designed by Cees Dam, the music theater was connected to a new *stadhuis* (city hall) on September 7, 1988.

HISTORICAL OVERVIEW
Background

The story of Amsterdam's first "opera house" goes back 338 years. In 1648, Jacob van Campen designed a *stadhuis* for Amsterdam, which opened seven years later. All went peacefully until 1808, when Louis Napoleon, then King of Holland, decided that the city hall was just the building he wanted for his palace. More than a hundred years passed before the city council decided it needed a new city hall and voted to include a proposal for an opera house as well. A competition was held and architect Staal won, but nothing further happened. Meanwhile, the Paleis voor Volksvlijt, the only theater suitable for opera, burned down. No action was taken until 1955, when the city council woke up and commissioned architects Berghoef and Vegter to design a new *stadhuis* to be located at the Waterlooplein. The following year, B. Bijvoet was commissioned to design an opera house to be located at the Frederiksplein. Nothing happened. Then in 1968, another competition was held to design a new city hall. This time architect Wilhelm Holzbauer won. Meanwhile, the site of the proposed opera house was moved to Ferdinand Bolstraat and Bijvoet and G. Holt were commissioned to prepare new opera house designs. Everything was finally approved and everyone was ready for action, but then the minister of state forbade any new building until Amsterdam's budget deficit was decreased. Next Holzbauer's city hall designs were scrapped because of the energy crisis: the plans were deemed energy wasteful. In 1979, Bijvoet died and Dam took his place. Meanwhile, Holzbauer suggested combining the two buildings at Waterlooplein. All went well until the first day of building in 1982. Riots erupted and a mini-*Götterdämmerung* resulted: cranes, site huts, and a pile-driven engine were set on fire. The operation was named "*van Opera naar Slopera*" (from opera to demolition). After four years of construction, Het Muziektheater opened in 1986.

The Theater

Het Muziektheater is a striking brick and natural stone building, its modern white Carrara marble, aluminum, and glass façade crowned with Frisian red brick masonry and blue-glazed bricks. The curved glass façade allows panoramic views of the Amstel River. The outside and inside fuse together in the forty-five-foot-high circular foyers that surround the auditorium. The foyers,

Top: Façade of Het Muziektheater (Photo by author)
Bottom: Auditorium, Het Muziektheater (Courtesy of De Nederlandse Oper, Photo by Pieper)

glass on the outside, pink salmon on the inside, and overlooked by shiny white balconies, are illuminated by specially designed lamps attached to white glass columns. A red velvet transition room transports you from the canals of Amsterdam into the semicircular world of opera. Two white-rimmed copper-colored tiers rise around bright red velvet high-backed orchestra seats. Maroon walls complement an open brownish-black ceiling (exposing technical equipment), which is transformed into a star-filled sky by hundreds of bulbs suspended on rods. Het Muziektheater seats 1,600.

Performance History

On December 31, 1680, Pietro Ziani's *Le fatiche d'Ercole per Deianira* inaugurated a theater on the Leidsegracht. This was the first opera performed in Amsterdam. Carolus Hacquart's *De Triomfeerende Min*, which was written to celebrate the Peace of Nijmegen, followed. Hendrik Anders and Servaas de Kunink tried to develop Dutch opera, but their attempts failed. Instead, the French and Italian repertory took hold and visiting troupes from Germany, France, and Italy performed at the Stadsschouwburg theater on Keizergracht. In 1772, this theater was destroyed by fire during a performance of Pierre-Alexandre Monsigny's *Le Déserteur*. Around the same time, Bartholomeus Ruloffs translated several of André Grétry's opéras comiques into Dutch, often inserting some of his own music.

In 1883, conductor Henri Viotta founded the Wagner Vereniging and most of Richard Wagner's operas were staged. The end of the nineteenth century saw the inauguration of an Italian season, which lasted from October to February and attracted well-known singers performing standard repertory masterpieces. The Nazi occupation of Holland put a sudden end to those productions.

After the war, the first homegrown opera company, De Nederlandse Opera, was formed. The company gave performances in Dutch, but

Top: *De materie*, World Première on June 1, 1989 (Courtesy of De Nederlandse Oper, Photo by Pieper)
Bottom: *Boris Godunov* (Courtesy of De Nederlandse Oper, Photo by Pieper)

their existence was short-lived. In 1965, the *nieuwe* Nederlandse Opera was born, with a more successful outcome. Since the opening of the music theater, the Netherlands Opera has instituted a regular season of around ten different operas comprising close to one hundred performances, with special interest in promoting works written especially for Het Muziektheater and Dutch opera. The first work was a children's opera, Kees Olthuis's *De Naam van de Maan*, introduced on December 25, 1988. Shortly thereafter, Philip Glass's *The Making of the Representative for Planet 8* was performed on January 8, 1989.

I saw a provocative production of Sergei Prokofiev's *Ognenniy angel*, sung in French under its French title, *L'Ange de feu*, that featured nightmarish scenes: weird black squiggly things crawling on walls and snakes thrown like baseballs. At times it was overpowering. (State-subsidized opera companies can afford to be very adventurous.) It was superbly sung and acted by Marilyn Zschau as Renata; Neil Howlett performed admirably as Ruprecht. Excellent conducting by Riccardo Chailly built the tension to a convincing climax. There were subtitles in Dutch.

PRACTICAL INFORMATION
Tickets

The box office (*kassa*) is located at 3 Amstel inside the theater building. The entrance is around to the left on the river side. Go through the revolving glass doors under a bulb-speckled black overhang. It is not easy to find because there are six entrances to the complex. The box office opens at 10:00 a.m. Monday through Saturday and stays open until curtain time. On Sundays and holidays, it opens at 12:00 noon. On days with matinee performances or no performances, the box office closes at 6:00 p.m. (*Openingstijden: maandag-zaterdag 10.00 uur tot aanvang voorstelling, zondag en feestdagen 12.00 uur tot aanvang voorstelling. Dagen zonder voorstelling en dagen et matinees tot 18.00 uur*). There are four windows, but usually only one or two are open. A price list is posted to the left of the window and a seating plan is under the window. Tickets go on sale one calendar month before the performance.

Tickets cannot be ordered by mail from the opera house. However, you can reserve tickets beginning two months ahead of the performance through the Netherlands Reservation Center.

TICKET TABLE	
Location	**Toegangsprijzen (Prices in f)**

1e Rang (1st level price category)
  zaal midden rij 8-17 (orchestra center, rows 8-17)
  le balcon midden rij 1-6 (1st balcony center, rows 1-6)
	80

2e Rang (2nd level price category)
  zaal midden rij 1-7 (orchestra center, rows 1-7)
  zaal links (orchestra left)
  zaal rechts (orchestra right)
	60

3e Rang (3rd level price category)
  le balcon links (1st balcony left)
  le balcon rechts (1st balcony right)
  2e balcon midden (2nd balcony center)
	40

4e Rang (4th level price category)
  2e balcon links (2nd balcony left)
  2e balcon rechts (2nd balcony right)
	20

$1 = f 1.85, but can change due to the fluctuating value of the dollar.
f is an abbreviation for the Dutch florin.

Write to:

Nationaal Reserverings Centrum
Postbus 404
2260 AK Leidschendam, The Netherlands

Tickets can be ordered by phone. Call (31) (20)255-455. (31) = country code, (20) = city code. In the Netherlands, dial (020)255-455. There are ten telephone lines, so usually there is no trouble getting through. You do not have to speak Dutch to order tickets by phone. Amsterdam is six hours ahead of Eastern Standard Time.

For ticket availability (returns) on *uitverkocht* (sold out) performances, call (020)551-8100.

Tickets are almost always available for lesser-known works and contemporary operas (except premières), which make up most of the reper-

tory. You are most likely to see *uitverkocht* (sold out) next to popular repertory operas, because so few are performed. Your best chance for tickets to these operas is to write two months ahead or telephone one month ahead. Reserved tickets must be picked up at least forty-five minutes before curtain time. Otherwise they will be resold.

Since the auditorium is raked, almost all the seats offer good views of the stage except the extreme sides. Avoid the last ten seats in the side sections on all levels. If you sit there, expect to see only part of the stage. With some productions, you will see nothing at all.

Tickets are easy to understand when you know the meaning of the words, so a translation of a sample ticket appears below.

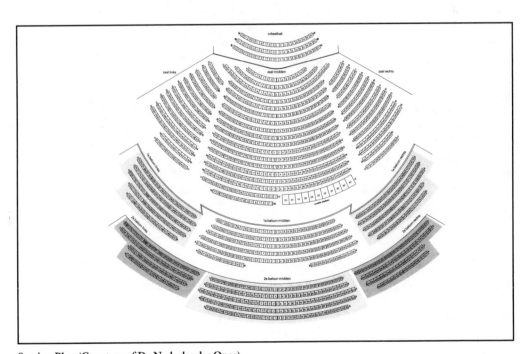

Seating Plan (Courtesy of De Nederlandse Oper)

TICKET TRANSLATION

Het Muziektheater				The Music Theater		
14 Jun 90		L'Ange de Feu		June 14, 1990		(Opera)
20:00 H			**Even**	**8 P.M.**		**Even (side)**
1E Balkon	**RIJ 3**		**Stoel 46**	**1st Balcony**	**Row 3**	**Seat 46**

Die Zauberflöte (Courtesy of De Nederlandse Oper, Photo by Pieper)

Operas begin at 8:00 p.m. (*20.00 uur*). Sunday matinees start at 1:30 p.m. (*13.30 uur*). There are exceptions. The monthly schedule (*maandagenda*) and the pamphlet *Amsterdam Cultural Life* both list the operas and their starting times. Latecomers are not seated until the intermission.

Finding Your Way

Het Muziektheater faces Amstel, bordered on the east by Waterloo. There is a map in front of the complex identifying each of its sections. You can reach the opera house by the following public transportation: metro, exit Waterlooplein, and tram 9 or 14. You can also arrive by water taxi, telephone 750-909.

The main entrance to Het Muziektheater faces the river on Amstel. Pass through the white marble lobby where the entrance to the theater is on the right. You are on the *begane grond* (ground floor). Go up the stairs to the *zaal* (orchestra) level, where you will be on the *oneven* (odd-numbered) or left side. If you hold tickets in the *zaal oneven*, use the entrance doors ahead, where signs *oneven stoelen* (odd-numbered seats) are posted. If you are in the *zaal even* (orchestra even number), continue around to the right side to the *even stoelen* (even-numbered seats) entrance. Go up one more flight for *1e balcon*, and two for the *2e balcon*. Look for the chocolate brown, red, and white signs to help you get oriented. If you still feel unsure of where your seat is, the ushers are recognizable by their bright red dresses.

Programs are for sale on the *begane grond*, where you enter, and cost fl5. The program (in Dutch) contains a synopsis in English, the complete libretto, as well as photographs and articles relevant to the opera. The cloakroom (*garderobe*) is located on your left as you enter. There is no charge. Bars are located at the extreme right end of the foyer on all levels, and the rest rooms (*toiletten*)—men's (*heren*) and ladies' (*dames*)—are behind the bars on the *zaal* and *2e balcon* levels. An exhibit of photographs from De Nederlandse Opera's productions is a half flight down from the *1e balcon* on the extreme left (where the walls are painted chicken yellow).

Così fan tutte (Courtesy of De Nederlandse Oper, Photo by Pieper)

There are eleven places, called *invaliden plaat-sen*, reserved for the disabled in the *zaal midden*, *rij* 17, *stoelen* 20-40 (center orchestra, row 17, seats 20-40). An audio aid system is available for those with hearing difficulties.

Planning Your Trip

OPERA SCHEDULE

The season runs from September through June. The repertory ranges from the very early operas to contemporary, with a strong emphasis on the baroque and modern operas. The 1990/91 season opened with Wagner's *Parsifal* (new production) on September 3 and closes on June 29 with Wolfgang Amadeus Mozart's *Idomeneo* (new production). Other new productions are Claudio Monteverdi's *Il ritorno di Ulisse in patria*, Christoph Willibald Gluck's *Iphigénie en Tauride*, Hector Berlioz's *Benvenuto Cellini*, Arnold Schönberg's *Die glückliche Hand*, Giuseppe Verdi's *Un ballo in maschera*, and Morton Feldman's *Neither*. Béla Bartók's *A Kékszakállú herceg vára* (Duke Bluebeard's Castle), Johann Strauß's *Die Fledermaus*, and Mozart's *Die Entführung aus dem Serail* complete the season.

De Nederlandse Opera is on a *stagione* system, which means only one opera is on the schedule at a time. To be sure your visit coincides with an opera, write for a schedule:

Het Muziektheater
Postbus 16822
1001 RH Amsterdam, Holland

TRAVEL INFORMATION

The best hotel in Amsterdam is the Amsterdam Marriott, Stadhouderskade 19-21, Amsterdam, Holland; telephone (31)(20)607-5555, fax (31)(20)833-834. For reservations in the United States, call toll-free, 1-800-228-9290. Singles start at $190, doubles at $220. The Amsterdam Marriott is a marvelous five-star hotel with 395 rooms, including 18 suites, offering all the comforts of home. Overlooking the Leidseplein, with a magnificent view of the city, it is located in the best section of town. Convenient to everything, the hotel is a delightful twenty-minute walk to the opera house. You can walk back after the opera with no problem, and the concierge can take care of all your last-minute ticket needs.

You will find a wide variety of restaurants near the opera house on Amstelstraat and at Rembrandtsplein. In addition, try the Grand Restaurant Waterloo, Zwanenburgwal 15, or Port O'Amsterdam in the Marriott.

The Netherlands Board of Tourism, 355 Lexington Ave, New York, NY 10017, 212-370-7360, can send you travel information as well as the opera schedule.

Spain

GRAN TEATRE DEL LICEU

Dies 14, 17, 20, 22 i 24 de maig de 1990

JENŮFA

Òpera en tres actes

Text
GABRIELA PREISSOVÁ

Música
LEOŠ JANÁČEK

L'àvia Buryja	Marita Knobel
Laca Klemeñ	Jan Blinkhof
Steva Buryja	Peter Straka
Kostelnička	Leonie Rysanek-Gausmann
Jenůfa	Linda Plech
Capatàs	Vicenç Esteve
El jutge	Alfonso Echeverría
La dona del jutge	Maria Uriz
Karolka	Rosa Maria Conesa
Barena	Begoña Alberdi
Jano	M.ª Antonia Martín-Regueiro
La Tia	Rosa Vilar
Serventa	M.ª Angels Sarroca
Veu interna	M.ª Angels Sarroca
Veu interna	Cristóbal Viñas

Directors d'orquestra
VACLAV NEUMANN (dies 14 i 17) - **RUDOLF KRECMER** (dies 20, 22 i 24)

Director d'escena i il·luminació
MARIO GAS

Escenògraf i vestuari
MARCELO GRANDE

Directors del cor
ROMANO GANDOLFI - VITTORIO SICURI

Assistent a la direcció d'escena   Assistent d'escenografia
JOSEP ANTONI GUTIERREZ   CARLOS MENDES-FAISCA

NOVA PRODUCCIÓ DEL GRAN TEATRE DEL LICEU, amb el patrocini de SEAT

ORQUESTRA SIMFÒNICA i COR DEL GRAN TEATRE DEL LICEU

Assistents musicals
Lucy Arner - Javier Pérez Batista - Laurent Wagner - Osias Wilenski

Mestre director d'estudis	Mestre apuntador	Violí concertino	Realització dels decorats	Ajudant a la direcció d'escena	Realització del vestuari
Enrique Ricci	Jaume Tribó	Josep M.ª Alpiste	Germans Salvador	Jaume Villanueva	Peris' 150

Servei de sabateria: Valldeperas   Serveis tènics del Gran Teatre del Liceu   Servei de perruqueria: Damaret

CONSORCI DEL GRAN TEATRE DEL LICEU

Dilluns 14 de maig, **21** h. (Funció n.º 76 - Torn D) - GALA   **Dimarts 22** de maig, **21** h. (Funció n.º 79 - Torn A)
Dijous 17 de maig, **21** h. (Funció n.º 77 - Torn C)   **Dijous 24** de maig, **21** h. (Funció n.º 80 - (Torn B)
Diumenge 20 de maig, **17** h. (Funció n.º 78 - Torn T)   Pròximes funcions: SIMON BOCCANEGRA

VENDA ANTICIPADA DE LOCALITATS de 8 a 15 h. dies feiners; dissabtes de 9 a 13 h. VENDA EL DIA DE LA FUNCIO d'11 a 13.30 h. i a partir de les 16 h.
Oficines del c. Sant Pau, 1, baixos. Tel 318 91 22

Impremta Barès - Barcelona   Dipòsit Legal B. 70.653 - 90

BARCELONA
Gran Teatre del Liceu

The Gran Teatre del Liceu, originally named Teatro del Liceo, bathed in the light of hundreds of wax torches, first opened its doors on April 4, 1847. The gala inauguration offered almost everything except opera: a symphony by the Catalan composer Gomis; a drama in verse, *Don Fernando, el de Antequera*, by Ventura de la Vega; a ballet, *Rondeña*, and a cantata, *Il Regio Imene*, written by Joan Cortada with music by Marià Obiols. Military music accompanied the audience into the theater, where the ladies received flowers and the men poems that praised the occasion. Even Queen Isabella II attended—not in person but in the form of a marble bust surrounded by three ladies representing the three Graces: Aglaia, Euphrosyne, and Thalia. Architect Miquel Garriga i Roca had been commissioned in 1845 to design the opera house, but Josep Oriol Mestres replaced him the following year.

The theater survived only fourteen years before fire consumed it as a grief-stricken Mestres watched. The rebuilt Teatro del Liceo, designed again by Mestres, was inaugurated on April 20, 1862, with a dazzling production of Vincenzo Bellini's *I Puritani*.

HISTORICAL OVERVIEW
Background

Barcelona's first theater, Teatro de la Santa Cruz, dates from 1579. Established near Las Atarazanas by the street La Rambla, the theater hosted its first opera in 1708. For more than a century, it was the only opera house in the city. In 1837, during an anticlerical movement, the Dominican Convent of Montesión was requisitioned as barracks for the Battalion of the National Militia. To help pass the time, three officers and a theatrical designer—Pere Vives, Josep M. Grau, Francesc Planas, and Josep Planella—formed the Sociedad Filodramática de Montesión. One of the founders heard of a "theater yard sale," and Teatro Montesión was born. When the Teatro Montesión opened in 1838, the Teatro de la Santa Cruz, not liking the competition, changed its name to Teatro Principal. The Principal suffered fire damage in 1787, 1915, 1924, and 1933 but was restored after each calamity, surviving today as a movie house.

Although the regiment eventually disbanded, the theater group expanded, changing its name to Liceo Filarmónico Dramático Barcelonés. Eight years later, when the nuns demanded their convent back, the group lost its Teatro Montesión. Three board members—Joaquim de Gispert, Manuel Gibert, and Manuel Girona—insisted on compensation. Eventually, they obtained land at the junction of La Rambla and calle de San Pablo. Here the cornerstone of the new Teatro del Liceo was laid on April 11, 1846. Although Barcelona had only 174,000 residents, Gispert had visions of an immense opera house, which he funded with the sale of stock in a newly formed Sociedad del Teatro and the purchase of permanent season tickets.

For the inauguration, every place in the 3,500-seat theater was taken. The rivalry that had developed between the Teatro Montesión and Teatro Principal (Teatro de la Santa Cruz) exploded with the establishment of the Teatro del Liceo. Known as the war of the *liceístas* and the *cruzados*, the rivalry was actually a struggle between the elder, merchant, and landed aristocracy of the Santa Cruz and the younger, industrial bourgeoisie of the Liceo. When the two administrations merged sometime later, peace was finally made.

In 1855, the Liceo's auditorium was repainted, and a new curtain by Fèlix Cagé was installed. Masked balls became an integral part of del Liceo's program, and the theater was decorated regularly in carnival style for these occasions. Then calamity struck shortly after 7:00 p.m. on April 9, 1861. The curtain was about to go up on Tomas Rubi's play, *Fortuna contra fortuna*, when fire broke out in the fourth-floor wardrobe area. Flames, visible for fifteen miles, raced through the building. Only the foyer, staircases, and entrance hall survived.

Undaunted by the catastrophe, the board of directors decided to rebuild immediately. Under Mestres's supervision, a new opera house was joined to the surviving sections, and one year after the fire, the rebuilt Teatro del Liceo opened. In 1865, a cholera epidemic struck Barcelona, forcing the opera house to close for several months. Then Queen Isabella II was deposed, causing havoc with the decorations. The plaque and crowns decorating the façade vanished, and her statue, which guarded the central staircase, was unceremoniously dumped into the sea. Del Liceo had become a center of political intrigue until the unthinkable happened. It was November 7, 1893, the opening night of the season. The second act of Gioacchino Rossini's *Guillaume Tell*, conducted by Leopoldo Mugnone, was beginning when Santiago Salvador Franch hurled two bombs from the fifth balcony. One fell harmlessly into the lap of a lady seated in row 25. The second exploded against the back of seat

Upper façade, Gran Teatre del Liceu (Courtesy of Gran Teatre del Liceu, Photo by Català)

24, row 13. Twenty people died and many more were wounded. In the ensuing chaos, Franch was able to leave the theater undetected. The theater closed its doors for several months, but the memory of elegantly dressed women dripping jewels and blood haunted the Liceo for years.

In 1977, Catalan became the official language of Catalonia, and the Gran Teatro del Liceo became Gran Teatre del Liceu. Del Liceu is still under private management, supported by the descendants of the original shareholders, who own their boxes. It is in the enviable position of rarely having any financial problems.

The Theater

The modest classical façade of the Gran Teatre del Liceu conceals one of the world's most magnificent opera houses. The exterior's eight pairs of Doric columns and pilasters flank three arched windows topped by a clock. Inscriptions pay homage to Mozart, Rossini, Calderón, and Moratín. The entrance hall, illuminated by several

Auditorium, Gran Teatre del Liceu (Courtesy of Gran Teatre del Liceu, Photo by Català)

View of stage (Courtesy of Gran Teatre del Liceu, Photo by Roca)

delicate chandeliers, combines a black and white marble floor with blue silk-covered walls. Two rows of beige and gold Ionic style columns divide the hall into three parts leading directly to three white marble staircases. The two lower ones go to the auditorium. The central grand staircase, watched over by the statue "Allegory of Music" by August Vallmitjana, leads to the grand foyer. Following Italian Renaissance canons, the grand foyer is adorned with mirrors, Ionic columns, and medallions of composers, singers, actors, and actresses. The ceiling, painted by Josep Mirabent, shows Apollo surrounded by the Muses, sitting on his throne at Parnassus above the foun-

tain of Castalia. Inscriptions honoring music encircle the room. The best: "Music is the only pleasure which cannot be misused by vice."

The plush red and gold, horseshoe-shaped, Renaissance-style auditorium boasts four tiers of boxes plus two balconies and a marvelous symmetry unspoiled by royal or presidential boxes. The lamps are the original gas lamps, which have been turned upside down to accommodate electric light bulbs. The proscenium arch, painted by Ramir Lorenzale, depicts scenes from Jules Massenet's *Manon*, Richard Wagner's *Die Walküre*, and Giuseppe Verdi's *Otello*. The ceiling is profusely decorated with eight allegorical panels executed by four artists, Ramon Marti i Alsina, Joan Vicens, Agusti Rigalt, and A. Caba. It displays scenes from *Guillaume Tell*, *Macbeth*, *The Frogs*, *El Acero de Madrid*, *The Persians*, and *Pope Marcelo's Mass*, as well as *Orpheus Taming the Wild Beasts* and *Athens Odeon*. The auditorium accommodates 3,000.

Performance History

Barcelona heard its first opera on August 7, 1708—Antonio Caldara's *Il più bel nome*. The first opera by a Catalan composer, Durán's *Antigono*, was performed in 1760. Other Catalan composers such as Carles Baguer, Domènec Terradellas, Ferran Sors, Ramon Carnicer, Mateu Ferrer, and Antoni Rovira all staged their premières here. Various Italian companies also offered opera. Christoph Willibald Gluck's *Orfeo ed Euridice*, which celebrated Carlos III's saint's day, was presented in 1780. The première of Vicenc Cuyàs's *La Fattuchiera* took place in 1838.

On February 3, 1838, Bellini's *Norma* was presented at the newly established Teatro Montesión. Several other Italian operas were staged during its short life. The first opera at the newly opened Teatro del Liceo was Gaetano Donizetti's *Anna Bolena*. For three years the competition between del Liceo and Principal stimulated superb seasons. Twenty-three operas were premiered locally in less than three years before the administrations of the two theaters merged, with Santiago Figueras at the helm. When the novelty of the Liceo wore off, the management offered entertainment of dubious quality along with opera in an effort to fill the house and stay afloat financially.

In 1848, a tradition was begun of bringing Spanish or Catalan operas to the stage on a regular basis. However, for many years they were sung in Italian. Of note were José Antonio Cappa's *Giovanna di Castiglia* in 1848 and Nicolas Guañabens's *Arnaldo d'Erill* in 1859.

Montserrat Caballé and Joan Pons in *La fiamma* (Courtesy of Gran Teatre del Liceu, Photo by Català)

The first season at the rebuilt Liceo lasted from April to June, with eleven different operas seeing the stage. The next year, Giacomo Meyerbeer's *Le Prophète* had its Barcelona première, ushering in an era of French operas, which shared the stage with plays and masked balls. More operas by Catalan composers emerged as well: Francesc Sánchez i Gavagnach's *Rahabba* in 1867, Marià Obiols's *Editta di Belcourt* and Felip Pedrell's *L'ultimo Abenzerraggio* in 1874, followed by Pedrell's *Quasimodo* the next year. Antoni Nicolau's *Constanza* was introduced in 1879 with only two of the opera's four acts performed. The tenor had cancelled his contract. Two years later, the first Catalan opera sung in Catalan, Joan Goula's *A la voreta del mar*, was premiered at the Teatro Principal.

The Teatro Principal also hosted the first Wagner opera to appear in Barcelona—*Lohengrin* on May 17, 1882. The next year *Lohengrin* moved to the Liceo, and five years later, the Catalan tenor Francesc Viñas made his debut in the title role on February 9. Viñas was the first to sing Wagner in Catalan. Since then, all Wagner's operas have been translated into Catalan and performed at the Liceo.

In 1892, the world première of the Tomás Breton's *Garín* took place and was a huge success. Pedrell's *Els Pirineus*, called "a kind of Catalan *Parsifal*," followed ten years later. Enric Morera's *Empòrium*, staged for the first time in 1905, was favorably received, but his *Bruniselda* was not as fortunate. Jaume Pahissa's *Gal la Placídia* graced the stage for the first time in 1913, followed seven years later by Amadeu Vives's *Balada de Carnaval* and Joaquim Cassadó's *Il monaco nero*, conducted by the composer.

Many leading artists of the period appeared on stage at the Liceu: Adelina Patti, Feodor Chaliapin, Enrico Caruso, Tita Ruffo, and Tito Schipa. Ironically, Caruso's debut was not an auspicious occasion. He was booed when he missed one of his high notes. Barcelona-born Maria Barrientos made her debut in 1899 in Meyerbeer's *L'Africaine*.

During the civil war, the Liceo managed to keep its doors open, but the opera pickings were meager. The last performance at the Liceo before Generalissimo Franco entered Barcelona took place on January 22, 1939. Georges Bizet's *Carmen*, advertised for January 24, was canceled. After the war, Carles Suriñach Wrokona's *El mozo que casó con mujer brava* and Xavier Montsalvatge's *El gato con botas* were both premiered.

Since 1945, three Barcelona-born artists have achieved international recognition: Victoria de los Angeles, Montserrat Caballé, and José Carreras. Caballé and Carreras appear regularly at del Liceo, along with other international circuit singers like Leonie Rysanek, Eva Marton, Mirella Freni, Nicolai Ghiaurov, Pilar Lorengar, and Plácido Domingo.

Barcelona traditionally opens the season with operas of Spanish interest. Two important world première openings were Manuel de Falla's *Atlàntida* in 1961, in which de los Angeles performed, and Leonardo Balada's *Cristobal Colón* on September 19, 1987. The latter opera was commissioned by the Spanish government to commemorate the 500th anniversary of Columbus's arrival in America. The celebrations are taking place over a five-year period.

I saw a fantastic and evocative new production of Leoš Janáček's *Jenůfa*. Leonie Rysanek was magnificent in the role of Kostelnicka. She received thunderous bravas and a fifteen-minute standing ovation. Linda Plech was most competent in the title role, well supported by Peter Straka as Steva Buryja and Jan Blinkhof as Laca Klemen. Rudolf Krecmer kept the dramatic tension with his crisp conducting. The lighting by Mario Gas was chillingly precise. Striking sets and costumes were created by Marcelo Grande. There were surtitles in Catalan.

PRACTICAL INFORMATION
Tickets

The box office (*la taquilla*) is located at Rambla dels Caputxins, 65, through the glass doors and to the left of the main entrance of del Liceu. It is open Monday through Friday from 8:00 a.m. to 3:00 p.m. and Saturday from 9:00 a.m. to 1:00 p.m. (*de dilluns a divendres de 8 a 15 h. i els dissabtes de 9 a 13 h.*). On performance days, the box office reopens at 4:00 p.m. and stays open until curtain time (*i des de les 16 h. fins a l'inici de la funció*). Tickets go on sale starting at the end of August for the entire season. You will find a seating plan but no prices posted in the box office. Pick up a program on the table to your right as you enter for prices.

Tickets still available on the day of the performance are sold at the box office between 11:00 a.m. and 1:30 p.m. and from 4:00 p.m. until curtain time.

Tickets can be reserved through the mail for any performance during the season starting the

TICKET TABLE

Tipus de Localitat (Type of Seat)	Preus Localitats (Prices in ptas.)
Llotges (boxes)	
Amfiteatre (1st Tier)	51.600
Platea-6 ent (orchestra-6 seats)	40.860
2n pis-5 ent (2nd tier-5 seats)	34.050
3r pis-4 ent (3rd tier-4 seats)	22.940
2n pis lateral-3 ent (2nd tier side-3 seats)	17.205
3r pis lateral-3 ent (3rd tier side-3 seats)	12.540
4t pis-4 ent (4th tier-stage-4 seats)	16.720
Butaques (seats)	
Platea i amfiteatre (orchestra and 1st tier)	8.600
3r pis la fila (3rd tier 1st row)	7.645
3r pis 2a fila (3rd tier 2nd row)	6.810
3r pis 3a fila (3rd tier 3rd row)	5.735
4t pis la fila central (4th tier 1st row center)	3.465
Entrada de llotja (entrance to box/standing)	3.465
4t pis 2a fila central (4th tier 2nd row center)	3.225
5è pis la fila central (5th tier 1st row center)	3.225
4t pis la fila lateral (4th tier 1st row side)	2.630
4t pis 3a fila (4th tier 3rd row)	2.630
5è pis 2a fila central (5th tier 2nd row center)	2.630
4t pis 2a fila lateral (4th tier 2nd row side)	2.150
5è pis la fila lateral (5th tier 1st row side)	2.150
5è pis 3a fila (5th tier 3rd row)	2.150
4t pis la fila extrem (4th tier 1st row extreme side)	1.670
5è pis 2a fila lateral (5th tier 2nd row side)	1.670
5è pis la fila extrem (5th tier 1st row extreme side)	1.315
Entrada general 4t i 5è pis (standing room/4th-5th tiers)	540

$1 = 101 ptas., but can vary due to the fluctuating value of the dollar.
Ptas. is an abbreviation for pesetas.

beginning of August. Write your name, address, telephone number, opera, date(s), number of tickets, and location of seat(s) on your request. Do not send any money. The Liceu will answer with the number and prices of tickets available for the requested date(s). If none are available, they will inform you of alternative choices. If you want any of the available tickets, you must send payment in pesetas either by international money order or by eurocheque immediately. After they receive payment, they will send you a confirmation of the reservation. Either the tickets will be mailed (if there is enough time) or they will be held at the box office. Write to:

Gran Teatre del Liceu
Department d'Abonaments i Localitats
Rambla dels Caputxins, 65
08001 Barcelona, Spain

You can order tickets by telephoning (34)(3) 318-9122 during box office hours. (34) = country code, (3) = city code. In Spain, dial (93)318-9122. You must speak Catalan or Spanish. Barcelona is five hours ahead of Eastern Standard Time.

The ticket table for del Liceu is very detailed, with the prices of tickets varying not only in each section but in each row. The cost of the ticket accurately reflects your ability to see the stage.

Since every performance is filled with big-name stars, tickets are extremely difficult to purchase. Your best chances for tickets are seeking nonsubscription performances (*función extraordinaria*), avoiding the opening night galas of each opera, getting your ticket requests in as early as possible, being flexible about dates, and, if neces-

sary, accepting seats with poor stage visibility. If you see *exhaurides* (sold out) next to the opera, choose another date. Black tie for the men and evening dress for the ladies is required at opening night galas. Otherwise, dark suits for the men and dressy attire for the ladies are requested.

Tickets are easy to understand if you know the crucial words, so a translation of a sample ticket appears below.

Evening performances (*les funcions de nit*) begin at 9:00 p.m. Matinees (*les funcions de tarda*) start at 5 p.m. Latecomers are not seated until intermission, but you can watch the performance on closed-circuit monitors located in the main entrance. The monthly publication *Agenda de la Ciudad Barcelona* lists the program at del Liceu for the month with the starting times.

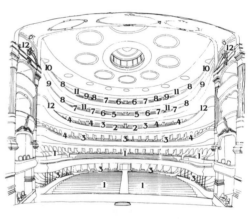

Seating Plan (Courtesy of Gran Teatre del Liceu)

TICKET TRANSLATION

Gran Teatre del Liceu				Grand Theater of the Liceu			
Jenůfa				(Opera)			
Dmg 20 Mai 1990 17H00				Sunday May 20, 1990 5 P.M.			
7.900				(Price)			
Butaca Platea				**Orchestra Seat**			
Funcio	Torn	Fila	Num	Performance Nr.	Subscription	Row	Seat
78	T	05	13	78	T	5	13

Finding Your Way

The Gran Teatre del Liceu faces Rambla dels Caputxins and is bordered on the west by Carrer de Sant Pau. It is easy to miss as you walk down La Rambla, since it is sandwiched between several buildings. You can reach the theater by metro line 3, exit Liceu.

The main entrance to the theater is located at 65 Rambla dels Caputxins. There are three entrance doors, and it is a mob scene when the doors open, with all the elegantly dressed Barcelonians pushing and shoving. Inside, however, everyone is polite once again. From the entrance hall, take either side staircase if you hold tickets in the *platea*. Everyone else goes up the central staircase. Since the auditorium was built sideways, not directly facing Rambla, you will be on the left side of the auditorium when you enter the hallway surrounding it. Turn right to reach the center doors, which sport a royal blue velvet curtain. Ushers, recognized by their dark blue suits, blue ties, and gold L surrounded by a wreath on their pockets, are stationed here. The *platea* contains twenty rows of seats separated by a large center aisle. The seat numbering begins with 1 on the extreme left aisle and increases sequentially to the extreme right aisle. You will find the seat numbers on top of each seat and the row numbers on the back of the first chair in the row. They refer to the row in front of the chair. The rows are wide enough that you do not have to stand up to allow people to pass.

The grand center staircase leads to the *1° pisa*. Around the front you will find the magnificent grand foyer. Take the inside staircase to reach the remaining tiers. Seat and box numbers for all tiers begin with 1 on the extreme left and increase sequentially to the extreme right.

Programs are for sale in the entrance foyer and cost 400 ptas. The program (in Catalan) contains a synopsis in English and articles about the opera and composer. Cloakrooms (*guardaroba*) are located on both sides of the hallway surrounding the *platea* and cost 100 ptas. The ladies' room

Alfredo Kraus in *Lucrezia Borgia* (Courtesy of Gran Teatre del Liceu, Photo by Català)

(*dones*) is to the right through the second door as you enter the *platea* hallway. The men's room (*homes*) is to the left, through the first door, and down the stairs. You will find the bar by taking the first door on your right or left from the *platea* hallway and going down the stairway. (Smoking permitted.) Access and parking for the handicapped are at Sant Pau 1, but be sure to notify the theater twenty-four hours in advance of your arrival.

Planning Your Trip
OPERA SCHEDULE

The opera season runs from September to the beginning of July. The 1990/91 season opened on September 5 with a ballet. The first opera was on September 18, Mozart's *Don Giovanni*. The season closes on July 6 with Mozart's *Die Zauberflöte*. The new productions are Donizetti's *Roberto Devereux* and Vicente Martín y Soler's *Una cosa rara*. Verdi's *Un ballo in maschera*, Wagner's *Die Walküre*, Ruggero Leoncavallo's *Pagliacci*, Ottorino Respighi's *Maria Egiziaca*, Richard Strauss's *Capriccio*, Rossini's *Il barbiere di Siviglia*, Donizetti's *Il campanello*, and Giacomo Puccini's *Tosca* complete the season.

Gran Teatre del Liceu is a *stagione* house, which means only one opera is performed at a time. Opera shares the stage with ballet, concerts, and recitals. To be sure your visit coincides with an opera, write for a schedule:

Gran Teatre del Liceu
Rambla dels Caputxins 65
08001 Barcelona, Spain

If you know Catalan or Spanish, you might be interested in joining L'Associació Amics del Liceu. Cost is 5,000 ptas. a year. For information, write to:

L'Associació
c/o Gran Teatre del Liceu
carrer de Sant Pau núm 1 bis
08001 Barcelona, Spain

TRAVEL INFORMATION

The Spanish railroads should be avoided if at all possible. They try to trick you into buying more expensive tickets by claiming what you have requested is sold out or only smoking seats are available if you requested no smoking. However, at the higher fares, what you have requested always seems to be available. And to add insult to injury, they do NOT accept Eurailpasses on the only modern through-trains they run. The alternative is changing trains three times during the wee hours of the morning to go to any country except France or Portugal. Otherwise, you must pay $150 for a $40 Eurailpass sleeper and $250 for a $75 Eurailpass sleeper. The $150 Eurailpass sleeper is $400. Fly instead.

It is also a pity that one of the world's great opera houses is located in such a hassle-filled city. To prevent all the inconveniences and problems of the city from interfering with your enjoyment of the opera (as they did mine), stay at the Hotel Ritz, Gran Via Cortes Catalanas, 668, 08010 Barcelona, Spain; telephone (34)(3) 318-5200, fax (34)(3) 318-0148. It is Barcelona's most luxurious hotel, and they will take care of all your needs. Singles start at $250, doubles $310. For reservations in the United States, call toll-free, 1-800-223-6800 (member of the Leading Hotels of the World). The Ritz is an elegant five-star hotel with 149 rooms and 12 suites, overlooking a grand tree-lined boulevard in a quiet section of town. The hotel's classical elegance and turn-of-the-century decor make it a great place to luxuriate on your opera trip. For an added treat, order a bottle of their fine champagne. Conveniently located in the best part of town, the hotel is a pleasant twenty-minute walk to the opera house. The concierge can take care of all your last-minute opera ticket needs.

Since La Rambla is the main avenue in Barcelona, there are many restaurants around the opera house. There is also the Restaurante Diana (gourmet and very expensive) in the Hotel Ritz.

The National Tourist Office of Spain, 665 Fifth Avenue, New York, NY 10022, 212-759-8822, can help you with travel material, but they take a long time to respond.

Sweden

Thomas Sunnegårdh and Solveig Faringer in *Gustaf Adolf och Ebba Brahe* at Drottningholms Slottsteater
(Courtesy of Kungliga Teatern, Photo by Rydberg)

STOCKHOLM
Kungliga Teater * Operan
Drottningholms Slottsteater

The first Kungliga Teater, originally called Kongliga Operan, was inaugurated on September 30, 1782, with a gala performance of Johann Gottlieb Naumann's *Cora och Alonzo*. Special stage effects, the likes of which had never before been seen, dazzled the opening night crowd as an earthquake destroyed the great temple amid erupting volcanoes. Cheers of approval greeted the opera and opera house. Designed by Carl Fredrik Adelcrantz, the royal opera house was considered one of the most beautiful buildings in Stockholm for more than a century, before its demolition in 1892. However, this opera house is probably more famous for being the site of King Gustav III's assassination in 1792 than for any opera ever performed there. The event was immortalized in Giuseppe Verdi's *Un ballo in maschera* and Daniel Auber's *Gustave III*.

The second Kungliga Teater, now known as Operan, was inaugurated on September 19, 1898, with Adolf Lindblad's *Frondörerna*, scenes from Franz Berwald's *Estrella di Soria*, and an inaugural cantata by Ivar Hallström. Designed by Axel Anderberg, the neoclassical opera house was grander and more ornate than its predecessor.

HISTORICAL OVERVIEW
Background

Stockholm's first theater was built at Drottningholm, an island near Stockholm, in 1754 by Queen Lovisa Ulrika. Designed by George Greggenhoffer, the *Slottsteater* (castle theater) not only hosted plays but also housed all the actors, actresses, and their families. The theater survived eight years before fire broke out in the middle of a performance. The audience thought it was part of the play when an actress raced on stage, screaming, "Fire, fire!" and fainted. When they realized the fire was real, panic broke out and four people perished. It was August 26, 1762.

Undaunted, Ulrika commissioned Carl Fredrik Adelcrantz to rebuild the theater, but she had little money to pay for it, so Adelcrantz used much of his own money. The result was a masterpiece of illusion. He created a fantasy of wealth by disguising cheap materials to look like the real thing. Drottningholms Slottsteater opened in July 1766. Eleven years later, King Gustav III purchased the theater from his mother. In 1791, the *Déjeunersalongen* (breakfast room) by Louis-Jean Desprez was added. When an assassin's bullet ended the life of Gustav III in March 1792, the Slottsteater was closed.

Meanwhile, in 1773, Gustav III had established Stockholm's first opera house, called Kongliga Svenska Operan, in a refurbished *bollhuset* (ball house) on a hill next to his castle. Nine years later, the first Kongliga Operan opened in Stockholm. After Gustav III's assassination, the opera house closed. His brother, Karl XIII, was appointed regent. When Gustav IV came of age, he attended the opera regularly, but the setting of his father's assassination tormented him, and in 1806, he closed the opera house, even attempting to have it demolished. When its shareholders objected, he accused them of wanting him murdered, too.

Two years later, the opera house was transformed into a field hospital when Sweden went to war against Russia over Finland, which ended up in Russian hands. Since the Swedes were none too happy about the outcome, they deposed King Gustav IV in 1809. Karl XIII, the former regent, became king and reopened the opera house with a coronation performance of Naumann's *Gustav Vasa*. However, it was not until 1812 that opera regularly graced the stage. Six years later, the *Riksdagen* (Swedish parliament) reduced its grant to the Kongliga Teater. The parliament suggested that the opera should be presented by visiting companies, paid for by a separate tax. At the same time, King Karl XIV resolved to abolish the theater. Fortunately, neither suggestion was acted on. After two months, the opera house reopened with a new name, Kongliga Stora Teater. Again in 1888 the *Riksdagen* voted to stop subsidizing the opera, feeling that taxpayers should not support an elitist institution. This crisis turned the opera into a private enterprise until state subsidies were restored. The Kongliga Stora Teater was renamed Kongliga Operan, but shortly thereafter the opera house was demolished, except for part of the façade, which was saved to be incorporated into the new opera house. Architects Magnus Isaeus and Axel Anderberg submitted plans for the new building. The twenty-seven-year-old Anderberg won the commission because his drawings were easier to execute. A theater construction consortium was formed, which was led by bank director K. A. Wallenberg. The consortium volunteered to built the new opera house and turn it over to the state. The new theater, called Kongliga Teater, opened in 1898.

One cold winter day in 1921, an inquisitive theater historian, Agne Beijer, uncovered Drottningholms Slottsteater buried under more than a century of dust. Amazingly, its fifteen sets of scenery and Donato Stopany stage machinery, including wave, thunder, wind, and cloud ma-

Top: Façade of Drottningholms Slottsteater (Courtesy of Drottningholms Theatermuseum)
Middle: Fire safety preparations for performance at Drottningholms Slottsteater (Photo by author)
Bottom: Auditorium, Drottningholms Slottsteater with eighteenth-century scenery (Courtesy of Drottningholms Theatermuseum)

chines, were still intact. The theater was restored to its former glory, with only the lighting brought up to the twentieth century. It reopened on August 19, 1922. Twenty years ago, specially designed flickering electric candles, invented for Drottningholm, were installed. Like candles, the lights stay at the same brightness before, during, and after the performance. The auditorium looks so authentic, you almost expect Gustav III to take his seat in the king's box.

The Theaters

The first Kungliga Teater was an imposing structure, presenting a façade of columns and rectangular windows. A center Corinthian tetrastyle portico supported four statues and was topped by the royal crown. Inside, the auditorium was oval shaped, surrounded by four tiers, and offered everyone good listening and a good view. In addition, it housed the royal apartment, schoolrooms, and the foyer. Sumptuously decorated with neoclassic medallions and pilasters, the foyer was the scene of King Gustav III's assassination.

The Operan is a majestic neoclassical building with Doric columns supporting its portico and Ionic columns supporting its window arches. Four Corinthian columns topped by four statues taken from the first Kungliga Teater complete the façade. As you enter, a marble grand staircase, partially covered with green carpet, looms before you as white marble busts greet you. Cherubs holding glass globes await you at the top of the stairs, where you will find a magnificent gold foyer boasting a ceiling with Swedish folk tales painted by Carl Larsson and the original gold-colored furniture, covered with Florentine brocade. A bust of Gustav III and a painting of Oscar II watch the happenings in the gold foyer from their central positions.

Top: Façade of Operan (Courtesy of Kungliga Teatern, Photo by Rydberg)
Middle: Golden Foyer (Courtesy of Kungliga Teatern, Photo by Rydberg)
Bottom: Auditorium, Operan (Courtesy of Kungliga Teatern, Photo by Rydberg)

The three-tier auditorium, intricately carved and sumptuously decorated in gold and red, is more circular and smaller than its predecessor. The arabesque arches buttress the gallery, lending a pseudo-Moorish look to the top gallery. The allegorical ceiling, depicting Music, Art, and Literature, was painted by Vicke Andrén. One angel carries a drawing of the opera house. High above the proscenium arch, you can spot a depiction of Gustav III. The curtain is a canvas painted to look like a curtain. Operan seats 1,239.

The perfectly preserved Drottningholms Slottsteater transports you back to a private eighteenth-century royal court theater. Located on the lush grounds of Drottningholms *slott* (palace), the plain yellow façade, which looks more like a manor house than a theater, hides a flawless jewel from the baroque period. But like most flawless jewels, it is a fake.

The auditorium, a blend of rococo and neoclassical with a baroque stage, is perfectly symmetrical and harmoniously balanced, even if it required the painting of fake doors. The room is constructed of wood, stucco, and papiermâché. Its ceiling is covered with cloth, the cartouches are made of plaster, and the rest is grisaille. The walls are plaster, painted to look like marble. The room is divided into three sections. The front section, which is underneath the boxes, was the royal section. The middle section was used by members of the court and guests. The back part, undecorated and separated from the rest of the auditorium by a painted curtain, was reserved for the servants. The steeply raked T-shaped auditorium allowed full view of the stage from every long, hard, backless bench. The benches now sport thinly padded blue backrests and cushions. "Democratic" sightlines were in use a century before Bayreuth was even built.

The auditorium has no balconies and only six boxes. Each box originally had its own purpose. The front two boxes were "gentlemen's boxes," where young men of the court flirted with the ladies during the performance. There was no view of the stage. The middle pair of boxes was reserved for the royal couple. Gustav III sat in the right box, and Sophie Magdalena sat in the left one. (They did not like each other.) The third pair was the "incognito" boxes, used by Gustav when he did not want his subjects to know he was present or if he had to depart in the middle of the performance. They were also used by young widows during their first year of mourning, when they were not supposed to be seen in public. The theater seats 454.

Performance History

Opera was first heard in Sweden during the reign of Queen Christina (1644-1654). By the mid-1700s, permanent French and Italian companies had been established. When King Gustav III ascended the throne in 1771, he was determined to establish a Swedish theater, but he cringed when he first heard a play performed in Swedish. (Swedish aristocracy, like Prussian aristocracy, used French as the language of culture.) Believing that music would absorb some of the shock of the Swedish language, he founded Swedish Opera in 1773. Since there were no Swedish operas, Gustav III proceeded to write one, which Francesco Uttini set to music. *Thetis och Pelée* opened the Kongliga Svenska Operan (*bollhuset*) on January 18, 1773. It was so popular, the opera played twenty-four times. Georg Friedrich Händel's *Acis and Galatea* came next, followed by the première of Christoph Willibald Gluck's *Orfeo ed Euridice* on November 25, 1773. Two years later, Uttini's *Aline, drottning av Golconda* was staged and in 1776, André Grétry's *Lucile* entertained the court. Naumann's *Amphion*, Grétry's *Zémire et Azor*, and Gluck's *Iphigénie en Aulide* were performed in 1778.

The first Kungliga Teater was to have been inaugurated with Josef Martin Kraus's *Aeneas i Cartago*, but "Dido" had to flee the country with her husband to avoid creditors, so Naumann's *Cora och Alonzo* got the honors. Another Naumann opera, *Gustav Vasa*, with libretto by Gustav III, was premiered on January 19, 1786. *Aeneas i Cartago* finally received its world première in 1799. Another opera written by Gustav III and set to music by Abbé Volger, *Gustav Adolf och Ebba Brahe*, was premiered on January 24, 1788.

Top: *Don Giovanni* with Lena Nordin and Stefan Dahlberg (Courtesy of Kungliga Teatern, Photo by Rydberg)
Bottom: *Gustaf Adolf och Ebba Brahe* at Drottningholms Slottsteater (Courtesy of Kungliga Teatern, Photo by Rydberg)

The Operan reopened on May 30, 1812, with the first Wolfgang Amadeus Mozart opera heard in Sweden, *Die Zauberflöte*. During most of the nineteenth century, foreign operas graced the stage. However, several homegrown operas did surface. Eduard Brendler's *Ryno* (completed by crown prince Oscar) in 1834, Adolf Lindblad's *Frondörerna* in 1835, Andreas Randel's *Värmlänningarne* in 1846, and Ivar Hallström's *Vita frun på Drottningholm* in 1847. Fifteen years later, Franz Berwald's *Estrella di Soria* was introduced on April 9, Hallström's *Den bergtagna* in 1874, his *Vikingarna* in 1877, and Per August Ölander's *Blenda* in 1876. The most illustrious performer to emerge in the nineteenth century was Jenny Lind, who made her debut as Agathe in Carl Maria von Weber's *Der Freischütz* on March 7, 1838. Six years later, she left Stockholm to continue her career abroad. During the 1847/ 48 season, she returned as a guest artist, dazzling the audience in Gaetano Donizetti's *La Fille du Régiment*, Vincenzo Bellini's *Norma*, and Mozart's *Le nozze di Figaro*.

After the new Kungliga Teater opened in 1898, operas continued in a Swedish vein, with the première of Wilhelm Stenhammar's *Tirfing* on September 19, 1898, Andreas Hallén's *Valdemarsskatten* the next year, and Stenhammar's *Gillet på Solhaug* in October 1902. Wilhelm Peterson-Berger's *Ran* was introduced on May 20, 1903, *Arnljot* on April 13, 1910, *Domedagsprofeterna* in February 1919, and *Adils och Elisiv* on February 27, 1927. The Swedish fare shared the stage with the usual repertory favorites. However, one popular Verdi opera was conspicuously absent from the schedule: *Un ballo in maschera*.

Gustaf Adolf och Ebba Brahe at Drottningholms Slottsteater (Courtesy of Kungliga Teatern, Photo by Rydberg)

248

Madama Butterfly (Courtesy of Kungliga Teatern, Photo by Rydberg)

Not until 1927 was Gustav III's assassination re-created, in the Boston version. It was not funny, but laughter rippled through the auditorium at the distortions: Gustav III was in reality a homosexual, not a lady's man, and his assassin, Anckarström, was certainly not his friend. Not until Göran Gentele produced his controversial *Maskaradbalen* in 1958, with several shapely pages prancing around the stage, did the laughter stop. Three years later, Ingmar Bergman made his debut as director at Operan with Igor Stravinsky's *The Rake's Progress*.

Meanwhile, the world première of Gunnar Frumerie's *Singoalla* took place on March 16, 1940. Oskar Lindberg's *Fredlös* was premiered in 1943, Heinrich Sutermeister's *Raskolnikov* on October 14, 1948, and Karl-Birger Blomdahl's *Aniara* on May 31, 1959. One hundred years after the death of Berwald, his opera, *Drottningen av Golconda*, was introduced on April 1, 1968. Hilding Rosenberg's *Hus med dubbel ingång* was staged for the first time in May 1970. The bicen-

tennial of Swedish opera was celebrated in 1973 with the world première of Lars Johan Werle's *Tintomara* on January 18. Five years later, Györgi Ligeti's *Le Grand Macabre* graced the stage for the first time on April 12, 1978, followed by Per Nørgård's *Siddharta* on March 18, 1983, and Hans Gefors's *Christina* in October 1986.

Some of the greatest singers of the twentieth century were Swedish and made their debut either at the Kungliga Teater or Drottningholms Slottsteater: Jussi Björling as Ottavio in Mozart's *Don Giovanni* in 1930, Birgit Nilsson as Agathe in Weber's *Der Freischütz* in 1946, Elisabeth Söderström as Bastienne in Mozart's *Bastien und Bastienne* in 1947, and Nicolai Gedda as Chapelou in Adolphe Adam's *Le Postillon de Longjumeau* in 1952.

Today, the Operan is weaning itself from Gustav III's dream of operas sung in Swedish. The impracticality of finding enough singers who can sing in Swedish combined with the lack of marketability of their Swedish-trained singers has forced the change. Although comic operas are performed in Swedish, tragic operas are usually sung in their original language with Swedish surtitles. A milestone of sorts was reached in April 1990 when Charles Gounod's *Faust* was sung in French.

I saw *Tosca* (sung in Italian) with Rolf Björling, Jussi Björling's son, as Cavaradossi, Jadwiga Koba as Tosca, and Björn Asker as Scarpia. Björling, looking very much like his father, performed admirably, as did Asker. Koba, however, shrieked more than she sang. The production was more than two decades old and looked in need of an overhaul. I would suggest attending a more current production for a delightful evening.

At the Slottsteater I saw *Gustav Adolf och Ebba Brahe*, a Swedish opera aimed at glorifying the monarchy, with the libretto by King Gustav III. Given the historical setting of Drottningholm, the opera fit perfectly. Delightful singing by Solveig Faringer as Ebba and Thomas Sunnegårdh as Gustav Adolf contributed much to an enjoyable evening. The orchestra, dressed in frock coats and powdered wigs, was conducted by Thomas Schuback. The scenery, copies of the originals by Louis Jean Desprez, was pure baroque. Opera at Drottningholms Slottsteater is unspoiled by the centuries that have passed since its inception.

PRACTICAL INFORMATION
Tickets
OPERAN

The box office (*biljettkontor*) is located at Jacobs Torg 2, along the left side of the opera house. It is open Monday through Friday from 11:00 a.m. to 7:30 p.m. and Saturday from 11:00 a.m. to 3:00 p.m. (*måndag-fredag 11-19,30, lördag 11-15*). It is closed on Sundays (*söndag stängt*). On performance days, it remains open until curtain time. You can buy tickets for a performance four weeks ahead. If there is a line when you enter the box office, take a number. There are three windows with price lists and seating plans posted next to the windows.

Tickets can also be reserved by mail. Write to:

Operan-Kungliga Teatern
P.O. Box 16094
10 322 Stockholm, Sweden

You can order tickets by telephoning (46)(8) 248-240 during box office hours. (46) = country code, (8) = city code. In Sweden, dial (08) 248-240. Stockholm is six hours ahead of Eastern Standard Time.

Tickets for Operan are not difficult to get, if you avoid *urpremiär* (world premières), *Sverigepremiär* (Sweden premières) and *nypremiär* (new productions). However, if you write ahead you should be able to get tickets in those hard-to-get categories. If a performance has *utsålt*

TICKET TABLE	
Location	Prices in Sek
Parkett (orchestra)	170
I:a Radens Fond (1st tier center)	200
I:a Radens Loger (1st tier boxes)	170
II:a Radens Fond (2nd tier center)	110
II:a Radens Sida (2nd tier side)	70
III:e Nedre Radens Fond (3rd tier front center)	70
III:e Nedre Radens Sida (3rd tier front side)	60
III:e Ovre Radens Fond (3rd tier rear center)	60
III:e Ovre Radens Sida (3rd tier rear side)	50

$1 = Sek 6, but can vary due to the fluctuating value of the dollar.
Sek is an abbreviation for Swedish krona. It is also abbreviated kr.

(sold out) or *helabonnerat* (closed performance) written next to it, plan on another date.

Your ticket will appear confusing, but it is crucial to understand it because there are no ushers at the Operan. Below is a translation of a sample ticket.

Most operas start at 7:30 p.m. (*kl.* 19.30), and no one is admitted after the opera begins. *På Operan*, available at the box office, lists the starting times and the opera schedule for both Operan and Drottningholms Slottsteater. The English language *Stockholm This Week* lists the operas and starting times as well.

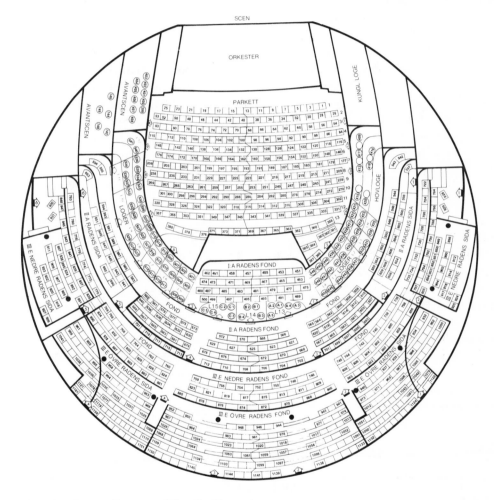

Seating Plan, Operan (Courtesy of Kungliga Teatern)

TICKET TRANSLATION					
Operan	Måndag	19:30 Tosca	Operan	Monday	7:30 P.M. (Opera)
Stora Scenen		11/6 1990	Great Stage		June 11, 1990
	Plats			Seat	
Parkett Vänster	131	170 Sek	Orchestra Left	131	(Price)
Dörr 9 Bänk 5			Door 9 Row 5		

251

DROTTNINGHOLMS SLOTTSTEATER

If you are in Sweden, six hundred post offices all over the country which bear the sign *Biljetter till Nöjen* become Drottningholms box offices at the end of March for one month.

Tickets are available to those from abroad throughout the season. Write to:

Drottningholms Slottsteater
Box 27050
10251 Stockholm, Sweden

Tickets can also be ordered by fax or by telephone starting the end of March. Telephone (46)(8)660-8225 or (46)(8)660-8281; fax (46)(8) 661-0194. Stockholm is six hours ahead of Eastern Standard Time.

If you venture to the Slottsteater without tickets, "turn backs" are resold, starting one hour before the performance, from a table set up in the theater's entrance foyer. The line forms outside, and as tickets become available (usually only a few per performance), a baroque-clad usher calls out the number, location, and price.

Since the theater is very small and the atmosphere unique, every performance is sold out. Your best chance for tickets is to write or fax as soon as the tickets go on sale at the end of March. A certain number of tickets are reserved for overseas visitors.

It is important to understand your ticket since the ushers only direct you to the correct entrance door. A translation appears below.

All operas begin at 8:00 p.m. (*kl.* 20.00), and no one is admitted after the opera begins. Check *På Operan* or *Stockholm This Week* for any change in the starting times.

TICKET TRANSLATION

Drottningholms Slottsteater	Tisdag 20:00 12/6 1990	Gustav Adolf Och Ebba Brahe
	Plats	
Mittenstol	**S12**	**400 Sek**

Drottningholms Castle Theater	Tuesday 8 p.m. June 12, 1990	(Opera)
	Seat	
Middle Chair	**S12**	**(Price)**

TICKET TABLE

Location	Prices in Sek
Bänk 5-7 (rows 5-7)	400
Bänk 1-4 (rows 1-4)	290
Bänk 8-12 (rows 8-12)	290
Bänk 13-16 (rows 13-16)	225
Bänk 17-20 (rows 17-20)	175
Bänk 21-27 (rows 21-27)	115
Bänk 28-31 (rows 28-31)	75

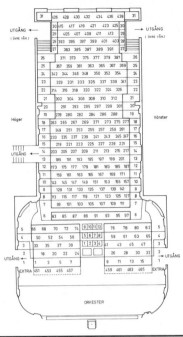

Top: Seating Plan (Courtesy of Drottningholms Slottsteater)
Bottom: 1990 Festival program (Courtesy of Drottningholms Slottsteater)

Finding Your Way

OPERAN

Operan faces Gustav Adolfs Torg and is bordered on the south by Strömgatan, on the east by Karl XII's Torg, and on the north by Jakobs Torg. You can reach the opera house by the following public transportation: buses 55 and 62, exit Gustav Adolfs Torg; buses 46 and 76, exit Karl XII's Torg; buses 43 and 59, exit: Jakobsgatan or Riksdagshuset. Also *Tunnelbana* 10 and 11, station Kungsträdgården, exit Gustav Adolfs Torg.

The main entrance to the Operan is located at Gustav Adolfs Torg. If you are seated in the *parkett* (orchestra), *först raden* (first tier), or *andra raden* (second tier), enter through the main doors. If you are seated in the *tredje raden* (third tier), enter through the door on Strömgatan. For those holding tickets in the *parkett* or *först raden*, go up the grand staircase. The first landing is the *parkett* level. You will be in the green hallway surrounding the orchestra. Match the door number on your ticket with the number next to the door. All the rows and seats served by each door are listed next to the door number. *Dörr* (doors) 6-10 are on the *vänster* (left) side, and doors 1-5 are on the *höger* (right) side. Brass and black seat numbers are on the backs of the seats. If you hold tickets in the *först raden*, continue to the top of the grand staircase. Those seated in the *andra raden* use the staircase at the extreme end of the entrance foyer.

Programs are sold at the coat check and cost Sek 20. The program (in Swedish) contains a synopsis in English, articles, and photographs relating to the opera. Cloakrooms (*garderob*) are located on the right and left sides in the hallway surrounding the *parkett*. There is no charge. The ladies' room (*damtoalett*) is on the right side of the hallway; the men's room (*herrtoalett*) is on the left side. Refreshments and nonalcoholic beverages are available at the extreme right side of the hallway and downstairs in the Opera Kafé. Neither smoking nor alcoholic beverages are allowed in the opera house. There are places for eight to ten wheelchairs in the orchestra. Wheelchair ramps are on both sides of the opera house.

DROTTNINGHOLMS SLOTTSTEATER

Drottningholms Slottsteater is located on one of the islands dotting the waters around Stockholm, on the Drottningholm Palace grounds, the current residence of the Swedish royal family. Boats depart from *stadshusbron* (city hall bridges) every half hour from May through September for Drottningholm and cost Sek 25 one way. The boats stop running at 7:00 p.m., so you will have to return by bus. The bus stop is a block from the theater. You change at Brommaplan for the "green line" *Tunnelbana* to T-Centralen. Sometimes a "theater bus" is waiting in the parking lot and goes directly into downtown Stockholm. The theater bus costs Sek 25.

The main entrance to Drottningholms Slottsteater faces south and is flanked by four pavilions. Gustav III's brothers and sisters lived in these buildings at one time. Currently the first one on the left is the Theater Museum, worth a visit. (Since the museum closes at 5:00 p.m., you will have to arrive early and have dinner on the grounds.)

Male ushers, attired in powdered wigs, blue waistcoats, and gray knickers, greet you at the door. Female ushers, dressed in long white Empire gowns with red sashes, take your ticket. If your ticket reads *vänster*, turn left in the entrance hallway; for *höger*, turn right. Those with *mitten* (center) can use either side. You will walk through several rooms, some with the original furniture and wallpaper, before reaching the doors leading into the auditorium. Rows 1-7 with seats 1-111 are in the front royal third of the auditorium and are best reached through the doors closest to the stage. Rows 8-20 with seats 113-301 are in the middle section, and rows 21-31 with seats 302-436 are in the old servants' section. The two red and gold royal chairs are reserved for the king and queen. Be careful when exiting the auditorium: a couple of the doors are fakes.

Programs are sold at the table on your left in the entrance foyer as well as in the *Déjeuner-salongen*. They cost Sek 35. The program, covering all the operas in the Drottningholm festival for that season, is in both Swedish and English. There are articles and illustrations relating to the operas and the composers. Cloakrooms (*garderob*) are also in the entrance foyer. There is no charge. The ladies' room (*damtoalett*) is through the doors on the right side of the entrance foyer, behind an unmarked gray door next to the fireplace. It is very easy to overlook. The men's room (*herrtoalett*) is through the doors on the left side of the entrance foyer near the stage. Nonalcoholic refreshments are sold in the *Déjeunersalongen*. There is no smoking inside the theater; fire alarms and stern warnings are posted all over.

If you cannot get a ticket to Drottningholms Slottsteater, you can tour the theater during the day for Sek 25. Tours in English are given once an hour. Round-trip by boat costs Sek 45. (Do not take the theater tour offered by the sightseeing boat companies. It is the identical tour, only more expensive.)

Planning Your Trip
OPERA SCHEDULE
OPERAN

The season runs from the end of August through mid-June. The repertory is varied, with an emphasis on classical opera. At least one Swedish opera is performed each season. The 1990/91 season opened on August 25 with Mozart's *Don Giovanni* and will close on June 19, 1991, with Mozart's *Die Entführung aus dem Serail*. In addition, Mozart's *Le nozze di Figaro*, Giacomo Puccini's *Tosca* and *Madama Butterfly*, Richard Wagner's *Lohengrin* and *Die Walküre*, Richard Strauss' *Salome*, Carl Orff's *Carmina Burana* (concert form), George Bizet's *Carmen*, Gounod's *Faust*, Jacques Offenbach's *Les Contes d'Hoffmann*, Dominick Argento's *The Aspern Papers*, and Sven-Erik Bäck' *Tranfjädrarna* are on the schedule. Many of the opera titles are in Swedish, so you might have to guess what opera you are going to see.

Operan is a repertory house with performances every night except Sunday and a matinee on Saturday. Opera shares the stage with ballet. To be sure your visit coincides with an opera, write or call for a schedule:

Operan—Kungliga Teatern
P.O. Box 16094
103 22 Stockholm, Sweden
Telephone (46)(8)203-515

If you read Swedish and visit Stockholm often, you might be interested in *Operavännerna vid Kungliga Teatern*. For Sek 100 per year, you will receive a monthly calendar on the happenings at the opera, a yearbook, invitations to artist receptions, discounts on purchases, and the opportunity to buy tickets before they go on sale to the public. For more information, write to:

Operavännerna vid Kungliga Teatern
Box 5110
102 43 Stockholm
Sweden
Telephone (46)(8)339-871

DROTTNINGHOLM

The opera season at Drottningholms Slottsteater runs from the end of May to mid-August. The 1990 season opened on May 31 with a new production of *Gustav Adolf och Ebba Brahe* and closed on August 11 with Mozart's *Trädgårdspiga På Låtsas* (*La finta giardiniera*). Mozart's *Enleveringen ur Seraljen* (*Die Entführung aus dem Serail*) and Gluck's *Ifigenia Bland Tauriderna* (*Iphigénie en Tauride*) completed the schedule. The castle theater is run on a *stagione* system, which means only one opera is performed at a time.

TRAVEL INFORMATION

The best hotel for operagoers in Stockholm is the SAS Strand Hotel, Nybrokajen 9, P.O. Box 16396, 10327 Stockholm, Sweden; telephone (46)(8)678-7800, fax (46)(8)204-436. Singles start at $200, doubles at $250. If you are visiting during the summer, ask about their special rates. A delicious Swedish breakfast is included. It is

Lohengrin (Courtesy of Kungliga Teatern, Photo by Rydberg)

a delightful five-star hotel with 120 rooms and 18 suites. Superbly situated in the best and quietest part of town, the hotel enjoys a great waterfront location. The view from the rooms is fantastic. Charmingly decorated in a Swedish style, the SAS Strand offers a free minibar in each room. Many famous opera singers have stayed there. It is only a five-minute walk to the opera house, and the front desk can take care of all your last-minute opera requests.

A complex of restaurants is located around the back of the Operan facing the adjacent park. Operakällaren offers gourmet food at very high prices, Café Opera offers lighter fare, and the Bakfickan is a reasonably priced upscale counter restaurant. In addition, the hotel's Strand Piazza offers great meals.

You do not have much choice if you eat at Drottningholm. There is only one restaurant, charming but overpriced: the Drottningholms Paviljongen.

Scandinavian National Tourist Offices, 655 Third Avenue, New York, NY 10017, 212-949-2333, can send you travel information only. Write far ahead. They take a long time to respond.

Switzerland

Yoko Watanabe in *Mefistofele* (Courtesy of Opernhaus Zürich, Photo by Schlegel)

GENEVA
Grand Théâtre de Genève

$\mathcal{G}$rand Théâtre de Genève, originally known as Théâtre Municipal de Genève, was inaugurated on October 4, 1879, with a gala performance of Gioacchino Rossini's *Guillaume Tell*. Numerous prominent guests, from the *Conseil fédéral* to the mayor of Saint-Julien, took part in the glorious festivities, which lasted until 2:00 a.m. Designed by J. E. Gosse, the opera house survived seventy-two years before a conflagration devoured the building. The Grand Théâtre de Genève, with its nineteenth-century façade and twentieth-century auditorium, reopened on December 10, 1962, with a glittering production of Giuseppe Verdi's *Don Carlos*.

HISTORICAL OVERVIEW
Background

The first theater in Geneva sprang up in 1766. Built entirely of wood, it was named Théâtre de Rosimond, after the impresario who managed it. Geneva being a Calvinist city, the locals were not enamored of the theater and referred to it as "*La grange des étrangers*" (the Barn of the Foreigners). The theater, seating 800, boasted three tiers of boxes and a huge chandelier, whose candles dripped unceremoniously on the hats and clothes of the audience. (Soon, the chandelier received a glass tray to catch the drippings.) The Théâtre de Rosimond was short-lived. On the night of January 29, 1768, a fire raged through the wooden building.

For over a decade the city had no theater.

Then on July 2, 1782, the troops of *Puissance* entered Geneva, and the first stones for the Théâtre de Neuve were laid. Designed by architect Matthey, Théâtre de Neuve opened on October 18, 1783. Later, political troubles boiled over, and the doors of the Théâtre de Neuve were shut on December 13, 1788. The doors reopened periodically until October 11, 1797, when all performances were banned. In 1798, French troops arrived in Geneva, proclaiming the Lemanic Republic, and on November 2, 1798, the theater reopened. Five years later, the Act of Mediation gave the Swiss cantons their independence and Neuve was closed and its doors locked until 1817.

As early as 1861, it had become evident that Geneva had outgrown its opera house. During Théâtre de Neuve's existence, the population of Geneva had tripled, and its tastes in opera had broadened. However, it was not until 1879 that the successor of the Théâtre de Neuve, the Théâtre Municipal de Genève, was inaugurated. For the occasion, the majestic façade was brilliantly lit by four candelabra flanking the three arched entrance doors. The architect, J. E. Gosse, was trained in Paris, and his French influence permeated the structure. The following year, the Théâtre de Neuve was demolished.

At the beginning of the 1910-11 season, the theater's name was changed from Théâtre Municipal de Genève to Grand Théâtre de Genève, although there was little in their programming to justify such a presumptuous change. Switzerland maintained strict neutrality during both world wars and the opera house remained unscathed.

Six years after World War II ended, on the morning of May 1, 1951, the company was rehearsing *Die Walküre*. To silence growing criticism of the opera house's technical capabilities, an oxygen tank was used to ''improve'' the fire surrounding Brünnhilde's rock. It was near the end of the third act, when Wotan raised his spear. As the Magic Fire Motif began and *"Loge hör! Lausche hierher"* resounded through the auditorium, a real flame six feet long shot forth, transforming the Grand Théâtre into a *Götterdämmerung*.

It took eleven years to replace what fire had destroyed in minutes. The current opera house, designed by the architects Schopfer and Zavelani-Rossi, is a masterful blend of the grandeur and glory of a bygone era with the practicality demanded by today's audiences.

The Theater

The Théâtre de Neuve had a noticeably plain façade: three large shuttered windows, flanked by six Ionic columns, and crowned by a clock. Posters announcing the upcoming performances were plastered beside the entrance doors. A huge central oil-burning chandelier illuminated the auditorium, which was described as comfortable and sumptuous. Boasting a parterre and three galleries, the theater accommodated 1,100 —940 seated and the rest as standees.

The Théâtre Municipal, a *Belle Époque*-style building, was a splendid affair. ''Tragédie—Poésie Lyrique—Comédie'' was carved high on its façade, along with the names Adam, Auber, Beethoven, Bellini, Donizetti, Gounod, Grétry, Halévy, Meyerbeer, Mozart, Rossini, and Rousseau. Various busts and gargoyles complemented four pairs of Corinthian columns flanking three suitably embellished windows. Statues of François Voltaire, William Shakespeare, Jean Racine, and Sophocles guarded the arched entrance doors.

Top: Façade of Grand Théâtre de Genève (Courtesy of Grand Théâtre de Genève)
Middle: Detail of façade (Photo by author)
Bottom: Auditorium, Grand Théâtre de Genève (Courtesy of Grand Théâtre de Genève)

The intimate auditorium, with three narrow horseshoe-shaped tiers, boasted medallions of Duprez, Déjazet, Talma, Rachel, Perlet, Lecouvreur, Thespis, Roscius, Mars, Baron, Dugazon, Elleviou, Arnould, Nourrit, and Falcon. A huge chandelier, carrying 400 gas jets, shed light over the surroundings. The auditorium accommodated 1,300 spectators—1,200 seated and 100 standing.

The rebuilt Grand Théâtre is a harmonious blend of the nineteenth and twentieth centuries. The exterior dates back to the original 1879 theater, with only one change: the elimination of the *marquise* entrance on the boulevard du Théâtre side, which led to the *loges* for the "privileged." The new entrance foyer displays two sculptures by Jakob Probst: "Genius" on the right and "Diane Chasseresse" on the left. One flight up, the grand foyer is as exquisite as ever, with its delicate crystal chandeliers, fresco ceiling inhabited by celestial beings, white and black marble fireplace, gold embellishments, mirrors, and horn-blowing cherubs. But the magnificent *Belle Époque* auditorium was lost forever, a victim of pragmatism. The modern auditorium, its ceiling transformed into a gold and silver galaxy-filled sky designed by Jacek Stryjenski, is paneled in dark wood with red velvet seats. The opera house holds 1,488.

Performance History

The Théâtre de Rosimond managed one complete season, 1766-67, during which 140 performances were given. André Grétry, then twenty-five years old, assisted Charles Simon Favart with *Isabelle et Gertrude*. But Grétry, finding the music so inadequate, composed his own version. *Isabelle et Gertrude* became Grétry's first French opera and Geneva's first *création mondiale* (world première).

Jeu de l'Amour et du Hasard inaugurated the Théâtre de Neuve on October 18, 1783. During the early years, opéra comique was the fare, with many Grétry operas in the repertory. One such

Top: Samuel Ramey in *Mefistofele* (Courtesy of Grand Théâtre de Genève (Photo by Meister)
Bottom: *Die Zauberflöte* (Courtesy of Grand Théâtre de Genève, Photo by Appelghem)

opera, *La Caravane du Caire*, had the distinction of employing a libretto by the Count de Provence, the future King Louis XVIII. Although Rossini's *Guillaume Tell* was first offered not long after its Paris première and was tremendously popular, Geneva seemed to lag behind in introducing new successful operas, especially those still found in today's repertory.

In 1850, Gilbert Duprez became *directeur*, and under his leadership the first *création mondiale* in eighty-six years appeared onstage: Bovy-Lysberg's *La Fille du Carillonneur* on April 17, 1854. Then *La Reine de Provence* by two inhabitants of Geneva was introduced on April 21, 1857. Seven years later, Kling's *Le Dernier des Paladins* was premiered followed by his *Le Flûtiste* on March 15, 1877.

During the almost one hundred years of existence of the Théâtre de Neuve, only twenty operas were produced which are performed more or less regularly today: Rossini's *Il barbiere di Siviglia* and *Guillaume Tell*; Gaetano Donizetti's *Don Pasquale, Lucia di Lammermoor, L'elisir d'amore*, and *La Fille du Régiment*; Vincenzo Bellini's *Norma, La sonnambula*, and *I Capuleti e i Montecchi*; Charles Gounod's *Faust*; Verdi's *Rigoletto, Il trovatore, Un ballo in maschera*, and *La traviata*; Wolfgang Amadeus Mozart's *Don Giovanni, Le nozze di Figaro*, and *Die Zauberflöte*; Richard Wagner's *Tannhäuser*; Ludwig van Beethoven's *Fidelio*; and Carl Maria von Weber's *Der Freischütz*.

Grand opera took center stage at the Théâtre Municipal. Giacomo Meyerbeer's *Les Huguenots* and Jacques Halévy's *La Juive* were performed, both unqualified triumphs. Then the Geneva première of Jules Massenet's *Hérodiade* took place, with Massenet present at the sold out performance. His *Sapho* was also a tremendous success with an overflowing crowd voicing its approval from the first act on. Again Massenet was there to receive the accolades. When the audience refused to leave after the performance, Massenet descended into the pit to congratulate the conductor and then climbed

onstage to lavish praise on the performers, the director, the excellent scenery, and the orchestra. His *Cendrillon* was also popular, but his *La Navarraise* just did not make it. Other Massenet operas performed were *Don César de Bazan*, which Massenet conducted himself, *Werther, Esclarmonde*, and *Thaïs*.

Municipal's first world première took place on December 16, 1886, with de Grisy's *Jacques Clément*. The work received seven performances before sinking into oblivion. Six years later, another now long forgotten opera received its world première, Louis Lacombe's *Winkelried*. The next world première, *Janie*, written by a well-known Geneva composer, Jacques-Delcroze, was officially deemed a success, but it went into a permanent sleep after four performances. There was great hope for Audran's *Photis*, introduced on February 28, 1896, but it, too, met a premature death after only five performances. Two seasons later, Jacques-Delcroze's *Sancho* appeared, followed by Delaye's *A bicyclette*, and Signan's *Anita* the next season.

After the turn of the century, the world premières of G. de Seigneux's *Tout s'arrange*, Maurice's *Le Drapeau blanc*, and L. Aubert's *La Forêt bleue* were seen at the Municipal. Other operas offered were Ruggero Leoncavallo's *La bohème*, presented before Giacomo Puccini's version; Amilcare Ponchielli's *La Gioconda*, performed after his death and conducted by his son; the French première of Umberto Giordano's *Siberia*; and Henri Rabaud's *Mârouf, Savetier du Caire*, conducted by the composer.

After a hiatus of a decade, the Grand Théâtre, as it was now called, hosted the world première of Knopf's *Les Baisers perdus*. However, soon management apathy set in, and productions became mediocre. When the Great Depression descended on Europe during the 1930s, the number of performances dropped to ten per season. During World War II, mainly operettas graced the stage. However, during the 1943-44 season, Dupérier's *Le Malade imaginaire*, an opéra comique, was premiered. Things picked up after the war, when operas new to Geneva's audience were introduced: Maurice Ravel's *L'Heure espagnole*, Gabriel Fauré's *Pénélope*, Richard Strauss's *Salome*, Modest Mussorgsky's *Boris Godunov*, and Nikolai Rimsky-Korsakov's *Zolotoy petushok* (The Golden Cockerel) sung in French under its French title, *Le Coq d'Or*. Then the fire closed the opera house for eleven years.

When the Grand Théâtre reopened, it was under the direction of Marcel Lamy. Rafaello de Banfield's *Alissa*, staged on May 14, 1965, was the first world première in the rebuilt opera house. Herbert Graf took the helm at the end of the 1964-65 season, introducing Darius Milhaud's *La Mère coupable* on June 13, 1966, as well as operas by two Geneva-born composers: Frank Martin's *Der Sturm* on April 11, 1967, and Ernest Bloch's *Macbeth* on October 29, 1968. In 1973,

Jean-Claude Riber took over as *directeur général*, followed by Hugues Gall in 1980. Gall was Rolf Liebermann's right-hand man in Paris, and he carried Liebermann's successful formula to the Grand Théâtre: grand productions, great singers, and captivating performances. In fact, Gall's tenure has been so outstanding that a marvelous book has been published which preserved forever those grand operatic moments, *Grand Théâtre de Genève—Operas Moments d'exception*, by Jean-Jacques Roth. Gall presented the world première of Girolamo Arrigo's *Il ritorno di Casanova* on April 18, 1985, and Liebermann's *La Forêt* on April 8, 1987. Both were stunning and provocative productions.

I saw a delightful performance of Georg Friedrich Händel's *Alcina* with Arleen Auger as Alcina, Della Jones as Ruggiero, and William

Lyubov' k tryom apel'sinam (The Love for Three Oranges) (Courtesy of Grand Théâtre de Genève, Photo by Appelghem)

Christie conducting. It was a stunning new production, admirably sung and well executed. For an opera company in a city of only 300,000 inhabitants, Geneva's performances rank with the best. There are surtitles in French.

Practical Information

TICKETS

The box office is located at Place Neuve, inside the opera house and identified with this sign on the door: *Entrée Location—Heures d'ouverture des guichets 10 à 19 jours ouvrable, samedi 10 à 17. Le premier jour de location des spectacles de 8h à 19h. Les soirs de spectacle: ouverture des guichets de location 1 heure avant le début de la représentation* (Box office entrance—open 10:00 a.m. to 7:00 p.m. workdays, Saturday 10:00 a.m. to 5:00 p.m. First day tickets are sold to an opera, the box office is open from 8:00 a.m. to 7:00 p.m. On performance evenings, the box office window opens one hour before the performance begins). You can buy tickets starting seven days before a performance.

There are eight box office windows, with opera tickets sold at windows 4 and 5. Price lists are posted around the box office, and color-coded seating charts are found under the windows. No credit cards are accepted, only cash and eurocheques. If you can, ask for your tickets *en français s'il vous plaît.*

Tickets are not available by mail. However, you can telephone (41)(22)212-311 for tickets, which can be picked up the evening of the performance. (41) = country code, (22) = city code. In Switzerland, dial (022)212-311. You should be able to speak French. Geneva is six hours ahead of Eastern Standard Time.

Since tickets are difficult to get, especially for the new productions (*nouvelle productions*), your best chance is to attend a nonsubscription (*hors abonnement*) performance. If that does not work into your plans, you will increase your odds if you avoid the première subscription night (*1 abonnement*). If you must see a new production on opening night, arrive at the box office at 8:00 a.m. seven days ahead of the first performance. Otherwise, you will be greeted with a *complet* (sold out) sign. Remember, black tie is desired for premières. If *représentation populaire à guichets fermé* is written before a date, it is a closed performance, so think of another date. Every seat offers a splendid view of the stage.

TICKET TABLE

Section	Price in SFr.
Parterre (orchestra)	
Orchestre I 1er au 14e rang (orchestra rows 1-14)	101/81
Orchestra II 15e au 17e rang (orchestra rows 15-17)	86/72
Balcon (1st tier)	
Loges (boxes)	101/81
Cordon (1st row)	101/81
Balcon face (center)	101/81
Balcon côté (side)	86/72
Galerie (second tier)	
Loges (boxes)	101/81
Cordon face (1st row center)	101/81
Cordon côté (1st row side)	86/72
Galerie face (center)	101/81
Galerie côté (side)	86/72
Amphithéâtre (third tier)	
Cordon (1st row)	73/50
1re série face 42e au 48e rang (rows 42-48 center)	73/50
2e série face 49e au 55e rang (rows 49-55 center)	62/44
Côté 1re série 42e au 48e rang (rows 42-48 side)	48/38
Côté 2e série 49e au 52e rang (rows 49-52 side)	30/16

The lower price applies only to certain operas.
$1 = SFr. 1.2, but can vary due to the fluctuating value of the dollar.
SFr. is an abbreviation for Swiss franc. It is also abbreviated Fr.

Your ticket might appear confusing, but understanding it will help you find your seat with no problem. First, the section is noted as a letter: **O** (orchestre), **B** (balcon), **G** (galerie), **A** (amphithéâtre), followed by the row number (1-55), and the seat number. A sample ticket appears below.

All performances start at 8:00 p.m. (20 *h*), and no one is admitted after the performance begins. Check the season program, available at the box office, for any exceptions. In addition, the bimonthly publication *Genève Flash* lists the performances at the opera house.

Statues in front of façade (Photos by author)

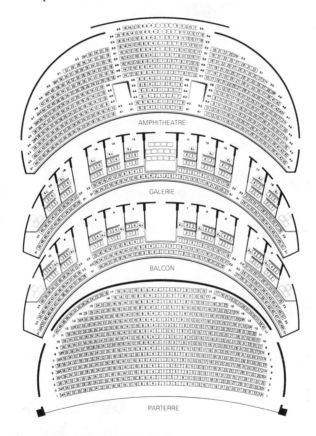

Seating Plan (Courtesy of Grand Théâtre de Genève)

TICKET TRANSLATION			
Grand Théâtre de Genève	Great Theater of Geneva		
13 Mai 1990 * 20.00	May 13, 1990 *		8:00 p.m.
O11/1	**Orchestra**	**Row 11**	**Seat 1**

Top: *Le nozze di Figaro* (Courtesy of Grand Théâtre de Genève, Photo by Meister)
Bottom: *Fidelio* (Courtesy of Grand Théâtre de Genève, Photo by Appelghem)

Finding Your Way

Le Grand Théâtre faces Place Neuve. It is bordered on the east by rue François Diday, on the west by boulevard du Théâtre, and on the north by rue Bovy Lyssberg. You can reach the opera house with these buses: 3, 5, and 17. No. 5 also stops at the Gare de Cornavin (central train station).

The main entrance to Le Grand Théâtre is at Place Neuve. In the entrance foyer you will find the sign *Parterre—Balcons—Galeries* above the center doors, which lead into a red-carpeted hallway. If you are holding tickets in any of these locations, go straight ahead. If you are seated in the *amphithéâtre* and have an odd-numbered seat (*impair*), go to the extreme left end of the foyer, where you will find *Amphithéâtre—Ascenseur—Impair* over the door. If you have an even-numbered seat (*pair*), go to the extreme right end of the foyer, where you will find *Amphithéâtre—Ascenseur—Pair* over the door. The elevators (*ascenseur*) are located there as well.

Doors going into the *parterre* are off the red-carpeted hallway on both sides. You enter the auditorium at row 11. Even numbers are on the right side, and odd numbers are on the left side. Seats 1 and 2 are located in the middle of each row, increasing sequentially to the side aisles. Black and silver seat numbers are on the floor. Since the seats stretch in unbroken rows across the orchestra, it is important to enter on the correct side. Those seated in the *balcon* and *galerie* take the staircase in the hallway. *Balcon* is at the first landing, and *galerie* at the top. Row numbers begin with 1 in the first row orchestra and continue to 55 in the last row of the *amphithéâtre*. Ushers are recognizable by their chocolate brown suits and beige blouses.

Programs are for sale in the entrance foyer and from the ushers. They cost SFr. 5. The program (in French) is filled with reproductions of etchings, engravings, and paintings relating to the opera as well as several articles. Cloakrooms (*vestiaire*) are located on both the right and left sides of the *parterre* hallway and cost SFr. 1.50. A bar is set up in the entrance foyer (smoking permitted), in the grand foyer on the *galerie* level (smoking prohibited), and down one flight off the *parterre* hallway (smoking permitted). Ladies' rooms (*toilette-dames*) and men's rooms (*toilette-messieurs*) are at the extreme ends of the *galerie* level and on the first landing leading down to the bar.

Planning Your Trip
OPERA SCHEDULE

The season runs from September through June. The repertory of operas ranges from baroque to contemporary, with a special emphasis on French opera. The 1990/91 season opened on September 11 with a new production of Verdi's *Simon Boccanegra* and will close on July 1 with a new production of Rossini's *Guillaume Tèll*. Other new productions are Jacques Offenbach's *La Vie parisienne*, Bellini's *I Capuleti e i Montecchi*, and Mozart's *Don Giovanni*. Richard Strauss's *Daphne* (in concert form) and *Intermezzo*, Benjamin Britten's *Peter Grimes*, and two ballets (*Romeo et Juliette* and *Axioma/Les sept péchés capitaux/Ghost dances*) complete the season. Many of the titles are in French, so occasionally you might have to guess what opera you are going to see.

Le Grand Théâtre is a *stagione* house, which means only one opera is presented at a time. Opera shares the stage with ballets, concerts, and recitals. To be sure your trip coincides with an opera, write for a schedule:

Grand Théâtre de Genève
Bureau de location, Place Neuve
1211 Geneva, Switzerland

If you read French, you might be interested in joining the *Association Genevoise des Amis de l'Opéra et du Ballet*. For more information, write to:

Association Genevoise des Amis de l'Opéra
Grand Théâtre de Genève
11, Boulevard du Théâtre
1211 Geneva, 11, Switzerland

TRAVEL INFORMATION

The best hotel for operagoers in Geneva is the Hotel Du Rhone, Quai Turrenttini 1, 1201 Genève, Switzerland; telephone (41)(22)731-9831, fax (41)(22)732-4558. For reservations call toll-free in the United States, 1-800-223-6800 (member of the Leading Hotels of the World). Singles start at $170, doubles at $260. Du Rhone is a luxurious five-star hotel with 272 rooms and 8 suites. Nonsmoking rooms are available. Superbly located in the best and quietest part of town, the hotel overlooks *Le Fleuve Rhône*. For a special treat, request a room on the *Bel Étage*. The rooms have VCRs with tapes of what to do and see in Geneva. They are also filled with neat gadgets, like an inside thermometer that tells you the temperature outside and curtains that open and close with a push of a button next to your bed. You will be in good company; many famous opera people stay here. The hotel is only a five-minute walk to the opera house, and it is safe to walk back after the performance. The hotel can arrange opera tickets for you. Since mail orders are not accepted, this is a big bonus. Contact the marketing department at the above address a few weeks ahead for all your opera ticket needs.

Several restaurants are near the opera house: Brasserie Landolt, 2, rue de Candolle, Le Lyrique, 12, boulevard du Théâtre, and La Terrasse, rue de la Corraterie. In addition, the Neptune is in the hotel.

The Swiss National Tourist Office, 608 Fifth Avenue, New York, NY 10020, 212-757-5944, can send you travel information only. Write far ahead. They take a long time to respond.

ZURICH
Opernhaus Zürich

The Opernhaus Zürich, originally known as the Stadttheater, was inaugurated on October 1, 1891, with a gala production of Richard Wagner's *Lohengrin*. Designed by Ferdinand Fellner and Hermann Helmer, the opera house was owned by its subscribers and managed by the municipality. Almost a century later, the Opernhaus underwent major restoration and expansion, reopening on December 1, 1984, with the world première of Rudolf Kelterborn's *Der Kirschgarten*, especially commissioned for the occasion.

HISTORICAL OVERVIEW
Background

In 1522, Zwingli and his followers loosened Catholicism's firm grip on Zurich and, in the process, converted the Barfüßer chapel from a place of worship to a grain storage center. The chapel took on a new life later in the sixteenth century when it became Zurich's first theater. However, its new role lasted only until 1624, when public performances were banned indefinitely.

More than two hundred years passed before a theater society was formed by private shareholders on October 24, 1832. Their task: find a suitable theater. They returned to the Barfüßer chapel, remodeled it, and renamed it the Aktientheater. Since many religious fanatics disagreed with the opening of a theater, the stockholders, fearing riots, did not post notices of its opening until a day before the performance. The the-

ater was active for more than fifty-five years, until fire ended its existence on New Year's night 1890.

After the demise of the Aktientheater, construction began on the Stadttheater Zürich. In 1925, a separate playhouse was erected, and the Stadttheater was renamed Opernhaus Zürich to reflect its new role, that of a theater devoted exclusively to opera, operetta, and ballet.

By the 1970s, the Opernhaus was in terrible shape: badly deteriorated, with antiquated stage facilities and a fire hazard besides. The Opernhaus was slated to be torn down and a modern theater complex constructed on the site. A competition was held for the best plans, and architect W. Dunkel was commissioned to develop his designs further, but the necessary funds did not materialize. Instead, 61 million francs were voted by the government to reconstruct the existing opera house and to build a concrete annex for the box office, administrative offices, dressing rooms, rehearsal halls, and a new Bernhard Theater.

Riots followed the voting of the renovation money, and hundreds of shop windows were broken. The rioters felt the money should not be spent on an "elitist" opera house. When the news spread that 18 million additional francs were required to complete the project, more rioting erupted, and fear spread that the opera house would be defaced and its glass portals smashed. The fear was so widespread that when the restored opera house reopened in 1984, the formally attired opening night audience had to

Top: Opernhaus before restoration (Courtesy of Opernhaus Zürich archives)
Bottom: Former carriage entrance after renovation (Photo by author)

pass through a police cordon before entering. The reopening coincided with the 150th anniversary of the first permanent theater in Zurich, the Aktientheater.

The Theater

The grand Opernhaus Zürich is an ornate fin-de-siècle building, with Teutonic inspiration. Built of white and gray stone, the neoclassical façade boasts a tetrastyle portico with busts of Carl Maria von Weber, Wolfgang Amadeus Mozart, and Wagner. Corinthian pilasters support two pediments and flank busts of Friedrich Schiller and Johann von Goethe. "MDCCCXC Stadt-theater Zürich MDCCCXCI" is etched in gold letters across the top. Busts of William Shakespeare and Gotthold Lessing and the inscriptions "Den Musen Ein Heim" (A Home for the Muses) and "Der Kunst Eine Stätte" (A Place for the Arts) adorn the side of the building. Four pairs of Doric columns support the former carriage entrance. Enclosed with glass walls and glass portals sporting brass handles, the entrance leads into a rococo auditorium, adorned with caryatids, cherubs, and garlands. Three ivory and gold parapets ascend from the plush red orchestra seats. Four oil paintings of allegorical beings, representing Music and Poetry, Comedy, Drama, and Love, by the Viennese painters Gastgeb, Peyfuss, and Gartner, encircle a celestial-like chandelier. Thirteen medallions complete the ornamentation. The curtain, distemper on fishbone canvas, depicts Muses from the arts: Erato, Polyhymnia, Clio, Melpomene, Euterpe, Urania, Thalia, Terpsichore, and Calliope. The concrete annex, nicknamed the "bunker" by Zurich's disenchanted inhabitants, is stark and modern. The Opernhaus Zürich seats 1,238.

Performance History

Religious and political pieces were performed in Zurich as early as the sixteenth century, including Johannes Haller's *Eydnossisch Spyll* in 1599. But within twenty-five years, presentations ceased. Not until the founding of the theater society in 1832 were performances revived, with Mozart's *Die Zauberflöte* inaugurating the Aktientheater on November 10, 1834. Five years later, Konradin Kreutzer directed his *Nachtlager von Granada*. Wagner, during his exile in Zurich between 1849 and 1858, was associated with the Aktientheater. He directed not only his *Der fliegende Holländer* and *Tannhäuser* but other operas as well.

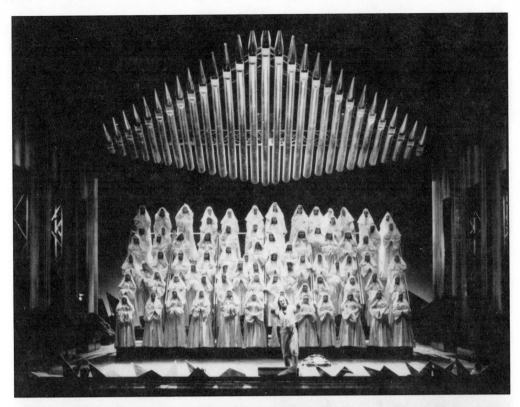

Top: *Mefistofele* (Courtesy of Opernhaus Zürich, Photo by Schlegel)
Bottom: *Lucia di Lammermoor* (Courtesy of Opernhaus Zürich, Photo by Schlegel)

Top: *Siegfried* (Courtesy of Opernhaus Zürich, Photo by Schlegel)
Bottom: Jean-Pierre Ponnelle with Thomas Hampson (Courtesy of Opernhaus Zürich, Photo by Schlegel)

After the Stadttheater opened, the world premières of Ferruccio Busoni's *Turandot* and *Arlecchino* took place on May 11, 1917. Five years later, Swiss composer Othmar Schoeck's *Venus* was introduced. On June 2, 1937, Acts I and II of Alban Berg's *Lulu* graced the stage for the first time. (His widow delayed the completion of Act III, only partially written at the time of his death, for more than forty years.) Paul Hindemith's *Mathis der Maler* was introduced on May 28, 1938, and the following year Helde Gueden made her debut as Cherubino in Mozart's *Le nozze di Figaro*. Immediately after the war, Beniamino Gigli and Kirsten Flagstad delighted the Zurich audience. Hindemith's revised *Cardillac* was performed on June 20, 1952, and the first staging of Arnold Schönberg's *Moses und Aron* took place on June 6, 1957. The *Uraufführung* of Bohuslav Martinů's *Řecké pašije* (*The Greek Passion*), was offered on June 9, 1961, followed by Paul Burkhard's *Barbasuk* on December 3. Armin Schibler's *Blackwood & Co.* was staged on June 3, 1962, with Gwyneth Jones making her debut. Rudolf Kelterborn's *Die Errettung Thebens* was world premiered on June 23, 1963, and his *Ein Engel kommt nach Babylon* appeared on June 5, 1977. A decade earlier, Heinrich Sutermeister's *Madame Bovary* had graced the stage for the first time on May 26 and Giselher Klebe's *Ein wahrer Held* was introduced on January 18, 1975.

Opernhaus Zürich was and still is a haven for young singers to try out new roles in an acoustically sympathetic auditorium. James McCracken sang his first *Prophète* there, Agnes Baltsa her first *Carmen*, and José Carreras his first *Werther*.

A few years ago, I saw a pleasant production of Strauss's *Der Rosenkavalier* with Mechthild Gessendorf as the Feldmarschallin, Helmut Berger-Tuna as Baron Ochs, Ute Walther as Octavian, and Cheryl Parrish as Sophie. Ralf Weikert was responsible for the conducting chores.

PRACTICAL INFORMATION
Tickets

The box office, (*Vorverkaufskasse*) is located at the Theaterplatz in the Informationszentrum down a flight of stairs. It is open Monday through Saturday from 10:00 a.m. to 6:30 p.m. (*Montag bis Samstag 10-18.30 Uhr*). It reopens one hour before curtain time (*Abendkasse*). Tickets go on sale seven days before the performance.

Tickets can be ordered by mail for any non-subscription opera for the entire season. To receive the schedule of nonsubscription performances and an order form (*Bestellkarte*), write to:

Opernhaus Zürich
Billetkasse
Falkenstraße 1
8008 Zurich, Switzerland

You can telephone the Opernhaus-Kasse at (41)(1)251-6922 or (41)(1)251-6923 to order tickets. (41) = country code, (1) = city code. In Switzerland, dial (01)251-6922. You should speak German. They will hold tickets up to thirty minutes before the performance for foreign visitors. Prepaid tickets can be picked up anytime, even after the performance has begun. Zurich is six hours head of Eastern Standard Time.

TICKET TABLE

Seat Location	Price in SFr	
	Stufe (Level)	
	II	III
Kategorie 1	101	111
Parkett, Reihen 1-16 (orchestra rows 1-16) Parkett-Galerie, Reihe 1 (1st tier, row 1) Parkett-Logen, Reihe 1 (1st tier boxes, row 1) 1. Rang, Reihe 1 (2nd tier, row 1) 1. Rang-Logen, Reihe 1 (2nd tier boxes, row 1)		
Kategorie 2	89	99
Parkett-Galerie, Reihe 2 (1st tier, row 2) 1. Rang, Reihen 2, 3 (2nd tier, rows 2, 3)		
Kategorie 3	78	88
Parkett-Galerie, Reihen 3, 4 (1st tier, rows 3, 4) 1. Rang, Reihen 4, 5 (2nd tier, rows 4, 5) 2. Rang Mitte, Reihe 1-3 (center 3rd tier, rows 1-3) 2. Rang Seite, Reihe 1 (side 3rd tier, row 1)		
Kategorie 4	46	52
Parkett-Logen, Reihe 2 (1st tier boxes, row 2) 1. Rang-Logen, Reihe 2 (2nd tier boxes, row 2) 2. Rang Mitte, Reihen 4-6 (center 3rd tier, rows 4-6) 2. Rang Seite, Reihe 2, Platz 1-12 (side 3rd tier, row 2, seats 1-12) 2. Rang Seite, Reihe 3, Platz 1-12 (side 3rd tier, row 3, seats 1-12) 2. Rang Seite, Reihe 4, Platz 1-13 (side 3rd tier, row 4, seats 1-13) 2. Rang Seite, Reihe 5 (side 3rd tier, row 5)		
Kategorie 5	17	19
Parkett-Logen, Reihe 3 (1st tier boxes, row 3) 1. Rang-Logen, Reihe 3 (2nd tier boxes, row 3) 2. Rang-Mitte, Reihe 7 (center 3rd tier, row 7) 2. Rang Seite, Reihe 2, Platz 13-20 (side 3rd tier, row 2, seats 13-20) 2. Rang Seite, Reihe 3, Platz 13-18 (side 3rd tier, row 3, seats 13-18) 2. Rang Seite, Reihe 6,7 (side 3rd tier, rows 6,7)		

$1 = SFr 1.2, but can vary due to the fluctuating value of the dollar.
SFr. is an abbreviation for Swiss franc. It is also abbreviated Fr.

Several different seating locations are identically priced, accurately reflecting your ability to see and hear the performance.

Some light comic operas and Singspiele fall under *Stufe* II. All the other operas fall under *Stufe* III. You should have no trouble buying tickets to *freier Verkauf* (nonsubscription) performances except on Saturday nights. Tickets to *Abonnement* (subscription) performances are noted with *beschränkter freier Verkauf* (limited ticket availability). *Premieren* (premières), *Galavorstellungen* (galas), and *Gastspiele* (international singers) are almost always *Ausverkauft* (sold out) far in advance. If you see *geschlossene Vorstellung* (closed performance), think of another date.

The tickets are easy to understand when you know the meaning of the German words, so below is a translation of a sample ticket.

The starting time is not printed on the ticket. Operas usually begin at 7:30 p.m. (19.30). However, longer operas start earlier, and shorter ones begin later, so consult the Zurich newspaper for the exact starting time. Latecomers are not admitted once the performance begins.

Finding Your Way

Opernhaus Zürich faces Theaterplatz and is bordered on the east by Theaterstraße, on the south by Falkenstraße, and on the west by Mozartstraße. It is one block from the Zürich-See. You can reach the opera house with buses 2, 4, 11, and 15. From the *Hauptbahnhof* (Main Railroad Station) it is a pleasant but long walk along the Limmat River and Zürich-See to the opera house.

The main entrance is at Theaterplatz. After entering the egg-shaped grand vestibule, those with tickets in the *Parkett* (orchestra) continue straight ahead, turning right if the ticket reads *rechts* or left if the ticket reads *links*. Since the seats stretch in unbroken rows across the auditorium in the *Parkett*, it is important to enter the row on the correct side. Seat 1 is on the left, with the numbers increasing sequentially to the right aisle.

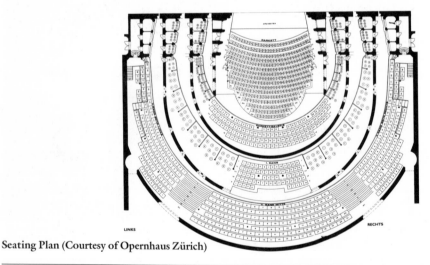

Seating Plan (Courtesy of Opernhaus Zürich)

TICKET TRANSLATION	
Opernhaus Zürich	Zurich Opera House
Parkett	Orchestra
Rechts	Right
Reihe 2 Sitz 20	**Row 2 Seat 20**
Dienstag 28.6.88	**Tuesday 6/28/88**

Top: *La Fille du Regiment* (Courtesy of Opernhaus Zürich, Photo by Schlegel)
Bottom: Thomas Hampson and László Polgár in *Don Giovanni* (Courtesy of Opernhaus Zürich, Photo by Schlegel)

Nello Santi and Daniel Schmid (Courtesy of Opern-haus Zürich, Photo by Schlegel)

Seats 14-16 are in the middle of the row, except for rows 22-26. The stairway closest to the *Parkett* entrance leads up to the *Parkett-Logen*, *Parkett-Galerie*, *1.Rang-Logen*, and *1.Rang*. The stairs closest to the main entrance on the left leads to *2.Rang links*, and the middle staircase on the right goes to the *2.Rang rechts*.

Programs are for sale in the entrance vestibule and from the ushers. They cost SFr. 7. The program (in German) contains articles and photographs pertaining to the opera, composer, and singers. Synopses in English are available separately. The ladies' rooms (*Damen*), men's rooms (*Herren*), cloakrooms (*Garderoben*), and bars are all located in the annex. Take the first staircase on the right side of the entrance vestibule down one flight and walk through the passageway. The cloakroom and rest rooms are on your left, and a bar is on your right. Additional cloakrooms, bars, and rest rooms are ahead. The cloakrooms are gratis, and they do **not** expect tips. In fact, you **must** check your coat, umbrella, and any packages you may have with you. Several guards keep a watchful eye at all entrances. I had a folded umbrella with me, which was inadvertently covered when I entered the theater. As I came out for the first intermission, a guard pounced on me, inquiring how I had smuggled the umbrella into the auditorium. I was told in no uncertain terms to check it before the next act. He explained the reason for their strict policy: many patrons

come dressed in fine clothes, and their evening could be ruined by having to climb over seats filled with wet items or dirty bundles.

Planning Your Trip
OPERA SCHEDULE

The opera season runs from September through June. The 1990/91 season opened on September 19 with Charles Gounod's *Romeo et Juliette* and closes on July 6 with Wagner's *Götterdämmerung*. The repertory ranges from baroque to contemporary, with special emphasis given to the baroque and French operas. Hector Berlioz's *Les Troyens*, Johann Strauß's *Der Zigeunerbaron*, Giacomo Puccini's *Tosca*, Richard Strauss's *Elektra*, Pyotr Il'yich Tchaikovsky's *Eugene Onegin*, and John Cage's *Europeras 1+2* are new productions. Mozart's *La clemenza di Tito*, *Die Zauberflöte*, and *Die Entführung aus dem Serail*, Gaetano Donizetti's *Lucia di Lammermoor* and *La Fille du Régiment*, and Verdi's *Il trovatore*, Wagner's *Das Rheingold*, *Die Walküre*, and *Siegfried* complete the schedule. Opera shares the stage with ballet. To be sure your visit coincides with an opera, write ahead for a schedule:

Opernhaus Zürich
Informationszentrum
Theaterplatz
8008 Zurich, Switzerland

TRAVEL INFORMATION

Two hotels are conveniently located behind the opera house: Hotel Opera, Dufourstraße 5, 8008 Zurich; telephone (41)(1)251-9090, singles start at $120, doubles at $190, including continental breakfast; Hotel Europe, Dufourstraße 4, 8008 Zurich, (49)(1)471030, singles start at $150, doubles at $210, including continental breakfast.

Several restaurants and sandwich shops are located near the opera house and in the *Altstadt* just to the north.

The Swiss National Tourist Office, 608 Fifth Avenue, New York, NY 10020, 212-757-5944, can send you travel information only. Write far ahead. They take a long time to respond.

Appendix

BOX OFFICE SURVIVAL
Essential Words

English	*Italian*	*French*	*German*
Box Office	Biglietteria	Bureau de location	Vorverkaufskasse
Ticket	Biglietto	Billet	Eintrittskarte
Sold Out	Tutto Esaurito	Complet	Ausverkauft
Closed Performance	Serata Riservata	Soirée Réservée	Geschlossene Vorstellung
Nonsubscription	Fuori Abbonamento	Hors Abonnement	Freier Verkauf
Subscription	Turno	Abonnement	Abonnement
Reservation	Prenotazione	Location	Vorbestellung

English	*Catalan*	*French (Belgium)*	*Flemish*
Box Office	La Taquilla	Bureau de location	Bespreekbureau
Ticket	Localitat	Billet	Ticket
Sold Out	Exhaurides	Complet	Uitverkocht
Closed Performance	–––––	à Bureaux Fermés	Besloten Voorstelling
Nonsubscription	Función Extraordinario	Vente Libre	Vrije Verkoop
Subscription	Torn	Abonnement	Abonnement
Reservation	Reserva	Réservation	Plaatsbespreking

English	*Danish*	*Swedish*	*Dutch*
Box Office	Billetkontor	Biljettkontor	Kassa
Ticket	Billet	Biljett	Kaart
Sold Out	Udsolgt	Utsålt	Uitverkocht
Closed Performance	Lukket Forestilling	Helabonnerat	–––––
Nonsubscription	–––––	–––––	Buiten Abonnement
Subscription	Abonnement	Abonnemang	Abonnement
Reservation	Forudbestilling	Förköp	Plaatsbespreking

Useful Phrases

English	Italian

English

Italian

I would like to buy a ticket for. . .
    today * this evening *
    tomorrow * tomorrow evening *
    this afternoon *
    tomorrow afternoon

Vorrei comprare un biglietto per. . .
    *oggi * questa sera (stasera) **
    *domani * domani sera **
    *questo pomeriggio **
    domani pomeriggio

    Monday * Tuesday * Wednesday *
    Thursday * Friday * Saturday * Sunday

    *lunedì * martedì * mercoledì **
    *giovedì * venerdì * sabato * domenica*

one * two * three * four * five *
six * seven * eight * nine * ten

*uno * due * tre * quattro * cinque **
*sei * sette * otto * nove * dieci*

How much does this ticket cost?
This ticket costs. . .

Quanto costa questo biglietto?
Questo biglietto costa . . .

Please write down the price.
It is sold out.

Per favore, scriva il prezzo.
È tutto esaurito.

That is rather expensive.

È piuttosto caro.

Do you have something less expensive?

Ha qualcosa di meno costoso?

I will take this ticket.

Prendo questo biglietto.

At what time does the performance start?
It begins at . . .
    7:00 p.m. *
    7:30 p.m. *
    8:00 p.m. *
    8:30 p.m.

A che ora comincia la rappresentazione?
Comincia alle. . .
    *le sette di sera (diciannove) **
    *le sette e mezza di sera **
    *le otto di sera (venti) **
    le otto e mezza di sera

Where is this seat?
    To the left *
    To the right *
    straight ahead

Dove si trova questo posto?
    *A sinistra **
    *A destra **
    sempre avanti

Front Orchestra
Rear Orchestra
Boxes
Gallery

Poltrone
Poltroncina
Palchi
Galleria

I am sorry, but I do not understand.

Mi scusi, ma non capisco.

Please speak more slowly.

Parli più lentamente, per favore.

Could you please repeat?

Può ripetere, per favore?

English	French

English

I would like to buy a ticket for. . .
    today * this evening *
    tomorrow * tomorrow evening *
    this afternoon *
    tomorrow afternoon

    Monday * Tuesday * Wednesday *
    Thursday * Friday * Saturday * Sunday

one * two * three * four * five *
six * seven * eight * nine * ten

How much does this ticket cost?
This ticket costs. . .

Please write down the price.
There are no more tickets

It is too expensive.

Do you have anything less expensive?

I will take this ticket.

At what time does the performance begin?
It begins at . . .
    7:00 p.m. *
    7:30 p.m. *
    8:00 p.m.

Where is this seat located?
    to the left *
    to the right *
    straight ahead

Orchestra
First Balcony
Second Balcony
Third Balcony

I am sorry, but I do not understand.

Would you please speak less quickly.

Would you please say that again.

French

Je voudrais acheter un billet pour. . .
    *aujourd'hui * ce soir ***
    *demain * demain soir ***
    *cet après-midi ***
    demain après-midi

    *lundi * mardi * mercredi ***
    *jeudi * vendredi * samedi * dimanche*

*un * deux * trois * quatre * cinq ***
*six * sept * huit * neuf * dix*

C'est combien ce billet?
Ce billet coûte . . .

S'il vous plaît, ecrivez le prix.
Il n'y a plus de billets

C'est trop cher.

Vous n'avez rien d'autre de moins cher?

Je prends ce billet.

A quelle heure commence la représentation?
Elle commence à . . .
    *dix-neuf heures (sept heures du soir) ***
    *dix-neuf heures et demie ***
    vingt heures (huit heures du soir)

Où se trouve cette place?
    *A gauche ***
    *A droite ***
    tout droit

Parterre
Premier Balcon
Deuxième Balcon
Troisième Balcon

Excusez-moi, mais je ne comprends pas

Voulez-vous parler moins vite, s'il vous plaît.

Voulez-vous répéter, s'il vous plaît.

English	German

English

I would like to buy a ticket for. . .or
I would like to buy a ticket for. . .

    Today * This evening *
    Tomorrow * Tomorrow evening *
    This Afternoon
    Tomorrow Afternoon

    Monday * Tuesday * Wednesday *
    Thursday * Friday * Saturday, * Sunday

one * two * three * four * five *
six * seven * eight * nine * ten

How much does this ticket cost?
This ticket costs. . .

Please write down the price.
There are no more tickets.

That is too expensive

Do you have something cheaper?

I'll take this ticket.

At what time does the performance begin?
It begins at . . .
    7:00 p.m. *
    7:30 p.m. *
    8:00 p.m. *
    8:30 p.m.

Where is this seat located?
    On the left side *
    On the right side *
    straight ahead

Orchestra
First Balcony
Second Balcony
Third Balcony

I am sorry, but I did not understand you.

Please do not speak so fast.

Please say it again.

German

Ich möchte eine Karte für. . .kaufen.
or *Ich hätte gern eine Karte für. . .*

    *Heute * Heute Abend ***
    *Morgen * Morgen Abend ***
    *Heute Nachmittag ***
    Morgen Nachmittag

    *Montag * Dienstag * Mittwoch ***
    *Donnerstag * Freitag * Samstag, (Sonna-*
    *bend) * Sonntag*

*Eins * Zwei * Drei * Vier * Fünf ***
*Sechs * Sieben * Acht * Neun * Zehn*

Wieviel kostet diese Karte?
Diese Karte kostet . . .

Bitte schreiben Sie den Preis auf.
Es gibt keine Karten mehr.

Das ist zu teuer.

Haben Sie etwas Billigeres?

Ich nehme diese Karte.

Um wieviel Uhr fängt die Vorstellung an?
Sie fängt um . . .an.
    *Neunzehn Uhr ***
    *Neunzehn Uhr Dreißig (Halb Acht) ***
    *Zwanzig Uhr ***
    Zwanzig Uhr Dreißig (Halb Neun)

Wo finde ich diesen Platz?
    *Auf der linken Seite ***
    *Auf der rechten Seite ***
    Geradeaus.

das Parkett
der erste Rang
der zweite Rang
der dritte Rang

Es tut mir leid, aber ich habe Sie nicht verstanden.

Sprechen Sie bitte nicht so schnell.

Weiderholen Sie bitte.

BOOKS TO BUY

For those of you who would like to have enlightening souvenirs of your trip, I strongly recommend the following books and booklets, all of which I have read and own. Since many of the books on European opera houses are not available in English, I have grouped them according to the foreign language background necessary for understanding. Opera houses that are not on the list do not offer any worthwhile books or booklets at this time.

These books capture the essence of the opera houses and performances through pictures or annals, with little or no text, and require no knowledge of the foreign language:

Grand Théâtre de Genève Operas Moments d'Exception (Paris: Office du Livre Editions Vilo, 1987) by Jean-Jacques Roth [French]

Le Immagini-Teatro Regio Torino, Stagione Lirica 1986-87 (Turin: Teatro Regio Torino, 1988) [Italian]

Le Immagini-Teatro Regio Torino, Stagione Lirica 1988-89 (Turin: Teatro Regio Torino, 1990) [Italian]

25 Jahre Deutsche Oper Berlin (Berlin: Deutsche Oper Berlin, 1986) [German]

Teatro Regio Parma-Cronologia degli Spettacoli Lirici 1829-1989 4 Vols. plus Indici (Parma: Citta di Parma, Teatro Regio, 1979, 1980, 1981, 1982, 1990) [Italian]

These books require a basic knowledge of the foreign language and a good dictionary to understand the text and have so many delightful pictures that even if the text is not completely comprehensible, they are still enjoyable.

*Il Teatro La Fenice:I Progetti * L'Architetture * Le Decorazioni* (Venice: Albrizzi Editore, 1987) [Italian]

Il Teatro Comunale di Firenze (Florence: Studio GE 9, 1987) [Italian]

Teatro dell'Opera di Roma (Rome: Teatro dell' Opera di Roma, 1989) [Italian]

*Lo Spettacolo:La Musica * Il Teatro * Il Cinema* (Busto Arsizio: Bramante Editrice, 1987) [Italian][1]

Un Théâtre d'Opéra: L'Équipe de Gerard Mortier à la Monnaie (Paris: Duculot, 1986) [French] (A synopsis in English is available with the book.)

Historie du Théâtre de Genève (Geneva: Théâtre de Genève, 1978) by Roger De Candolle [French]

Das Frankfurter Opernhaus 1880-1980 (Frankfurt: Waldemar Kramer, 1980) by Albert Richard Mohr [German]

Berliner Forum 1/86-Die Deutsche Oper Berlin (Berlin, 1986) [German]

Operan 200 År: Jubelboken (Stockholm: Bokförlaget Prisma, 1973) by Klas Ralf (ed.) [Swedish]

Books/booklets originally written or translated into English:

A History of the Royal Opera House Covent Garden 1732-1982 (London: The Royal Opera House, 1982)

Gran Teatro del Liceo (Barcelona: Escudo de Oro, 1979)

Drottningholms Slottsteater (Uddevalla, Bohuslänin-gens, 1985)

The Drottningholm Theater Museum (Borås, Centraltryckeriet, 1984)

Gran Teatro La Fenice (Venice: Teatro La Fenice, 1985)

Teatro Regio Torino (Turin, 1978) (Only the history section is in English)

Inbel-The Royal Theatre of La Monnaie (Brussels, 1988)

Oper der Stadt Köln (Cologne, 1989)

The Salzburg Festival and Its Halls (Salzburg: Salzburg Festival)

Yearbooks which require a good background in the foreign language:

Jahrbuch: Bayerischen Staatsoper [German]

Jahrbuch: Oper Hamburg [German]

Jahrbuch: Opernhauses Zürich [German]

Årsbok: Operan [Swedish]

---

[1] Bramante Editrice, via generale biancardi, 1/b, 21052 Busto Arsizio, Italy, also publishes a twelve volume history of Italian music, *Storia della Musica Italiana da Sant'Ambrogio a Noi* with Italian opera covered in *La Musica Italiana nell'ottocento* and *La Musica Italiana nel Novecento* volumes. If you read Italian, it is worth investigating.

Bibliography

GENERAL BOOKS: opera history, houses, architecture, composers, and encyclopedias

Aloi, Robert: *Teatri e Auditori* (Milan, 1972)

Beijer, Agne: *Court Theaters of Drottningholm and Gripsholm* (New York, 1972)

Burchard, John: *The Voice of Phoenix: Post War Architecture in Germany* (Cambridge MA, 1966)

Ewen, David: *Encyclopedia of the Opera* (New York, 1963)

Gishford, Anthony (ed.): *Grand Opera: Story of the World's Leading Opera Houses* (New York, 1972)

Graubner, Gerhard: *Theaterbau Aufgabe und Planung* (Munich, 1968)

Grout, Donald Jay: *A Short History of Opera* (New York, 1963)

Grun, Bernard: *The Timetables of History* (New York, 1979)

Gutman, Robert: *Richard Wagner: The Man, His Mind and His Music* (New York, 1968)

Hadamowsky, Franz: *Barocktheater am Wiener: Kaiserhof mit einem Spielplan (1625-1740)* (Vienna, 1955)

Hamilton, David (ed.): *The Metropolitan Opera Encyclopedia* (New York, 1987)

Harewood, Earl of: *The Definitive Kobbé's Opera Book* (New York, 1987)

Huges, Patrick Cairns: *Great Opera Houses: A Traveler's Guide to their History & Tradition* (London, 1956)

Hürlimann, Martin: *Vom Stadttheater zum Opernhaus: Zürcher Theatergeschichten* (Zurich, 1980)

Izenour, George C.: *Theater Design* (New York, 1977)

Jacob, Naomi and James C. Robertson: *Opera in Italy* (Freeport, N.Y., 1970)

Landon, H.C. Robbins: *1791 Mozart's Last Year* (New York, 1988)

Osborne, Charles: *The Complete Operas of Verdi* (New York, 1987)

Osborne, Charles: *The World Theatre of Wagner* (New York, 1982)

Pitou, Spire: *Paris Opera: An Encyclopedia of Operas, Ballets, Composers and Performers, Genesis & Glory 1671-1715* (Westport, 1983)

Rosenthal, Harold & John Warrack: *The Concise Oxford Dictionary of Opera* (Oxford, 1989)

Sachs, Edwin O., and Ernest A. Woodrow: *Modern Opera Houses and Theaters*, 3 Vols. (London, 1897-1898; reissued, New York, 1968)

Sadie, Stanley: *Handel* (New York, 1968)

Sadie, Stanley (ed.): *History of Opera* (New York and London, 1990)

Sadie, Stanley: *The New Grove Mozart* (New York and London, 1980)

Santarelli, Cristina, Franco Pulcini, Marco Salotti, Gianni Rondolino: *Lo Spettacolo-La Musica * Il Teatro * Il Cinema* (Busto Arsizio, 1987)

Saracino, Egidio: *Invito all'Ascolto di Donizetti* (Milan, 1984)

Schubert, Hannelore: *The Modern Theater: Architecture, Stage Designing, and Lighting*, translated by J.C. Palmes (New York, 1971)

Shaw, George Bernard: *The Perfect Wagnerite* (New York, 1967)

Vance, Mary A.: *Opera Houses: A Bibliography* (Monticello, Ill., 1982)

Various authors: *Bellini* (Catania, 1988)

Various authors: *Bellini* (Catania, 1989)

Vickers, Hugh: *Great Operatic Disasters* (New York, 1979)

Weaver, Robert Lamar, and Norma Wright Weaver: *A Chronology of Music in the Florentine Theater 1590-1750* (Detroit, 1978)

Wechsberg, Joseph: *The Opera* (New York, 1972)

Wechsberg, Joseph: *Verdi* (New York, 1974)

Worsthorne, Simon Towneley: *Venetian Opera in the Seventeenth Century* (London, 1954)

Zöchling, Dieter: *Opernhäuser in Deutschland, Österreich und der Schweiz* (Düsseldorf, 1983)

BOOKS on individual opera houses

Arruga, Lorenzo: *La Scala* (New York, 1976)

Brusatin, Manlio/Giuseppe Pavanello: *Il Teatro La Fenice I Progetti * L'Architetture * Le Decorazioni* (Venice, 1987)

Cervetti, Valerio, Claudio del Monte, and Vincenzo Raffaele Segreto (eds.): *Teatro Regio-Cronologia degli Spettacoli Lirici 1829-1989* 4 Vols. plus Indici (Parma, 1979, 1980, 1981, 1982, 1990)

Charlet, Gerard: *L'Opéra de la Bastille Genese et Realisation* (Milan-Paris, 1989)

De Candolle, Roger: *Historie du Théâtre de Genève* (Geneva, 1978)

Hillestron, Gustaf: *Drottningholmsteatern Förr och Nu* (Stockholm, 1956)

Huges, Patrick Cairns: *Glyndebourne: A History of the Festival Opera* (London, 1981)

Huwe, Gisela: *Die Deutsche Oper Berlin* (Berlin, 1984)

Mohr, Albert Richard: *Das Frankfurter Opernhaus 1880-1980* (Frankfurt, 1980)

Ralf, Klas: *Operan 200 År: Jubelboken* (Stockholm, 1973)

Rosenthal, Harold D.: *Opera at Covent Garden: A Short History* (London, 1967)

Rosenthal, Harold: *Two Centuries of Opera at Covent Garden* (London, 1958)

Roth, Jean-Jacques: *Grand Théâtre de Genève Operas Moments d'Exception* (Paris, 1987)

Sàbat, Antoni: *Gran Teatro del Liceo* (Barcelona, 1979)
Secchi, Luigi: *Il Teatro alla Scala* (Milan, 1978)
Thubron, Colin: *The Royal Opera House-Covent Garden* (London, 1982)
Tommasi, Rodolfo: *Il Teatro Comunale di Firenze* (Florence, 1987)
Various authors: *A History of the Royal Opera House Covent Garden 1732-1982* (London, 1982)
Various authors: *Propos d'Opera-Images de la Bastille* (Paris, 1989)
Various authors: *Teatro dell'Opera di Roma* (Rome, 1989)
Various authors: *Un Théâtre d'Opéra:L'Équipe de Gerard Mortier à la Monnaie* (Paris, 1986)
Walsh, T.J.: *Monte Carlo Opera 1879-1909* (Dublin, 1975)
Wenzel, Joachim E.: *Geschichte der Hamburger Oper 1678-1978* (Hamburg, 1978)
25 Jahre Deutsche Oper Berlin (Berlin, 1986)

BOOKLETS on individual opera houses
Berliner Forum 1/86-Die Deutsche Oper Berlin (Berlin, 1986)
Drottningholms Slottsteater (Uddevalla, 1985)
The Drottningholm Theater Museum (Borås, 1984)
Duecento Anni alla Scala (Milan 1978)
Gran Teatro La Fenice (Venice, 1985)
Het Muziektheater (Amsterdam, 1986)
Kleine Geschichte der Münchner Oper (Munich)
Das Kölner Opernhaus am Offenbachplatz 1957- 1987 (Cologne, 1987)
Il Maggio Musicale Fiorentino (Florence)
Opera House Guide, Vienna State Opera Building History (Vienna)
Opéra National/Théâtre Royal de la Monnaie- Nationale Opéra/Koninklijke Muntschouwburg (Brussels, 1963)
Oper der Stadt Köln (Cologne, 1989)
Teatro Massimo Bellini (Catania)

Il Teatro Regio (Parma, 1962)
Inbel-The Royal Theatre of La Monnaie (Brussels, 1988)
The Royal Theatre Past and Present (Copenhagen, 1967)
The Salzburg Festival and Its Halls (Salzburg)
La Scala-Breve storia attraverso due secoli (Milan, 1981)
Teatro di San Carlo (Naples, 1987)
Teatro Regio Torino (Turin, 1978)

PERIODICALS (selected issues) and YEAR-BOOKS
Årsbok 1988-89-Operan (Stockholm, 1989)
Das Opern Glas (Hamburg)
Italian Journal (New York)
Jahrbuch der Bayerischen Staatsoper 1989/90 (Munich, 1989)
Jahrbuch 89/90 des Opernhauses Zürich (Zurich, 1989)
Le Immagini-Teatro Regio Torino, Stagione Lirica 1986-87 (Turin, 1988)
Le Immagini-Teatro Regio Torino, Stagione Lirica 1988-89 (Turin, 1990)
L'Opera (Milan)
Musica Viva (Milan)
Newsweek (New York)
Opera (London)
Opera International (Paris)
Opera News (New York)
Opera Now (London)
Oper Frankfurt Saison 89/90 (Jahrbuch) (Frankfurt, 1989)
Oper in Hamburg 1984-1988 (Jahrbuch) (Hamburg, 1988)
Oper in Hamburg 1989 (Jahrbuch) (Hamburg, 1990)
Opernwelt (Zurich)
SM-Sicilia Magazine (Rome-Palermo)
Teatro Bellini-31 Maggio 1890-1990 (Catania, 1990)
Theatre National de L'Opéra (Paris, 1972)
Time (New York)

Index

284

Other Books from John Muir Publications

Adventure Vacations: From Trekking in New Guinea to Swimming in Siberia, Richard Bangs (65-76-9) 256 pp. $17.95

Asia Through the Back Door, 3rd ed., Rick Steves and John Gottberg (65-48-3) 326 pp. $15.95

Being a Father: Family, Work, and Self, *Mothering* Magazine (65-69-6) 176 pp. $12.95

Buddhist America: Centers, Retreats, Practices, Don Morreale (28-94-X) 400 pp. $12.95

Bus Touring: Charter Vacations, U.S.A., Stuart Warren with Douglas Bloch (28-95-8) 168 pp. $9.95

California Public Gardens: A Visitor's Guide, Eric Sigg (65-56-4) 304 pp. $16.95

Catholic America: Self-Renewal Centers and Retreats, Patricia Christian-Meyer (65-20-3) 325 pp. $13.95

Complete Guide to Bed & Breakfasts, Inns & Guesthouses, 1991-92 ed., Pamela Lanier (65-43-2) 520 pp. $16.95

Costa Rica: A Natural Destination, Ree Strange Sheck (65-51-3) 280 pp. $15.95

Elderhostels: The Students' Choice, Mildred Hyman (65-28-9) 224 pp. $12.95 (2nd ed. available 5/91 $15.95)

Environmental Vacations: Volunteer Projects to Save the Planet, Stephanie Ocko (65-78-5) 240 pp. $15.95

Europe 101: History & Art for the Traveler, 4th ed., Rick Steves and Gene Openshaw (65-79-3) 372 pp. $15.95

Europe Through the Back Door, 9th ed., Rick Steves (65-42-4) 432 pp. $16.95

Floating Vacations: River, Lake, and Ocean Adventures, Michael White (65-32-7) 256 pp. $17.95

Gypsying After 40: A Guide to Adventure and Self-Discovery, Bob Harris (28-71-0) 264 pp. $14.95

The Heart of Jerusalem, Arlynn Nellhaus (28-79-6) 336 pp. $12.95

Indian America: A Traveler's Companion, Eagle/Walking Turtle (65-29-7) 424 pp. $16.95 (2nd ed. available 7/91 $16.95)

Mona Winks: Self-Guided Tours of Europe's Top Museums, Rick Steves and Gene Openshaw (28-85-0) 456 pp. $14.95

Opera! The Guide to Western Europe's Great Houses, Karyl Lynn Zietz (65-81-5) 280 pp. $18.95

Paintbrushes and Pistols: How the Taos Artists Sold the West, Sherry C. Taggett and Ted Schwarz (65-65-3) 280 pp. $17.95

The People's Guide to Mexico, 8th ed., Carl Franz (65-60-2) 608 pp. $17.95

The People's Guide to RV Camping in Mexico, Carl Franz with Steve Rogers (28-91-5) 320 pp. $13.95

Preconception: A Woman's Guide to Preparing for Pregnancy and Parenthood, Brenda E. Aikey-Keller (65-44-0) 232 pp. $14.95

Ranch Vacations: The Complete Guide to Guest and Resort, Fly-Fishing, and Cross-Country Skiing Ranches, Eugene Kilgore (65-30-0) 392 pp. $18.95 (2nd ed. available 5/91 $18.95)

Schooling at Home: Parents, Kids, and Learning, *Mothering* Magazine (65-52-1) 264 pp. $14.95

The Shopper's Guide to Art and Crafts in the Hawaiian Islands, Arnold Schuchter (65-61-0) 272 pp. $13.95

The Shopper's Guide to Mexico, Steve Rogers and Tina Rosa (28-90-7) 224 pp. $9.95

Ski Tech's Guide to Equipment, Skiwear, and Accessories, edited by Bill Tanler (65-45-9) 144 pp. $11.95

Ski Tech's Guide to Maintenance and Repair, edited by Bill Tanler (65-46-7) 160 pp. $11.95

Teens: A Fresh Look, *Mothering* Magazine (65-54-8) 240 pp. $14.95

A Traveler's Guide to Asian Culture, Kevin Chambers (65-14-9) 224 pp. $13.95

Traveler's Guide to Healing Centers and Retreats in North America, Martine Rudee and Jonathan Blease (65-15-7) 240 pp. $11.95

Understanding Europeans, Stuart Miller (65-77-7) 272 pp. $14.95

Undiscovered Islands of the Caribbean, 2nd ed., Burl Willes (65-55-6) 232 pp. $14.95

Undiscovered Islands of the Mediterranean, Linda Lancione Moyer and Burl Willes (65-53-X) 232 pp. $14.95

A Viewer's Guide to Art: A Glossary of Gods, People, and Creatures, Marvin S. Shaw and Richard Warren (65-66-1) 152 pp. $10.95

2 to 22 Days Series
These pocket-size itineraries (4½" × 8") are a refreshing departure from ordinary guidebooks. Each offers 22 flexible daily itineraries that can be used to get the most out of vacations of any length. Included are not only "must see" attractions but also little-known villages and hidden "jewels" as well as valuable general information.

22 Days Around the World, Roger Rapoport and Burl Willes (65-31-9) 200 pp. $9.95 (1992 ed. available 8/91 $11.95)

2 to 22 Days Around the Great Lakes, 1991 ed., Arnold Schuchter (65-62-9) 176 pp. $9.95

22 Days in Alaska, Pamela Lanier (28-68-0) 128 pp. $7.95

22 Days in the American Southwest, 2nd ed., Richard Harris (28-88-5) 176 pp. $9.95

22 Days in Asia, Roger Rapoport and Burl Willes (65-17-3) 136 pp. $7.95 (1992 ed. available 8/91 $9.95)

22 Days in Australia, 3rd ed., John Gottberg (65-40-8) 148 pp. $7.95 (1992 ed. available 8/91 $9.95)

22 Days in California, 2nd ed., Roger Rapoport (65-64-5) 176 pp. $9.95

22 Days in China, Gaylon Duke and Zenia Victor (28-72-9) 144 pp. $7.95

22 Days in Europe, 5th ed., Rick Steves (65-63-7) 192 pp. $9.95

22 Days in Florida, Richard Harris (65-27-0) 136 pp. $7.95 (1992 ed. available 8/91 $9.95)

2 to 22 Days in France, 1991 ed., Rick Steves (65-86-6) 192 pp. $9.95

22 Days in Germany, Austria & Switzerland, 3rd ed., Rick Steves (65-39-4) 136 pp. $7.95

2 to 22 Days in Great Britain, 1991 ed., Rick Steves (65-85-8) 192 pp. $9.95

22 Days in Hawaii, 2nd ed., Arnold Schuchter (65-50-5) 144 pp. $7.95 (1992 ed. available 8/91 $9.95)

22 Days in India, Anurag Mathur (28-87-7) 136 pp. $7.95

22 Days in Japan, David Old (28-73-7) 136 pp. $7.95

22 Days in Mexico, 2nd ed., Steve Rogers and Tina Rosa (65-41-6) 128 pp. $7.95

2 to 22 Days in New England, 1991 ed., Anne Wright (65-88-2) 176 pp. $9.95

2 to 22 Days in New Zealand, 1991 ed., Arnold Schuchter (65-58-0) 176 pp. $9.95

2 to 22 Days in Norway, Sweden, & Denmark, 1991 ed., Rick Steves (65-87-4) 184 pp. $9.95

2 to 22 Days in the Pacific Northwest, 1991 ed., Richard Harris (65-89-0) 184 pp. $9.95

22 Days in the Rockies, Roger Rapoport (65-68-8) 176 pp. $9.95

22 Days in Spain & Portugal, 3rd ed., Rick Steves (65-06-8) 136 pp. $7.95

22 Days in Texas, Richard Harris (65-47-5) 176 pp. $9.95

22 Days in Thailand, Derk Richardson (65-57-2) 176 pp. $9.95

22 Days in the West Indies, Cyndy & Sam Morreale (28-74-5)136 pp. $7.95

"Kidding Around" Travel Guides for Young Readers
Written for kids eight years of age and older. Generously illustrated in two colors with imaginative characters and images. An adventure to read and a treasure to keep.

Kidding Around Atlanta, Anne Pedersen (65-35-1) 64 pp. $9.95

Kidding Around Boston, Helen Byers (65-36-X) 64 pp. $9.95

Kidding Around Chicago, Lauren Davis (65-70-X) 64 pp. $9.95

Kidding Around the Hawaiian Islands, Sarah Lovett (65-37-8) 64 pp. $9.95

Kidding Around London, Sarah Lovett (65-24-6) 64 pp. $9.95

Kidding Around Los Angeles, Judy Cash (65-34-3) 64 pp. $9.95

Kidding Around the National Parks of the Southwest, Sarah Lovett 108 pp. $12.95

Kidding Around New York City, Sarah Lovett (65-33-5) 64 pp. $9.95

Kidding Around Paris, Rebecca Clay (65-82-3) 64 pp. $9.95

Kidding Around Philadelphia, Rebecca Clay (65-71-8) 64 pp. $9.95

Kidding Around San Francisco, Rosemary Zibart (65-23-8) 64 pp. $9.95

Kidding Around Santa Fe, Susan York (65-99-8) 64 pp. $9.95

Kidding Around Seattle, Rick Steves (65-84-X) 64 pp. $9.95

Kidding Around Washington, D.C., Anne Pedersen (65-25-4) 64 pp. $9.95

Environmental Books for Young Readers
Written for kids eight years of age and older. Examines the environmental issues and opportunities that today's kids will face during their lives.

The Indian Way: Learning to Communicate with Mother Earth, Gary McLain (65-73-4) 114 pp. $9.95

The Kids' Environment Book: What's Awry and Why, Anne Pedersen (55-74-2) 192 pp. $13.95

No Vacancy: The Kids' Guide to Population and the Environment, Glenna Boyd (61-000-7) 64 pp. $9.95 (Available 8/91)

Rads, Ergs, and Cheeseburgers: The Kids' Guide to Energy and the Environment, Bill Yanda (65-75-0) 108 pp. $12.95

"Extremely Weird" Series for Young Readers
Written for kids eight years of age and older. Designed to help kids appreciate the world around them. Each book includes full-color photographs with detailed and entertaining descriptions.

Extremely Weird Bats, Sarah Lovett (61-008-2) 48 pp. $9.95 paper (Available 6/91)

Extremely Weird Frogs, Sarah Lovett (61-006-6) 48 pp. $9.95 paper (Available 6/91)

Extremely Weird Spiders, Sarah Lovett (61-007-4) 48 pp. $9.95 paper (Available 6/91)

Automotive Repair Manuals

How to Keep Your VW Alive, 14th ed., (65-80-7) 440 pp. $19.95

How to Keep Your Subaru Alive (65-11-4) 480 pp. $19.95

How to Keep Your Toyota Pickup Alive (28-81-3) 392 pp. $19.95

How to Keep Your Datsun/ Nissan Alive (28-65-6) 544 pp. $19.95

Other Automotive Books

The Greaseless Guide to Car Care Confidence: Take the Terror Out of Talking to Your Mechanic, Mary Jackson (65-19-X) 224 pp. $14.95

Off-Road Emergency Repair & Survival, James Ristow (65-26-2) 160 pp. $9.95

About the Author

Karyl Lynn Zietz has had a lifelong fascination with opera and has recently revisited all of the 28 houses described here. Ms. Zietz has written articles for *Opera News* and *Dossier.* She lives in Washington, D.C., and works as an independent T.V. producer and filmmaker.